Illumination of the Hidden Meaning

Yogic Vows, Conduct, and Ritual Praxis

(*sbas don kun gsal*)

Part II: Chapters 25–51

Treasury of the Buddhist Sciences series

The *Treasury of the Buddhist Sciences* series is copublished by the American Institute of Buddhist Studies and Wisdom Publications in association with the Columbia University Center for Buddhist Studies and Tibet House US.

The American Institute of Buddhist Studies (AIBS) established the *Treasury of the Buddhist Sciences* series to provide authoritative translations, studies, and editions of the texts of the Tibetan Tengyur (*bstan 'gyur*) and its associated literature. The Tibetan Tengyur is a vast collection of over 4,000 classical Indian Buddhist scientific treatises (*śāstra*) written in Sanskrit by over 700 authors from the first millennium CE, now preserved mainly in systematic 7th–12th century Tibetan translation. Its topics span all of India's "outer" arts and sciences, including linguistics, medicine, astronomy, socio-political theory, ethics, art, and so on, as well as all of her "inner" arts and sciences such as philosophy, psychology ("mind science"), meditation, and yoga.

The present work is contained in a related series comprising the collected works of Tsong Khapa Losang Drakpa (1357–1419) and his spiritual sons, Gyaltsap Darma Rinchen (1364–1432) and Khedrup Gelek Pelsang (1385–1438), a collection known in Tibetan as rJey Yab Sras gSung 'Bum. This collection also could be described as a voluminous set of independent treatises and supercommentaries, all based on the thousands of works contained in the Kangyur and Tengyur collections.

THE DALAI LAMA

Message

The foremost scholars of the holy land of India were based for many centuries at Nālandā Monastic University. Their deep and vast study and practice explored the creative potential of the human mind with the aim of eliminating suffering and making life truly joyful and worthwhile. They composed numerous excellent and meaningful texts. I regularly recollect the kindness of these immaculate scholars and aspire to follow them with unflinching faith. At the present time, when there is great emphasis on scientific and technological progress, it is extremely important that those of us who follow the Buddha should rely on a sound understanding of his teaching, for which the great works of the renowned Nālandā scholars provide an indispensable basis.

In their outward conduct the great scholars of Nālandā observed ethical discipline that followed the Pāli tradition, in their internal practice they emphasized the awakening mind of *bodhichitta*, enlightened altruism, and in secret they practised tantra. The Buddhist culture that flourished in Tibet can rightly be seen to derive from the pure tradition of Nālandā, which comprises the most complete presentation of the Buddhist teachings. As for me personally, I consider myself a practitioner of the Nālandā tradition of wisdom. Masters of Nālandā such as Nāgārjuna, Āryadeva, Āryāsaṅga, Dharmakīrti, Candrakīrti, and Shāntideva wrote the scriptures that we Tibetan Buddhists study and practice. They are all my gurus. When I read their books and reflect upon their names, I feel a connection with them.

The works of these Nālandā masters are presently preserved in the collection of their writings that in Tibetan translation we call the Tengyur (*bstan 'gyur*). It took teams of Indian masters and great Tibetan translators over four centuries to accomplish the historic task of translating them into Tibetan. Most of these books were later lost in their Sanskrit originals, and relatively few were translated into Chinese. Therefore, the Tengyur is truly one of Tibet's most precious treasures, a mine of understanding that we have preserved in Tibet for the benefit of the whole world.

Keeping all this in mind I am very happy to encourage a long-term project of the American Institute of Buddhist Studies, originally established by the late Venerable Mongolian Geshe Wangyal and now at the Columbia University Center for Buddhist Studies, and Tibet House US, in collaboration with Wisdom Publications, to translate the Tengyur into English and other modern languages, and to publish the many works in a collection called *The Treasury of the Buddhist Sciences.* When I recently visited Columbia University, I joked that it would take those currently working at the Institute at least three "reincarnations" to complete the task; it surely will require the intelligent and creative efforts of generations of translators from every tradition of Tibetan Buddhism, in the spirit of the scholars of Nālandā, although we may hope that using computers may help complete the work more quickly. As it grows, the *Treasury* series will serve as an invaluable reference library of the Buddhist Sciences and Arts. This collection of literature has been of immeasurable benefit to us Tibetans over the centuries, so we are very happy to share it with all the people of the world. As someone who has been personally inspired by the works it contains, I firmly believe that the methods for cultivating wisdom and compassion originally developed in India and described in these books preserved in Tibetan translation will be of great benefit to many scholars, philosophers, and scientists, as well as ordinary people.

I wish the American Institute of Buddhist Studies at the Columbia Center for Buddhist Studies, Tibet House US, and Wisdom Publications every success and pray that this ambitious and far-reaching project to create the *Treasury of the Buddhist Sciences* will be accomplished according to plan. I also request others, who may be interested, to extend whatever assistance they can, financial or otherwise, to help ensure the success of this historic project.

May 15, 2007

Illumination of the Hidden Meaning

Yogic Vows, Conduct, and Ritual Praxis

(sbas don kun gsal)

Part II: Chapters 25–51

By Tsong Khapa Losang Drakpa

Introduction and Translation by
David B. Gray

TREASURY OF THE BUDDHIST SCIENCES SERIES

TENGYUR TRANSLATION INITIATIVE

COMPLETE WORKS OF JEY TSONG KHAPA AND SONS COLLECTION

COPUBLISHED BY

THE AMERICAN INSTITUTE OF BUDDHIST STUDIES AND WISDOM PUBLICATIONS

IN ASSOCIATION WITH THE COLUMBIA UNIVERSITY CENTER

FOR BUDDHIST STUDIES AND TIBET HOUSE US

Wisdom

Treasury of the Buddhist Sciences series
Tengyur Translation Initiative
Complete Works of Jey Tsong Khapa and Sons collection
A refereed series published by:

American Institute of Buddhist Studies
Columbia University
80 Claremont Avenue, Room 303
New York, NY 10027
www.aibs.columbia.edu

Wisdom Publications
199 Elm Street
Somerville, MA 02144
www.wisdompubs.org

In association with Columbia University's Center for Buddhist Studies
and Tibet House US.
Distributed by Wisdom Publications.

Library of Congress Cataloging-in-Publication Data is available.
LCCN 2018050210.

ISBN 978-1-949163-04-9 (hardcover)   ebook ISBN 978-1-949163-05-6

23 22 21 20 19   5 4 3 2 1

Cover and interior design by Gopa&Ted2. Set in Diacritical Garamond Pro 11/13.9.

Printed on acid-free paper and meets the guidelines for permanence and durability of the Production Guidelines for Book Longevity of the Council on Library Resources.

♻ This book was produced with environmental mindfulness.
For more information, please visit wisdompubs.org/wisdom-environment.

Printed in the United States of America.

This work is gratefully dedicated to
all gurus everywhere, and especially to Robert A.F. Thurman,
whose inspiration made it possible.

Contents

Series Editor's Preface

THIS *TREASURY* SERIES is dedicated to making available in English and other languages the entire Tengyur (*bstan 'gyur*), the collection of Sanskrit works preserved in Tibetan translations, and the originally Tibetan learned commentaries and treatises based upon them.

I am delighted to publish here the long-awaited second volume of Jey Tsong Khapa's master commentary on the *Chakrasaṁvara Tantra*, the *Illumination of the Hidden Meaning* (*sbas don kun gsal*), well translated by Professor David Gray, who previously translated the first volume of the *Illumination* (Gray 2017) as well as the *Chakrasaṁvara Tantra* itself (Gray 2007). Building on the work of his eminent predecessors in India and Tibet, Lama Tsong Khapa's *Illumination* (the second half of which is introduced and translated herein) clarifies the esoteric, often enigmatic contents of the abridged root tantra, widely considered the most important of the "mother tantra" category of the unexcelled yoga tantras.

Professor Gray's translation of the *Illumination* has now been completed. I am quite relieved that now have we succeeded in properly following H.H. the Dalai Lama's advice to us, that root tantras of the unexcelled yoga category should not be published without being accompanied by extensive commentaries. This is because the root tantras tend to have shocking statements about transgressive thoughts and acts, which can give rise to serious misunderstandings, perhaps even more intense than the misunderstandings that still arise in some from learning of the Freudian discoveries of the transgressive contents of the human unconscious. After all, there are elements of clearly negative magic in the root texts: elements which have to be understood—in the context of the Indic culture of those ancient times—as intending to defend the dedicatedly altruistic Buddhist tradition with the exceptional use of surgical violence in a curative way by highly advanced adept yogis; elements which were previously kept esoteric in the effort to avoid creating a dangerous slippery slope that might easily lead less developed practitioners toward the dark side. These works are no longer hidden in esoteric circles, and they have already been misunderstood in some quarters. However, with translation of the commentaries from the authoritative scholar-practitioners of the tradition, students can begin to gain a clearer sense of the extraordinary world of the Buddhist tantras; how they aim to fulfill, and do not depart from, the Mahāyānist bodhisattva drive to transform the world for the betterment of all sentient beings.

In our first edition of the first half of the *Illumination* (Gray 2017), I already commented on some of the circumstances surrounding Jey Tsong Khapa's composition of this commentary, which I need not repeat here. Let me just add here that the work was written in in 1419, in the last year of his life. Worthy of mention also is the depth and intensity of Tsong Khapa's personal practice of the central yogas of the *Chakrasaṁvara Tantra*, as witnessed in his pilgrimage to a holy Chakrasaṁvara site on Mount Tsari in southern Tibet in the fall of 1396. It is said that his connection to the deities of the Saṁvara mandala, the network of ḍākinīs (*ḍākinījāla*), was so strong that he was physically unable to leave the high peak of the mountain without performing the celebratory feast ritual (*gaṇacakrapūja, tshogs mchod*) for their mandala, due to his mysterious sudden experience of crippling pains in his legs (which disappeared the minute the ritual was completed). Further, before he wrote this commentary on the abridged root tantra itself, he had already written a number of important texts on the practice of the Chakrasaṁvara yogas of the creation and perfection stages, based on the practice-oriented writings of the great adepts such as Lūipa, Ghaṇṭapa, Kaṇhapa, Kambalika, and Nāropa, as well as on the numerous scholarly works of the great Indian commentators on the *Chakrasaṁvara*. So this *Illumination* can be seen from the biography to be the capstone for the majestic gateway arch of all of Tsong Khapa's teachings on the mother or yoginī category of the unexcelled yoga tantras.[1]

I must here again express my unstinting admiration for Professor Gray's breadth of scholarship in accomplishing this landmark work, on top of his authoritative translation of the *Chakrasaṁvara Tantra* itself. He is one of the few contemporary scholars who has read very widely and carefully in the

1. This process is beautifully described in a forthcoming biography written by Dr. Thupten Jinpa.

Indian and Tibetan tantric spiritual scientific treatises. These still survive in a few cases in corrected Sanskrit, but most of them must be studied in the Tibetan Tengyur translations, where accurate editions of the important works from the libraries of the great Indian Buddhist monastic universities have been preserved in Tibetan. Therefore, Dr. Gray and his colleagues have accomplished a monumental effort in providing primary source evidence on which religious studies scholars interested in tantra can further develop their interpretations.

I congratulate Professor Gray for his great scholarly and intellectual achievement in producing these three books, maintaining his focus through many years of strenuous labor and unrelenting critical insight. I add my sincere thanks to the international group of fine scholars he has remembered and thanked for their skilled assistance, and I give a special acknowledgment of the labor of love and skill given by Professor Thomas Yarnall, our designer, meticulous scholarly colleague, and executive editor.

Robert A.F. Thurman (Ari Genyen Tenzin Choetrak)
Jey Tsong Khapa Professor of Indo-Tibetan Buddhist Studies,
Columbia University
Director, Columbia Center for Buddhist Studies
President, American Institute of Buddhist Studies
President, Tibet House US

Ganden Dechen Ling
Woodstock, New York
June 27, 2018 CE
Tibetan Royal Year 2145, Year of the Earth Dog

Abbreviations and Sigla

THE FOLLOWING is a list of the two-letter abbreviations and one-letter sigla used throughout this text, along with the corresponding shorthand names, text titles, etc. to which they refer. Complete bibliographic details for each of these entries can be found in the bibliography (p. 377ff.).

AM	Abhayākaragupta. *Sheaf of Esoteric Instructions* (*Āmnāyamañjarī*)
AU	*Discourse Appendix Tantra* (*Abhidhānottara Tantra*)
B	TBRC scan of the *bla brang bkra shis 'khyil* print of KS
BC	Bhavyakīrti, *Heroes' Delight, a Commentary on the Shrī Chakrasaṁvara* (*Śrīcakrasaṁvarapañjikā-śūramanojñā-nāma*)
CP	Jayabhadra, *Commentary on the Chakrasaṁvara* (*Cakrasaṁvarapañjikā*)
CT	*Chakrasaṁvara Tantra*
CV	Bhavabhaṭṭa, *Detailed Commentary on the Chakrasaṁvara* (*Cakrasaṁvaravivṛtti*)
D	TBRC scan of the *de dge dgon chen* print of KS
DV	*Ḍākinīs' Vajra Pavillion* (*Ḍākinīvajrapañjara*)
GT	*Esoteric Communion Tantra* (*Guhyasamāja Tantra*)
H	*Discourse Appendix Tantra* (*Abhidhānottara Tantra*). IASWR microfiche no. MBB-I-100
HA	*Origin of Heruka* (*Herukābhyudaya*)
HT	*Hevajra Tantra*

I	*Discourse Appendix Tantra* (*Abhidhānottara Tantra*). IASWR microfiche no. MBB-I-26
IC	Indrabhūti, *Saṁvara Compendium on the Shrī Chakrasaṁvara King of Tantras, a Commentary* (*Śrīcakrasaṁvaratantrarāja-saṁvarasamuccaya-nāma-vṛtti*)
J	*Discourse Appendix Tantra* (*Abhidhānottara Tantra*). Lokesh Chandra 1981 reproduction
JS	*Network of Ḍākinīs, Unification of all Buddhas Tantra* (*Sarvabuddhasamāyoga-ḍākinījālasaṁvara-nāma-uttaratantra*)
K	Kambala, *Treasury of Practice Manuals, a Commentary on the Shrī Chakrasaṁvara* (*Sādhananidhi-śrīcakrasaṁvara-nāma-pañjikā*) (Sanskrit version)
KS	Tsong Khapa, *bde mchog bsdus pa'i rgyud kyi rgya cher bshad pa sbas pa'i don kun gsal ba*
L	*Kiss Tantra* (*Saṁputa Tantra*) (IASWR Microfiche edition)
LA	Sumatikīrti, *Intended Import of the Chapters of the Concise Saṁvara Tantra* (*Laghusaṁvaratantrapaṭalābhisandhi*)
M	*Origin of Saṁvara Tantra* (*Saṁvarodaya Tantra*). IASWR microfiche no. MBB-II-89
MT	*Great Seal Drop* (*Mahāmudrātilaka Tantra*)
NS	Butön Rinchendrup, *Illumination of the Hidden Reality* (*bde mchog rtsa rgyud kyi rnam bshad gsang ba'i de kho na nyid gsal bar byed pa*)
PD	Vīravajra, *Illumination of the Meaning of the Words, a Commentary on the Shrī Saṁvara Root Tantra* (*Padārthaprakāśikā-nāma-śrīsaṁvaramūlatantraṭīkā*)
PG	Sachen Kunga Nyingpo, *Pearl Garland* (*dpal 'khor lo bde mchog gi rtsa ba'i rgyud kyi ṭī ka mu tig phreng ba*)
PM	Prajñākīrti-Mardo revised translation of CT (edited in Gray 2012)
PTT.	Refers to the numbers assigned in *Tibetan Tripitaka: The Peking Edition* (Suzuki 1955–1961)

Q The Otani reprint of KS in the Tibetan Tripitaka, Beijing edition

RG Durjayachandra, *Jewel Assembly, a Commentary [on the Chakrasaṁvara]* (*Ratnagaṇa-nāma-pañjikā*)

SG Vīravajra, *Abode of Universal Virtue, a Commentary [on the Chakrasaṁvara Tantra]* (*Samantaguṇaśālinī-nāma-ṭīkā*)

SL Sumatikīrti-Malgyo revised translation of CT (edited in Gray 2012)

SM Sumatikīrti-Mardo revised translation of CT (edited in Gray 2012)

SN Kambala, *Treasury of Practice Manuals, a Commentary on the Shrī Chakrasaṁvara* (*Sādhananidhi-śrīcakrasaṁvara-nāma-pañjikā*) (Tibetan)

SS Devagupta, *Storehouse for Shrī Chakrasaṁvara Practice Manuals, a Commentary* (SS) (*Śrīcakrasaṁvarasādhana-sarvaśālā-nāma-ṭīkā*)

ST *Kiss Tantra* (*Saṁpuṭa Tantra*)

SU *Origin of Saṁvara Tantra* (*Saṁvarodaya Tantra*)

T *bkra shis lhun po par rnying* edition of KS

Tōh. Refers to the numbers assigned in the Tōhoku Catalogue of the Derge Canon (Ui 1934)

UN Tathāgatarakṣhita, *Twofold Commentary* (*Ubhayanibandha*)

VD *Vajraḍāka Tantra*

VV Bhavabhaṭṭa, *Commentary on the Shrī Vajraḍāka, Great King of Tantras* (*Śrīvajraḍāki-nāma-mahātantrarājasya-vivṛtti*)

YS *Conduct of the Yoginīs [Tantra]* (*Yoginīsaṁcāra*)

Typographical Conventions

To facilitate pronunciation for the non-specialist, we have striven to present Sanskrit proper names, shorter text titles, and some terms in a phonetic form. Toward this end, while in such cases we generally have maintained conventional diacritics, we have added an *h* to convey certain sounds (so *ś*, *ṣ*, and *c* are rendered as *sh*, *ṣh*, and *ch* respectively), and we have rendered *ṛ* as *ṛi*. For Sanskrit terms that have entered the English lexicon (such as "nirvana" or "mandala"), we use no diacritical marks. Likewise, we have rendered Tibetan proper names in a phonetic form. A complete list of Wylie transliterations for such Tibetan proper names may be found in Appendix II (p. 349ff).

In more technical contexts—italic Sanskrit or Tibetan terms in parentheses; the longer names of Sanskrit texts (which are treated as technical terms); Sanskrit or Tibetan passages cited in footnotes; bibliographical citations; and so on—we use standard diacritical conventions for Sanskrit and Wylie transliterations for Tibetan. Standard Sanskrit diacritics and Wylie Tibetan transliterations will also be found for all terms in the trilingual glossaries (p. 351ff).

Throughout the translation, text in square brackets has been added by the translator for clarity. Words in bold represent text quoted from a root text (generally the CT, unless otherwise noted or evident from context). Light gray numbered outline entries have been inserted throughout from Tsong Khapa's general outline (*sa bcad*), the entirety of which may be found in Appendix I (p. 313ff).

Part One

Introduction

Introduction

Translator's Introduction: Writing about Ritual

Having already provided a general introduction to Tsong Khapa's *Illumination of the Hidden Meaning* commentary on the *Chakrasaṁvara Tantra* in the introduction to the first volume of my translation of this work (Gray 2017), here I would like to focus on a specific issue, namely the challenge of writing about ritual, meditative, and yogic practices, and the strategies employed by Tsong Khapa to meet this challenge. First, it should be noted that this is a challenge that is generally faced by all who delve into the genre of tantric literature. Usually, this is attributed to the secrecy of tantric traditions. Secrecy is, after all, a defining feature of these traditions. Tibetans refer to this tradition as that of "secret mantra" (*gsang sngags*), while in East Asia it was referred to as "esoteric teachings" (密教) or "esoteric Buddhism" (密宗佛教). The tantras are known for their secrecy; this was in fact a strategy used by advocates of tantric traditions to create the space for new revelations. The authority figures of Mahāyāna Buddhism either existed in the distant past, i.e., Shākyamuni, or far off in "space," i.e., the cosmic buddhas such as Mahāvajradhara who dwelled in alternate reality buddhalands. For most tantric traditions, the "secret" is a new revelation recently made available in the human realm. The *Chakrasaṁvara Tantra*, after all, opens with the following two lines:[2]

> Now I will explain the secret,
> Concisely, not extensively.

2. CT 1.1ab: *athāto rahasyaṁ vakṣye samāsān na tu vistarāt*, Gray 2012, 49; cf. Gray 2007, 155.

This promises the disclosure of a secret: teachings that were hitherto secret, unknown in the human realm, are now being revealed by this work. Secrecy here is a strategy permitting the revelation of new teachings in an otherwise conservative religious community, and this idea permitted the canon of Mahāyāna Buddhism to remain theoretically open until the present day.[3] As Ronald Davidson has noted, the tantras have involved an ongoing evocation of secrecy. He argued that:

> Indian tantric secrecy is a self-disclosing idiom of scriptural development, a rubric that continues to require both self-emptying and self-filling, a kenotic process that discharges a horizon of expectations so that the real scriptures are continually being revealed, the new mandalas and new sacraments continually unfolding, while the yogins try to avoid suspicion by acting suspiciously themselves. The esotericness of tantric Buddhism was a self-perpetuating strategy that ensured its continued independent maturation. (2006, 74)

Throughout the history of tantric Buddhism in India, new traditions have emerged with the discovery of a "new" scripture that, almost always, invokes the concept of secrecy. This is partly because these scriptures typically do not claim to be new, but rather ancient works attributed to Shākyamuni or other buddhas, which were either hidden away or lost and newly rediscovered, or timeless works that are newly revealed, as advocates of the Chakrasaṁvara tradition claim. This is discussed in the first volume of this work. The works themselves are thus newly revealed secrets. They often claim to teach "new" or newly revealed practices, these being secrets that these texts and their traditions are intent on disclosing, albeit in a controlled manner, to properly qualified students.

Root tantras such as the *Chakrasaṁvara* promise disclosure of "the secret," but the text's brevity and ambiguity arguably prevent this from being accomplished. The history of tantric literature is, from a certain perspective, the history of attempts to fulfill this promise of disclosure in a recursive manner. That is, tantric traditions are characterized by cycles of

3. I explore this concept in my 2010 article "On the Very Idea of a Tantric Canon: Myth, Politics, and the Formation of the Bka' 'gyur."

revelation, which promise disclosure, and commentary, which attempt to disclose, in turn giving rise to a new cycle of revelation and commentary that builds upon the foundation of the older revelations and systematizations. So, as I have argued previously, we see a process of "primary revelation," new tantras attributed to awakened buddhas, which give rise to "primary exegesis," initial attempts to explain the meaning of these works, typically in commentaries. Tantras that become popular, the basis of new practice traditions, will sometime give rise to "secondary revelation," new revelation in the so-called explanatory tantras (*vyākhyātantra*), subsidiary tantric works that typically reveal the secret practices in greater detail. Through this process, the primary tantra becomes recognized as a "root tantra" (*mūlatantra*), the foundation of this new and growing scriptural tradition. We might include in this category works attributed to great saints such as Nāropa, which, due to the great prestige of their authors, come to be recognized as authoritative as well. These works can include commentaries, ritual texts, and "oral instructions" (*upadeśa*), which were transformed into a written genre, which in turn spawned more commentary, leading to a final level of exegetical development, "secondary exegesis," i.e., commentaries on these works of commentary.[4]

It is in this way that a tantric tradition or "cycle" (*skor*) of literature surrounding a root tantra becomes established. Once a tradition is fully elaborated in this manner, invariably new scriptures are revealed that borrow from it and hence build upon its foundation, giving rise to new cycles of revelation and commentary, and hence new traditions of scripture and practice. Thus, the cycle of the development of tantric literature and practice comes full circle and begins a new recursive cycle.

While tantric texts and traditions are seemingly focused on the disclosure of secrets, this disclosure—when mediated by texts—is always imperfect and incomplete since these texts and traditions are focused on practices that are not readily or entirely communicable via written text. The tantras in general tend to focus primarily on practice; tantric literature—by which I mean the tantras themselves as well as the commentaries, ritual manuals (*maṇḍalavidhi*, *abhiṣekavidhi*, etc.), and meditation manuals (*sādhana*)—tends to share this focus. They are thus "self-secret" (*rang gsang*), incapable of complete disclosure via words alone. For when reading about ritual,

4. For a more extensive discussion of these categories see Gray 2001, 299–314.

yogic, or meditation practices that one has never personally experienced, it is arguably impossible to fully understand these practices simply by reading the text, even if one's ability to read and understand the words of the text is perfect.

The task then of commenting upon ritual texts is a very challenging one, and it is arguably not directed toward total neophytes at all. Rather, the ideal reader for texts such as Tsong Khapa's commentary is someone who, having been initiated and introduced to the practices, already has had exposure to the practice tradition and is seeking a deeper understanding. Such a reader might gain a great deal from works of tantric exegesis. Those with no exposure to the traditions might find them impossible to understand, regardless of how well or poorly these works are translated and presented.

In seeking to compose a commentary on the *Chakrasaṁvara Tantra*, Tsong Khapa had a great number of resources to draw upon. When Tsong Khapa gave the lectures that were eventually compiled into this commentary at Ganden Monastery during the early fifteenth century, approximately 500 to 600 years had passed since the root text was initially composed.[5] He was thus commenting upon the root text of a tradition that was, on account of its popularity, very well established. In addition to the root text itself, he was thus able to draw upon at least five explanatory tantras—most of which were considerably longer than the *Concise Saṁvara* root text—and he therefore treated the rituals and contemplative practices of the root text in greater depth. There were also a dozen Indian commentaries preserved in the Tibetan canon, if one does not count Sumatikīrti's one-and-a-half-folia *Intended Import of the Chapters of the Concise Saṁvara Tantra*, and many dozens of ritual texts, meditation manuals, and commentaries. He also had several centuries of Tibetan scholarship on which to rely.

Tsong Khapa relied on all five of the explanatory tantras that he deemed authoritative,[6] the twelve Indian commentaries as well as Sumatikīrti's chapter synopsis, which he quoted in its entirely. Among the various ritual and contemplative texts, he focuses on those attributed to the mahāsiddha

5. The date of the composition of CT is impossible to set precisely; it may have been composed as early as the late eighth century to as late as the tenth century, when Rinchen Zangpo's intitial Tibetan translation was made. Regarding the dating of this work see Gray 2007, 11–14, Gray 2012, 6–8, note 14, and Sanderson 2009, 162–63.

6. Published in the first volume of this translation, see Gray 2017, section 2.1.1.

trio, Lūipa, Ghaṇṭapā or Vajraghaṇṭa, and Kāṇha or Kṛiṣhṇāchārya, who are major figures in the development of the Chakrasaṁvara tradition in India.[7] Regarding the tradition of Tibetan scholarship on this work that preceded him, Tsong Khapa mentions by name, and comments upon, the commentaries composed by Sachen Kunga Nyingpo, Butön Rinchendrup, and Mardo. As discussed in my introduction to the first volume of this translation, he relies generally on the former two, and particularly on the latter. Mardo's commentary, entitled the *Summary and Detailed Commentary on the Saṁvara Root Tantra by the Translator Mardo Chökyi Wangchuk*, (*mar do lo tsā ba chos kyi dbang phyug gi bde mchog rtsa rgyud kyi bsdus don dang ṭikka rgyas pa*), is evidently lost, so it is not currently possible to estimate the degree to which Tsong Khapa relied upon it. I believe, however, that many of the quotes from unidentified sources may be from this work.[8]

In commenting upon the *Chakrasaṁvara Tantra* in general, and in the latter half of this work in particular, Tsong Khapa was faced with the challenge of explaining ritual and contemplative practices that are presented in a very bare-boned manner in the root text. In doing this, he relied on all of the sources available to him. However, he relied primarily on the more extensive Indian commentaries that comment on the ritual practices in more detail. These include Bhavabhaṭṭa's (CV) commentary, which is one of the longest commentaries, at over one hundred folia long in Tibetan translation. However, the work on which he most relies is Kambala's *Treasury of Practice Manuals* commentary (*Sādhananidhi-śrīcakrasaṁvara-nāma-pañjikā*). A relatively long work (seventy-seven folia in length in Tibetan translation), it is indeed a "treasury of practice manuals," as the title promises. Here in the title of the text, the term *sādhana* refers not only to meditation manuals but to any sort of practice manual.[9] Kambala's commentary provides more detailed explanations for many of the text's ritual and meditative practices, and as this text is also attributed to a mahāsiddha, it served as an indispensable source for those interested in understanding the root text. For Tsong

7. See also Gray 2017, 7.

8. Regarding these commentaries see Gray 2017, 8.

9. As I noted in my 2012 edition, the title for Kambala's commentary is mislabeled in the Tibetan translation as "context for practice manuals," *sādhananidāna/sgrub pa'i thabs kyi gleng gzhi*. This title makes much less sense than the title preserved in the Sanskrit manuscript, the *Śrīherukābhidhāna-sādhananidhi-pañjikā*. See Gray 2012, 41.

Khapa, it was particularly important as the translation he preferred, the "dual translation" jointly revised by Mardo and Sumatikīrti, was itself a secondary revision of the revised translation by the India scholar Sūryagupta and the Tibetan translator Gö Lotsawa Shönu Pal, who also translated Kambala's commentary into Tibetan.[10] Kambala's commentary was thus a major influence on the Tibetan translation that Tsong Khapa preferred, so it is natural that he would find it particularly helpful for facilitating his understanding of the root text.

In addition to Chakrasaṁvara literature, Tsong Khapa ranges beyond it, drawing upon scholarship from other traditions, particularly the highly influential Esoteric Communion (*Guhyasamāja*) and Hevajra traditions. Here he followed in the footsteps of his Indian predecessors, including Kambala, who also made reference to major works from these traditions. Lastly, Tsong Khapa also refers to classic works from the Mahāyāna tradition, such as Asaṅga's *Bodhisattva Stages* and Asaṅga/Maitreyanātha's *Ornament of the Universal Vehicle Sutras* and Haribhadra's *Splendid Ornament* commentary on the *Eight-thousand-stanza Perfection of Wisdom Sutra*. In so doing, he contextualized the *Chakrasaṁvara Tantra* within the larger Mahāyāna tradition and furthered the integration of exoteric and esoteric Buddhist traditions.

10. See Gray 2012, 31.

Part Two

Annotated English Translation

Chapter 25

Chapter 25 Outline

3.3.3. 2.2.2. 4. Showing the root mantra and the detailed explanation of the commitments to be protected

The fourth part, showing the root mantra and the detailed explanation of the commitments to be protected, has two sections: (1) the clear exposition of the root mantra, and (2) showing the eight commitments.

3.3.3. 2.2.2. 4.1. The clear exposition of the root mantra

The first part has three sections: (1) the way in which the root mantra is made unclear, (2) the way in which the root mantra is clarified in this chapter, and (3) showing the name of the chapter.

3.3.3. 2.2.2. 4.1.1. The way in which the root mantra is made unclear

Now, after the twenty-fourth [chapter], that to which one should aspire, which accomplishes **the aims of all** sentient beings, is supreme bliss. The root mantra is clarified for the yogin who has the yoga of that. What is the mantra like? It is that which should be **hidden** from those who are not suitable vessels. **The end of the eight** is the eighth [letter] counting from *y*, i.e., *h*. As for that which is **joined** to *h*, it is the *u* [vowel] together with the *anusvāra*, [yielding] *huṁ*; this is Kambala's assertion.[11] The application of *oṁ* to the beginning of the root mantra and *huṁ huṁ phaṭ* to its end was previously explained in chapter seven. Here, *huṁ* is shown because *huṁ huṁ phaṭ* is joined to the end of both the eight-lined [root mantra] as well as the [mantras of the] twenty-four [deity couples].[12] One should also know that [such is the case] also with respect to *oṁ* at the beginning.

Why must that be hidden? It is hidden in order to protect it from slander by **deluded** heretics who have **minds ignorant** of the profound meaning, and those **of little faith** (25.1) in the secret mantra Mahāyāna, such as the disciples and so forth.

3.3.3. 2.2.2. 4.1.2. The way in which the root mantra is clarified in this chapter

The second part has two sections: (1) explaining in terms of the interpretable meaning, and (2) explaining in terms of the definitive meaning.

3.3.3. 2.2.2. 4.1.2. 1. Explaining in terms of the interpretable meaning

The translation reads,[13] "**With respect to that, the mantra clearly stated by the heroes and yoginīs is as follows** (25.2)," [meaning that] "it was stated by the Blessed Lord in the appearance of the heroes and yoginīs." Lochen's translation has "not clearly stated by the heroes and yoginīs." In Durjayachandra's commentary it is explained that "the ends of the mantra were not stated by the heroes and yoginīs."[14]

11. See SN 39b.

12. Tsong Khapa is presumably referring here to the names of the twenty-four heroes and heroines, whose mantras are their names bracketed by *oṁ* and *hūṁ hūṁ phaṭ*.

13. This is the text preserved in both in the PM and SL translations; see Gray 2012, 330, 448.

14. Durjayachandra does not specifically say this, but he does state that the seed syllables that terminate the mantra are "that which is hidden" (RG 286b).

Oṁ[15] gathers into one the three, *a*, *u*, and *m*. That is, it gathers the three vajras into one, taking hold of merit.[16] *Namo* is the salutation. *Bhagavate* refers to the "Blessed Lord." **Vīreshyāya** means the "lord of heroes." **Mahākalpā** means "great eon." *Agni*, which is joined to the [terminal] *a* of [*kal*]*pa*, means "fire." **Sannibhāya** means "like." **Jaṭā** means "dreadlock." **Makuṭa** means "crest," [the terminal *a* of which] combines with [the *u* of *u*]*tkaṭāya*—which means "tied up," "tucked up," or "unbearable"—yielding [the sandhi] *o*.[17] **Daṁṣhṭra** means "fang," and **karāla** "to bare." **Ugra** means "awful," **bhīṣhaṇa** "terrible," and **mukhāya** "to the mouth." **Sahasra** means "a thousand," **bhuja** "arm," **bhāsurāya** "possessed of blazing light." **Parashu** means "axe," **pāsha** "lasso," **udyata** "upraised," **shūla** "spear," and **khaṭvāṅgadhāriṇe** "wielding a skull staff."[18] **Vyāghra** means "tiger," **ajina** "hide," **ambara** "garment," and **dharāya** "wearing." **Mahā** means "great," and **dhūmra**[19] "smoke." **Andhakāra** is explained by some as "causing death" (*antakara, mthar byed*), by others as a type of "darkness."[20] **Vapuṣhāya** means "to the body."

The two **kara** both mean "do!"[21] **The** two **kuru** both mean "do!" **The**

15. Tsong Khapa here gives a word by word explanation of the root mantra, which is: *oṁ namo bhagavate vīreśāya / mahākalpāgnisannibhāya / jaṭāmakuṭotkaṭāya / daṁṣṭrākarālograbhīṣaṇamukhāya / sahasrabhujābhāsurāya / paraśupāśodyataśūlakhaṭvāṅgadhāriṇe / vyāgrājināmbaradharāya / mahādhūmrāndhakāravapuṣāya /*. Note that he, in some but not all instances, takes into account the dative terminations of the final terms in the compounds.

16. This presumably refers to the creation stage meditation involving the visualization of vajras marked by the syllables *oṁ*, *āḥ*, and *hūṁ*, described in GT ch. 11; see Matsunaga 1978, 36–37.

17. The term *utkaṭa* usually means "endowed with" or "abounding in." However, it could be interpreted as Tsong Khapa does when in compound with *jaṭāmakuṭa*.

18. Tsong Khapa seems to understand *dhāriṇe* in reference to *khaṭvāṅga* only, but clearly the term extends to all of the other implements in the compound as well.

19. Tsong Khapa here reads *dhūmbra/dhūmvra*, but this is clearly a misreading of *dhūmra*. This reading seems to derive from the SM translation that Tsong Khapa favors (Gray 2012, 525) as well as Butön (NS 154a). The different editions of the PM translation vary here, with some containing the correct reading while others have various incorrect readings (Gray 2012, 331, n. 1952).

20. The latter interpretation is the correct one. Tsong Khapa here again follows Butön (NS 154a).

21. Tsong Khapa here comments upon the translatable portions of the *kara kara* mantra. The mantra occurs in the Sanskrit root text as follows: *kara kara kuru kuru bandha*

two **bandha** both mean "bind!" The two **trāsaya** both mean "terrify!" The two **kṣhobhaya** both mean "incite!" The two **daha** both mean "burn!" The two **pacha** both mean "cook!" The two **bhakṣha** both mean "eat!" **Vasa** means "grease," **rudhira** "blood," **antra** "entrail," **mālāva** "garland," and **lambine** "hanging."[22] The two **gṛihṇa** both mean "take!" **Sapta** means "seven," **pātāla** "underworld," **gata** "to reside in," **bhujaṅgāṁ**[23] "snake,"[24] and **sarpaṁvā** "serpents."[25] The two **tarjaya** both mean "threaten!" The two **ākaḍḍha** both mean "summon!"

With regard to the root mantra, in the *Discourse Appendix* there are two [augments called for, namely] an affix at the beginning of the eight-line [mantra] as was stated in this [tantra],[26] and it does not add augments in the *kara kara* mantra.[27] There are a few differences, such as, in the *Vajraḍāka* and the *Origin of Heruka*, the lack of an affix at the beginning of the eight-line [mantra], and the addition [of augments] in *kara kara* mantra.[28]

---

bandha trāsaya trāsaya kṣobhaya kṣobhaya hrauṁ hrauṁ hraḥ hraḥ pheṁ pheṁ phaṭ phaṭ daha daha paca paca bhakṣa bhakṣa vasarudhirāntramālāvalambine gṛhṇa gṛhṇa sapta-pātālagatabhujaṅgaṁ sarpam vā tarjaya tarjaya ākaḍḍha ākaḍḍha hrīṁ hrīṁ jñauṁ jñauṁ kṣmāṁ kṣmāṁ hāṁ hāṁ hīṁ hīṁ hūṁ hūṁ kili kili sili sili cili cili dhili dhili hūṁ hūṁ.

The transliterations in the Tibetan translation differ from this at several points that will be noted.

22. Tsong Khapa here incorrectly analyzes the compound *mālāvalambine* as *mālāva+lambine*, rather than *mālā+avalambine*, which is the correct analysis, as Butön notes (NS 155a).

23. Tsong Khapa's reading *bhujaṅgāṁ*, with its feminine termination, is unattested elsewhere. The Sanskrit sources here read *bhujaṅga*.

24. Tsong Khapa, following Butön (NS 155b), gives the literal but inaccurate translation *lag 'gro*. This is inaccurate because here *bhujaṁ* does not mean "hand," but rather "bend," i.e., a snake is an animal that moves by bending its body.

25. Unfortunately, here Tsong Khapa does not follow Butön, who correctly analyzes *sarpaṁ* as "serpent" and *vā* as a grammatical particle (NS 155b).

26. Tsong Khapa here refers to the syllable *oṁ*, which is not coded for in the mantra selection process, but which is called for at the end of CT ch. 7, as well as in the parallel passage in AU (AU 354b).

27. The *kara kara* mantra occurs twice in AU, and it does not add such augments as Tsong Khapa noted (AU 299b, 352a).

28. HA ch. 3a omits any reference to the augmented syllables at the beginning and end of the mantra. HA and VD both add seed syllables between some of the pairs of reduplicated words (HA 3a, VD 71b–72a).

3.3.3. 2.2.2. 4.1.2. 2. Explaining in terms of the definitive meaning

The second part has two sections: (1) the definitive meaning of the first set of eight, and (2) the definitive meaning of the latter set of eight.

3.3.3. 2.2.2. 4.1.2. 2.1. The definitive meaning of the first set of eight

An explanation of the definitive meaning of the root mantra from *kara kara* onward is stated in the explanatory tantra.[29] As is stated previously in chapter nine, one who longs for power without knowing the reality (*tattva*) of the root mantra is like one who, desiring grain, threshes chaff. The effort of one who desires yoga without knowing the reality of mantra is in vain.[30] Therefore, knowledge of the reality of mantra is very important. Moreover, the *Vajraḍāka* states that:[31]

> Karma past acquired is the end-maker,
> Endowed with fire, it is recited twice.
> *Kuru kuru* is free of intention.

As for its interpretable meaning, "past acquired" refers to the former member of the class of consonants as *ka*, and at its end as fire, so possessed of *ra* [yields] two *kara*. With regard to its definitive meaning, "past" refers to the obscurations of karma such as the five inexorable sins[32] etc. that were previously accumulated. They are "endowed with fire," meaning that one suffers as they ripen, like fire. The pair of *kara* signifies "making," making the end

29. As will become obvious below, Tsong Khapa's commentary relies on the explanation of the *kara kara* mantra that occurs in VD ch. 2, which he quotes below. He also relies on Bhavabhaṭṭa's commentary on this text, which he widely paraphrases. See VV 25a–29b.

30. Tsong Khapa here paraphrases a passage that occurs at the end of CT ch. 9, commented upon above.

31. Tsong Khapa quotes this passage as: *sngon bsags las ni mthar byed pa / me dang bcas te lan gnyis bzlas / ku ru ku ru sems pa bral.* This quote occurs as follows in VD ch. 2: *sngon bsags las ni mthar byed pa / me dang bcas te lan gnyis bzla / ku ru ku ru sems dpa' bral* (VD 5b.5). I follow Tsong Khapa's reading of *sems pa bral* rather than *sems dpa' bral.*

32. The *pañcānantarīya*, which are (1) *pitṛghāta*, killing one's father; (2) *mātṛghāta*, killing one's mother; (3) *arhatghāta*, killing an arhat; (4) *tathāgatasyāntike duṣṭicittarūdhirotpādanam*, drawing the blood of a tathāgata with an ill intention; (5) *saṁghabheda*, causing a schism in the saṁgha (Rigzin 1986, 343).

or exhausting those obscurations. "Twice" is an illustration, signifying that the exhaustion of the obscurations is done over and over again. Moreover, the absence of non-assembly of the two, *ka* and *ra*,[33] points to the cause of that which is to be exhausted. So, if one wonders how one eliminates the obscurations of karma, [the answer is] "Make oneself 'free of the mind' which is attached, i.e., the mentality of attachment, to the true existence of subjectivity and objectivity, which is the root of all evil karma." This is the significance of *kuru*. Its statement twice is as was previously [explained]. Moreover [the *Vajraḍāka*] also [states]:

> **Bind** is known as flashing dreadlocks;
> That should be repeated once more.
> Being without a worldly form,
> To **terrify** is a falsehood.[34]
> Repeat that excellent one twice.
> **Kṣha** is endowed with the **o** sound,
> And **bhaya** exists at its side
> That should be repeated once more.[35]

Having called out "bind the copious dreadlocks," the definitive meaning of this is "bind the hatreds." The "dreadlocks" are the assembly of the tathāgata clan. "Flashing" means that ultimately [things] lack intrinsic reality, although they appear to exist as conventionally real. Their binding means that through the wheel of selflessness they should be taken to be one, i.e., should be taken as inseparably, experientially unified. This should be repeated twice as previously [explained].

If one thinks that since one visualizes the tathāgatas through the method

33. That is, the fact that they are combined in a single word rather than appearing as disjointed syllables.

34. This translates Tsong Khapa's text *'jig rten gzugs dang bral ba yi*. The Derge text is corrupt here, reading *'jig rten gzugs rang bral ba yi* (VD 5b).

35. Tsong Khapa relates this text as follows: *ral pa gya gyu bandha gsal / de ni slar yang bzlas par bya / 'jig rten gzugs dang bral ba yi / trā sa ya zhes bya ba brdzun / dam pa de ni lan gnyis bzla / ka ṣa zhes bya o sgrar ldan / glo na bha ya yang dag gnas / de yang slar ni bzlas par bya*.

It occurs as follows in VD ch. 2: *ral pa gya gyu ban dha gsal / de ni slar yang bzlas par bya / 'jig rten gzugs rang bral ba yi / trā sa ya zhes bya ste brdzun / dam pa de ni lan gnyis bzla / kṣa zhes bya ba o sgrar ldan / glo na bha ya yang dag gnas / de yang slar ni bzlas par bya* (VD 5b.5–6).

of endowing them with characteristics such as faces, hands, etc., they are of cyclic existence, since it is shown that they lack any worldly forms, i.e., essential natures, "terrify" means "produce the terror of suffering [resulting from] habitual attachments to things. Repeated it twice is as was previously [explained.] Thus, although one visualizes the deities as having characteristics such as faces and hands, and so forth, it is not the case that they do not liberate [beings] from cyclic existence.

The equivalent term of "false" (*mrdzun*), *alīka*, has two meanings.[36] If taken in reference to the falsity of beings, and if one analyzes by means of the valid means of knowledge for investigating reality, then, as they lack essential natures, one abandons worldly terrors. Thus, it should be shown that things "are false in the manner that they appear conventionally and exist as do illusions." Furthermore, if *alīka* is taken as meaning "beast" (*phyugs*), [then it means] "terrify the beastly fools."[37]

Stacking *k* and *ṣh* yields *kṣh*. Since it is endowed with an *o*, it is *kṣho*. The two, *k* and *ṣh*, sharpen; it is the conventional truth that is like a whetstone. Why is that? One should sharpen, i.e., analyze, the ultimate truth. And just as *o* consists of the pair, *a* and *u*, there is the pair of wisdom and art. The syllable is the experience of art and wisdom and the possession of that.

As for clearly indicating art and wisdom, *bhaya* is the vulva (*bhaga*), which is wisdom (*prajñā*). It is positioned at the side of *kṣho*, the conventional truth it is similar to, i.e., equipoised with. If one analyzes the conventional truth that is like a whet[stone] in the manner of the ultimate truth that is like gold, then the two truths become similar, i.e., inseparable, just like a golden image clings to stone. Furthermore, as *kṣh* sharpens, it is also a valid means of knowledge. If one analyzes and sharpens with a valid means of knowledge, then one exhausts and reaches the limit of the gold-like conventional truth and the image-like ultimate truth.[38]

36. These are (1) unpleasant, disagreeable, and (2) false. Tsong Khapa transliterates the term incorrectly, as *alika*.

37. The term *alīka* does not mean "beast." Tsong Khapa seems to have gotten this idea from Bhavabhaṭṭa's VV commentary, which reads, "**False** refers to the vowels and consonants (*ālikāli*). If taken in terms of 'beast,' then *trāsaya* means 'terrify the beastly, foolish men.'" (VV 26a.4: *brdzun pa ni ā li kā li ste / phyugs la bya la phyugs dang 'dra ba'i skye bo blun po rnams tra say a ste skrag par gyis shig pa'*) It seems likely that Bhavabhaṭṭa's text is mistranslated or corrupt here; *alīka* may have been misconstrued as *ālikāli*.

38. I am not sure why the metaphors switch here. Tsong Khapa closely follows Bhavabhaṭṭa's text at VV 26b.

However, it is said that this is not the case by some scriptural epistemic authorities.[39] [These sources] state that [*kṣh*] possesses the sound *o*, which is engagement by means of faith. Possessing it means that one analyzes it by means of reason.[40] While it is acceptable here to analyze by means of scripture and reason, it is not done by faith alone.

Bhaya can be taken to be *bhava*, the equivalent term for which is "existence" (*gnas pa*), and also, by extension, "exhaustion" (*zad pa*, *kṣaya*). This means that "if one analyzes and sharpens with reason, one exhausts the noose which is [wrong belief in] the existence of the object etc."[41] Also, [the *Vajraḍāka*] states:[42]

> After *sa* is the solar seat,
> Ten arrows on the moon, drop filled,
> That too should be stated again.
> After *sa* is the refined gold,
> And "please approach" is at its side.
> It should be repeated as well.

[This text] has shown the need for exhausting the obscurations of karma, and also the need for exhausting attachment to true existence that is the root of obscurations of karma. And, to exhaust that, [it shows] the necessity of realizing the illusory falsehood that terrifies those who cling to the true existence [of things] (*bden 'dzin can*, *satyagrāhin*), as well as inseparability of the two truths. [It also shows] the need for establishing well with reason the import of scriptures of definitive meaning.

Now, to show the need for integrating that with bliss, the definitive

39. Tsong Khapa is here directly drawing from Bhavabhaṭṭa's commentary (VV 26b). Neither author identifies which scriptural sources are being referred to here.

40. Here I read *rigs pa*, following Bhavabhaṭṭa's text quoted below, rather than the *rig pa* of Tsong Khapa's text. The correct reading *rigs pa* occurs later in Tsong Khapa's text as well.

41. The quotation occurs in Bhavabhaṭṭa's text. The source is not indicated. It occurs as follows: *rigs pas rnam par dpyad cing bdar na bzung ba la sogs pa'i srid pa'i zhags pa zad par 'gyur zhes bya ba'i don to* (VV 26b.5).

42. This quotation occurs in VD ch. 2 as follows: *sa yi mtha' ni nyi stan gnas / mda' bcu zla dum thig les dgang / de yang slar ni brjod par bya / 'od byed sbyangs pa sa yi mtha' / gshegs su gsol ba glo na gnas / nyis 'gyur du ni bya ba yin* (VD 5b.6–7).

meaning of [the syllables] *hrauṁ* etc. [are explained] as follows. [The letter] *h*, its *r* affix serving as its "seat," the vowel *o* on top, a half-moon and a drop, illuminate art and wisdom as previously explained. Since [the letter] *r* is the solar seed, it is said to be the sun. Furthermore, it is the vajra of art, because it gives rise to the luminance of natural gnosis. The "seat" of that sun is the consort's vulva, because it serves as the vajra's place. After [the letter] *s*, in [the sibilant series] *sh*, *ṣh*, *s*, *h*, is [the letter] *h*. Through the union of the sun and the seat is the lily-like seminal essence that is generated as a distinctive feature in all bodies. The crescent moon that exists on the crown of *h* trickles from the crown as the first spirit of awakening.

What does it do? The equivalent term to "arrow," *bāṇa*, which can also designate "forest,"[43] here refers to the five aggregates. The "ten" are the five sense powers and five sense objects. Regarding that, the tenth vowel, when the four hermaphrodites[44] are excluded, is *au*, which is affixed to *h*, to which the meaning of *o* is also applicable. [The term] "piece" indicates that they appear to be numerous.[45] "Drop" is an image of the realization of emptiness. That which is filled by them is the five sense powers, sense objects, and aggregates, and so forth. Having been drawn as an image of the realization of emptiness, they are taken to be experientially unified. These indicate that when the seminal essence abides within the jewel of the vajra due to the equal union of the sun and seat, all of the natures of conceptualization wane, and one realizes the natural nature (*sahajaprakṛti*, *lhan cig skyes pa'i rang bzhin*). When one discovers this sort of natural bliss, this means that one is united with emptiness, as I have previously established. These are the meanings of *hrauṁ*. "Stating it twice" means that one should be practiced in this again and again.

With regard to *hraḥ*, "after *s*," has the previously explained meaning of *h*. The *r* affix is the "illuminator," i.e., fire, which is the blood of the consort.

43. Tsong Khapa here writes *bāna*, although the Sanskrit for "arrow" is actually *bāṇa*. The term *vāna* can mean forest, but the Tibetan script does not distinguish between the Sanskrit letters *b* and *v*.

44. These are, presumably, the four long vowels, *ā*, *ī*, *ū*, and long *ṛ*, but they may be the four retroflex and dental vowels, even though long *ḷ* does not actually occur in Sanskrit.

45. Tsong Khapa here is not following the text of VD as is preserved in the Kangyur and as he quoted it above, which reads *zla du*, "on the moon," here. Instead, he follows Bhavabhaṭṭa's commentary, which reflects a textual variant here, *dum bu* or *khaṇḍa* (VV 26b, 27a).

When it is refined, it has the import taught in the root tantra, that is, the "illuminator" should be taken to be the "seat." This refers to the mixture of the two seminal essences. The *visarga*[46] [is coded by] "please come," meaning that the semen and blood are brought down to the consort's lotus. These two [*visarga* dots, or, seminal fluids] are "at its side," that is, "eaten," meaning one is satisfied by enjoying them. The *hraḥ* is stated twice, as previously [explained].

Also, [the *Vajraḍāka*] states:[47]

> The young moon,[48] the clear drop, is *phe*.
> That should also be repeated.

Phe means that the subject ultimately does not exist. If it does not exist, what then apprehends entities? It [the subject] does, since [these] depend upon that. The "young moon" refers to the first day of the lunar month, and it is ornamented by a drop upon *phe*; this drop is a star. While with these two there is power of illumination with respect to oneself, this is not the case with respect to others. This is because one sees directly with eyes possessed of darkness even when these have arisen in this way. With these there is no power of illuminating darkness. By what then is [darkness illuminated]? It is only by the full moon that illuminates both self and other. In this way, there is no power to accomplish the aims of beings with only the selflessness that is an empty image, and that is like the [first] lunar day. Nor is there [such power] with just the body of the deity, which is the star-like conventional truth. However, it is shown that there is [such] power, but only by means of full moon-like body of non-dual integration of the two truths. As for the meaning of "should be repeated," just as darkness is dispelled even by stars when they are accompanied by the full moon, likewise all actions follow after the body of non-dual integration.[49]

46. These are the *tsheg drag gnyis*, the two "dots" that graphically represent the *visarga* in Sanskrit. For Tsong Khapa, these symbolize the male and female seminal essences.

47. The canonical version of the VD ch. 2 reads: *zla zhon thig gsal phe zhes bya / de yang slar ni bzlas par bya* (VD 5b.7).

48. VD here reads *zla zhon*, but this is corrected to *zla gzhon* by Tsong Khapa and Bhavabhaṭṭa (VV 27a).

49. This concludes a long paraphrase from Bhavabhaṭṭa's commentary. See VV 27ab.

In this way, the clear light gnosis of emptiness is illustrated by the [first] lunar day, and the magic deity body is illustrated by the star-like drop. The non-distinct association of these two is their integration. [The syllable] *phe*, which completes and assembles these two, is the individual who integrates the empty self of clear light. These previous [points] have shown the need for the inseparability of bliss and emptiness, which, in turn, demonstrate the need for the inseparable integration of the two truths.

3.3.3. 2.2.2. 4.1.2. 2.2. The definitive meaning of the latter set of eight

Phaṭ is the gnosis of clear light of selflessness. *Daha* means "**Burn** the wood of conceptualization that perceives things as having attributes!"[50] *Pacha* means "**Cook** the defiled aggregates!" *Bhakṣha* means "**Eat** the devil[s] of conceptualization!" which means that they are destroyed by the previously [explained] gnosis of bliss and emptiness. [The text] from *vasa* to *lambine*[51] is called out in praise of the deity. *Grihṇa* and *tarjaya* mean "seize!" and "threaten!" i.e., "destroy!" What is seized? [It is indicated by the text] from *sapta* to *sarpaṁ vā*,[52] that is, the conceptualization that perceives things as having attributes that is like the poisonous serpents of the seven levels of the underworld. [One should] seize and destroy them.

Also, [with regard to the term *ākaḍḍha*,] *ā* [indicates] *ākāra*, "form,"[53] and *ka* "throat" (*kaṇṭha*), meaning that one should gulp down in a one-tasted manner the various forms.[54] What does that gullet gulp down? It is *ḍḍha*, i.e., the mind, that should be gulped down there. [Mind] is said to both have and lack form, and as both of these are faulty, one should ascertain it, i.e., meditate upon it, by means of both scriptural epistemic authority and reason in the natural clear light that is the nature of the three

50. This is an expansion of the text at VD 5b.7: *rnam par rtog pa kun gyi shing / da ha da ha mkha' 'gro'i sdom*.

51. That is, *vasarudhirāntramālāvalambine*.

52. That is, *saptapātālagatabhujaṅgaṁ sarpam vā*.

53. Tsong Khapa's text follows Bhavabhaṭṭa's commentary (VV 28a) in giving the (presumably) incorrect transliteration *akara*, followed by the translation, *rnam pa*.

54. Tsong Khapa here expands upon Bhavabhaṭṭa's gloss of *a* as *akara* and *ka* as *mid pa* (VV 28a.3). His comment involves a pun on the Tibetan word *mid pa*, which as a noun means "throat," and as a verb "gulp down, swallow."

liberations[55]—this is the meaning of *ya*.[56] As for that, there is a commentary on the *Vajraḍāka* that selects the syllable *ya* in [the term] *ākaḍḍha*, but *ya* is not selected in the root tantra.[57]

The *h* of *hrīṁ* signifies Heruka who pervades all beings, namely art, while the *r* affix is the "sun," namely wisdom.[58] [The letter] *ī* is the fourth vowel, which is Heruka's leftover fourth class.[59] The *anusvāra* is as occurs below.[60] Regarding stating it twice, this means that the portion of wisdom is joined to art. Regarding [the syllable] *jñauṁ*, it seems that it is not selected in the *Vajraḍāka*, but is selected in the root tantra. [The letter] *jña*, by means of the method of alliterative etymology, [designates] *jñāna*, gnosis, while *au* is the tenth vowel, designating the five sense powers and five sense objects. It is a lunar day, and a classification of aggregates, sense elements, and sense media. It is said that *anusvāra* designates that everything is experientially unified in the inseparability of emptiness and compassion.

The *kaṁ* of *kṣhmāṁ* means bliss. [The letter] *sh* or *ṣh* is the experience of that. The gnosis that is the self-awareness of great bliss is *kṣha*. The letter *m*, of the fifth palatal class, illustrates the five conceptual imputations of the subject and object. Existing at the end of the palatal class, it reaches the limit of the absence of conceptual imputation. Long *ā* has the form of bliss. The *anusvāra* is emptiness. The *m* serves as the seat of *kṣh*, which possesses bliss. Therefore, its seat is seminal essence. The *kṣh* abides on that seat in the manner of the arising of natural bliss. Regarding stating it twice, if beings have the nature of great bliss, but are obscured by taints, then one should recollect [this syllable] with just the thought "Ignorance of reality is exhausted!"

Since the *h* of *haṁ* has the nature of two *nāda*, i.e., sounds, it is joined

55. These are the three *vimokṣamukha*, namely emptiness (*śūnyatā*), signlessness (*animittatā*), and wishlessness (*apraṇihitatā*). See Thurman 1976, 148.

56. Tsong Khapa here very concisely summarizes Bhavabhaṭṭa's longer commentary at VV 28a.

57. Tsong Khapa is correct that CT reads here *ākaḍḍha*. VD is cryptic here (6b), but Bhavabhaṭṭa does interpret it as coding *ākaḍḍhya* rather than *ākaḍḍha* (VV 28a).

58. The *h* is coded in VD as "the end of *s*," while the *r* is coded as "sun" (VD 6a). Tsong Khapa here follows Bhavabhaṭṭa's commentary (VV 28b).

59. This, presumably, is a reference to Kambala's association of Heruka with the fourth or *shūdra* social class, discussed above in the context of chapter 16. See SN 35a.

60. That is, as Tsong Khapa explains with respect to the syllable *kṣhmāṁ* below.

with the long *ā*. The relevance of the [letter] *h*, the lunar day, and the *anusvāra* is as previously explained. The third vowel, *i*, of *hiṁ*, is the realization of discerning gnosis, the third gnosis. The fifth vowel, *u*, of *huṁ*, is the nature of the five gnoses. The rest should be known from what has been previously explained.[61]

Kaṁ, i.e., the *k* of *kili* to which an *anusvāra* has been given, means bliss. [The letters] *s* and *c*, [of the expressions *sili* and *cili*], are combined or bound together. That is, they are bliss and emptiness inseparably combined. The *dhi* [of *dhili*] is the extremely pure intelligence that enjoys non-dual bliss. In the *Vajraḍāka* there is no *hili*; it selects *cili* instead. While the root tantra selects *hili*, this is acceptable, since it is explained that *s* and *h* are combined.[62] Since the application of [the vowel] *i* to the four [consonants], *k* etc. is explained as meaning "supreme," and as it seems that the application of [the vowel] *i* to [the four] [consonants], *k* and so forth, is also like that, it appears to be appropriate to apply the explanation of the former letters to the [letter] *l* [that follows them].

The two *hu* are the portion of art, and the crescent moon and drop (*candrabindu*) are the portion of wisdom, so *huṁ* is the inseparability of art and wisdom that unite them. In the context of the explanation of the root [tantra's] intention in the *Vajraḍāka*, two *huṁ*, two *phaṭ*, and *svāhā* are joined to the end [of the mantra].[63] In the root tantra's seventh chapter and in this chapter, two *huṁ* and one *phaṭ* are applied,[64] while the *Discourse Appendix* applies two *hūṁ* and two *phaṭ*.[65]

Regarding the placement of the entire root mantra at the end of "the section on the messenger" (*dūtīkalpa*) in ten chapters,[66] it is for the sake of

61. That is, the meaning of the letter *h* etc.

62. The Sanskrit text of CT, like VD, reads *cili cili* (Gray 2012, 149), and this is supported by Bhavabhaṭṭa's commentary (Pandey 2002, 58), which reads *cili cili*. The Tibetan translation reads *hili hili*, following the AU reading.

63. CT reads only *hūṁ hūṁ* (not *huṁ huṁ*) and omits *phaṭ phaṭ svāhā*. VD does code *huṁ* and adds *phaṭ* as well (VD 6a). Bhavabhaṭṭa reads *hūṁ hūṁ phaṭ phaṭ svāhā* here (VV 29b).

64. Both Tibetan translations read *hūṁ hūṁ phaṭ* here (PM 230b and SL 118b).

65. AU reads *hūṁ hūṁ phaṭ phaṭ* in the context of chapter 57 (AU 352a).

66. This refers to the ten chapters from chapter 14 through chapter 24, all of which deal with the classes of female practitioners and the methods for identifying them and communicating with them.

knowing the union of bliss and emptiness in reliance upon the messenger. This is explained to be the definitive meaning of the root tantra, as very clearly explained in the explanatory tantras and commentaries. That is, it is seen as the essence of the path.

3.3.3. 2.2.2. 4.1.3. Showing the Name of the Chapter

In the *Concise* ***Shrī Herukābhidhāna Tantra***, this is **the twenty-fifth chapter** on **the procedure of the secret** definitive meaning **of the root mantra.**[67] This is the explanation of the twenty-fifth chapter in the *Illumination of the Hidden Meaning, A Detailed Exegesis of the Concise Saṁvara Tantra Called "The Chakrasaṁvara."*

67. The Sanskrit title for this chapter of the root tantra, preserved by Bhavabhaṭṭa, reads, "The Procedure of Completely Hiding the Root Mantra," *mūlamantrasarvagopyavidhi* (Pandey 2002, 131). This corresponds exactly to the SL title, *rtsa ba'i sngags thams cad sbas pa'i cho ga* (Gray 2012, 449), but the PM and SM translations' title, which Tsong Khapa follows, is a bit different, reading "The Procedure of the Secret of the Root Mantra," *rtsa ba'i sngags kyi gsang ba'i cho ga* (Gray 2012, 332, 526).

Chapter 26

Chapter 26 Outline

3.3.3. 2.2.2. 4.2. Showing the eight commitments

The second part, showing the eight commitments, has six sections: (1) demonstrating the greatness of the root mantra, (2) the bestowal of all powers through the worship of the messenger, (3) the procedures of the commitments and vows, (4) the cause of delighting the messenger, (5) the procedure of examining the disciple, and (6) showing the name of the chapter.

3.3.3. 2.2.2. 4.2.1. Demonstrating the greatness of the root mantra

After the twenty-fifth [chapter], [the text reads] "**Furthermore**," [implying] "I will also explain other [matters] than that which is explained in chapter twenty-five."[68] **Having known** well the definitive meaning of **Shrī**

68. Tsong Khapa takes the conjunction *de nas gzhan yang*, "furthermore," and breaks it into portions that he analyzes as separate terms.

Heruka's root **mantra**, regarding which there **exists no** other mantra as supreme **in** this **triple world** or three realms,[69] one **disregards**, i.e., rejects, primary adherence to **the all** of the literal meanings of **mantras (26.1)** and adheres primarily to that very definitive meaning of mantra.[70]

3.3.3. 2.2.2. 4.2.2. The bestowal of all powers through the worship of the messenger

Since it appears that [the text] **in the usual or reverse order** is explained as [meaning] not transgressing the stages of the teaching of yoga, "the usual order" means upholding that which is to be upheld, and "reverse order" not skipping over the rejection of that which is to be abandoned.[71]

The messengers, since they are like messengers, will certainly bestow the awakened state, and they are **present**, exist truly, everywhere, through the method of giving rise to joy and the nature of non-dual joy. It is explained that they **bestow powers** that are **below**, i.e., mundane, whatever exists in the underworld, and those that are **above**, i.e., the power of the great seal.[72]

Another commentary explains:[73]

> Regarding the messengers who **are placed in the usual order**, they are placed, in descending order, from Prachaṇḍā to Mahāvīryā. **Placed in reverse order** refers to their placement

69. Tsong Khapa glosses *'jig rten gsum* with the synonym *sa gsum*, which likewise refers to the heavens, earth, and underworlds.

70. Tsong Khapa is clearly uncomfortable with the root text's statement that "all [other] mantras should be disregarded," and seeks to explain it in terms of discriminating between the definitive versus literal interpretations of mantras, rather than between the mantras themselves.

71. Tsong Khapa may here be following Devagupta, who wrote, laconically, that "**in the usual or reverse order** means that one should train in accordance with the stages" (SS 110a). All of the other Indian commentators interpret this line, "The messengers are placed in the usual or reverse order" as a reference to the twenty-four ḍākinīs of chapter 4, which Tsong Khapa discussed below. This interpretation is also followed by Sachen (PG 336.3) and Butön (NS 156b).

72. Tsong Khapa here paraphrases Kambala's commentary at SN 39b.

73. Tsong Khapa here paraphrases Bhavabhaṭṭa's commentary at CV 202a; for the Sanskrit see Pandey 2002, 483.

> in ascending order, from Mahāvīryā to Prachaṇḍā. If one meditates having thus previously arranged them positioned **below** and **above**, then **power** is **bestowed**.

In practicing the supreme, with whom does one practice? It is **my messenger**. She **goes to all** (**26.2**) places[74] through the mode of bestowing kisses and embraces etc. to all for the purpose of achieving the aims of fortunate beings.[75] If **that messenger** who is like this **bestows all powers** even by **looking** with the eye, **touching** with the body, or hearing, what need is there to mention her bestowing power through being propitiated continually and correctly? This is the explanation of the three scholars.[76]

Regarding the messenger's system of bestowing power by means of looking and so forth, it is through a process of giving rise to great bliss. The *[Ḍākinīs'] Vajra Pavillion* states:[77]

> There is bliss through seeing a good woman,
> Good too is the bliss from hearing her song.
> The bliss from smelling her scent is greater,
> And even greater touching her vulva.
> No one can turn away from union's bliss,
> For it's the draught of the supreme savor.

Thus, the blazing of great bliss from the sight and so forth of the supreme messenger is the "melting bliss" (*zhu bde*). One must melt the body's seminal essence to give rise to that bliss, and for that [to happen] it is essential that the fury fire blaze. Since the fire is kindled through the force of the accumulated winds, if one is blessed by the supreme messenger, just as soon

74. Tsong Khapa here glosses the term "omnipresent" (*sarvagāḥ, kun 'gro*) as *gnas kun tu 'gro ba'o*.

75. Tsong Khapa here comments on the text *don kun ster* (Gray 2012, 333), which might translate *sarvārtha*, corresponding somewhat to Bhavabhaṭṭa's reading *sattvārthasiddhidam* (Pandey 2002, 483). Jayabhadra, however, reads here *sarvasiddhidāṁ* (Sugiki 2001, 125), which corresponds to Sumatikīrti's reading (SL: *kun grub ster*, Gray 2012, 449).

76. Tsong Khapa here expands upon Butön's commentary at NS 157a.

77. The text occurs as follows in the canonical translation: *bud med bzang mo mthong bas bde / rna bas glu yi bde bas bzang / snom pas dri yi bde ba che / skye gnas reg pa'i bde chen dang / ro yi btung ba'i sbyor ba las / gang gis bde 'gog par byed* (DV 57b.4–5).

as she is seen one will generate great bliss continually and without reversal, even if there are contradictory conditions, through the force of the accumulated powers of wind that draw forth great bliss. Thus, one will very quickly [progress on] the path of the messenger.

One should **always**, i.e., continually, kiss and embrace the messenger. Furthermore, [one should] **especially** [kiss and embrace] **the seat**, i.e., distinctive place, in which occurs **the yoga** of the non-dual union of bliss and emptiness, that is, the supreme lotus.[78] It is there that **the kissing** (26.3) should be done, meaning that one rubs it by moving about the tip of one's tongue. Having delighted one's mind with beer drinking, one should engage in love play, uniting the vajra and lotus. One engages in love play **so long as** one knows **the yoga** spoken by Vajrasattva, which is **the host of**[79] sexual positions (*karaṇa*)[80] explained in the treatises on love (*kāmaśāstra*). **It is said that** [doing this] causes **the production of all powers.**[81]

Another commentary explains that:[82]

> **The messengers** who live at **the seats of yoga**, i.e., the seats (*pīṭha*), subsidiary seats (*upapīṭha*), etc. **bestow all powers**, meaning that [the messengers] will [bestow] power if one has been instructed in the stages explained in the treatises on love such as **kissing** and **embracing**.

78. Tsong Khapa is commenting here upon the text *yogapīṭhaṁ viśeṣataḥ, rnal 'byor gnas kyi khyad par.*

79. Tsong Khapa here is commenting on the term *yogasaṁghātāḥ, rnal 'byor tshogs rnams.* One should note that Bhavabhaṭṭa interprets this compound differently, explaining that it refers to "a community of yoginīs" (Pandey 2002, 484: *yogasaṁghātā iti yoginīsamūhā ity arthaḥ*).

80. This is transliterated by Tsong Khapa incorrectly as *ka ra na.*

81. Tsong Khapa here closely follows Kambala's commentary at SN 40a.

82. Tsong Khapa here quotes this passage as: *gnas dang nye ba'i gnas la sogs pa rnal 'byor gyi gnas la gnas pa'i pho nya mos ni / dngos grub thams cad ster te tsumba na dang 'khyud pa 'dod pa'i bstan bcos las bshad pa'i rim pas bsten na dngos grub tu 'gyur ro.* It occurs as follows in Bhavyakīrti's commentary (BC 22b.1–2): *gnas dang nye ba'i gnas la sogs par gnas pa'i rnal 'byor ma rnams dngos grub ster bar 'gyur ba ste / tsumba na dang 'khyud pa 'dod pa'i bstan bcos las bshad pa'i rim pas bstan na de la pho nya ma rnams dngos grub ster bar 'gyur ro.* The words in brackets are words omitted by Tsong Khapa that are included in the original text. Interestingly, these omissions serve to downplay the positive contribution of the female messenger here.

If one sees a yoginī who is possessed of **the real thing**, or honesty, or the commitments, they, meaning food, feasts, beer, and the signs, **should be offered** [to her]. **It is never otherwise**, (26.4) meaning that they should never be offered to one who lacks the commitments.

Who are the messengers? **One's mother, sister, daughter**, and **wife can serve as messengers**. Furthermore, the "field-born," "mantra-born," and "natural" are the "mother" and so forth, and it is said that they should be worshipped by one who is meditatively absorbed in the goddess Lochanā etc.[83]

As for them, to whom does the messenger always **bestow the mantra**? It is explained that **the procedure** (26.5) for this is that one who has been made a suitable vessel by consecration etc. serves the messenger. Someone might say that the "mother" is the consort, and that having intercourse with one who is one's mother would be having intercourse by means of religious deception. In response to this, while it is the messenger that bestows the mantra, since there is no contact with her vulva, there is no contradiction. It is explained that: "The guru's seal (consort) is the 'mother,' one's fellow student is the 'sister,' she to whom one teaches the Dharma is **the daughter**, and she who is given by the guru is the **wife**."[84] Kambala explains that the literal meaning of "mother" etc. is intended for exalted yogins. For the inferior ones, "mother" etc. should be taken as just explained.[85]

3.3.3. 2.2.2. 4.2.3. The procedures of the commitments and vows

The third part has four sections: (1) the promise to explain, (2) heteropraxy together with worship, (3) showing each of the commitments, and (4) their concise meaning.

83. None of the commentaries that I have consulted correlate the messengers to deities such as Lochanā.

84. Tsong Khapa here quotes the text of Durjayachandra, as follows: *bla ma'i phyag rgya ni ma'o / lhan cig nyan pa ni sring mo'o / rang gi chos bstan pa ni bu mo / bla mas byin pa ni chung ma'o* (RG 288a.2–3). Tsong Khapa closely paraphrases him in the previous objection. Butön also quotes this text (NS 157b).

85. This is not what Kambala states; he simply states that "**mother, sister**, etc. are to be taken literally" (SN 40a.4: *ma dang sring mo zhes bya ba la sogs pa rnams ni sgra ji bzhin pa'o*).
The claim that this is only the case for exalted yogins appears to be Tsong Khapa's.

3.3.3. 2.2.2. 4.2.3. 1. The promise to explain

Now, following the worship of the messenger, **I**, Vajradhara, **will explain the commitments** that delight the messenger. What are the commitments like? They are very **difficult to obtain in the** lower **yoga tantras.** "In the yoga tantras" has been taken as referring to the father tantras, and that which is difficult to find in those tantras are the "eight extraordinary commitments of the yoginī tantras." This interpretation should not be accepted, since, with the exception of the heteropraxical commitment only, the others are similar to those in the father tantras.[86]

3.3.3. 2.2.2. 4.2.3. 2. Heteropraxy together with worship

If **a man or woman** sees a yoginī, he or she should **go** placing her to **the left**, and she bestows **the** fruit **desired** in his or her mind (**26.6**). **Those who stay in houses and fields even if** they stay in **far away** places, **should be recognized**, and one should practice heteropraxy. Here women are said to be yoginīs, and men are also known to be yogins; they are not simply men and women. Those who live "far away" are evidently ones who live in excellent "fields" (*kṣetra*). Moreover, it is also said that:[87]

> When you see women, circle them three times left-wise, and, bowing your head as well, supplicate them three times, [saying]:
>
> You are my mother, and I am your son.
> Until awakening occurs, guard me
> By means of your milk that originates
> From the factors of awakening's breast.

Regarding this supplication "You are the mother" etc., although this can be made openly, it is a commitment that this must be done mentally. Bhavabhaṭṭa explains that:[88]

86. Tsong Khapa here refers to Sachen's argument at PG 337.2. This edition of Sachen's text reproduces five folio sides per page, so citations refer to page number, folio side, and, when necessary, line numbers.

87. I am not sure what the source is for this passage. It does not occur in any of the sources I have consulted. Tsong Khapa quotes it as follows: *khyod ma bdag ni bu yin te / ji srid byang chub 'byung bar du / byang chub yan lag nu ma las / byung ba'i rang gi 'o mas skyongs.*

88. This is a translation of the text as it occurs in Bhavabhaṭṭa's commentary, which is:

> It is known that **the man or woman** [who] **goes**, having placed another man or woman **to the left**, is a yogin or yoginī in Shrī Chakrasaṁvara. On account of [it is certain that] he or she **proceeds to** his or her **desired power. Therefore** [it is said that they **should be recognized, even if far away**.] Even if one does not see the previously stated characteristics, the [male or] female messenger is characterized by his or her going, turning to the left. [Where is the messenger? **The house** etc.]

Since **there is no yoga** greater than Shrī **Heruka's** yoga, Shrī **Heruka's** yoga is the best yoga. Thus, since **the master** who holds this yoga is the creator **of the** supreme **yoga**, he is **the mother** and father of the yogas (**26.7**). **The adept**, i.e., yogin, who is consecrated **in this** *Saṁvara Tantra* is **excellent**, i.e., supreme. Therefore, they[89] **should not be disparaged**, i.e., deprecated, **nor should they be insulted**, i.e., slandered. **They should be worshipped with devotion** (**26.8**) to the best of one's ability.[90]

Since **Kākāsyā** etc. occur after the explanation of the eight commitments in Kambala's and Devagupta's commentaries, I will not quote it in the

---

vāmena naraṁ striyaṁ sthāpayitvānyaḥ puruṣaḥ striyo vā yāti sa ca śrīcakrasaṁvare yogī yoginī veti jñāyate / ataś ca siddhir iṣṭāni gacchati niyatā bhavati / ata āha vijñāyate sudure 'pīti / pūrvoktalakṣaṇādarśane 'pi vāmāvartagamanāl lakṣyate dūto dūtī vā / kurta dūta ity āha gṛha ity ādinā / (Pandey 2002, 485); *g.yon du skyes pa'am bud med bzhag nas gzhan skyes pa'am bud med 'gro ba gang yin pa de ni dpal 'khor lo sdom pa'i rnal 'byor ma'am rnal 'byor par shes par bya'o / de'i phyir yang 'dod pa'i dngos grub tu 'gyur ro zhes nges pa yin no / de bas na shin tu ring ba yang shes par 'gyur / zhes gsungs te/ sngon du bstan pa'i mtshan nyid ma mthong yang g.yon nas bskor zhing 'gro bas mtshon pa ni pho nya'am pho nya mo'o / pho nya gang nas zhes pa la pho nya zhes bya ba la khyim dang zhes bya ba la sogs pa gsungs so/* (Pandey 2002, 606).

Tsong Khapa's version of this text is abbreviated: *rang gi g.yon du skyes pa'am bud med bzhag nas 'gro ba'i skyes pa'am bud med ni / bde mchog gi rnal 'byor pa'am rnal 'byor mar shes par bya'o / de'i phyir yang 'dod pa'i dngos grub tu 'gyur ro / de bas na shin tu ring ba ste sngar bshad pa'i mtshan nyid ma mthong yang / g.yon nas bskor zhing 'gro bas mtshon pa ni pho nya mo ste / de yang khyim dang zhing na gnas pa zhes 'chad do.*

The text that Tsong Khapa omits is included in square brackets. Note that in place of the final line of the passage, Tsong Khapa adds the following: "She also lives in a house and field."

89. It is not clear to whom the plural pronoun here refers, since the plural referents in the root text, the "master and mothers of yoga" are apparently reduced by Tsong Khapa to the singular and masculine figure of the guru.

90. Tsong Khapa gives both of the two textual variants here, *bhaktitaḥ*, "with devotion," and *śaktitaḥ*. Regarding this, see Gray 2012, 151–52, n. 1911.

context of the eight commitments.[91] Although other commentaries explain them in this context, I will not quote them in the context of the eight commitments. What then is the explanation here? The explanation of the previous ones, that it is for the sake of revering Kākāsya etc., as well as their corresponding animals,[92] is incorrect. With regard to this, it is said that if the adept worships with devotion the Saṁvara yogins in the same manner that the eight gate keepers are worshipped, he will be mentally blessed. As Bhavabhaṭṭa previously explained with respect to "worshipped with devotion," [the text] "states Kākā, etc., indicating that **these eight** [goddesses], **Kākāsyā and so forth, truly promote devotion and faith**, and they are **the cause of the powers**."[93]

Always, i.e., continually, being devoted to the guru and yogins is **the cause of the powers (26.9abc)**. Since the gatekeeper goddesses turn back the hindering, obstructing spirits in order to promote more and more devotion and faith, [the statement that] the gatekeeper goddesses are the cause of promoting the powers is very good. Since the equivalent term of "liberation" (*'grol ba*, *mukti*) seems to also apply to devotion and aspiration, here the translations "aspiration" (*mos pa*) and "devotion" (*gus pa*) are better.[94]

91. Tsong Khapa is here referring to the text "these eight, Kākāsyā and so forth, who truly promote devotion and faith." While it is true that Kambala and Devagupta discuss these lines following the eight commitments (SN 40b and SS 111a), Tsong Khapa's position here is weak, as this text occurs before the list of the eight commitments in the surviving Sanskrit texts as well as the Tibetan trans. In fact, these eight guardian goddesses (*kākāsyādayo 'ṣṭau hy ete*) clearly decline with the gerundives of the previous verse (*nāvamantavyāḥ, nāpy adhikṣeptavyāḥ, pūjanīyāś ca*; see Pandey 2002, 485) indicating that they are the objects of these actions. As we shall see, Tsong Khapa does not agree with this interpretation, which fits his tendency to seek to replace the female objects of devotion with male objects.

92. This argument is made by Sachen at PG 337.3.

93. As before, Tsong Khapa's version of Bhavabhaṭṭa's text is slightly abbreviated, with the term "goddesses" omitted. The text occurs in Bhavabhaṭṭa's commentary as follows: *kāketyādi kākāsyādayo 'ṣṭau devyo bhaktiśraddhāvivardhikāḥ bhavanti / tāś ca kāraṇaṁ siddhīnām* (Pandey 2002, 485); *khwa gdong ma la sogs zhes gsungs te khwa gdong ma la sogs pa lha mo brgyad pa 'di gus pa dang dad pa 'phel bar byed pa yin no / de yang dngos grub rnams kyi rgyu yin no,* (2002, 608). Tsong Khapa quotes this passage as follows: *ka ka sogs kyis ston pa la khva gdong ma la sogs pa brgyad po 'di gus pa dang dad pa 'phel bar byed pa yin no / de yang dngos grub rnams kyi rgyu yin no.*

94. Here Tsong Khapa is referring to the PM translation of 26.9b, *grol dang dad pa phel byed pa* (Gray 2012, 333–34), which may be misreading of *bhakti* as *mukti*, or a genuine textual variant. All extant Sanskrit mss. read here either *bhaktiśraddhāvivardhikāḥ* or

3.3.3. 2.2.2. 4.2.3. 3. Showing each of the commitments

The protection of the commitments (**28.9d**) to renounce disparaging and slandering the previously explained heteropraxy is the first. "**Moreover**" (*ca, kyang*) is for emphasis exclusively on the act of protecting. The previous explanation of heteropraxy was just an example. One should abide in all [types of] heteropraxy.

The second commitment is renouncing **union with another goddess**, i.e., consort, on account of being **stupefied** and attached to **lust**. Kambala explains that this [prohibits] renouncing the method of the supreme yoga and relying on another [system of] yoga.[95] Vīravajra also states [that this passage means] "becoming attached to **lust** for **union with other goddesses**."[96]

Regarding the third commitment, it is said that one should avoid dichotomizing self and other. It seems that this is stated for the sake of those who are not devoid of the realization of non-duality. Furthermore, since this means that one should make oneself non-devoid of, i.e., that one should protect, the realization of thatness, [the text] should be read as "not taking as two" or "**non-dual.**"

Unobstructed is explained as meaning that no one whatsoever is able to oppress one. That is, being unable to instruct [others] in [subjects] other than the extraordinary tantric perspective is the fourth commitment. If [the text] seems to read "not being unobstructed," this means that one should avoid that.

The commitment is the goddess or consort. **Performance** means the performance of sexual passion (*kāma, 'dod pa*). Being **occupied** (**26.10**)

śraddhābhaktivivardhikāḥ (Gray 2012, 152, n. 1913). In place of *grol*, the SL and SM translations read *mos* and *gus*, respectively (Gray 2012, 450, 527).

95. Tsong Khapa here condenses Kambala's commentary. He wrote that "He who desires power by renouncing the method of the supreme yoga of delighting in great compassion, and relying on another [system of] yoga for the sake of achieving the powers of the desire realm deities, is **stupified** like a blind man." (SN 40a.6–7: *snying rje chen por rab dga' ba'i / rnal 'byor mchog gi thabs spangs nas / 'dod lha'i dngos grub bsgrub don du / rnal 'byor gzhan la brten byas pas / gang zhig dngos grub 'dod gyur pa / dmus long bzhin du rnam par rmongs*).

96. This text does not occur in either of Vīravajra's commentaries. The text *'dod la chags pa* does occur in Jayabhadra's (CP 57a) and Bhavabhaṭṭa's (CV 203a) commentaries, but in these cases, it is simply an alternate translation corresponding to the Sanskirt *kāmavimohitaḥ*.

means doing that. The sphere of that is the actual and gnostic seals.[97] With regard to this, when one practices this, the third [commitment] prohibits its performance for one who lacks the view of thatness, and, through the fourth, one produces a mentality that is not otherwise [than this]. [This is] the fifth commitment.

Koṅkana [Jayabhadra] claims that relying upon a human female (*nārī, mi mo*), i.e., **woman**, one should not lack mastery (*aiśvarya, dbang phyug nyid*) when uniting the vajra and lotus. Regarding this Bhavyakīrti explains that one should not lack a lady (*īśvarī, dbang phyug mo*).[98] One brings about [the state of] not lacking [her] by being "well-united" or "extremely united."[99] That one should not lack [her] for as long as one has not perfected the ability to draw forth natural bliss is the sixth commitment.

Just as it is explained that there is no deprivation in the sixth commitment, the seventh commitment is that one should **observe chastity** wherein there is no outward release from the tip of the secret place when seminal essence trickles down from the head, the repository of bliss.[100]

97. That is, the *karmamudrā* practices, which entail union with a physical seal, or the *jñānamudrā* practices, which involve union with a visualized seal.

98. Tsong Khapa's source here is Bhavyakīrti, who quotes Jayabhadra's commentary then and comments upon it as follows: "Regarding **united with a woman**, Koṅkana claims that, when uniting the vajra and lotus, if there is no master one should not lack mastery; otherwise, it should be done in a masterful manner. This is the sixth [commitment]. I, Bhavyakīrti, hold that when [engaged in] sexual pleasure, the yoginī alone is the central figure." (BC 23b: *bud med dbang phyug shin tu sbyor / zhes bya ba ni rdo rje dang padma mngon par 'du bya ba'i dus su dbang phyug med cing dbang phyug dang bral bar mi bya'i / gzhan du na dbang phyug nyid du bya'o zhes bya ba ni drug pa'o zhes koṅka na'i zhal sna nas bzhed doskal ldan grags pa ni rab tu dga' ba'i dus su rnal 'byor ma nyid gtso bo yin no zhes 'dod do*). Cf. Sugiki 2001, 126 and CP 57a.

99. Tsong Khapa here glosses the Tibetan translations *legs par sbyor* (PM, SM) and *shin tu sbyor* (SL), which are poor translations of the Sanskrit *sumanthāna*, "excellent churning stick."

100. The Sanskrit here, as preserved in the AU mss. and Jayabhadra's commentary, is "yet observe chastity in meditation," *brahmacaryaṁ tathā dhyāne* (CT 26.11b and Gray 2012, 152), a reading attested by all of the Tibetan translations. Bhavabhaṭṭa's commentary, however, attests the variant noted by Tsong Khapa, namely *brahmacaryaṁ tathādhāne* (Pandey 2002, 486). The root meaning of *ādhāna* is "to deposit," and it can have the sense of "impregnate," but it can also have the opposite meaning, "to receive," "take," "conceive." The Tibetan translation of Bhavabhaṭṭa's commentary takes it in the latter sense of the word, and also makes it clear that it is the ejaculation of semen that is implied here: "**Yet observe chasity in reception** refers to the taking up of the spirit of awakening that has the

The three commentaries read "yet observe chastity in the receptacle."[101]

"Transfer in the hole"[102] is practicing without hostility at the time of taking up the spirit of awakening with the tongue from the woman's lotus. The meaning of **not hostile** is (**26.11abc**), as Vīravajra explains: "at the time of taking up the spirit of awakening, one should not give rise to the conception that it is filth."[103] Since the conception of filth or repulsiveness is a [state of] non-desire in which one turns one's back to its object, [the text] "hatred" toward that, which is like that, also occurs elsewhere. This is the eighth commitment.

---

form of reality. Taking it up without attachment is the seventh." (Pandey 2002, 609–10: *tshang par spyod pa de bzhin blangs zhes gsungs te de bzhin nyid kyi ngo bo nyid byang chub sems blang ba ni mngon par zhen pa med pas blang ba ste bdun pa'o*).

In the original Sanskrit text, Bhavabhaṭṭa glosses *ādhāna*, "to deposit, release," with its antonym, *ādāna*, "to take, draw to oneself," a subtlety that was evidently missed by the Tibetan translators. The Sanskrit text of his commentary reads, "**Yet in reception** refers to the deposition of the seminal essence that has the form of reality; drawing it up without attachment is the seventh" (2002, 486: *tathādāna iti tathatā[rūpa]sya bodhicittasyādhānam ādānaṁ tatrānabhiniveśaḥ saptamaḥ*; the bracketed text is my correction).

At issue here is the challenge presented by sexual yogas to the vows of celibacy taken by monks. The canonical text, "observe chastity in meditation," implies that these practices can be fruitfully undertaken via visualization only. Bhavabhaṭṭa's comment implies the arguably more transgressive, alternative, namely seminal emission followed by reabsorption.

101. Tsong Khapa refers to another variant of this line, *tshangs par spyod pa de bzhin gzhi*, with *gzhi/ādhāra* in place of *dhyāna*, occurs in the translations of the commentaries by Jayabhadra, Bhavyakīrti, and Vīravajra (BC 23b.2: *tshang par spyod pa de bzhin gzhi*; PD 404a.2: *tshang par spyod dang de bzhin gzhi*; CP 57a.6: *tshang par spyod pa de bzhin bzhi*). However, the Sanskrit text of Jayabhadra's commentary attests *dhyāne*, which he glosses as *ādhāre*, as follows: "**Yet observe chasity in meditation** means that, at the time of the trickling of seminal essence in the receptacle, one should observe, i.e., practice, chastity" (Sugiki 2001, 126: *brahmacaryaṁ tathā dhyāna ity ādhāre bodhicittasravaṇakāle brahmatattvaṁ cared ācared ity arthaḥ*).

102. The Sanskrit here reads *srotasaṁcāre*, "in the transfer of fluid," which is correctly translated as *rgyun gyi kun tu spyod* in the SL translation (Gray 2012, 450). In place of *rgyun gyi*, the SM and PM translations give the variant readings *bu gar* and *sbubs su* (Gray 2012, 527, 334), with *sbubs* meaning an interior hollow space, a cavity, tube, or the womb. Tsong Khapa follows the SM translation, reading "in the hole," *bu gur*.

103. Tsong Khapa quotes Vīravajra's text as follows: *byang sems len pa'i dus su btsog pa'i 'du shes mi bya ba*; the text occurs as follows: *byang chub sems len pa'i dus su bcog pa'i 'du shes mi bya ba* (SG 190a5). Note that Tsong Khapa's text has the correct reading *btsog pa'i 'du shes*.

3.3.3. 2.2.2. 4.2.3. 4. Their concise meaning

Upholding **these eight** previously explained [commitments] is **the conduct of the commitments** (**26.11d**). They **should always**, i.e., continually, **be known**, i.e., not forgotten, **by adepts** who are engaged in spiritual practice correctly without settling for mere knowledge. These commitments are **common to all** of **the tantras** of the action (*kriyā*), practice (*caryā*), yoga, higher yoga (*rnal 'byor bla ma*), and yoginī tantra [classes]. They **cannot be destroyed**, i.e., broken, by one who exerts himself the manner of action [tantras], because those lower tantra classes lack the cause of awakening in the manner of the higher tantra classes. This is the explanation of Kambala and Devagupta.[104] According to Koṅkana, since they are common to all tantras, i.e., general, they are secret. Even those who know other tantras do not realize this implication. Since they do not realize the implication, they **lack** the cause, i.e., true **reason** (**26.12**), that cannot be destroyed, i.e., refuted, by other means of knowledge.[105]

Why is this so? They should be **apprehended through the faith** of trust in the tantra. They are not like the forms that can be seen **by the eye**, or the tangible forms touched **by the hand**. With respect to these **secret** commitments, even their name **is not brought to light** for unsuitable vessels but **should be vigorously concealed** (**26.13**); they should be explained to suitable vessels [only].

3.3.3. 2.2.2. 4.2.4. The cause of delighting the messenger

The wise one should move his little finger, that is, stimulate the channel called "crow face" in the messenger's lotus. What is the purpose of this?

104. Tsong Khapa here paraphrases the commentaries contained at SN 40b and SS 111a.

105. Tsong Khapa here glosses Jayabhadra's comments at CP 57b.1, although he downplays the notion of secrecy, and also differs with respect to the gloss of *hetubhiḥ/rgyu yis*. Jayabhadra's full commentary reads as follows: "**Common to all tantras** means that this is the secret of all tantras that is common [to them]. While this secret is implied, those who know other tantras do not know it. Hence [the text] **cannot be destroyed by causes** is stated. That is, they cannot be destroyed by causes, namely by means of knowledge such as direct perception, etc." (Sugiki 2001, 126: *sāmānyaṁ sarvatantrāṇām iti etad rahasyaṁ sarvatantrāṇām iti sāmānyam / ata eva rahasyaṁ abhisaṁdhānam anyatantravido na vidanti / ato na hantavyā hetubhir ity uktaṁ / hetubhiḥ pratyakṣādibhiḥ pramāṇair na hantavyaḥ*).

It is for the sake of the flow of the liquor that exists within **the messenger** (26.14). It is said that that which stimulates [the channel] moves with the concave space [formed by] the tips of the ring and middle fingers.[106] Koṅkana explains that if, when worshipping the goddess with the movement of the little finger, one is unable to find a [woman] who is endowed with the yoga of the deity or well educated in mantra and seal, then one worships another consort, taking her as having the nature of the deity.[107] [He also] explains that **the messengers are positioned** means that, at the time of that [worship], all of the messengers are pleased with the yogin.[108]

Durjayachandra claims that "**the little finger** is the center of the blessed lotus; one should move that."[109] Also, Kambala states that **the little finger** is the joint of an eleven-year-old, and if you take up with the tongue and

106. Tsong Khapa here relies on Bhavabhaṭṭa's commentary, which occurs as follows: "The rite of loving the messenger is indicated by **little finger**, etc. The channel called 'bird face,' *khagamukhā*, which is like a *bandhūka* flower, should be moved, i.e., stimulated, by the concave space [formed] by the tips of the ring and middle fingers as if around a seed, inserted within the flower. What is the purpose of this? The messengers, etc. indicate that [it is done in order to stimulate] the descent of the streaming intoxicant which exists within the messenger" (Pandey 2002, 487: *dūtyanurāgaṇavidhim āha kaniṣṭhām ityādi / khagamukhānāḍīṁ bandhūkakusumasadṛśīṁ kusumasadṛśena kiṁbījenānāmikā-madhyamāgra-saṁpuṭanyastena cālayec codayet / kimartham āha dutaya ityādi / dūtīnāṁ samvyasthānaṁ svavasthānaṁ sravanmadatvam*). Note that Tsong Khapa gives an alternate name for the channel, "crow face" (*kākāsyā, bya rog gdong*).

107. Jayabhadra comments here that: "**The wise one should move his little finger** means that he has union with the goddess at the time of worshipping the goddess. But if a woman who is well educated in mantra and tantra has not been obtained, then cultivating some other uncultivated woman, she should be worshipped (Sugiki 2001, 126–27: *kaniṣṭhāṁ cālayed dhīmān iti devīpūjākāle devatāyogavān ity arthaḥ / athavā mantratantrasuśikṣitā yadi na labhyata itarām apy aprākṛtaṁ kṛtvā pūjāyed iti*; cf. CP 57b.2–3).

108. Tsong Khapa here glosses Jayabhadra's commentary, which is grammatically ambiguous in its Tibetan translation. The commentary reads as follows: *pho nya mo rnams yang dag gnas / zhes bya ba ni / de ltar dus de'i tshe blo dang ldan pa zhes bya ba pho nya mo thams cad dga' bar 'gyur ro zhes bya ba'I don to* (CP 57b.3–4).

This text is ambiguous because it does not indicate the grammatical connection between the wise one/yogin and the rest of the sentence. Tsong Khapa assumes a locative relationship, i.e., the messengers are pleased with the yogin. The Sanskrit, however, reads differently, as follows: "The messengers are positioned means that at that very time all of the messengers are pleased by the wise one, i.e., the yogin" (Sugiki 2001, 127: *dūtayaḥ saṁvyavasthitā ity evaṁ tatkāle dhīmato yoginaḥ sarvā dūtyaḥ suprasannā bhavantītyarthaḥ*).

109. Durjayachandra's commentary here occurs as follows: *blo ldan mthe'u chung bskyod par ni / zhes bya ba la sogs pa smos te / padma'i mthe'u chung ste byin gyis brlabs pa'i lte ba du mthe'u chung ste bskyod par bya zhes sbyar ro /* (RG 289a.7–b.1).

drink the nectar [that flows from] holding and playing with it, it will be the cause that gives rise to great bliss for one who is accomplished in alchemy (*rasāyāna*).[110]

3.3.3. 2.2.2. 4.2.5. The procedure of examining the disciple

There are three types of persons who have the qualities of an **adept, the pure, impure and mixed.** The first, **the purified one**, gives rise to power. The second, **the aspirant**, does not give rise to power. The third, **the illuminating**, is middling; he gives rise to a little bit of power and knows the import of the treatises. Moreover, the aspirant reveres and is skilled in mantra and yoga. **The man** who is **virtuous** and who knows the import of the treatises is **illuminating.** Since he is lamp-like, he is able to act for the benefit of sentient beings. This is what Koṅkana intended, and it is also similar to Vīravajra's explanation.[111]

3.3.3. 2.2.2. 4.2.6. Showing the Name of the Chapter

In the *Concise* ***Shrī Herukābhidhāna Tantra***, this is **the twenty-sixth chapter** on **the procedure of inspecting the disciple**, i.e., the characteristics of superior and inferior disciples, **and the observances**, i.e., the eight

110. Tsong Khapa here expands upon Kambala's comment that occurs as follows: "**Little finger** is one who has the joint of a little finger. Holding the body of an eleven-year-old and taking it up with one's tongue is the cultivation of the achievement of alchemy, which is the cause of great bliss." (SN 40b.6–7: *mthe'u chung zhes bya ba mthe'u chung ni tshigs dang ldan pa ste / lo bcu gcig pa'i bdag nyid bzung nas / lce yis blangs te ra sa ya na'i dngos grub brtsam pa ni bde ba chen po 'byung ba'i rgyu'o*).

111. Tsong Khapa here paraphrases Vīravajra's commentary, which begins by distinguishing the three types of adepts in terms of their capability, and then restates Jayabhadra's commentary; see SG 190b. Jayabhadra's commentary here occurs as follows: "**The aspirant, the purified one, and the illuminating virtuous man** refers to the three types of yogins. The aspirant has not given rise to inspiration (*pratibhā*), the purified one has given rise to competence. The illuminating one is middling, having given rise to some inspiration, and awakening for the sake of self and others. In addition, the aspirant worships the deity through the discipline of *mantrayoga*. The illuminating one who is virtuous and who knows the meaning of the treatises is like a lamp, and is able to accomplish the aims of all beings." (Sugiki 2001, 127: *ārādhako viśuddhaś ca dīpako guṇavān nara iti yogi tridhā vidyate / ārādhaka ity anutpannapratibhāḥ, viśuddha ity utpannasamarthyaḥ, dīpaka iti madhyadīpakaḥ kiṁcidutpannapratibhāḥ svaparārtha-bodhakaś ca / atha vā ārādhako*

commitments. This is the explanation of the twenty-sixth chapter in the *Illumination of the Hidden Meaning, A Detailed Exegesis of the Concise Saṁvara Tantra Called "The Chakrasaṁvara."*

---

mantrayogābhyāsena devatārādhakaḥ, guṇavān śāstrārthavettā, dīpakaḥ pradīpavat sarvasattvārthakriyāsamarthaḥ /; cf, CP 57b.4–6).

Interestingly, Vīravajra, in his other commentary, distinguishes the three types of adept in terms of their mode of practice, writing that "**the pure** one meditates on the creation stage, and **the impure** one meditates on the perfection stage in which the five types of nectar are enjoyed. **The mixed** one meditates on both the creation and perfection stages" (PD 404b: *dag pa ni bskyed pa'i rim pa bsgom pa'o / ma dag pa ni bdud rtsi rnam pa lnga la longs spyod pa'i rdzogs pa'i rim pa bsgom pa'o / 'dres pa ni bskyed rdzogs gnyis ka bsgom pa'o*). This inverts the hierarchy assumed by commentators such as Jayabhadra.

Chapter 27

Chapter 27 Outline

3.3.3. 2.2.2. 5. The detailed exegesis of the conceptually elaborate practices

The fifth part, the detailed exegesis of the conceptually elaborate practices, has two sections: (1) the general arrangement of practices, and (2) the conceptually elaborate practices shown by three chapters.

3.3.3. 2.2.2. 5.1. The general arrangement of practices

In general, there are two contexts for the performance of practices. These are creation stage practices that support the attainment of mundane powers, and perfection stage practices that support the rapid attainment of the supreme power. The creation stage practices are done in the state of being very stable in the deity yoga and so forth, and I have explained in detail elsewhere the three contexts for the performance for perfection stage practices.[112] In the literature of this tantra, the *Conduct [of the Yoginīs Tantra]*[113] states that:[114]

> First, the yogin who's equipoised
> Gives rise to power zealously.
> Later, giving rise to power,
> The great hero wanders about
> As he desires in his mind,
> In the observance of his vow,
> So as to benefit beings.

The *Origin of Saṁvara [Tantra]* and *Kiss [Tantra]* also state that one should practice having attained the heat [aid to penetration].[115] This is explained in the twenty-ninth chapter [of the *Chakrasaṁvara*], which states that "one will be awakened through constant practice in the nature of the exercises of heat (**29.7ab**)." Kambala explains that the attainment of heat is the heat that is one of the four [aids to penetration on the] path of application.[116]

The *Sheaf of Esoteric Instructions* explains that distinctive power is attained [through this, as follows]:[117]

112. In his *rim lnga gsal sgron*, he describes these as the occasions of birth, death, and the between state. See *sku 'bum par ma* vol. ja, fol. 68a ff.

113. While Tsong Khapa transliterates this text as the *Yoginīsaṁcārya*, I, following the Pandey 1998 edition, quote this text's title as the *Yoginīsaṁcāra*.

114. This text occurs at the beginning of YS ch. 15, as follows: *prathaṁ samāhito yogī śaktim utpādya yatnataḥ / paścād utpannasāmarthyo vratacaryāṁ manopsitām / paryaṭati mahāvīraḥ sattvānugrahahetunā /* (Pandey 1998, 133, 331; cf. YS 42a).

115. Tsong Khapa here refers to the "heat" aid to penetration, *uṣmanirvedabhāgiya*, of the "path of application" (*prayogamārga*), described by Vasubandhu in his commentary on Asaṅga/Maitreyanātha's *Ornament of the Universal Vehicle Sutras* (ch. 14 following v. 26, see Bagchi 1970, 91 and the translation in Jamspal et al. 2004, 180–81).

116. Kambala, in his comments on this line in CT ch. 29, does not connect "the exercise of heat" (*uṣmākriyā, dro ba'i bya ba*), with the path of application (SN 57a). Jayabhadra makes this connection, however. See my note on this text in chapter 29 below.

117. This passage occurs as follows: *drod ni rnal 'byor gyi mthu ste / gang las 'di rnal 'byor*

> Heat is the power of yoga and is that by which [yogīs] are delighted on account of enjoying yoga. Opportunists, however, cannot endure this.[118] They [yogīs] become powerful in destroying and conferring benefit, and are not oppressed by heat, cold, and so forth.

"Practice" is of three [types]—conceptually elaborate, unelaborate, and extremely unelaborate. The defining characteristics of these three [types] are unclear in other texts. I will summarize and extensively explain [these types of] practice. The *Sheaf of Esoteric Instructions*, on account of its summary of practice, explains these three [types] of practice, which is excellent.[119]

The conceptually elaborate includes the yogī or yoginī who identifies him or herself with the quantity of deities in the mandala engaging with the appearances of each of the deities. At the conclusion of the *sādhana* visualization, he or she practices for the sake of objects of desire by means of the manifold elaborations that he or she has, such as the hand gestures (*hastamudrā*, *lag pa'i phyag rgya*), the responses to these, as well as song and dance and their responses.

The unelaborate is practicing for the sake of objects of desire, leaving behind the manifold elaborations such as hand gestures and so forth. It is explained that there are three [types of elaborations], the manifold, in which the yogī or yoginī self-identifies with the full count of [mandala] deities, the middling, in which this is done together with the five or four seals (*mudrā*), and the concise, done together with one. In these two [the elaborate and unelaborate practice modes], one practices relying on an actual seal (*karmamudrā*).

In the extremely unelaborate [practice mode], one leaves behind all outer

---

la dga' bas rab tu mgu bar 'gyur ba dang / klags 'tshol ba rnams kyis kyang 'di la mi bzod pa dang / tshar gcod pa dang rjes su 'dzin par nus par 'di rnams 'gyur ba dang grang ba dang rlung la sogs pa rnams kyis zil gyis mi non pa'o (AM 186a1–2). Tsong Khapa quotes the passage as follows: *drod ni rnal 'byor gyi mthu ste gang las 'di rnal 'byor la dga' bas rab tu mgu bar 'gyur ba dang / glags tshol ba rnams kyis kyang 'di la mi bzod pa dang / tshar gcod pa dang rjes su 'dzin par nus par 'di rnams 'gyur ba dang / grang ba dang rlung la sogs pa rnams kyis zil gyis mi non pa'o.*

118. That is, *glags tshol ba rnams kyis kyang 'di la mi bzod pa.* I presume that this means that opportunists, who do not actually enjoy the yoga but simply see it as a means to a desired end, cannot endure the arduous requisite training in yoga.

119. See AM 177b.

elaborations, and meditates upon the great seal relying solely upon the gnostic seal (*jñānamudrā*). Here this is also called "the practice of *bhusuku*." In regard to the first syllable [*bhu*], adding syllables yields *bhuñjana*, meaning "eating," if explained etymologically.[120] Likewise, [*su*] is explained as *sutana*, meaning "sleeping,"[121] and [*ku*] is explained as *kuṭisara*, meaning "going out for the purpose of defecation or urination."[122] One renounces distractions, with the exception of just those three conceptions. One guards the mixing of sleep and clear light without any thought whatsoever for one's body, life, sense objects, or sense powers.[123] Someone explains that: "*bhu* means 'eating' if one derives it from *bhuktā*."[124]

The *Esoteric Accomplishment* states that, with regard to practice, there are two [modes], namely, practice wandering like a goblin,[125] and, if one is unable to abandon one's home, practice in one's own home.[126] Since the *Origin of Saṁvara* also states that one should do what one wishes from among the three, i.e., wandering like a leaf in motion, practicing in a charnel ground or at a tree etc., or practicing in one's own home, there is no definitive need to go to many places.[127] The *Kiss [Tantra]* also mentions the

120. This would appear to be an attempt to connect *bhu* with the verbal root *bhuj*, which does mean "to eat." The term *bhuñjana* does not appear to be an actual word or verb form, but it is close to genuine forms such as *bhuñjati* and *bhuñjanti*.

121. This appears to represent an attempt to connect the syllable *su* with the verbal root *svap*, "to sleep."

122. The term *kuṭisara* appears to be a compound meaning "going to the hut," with "hut" here possibly being a euphemism for an outhouse.

123. Tsong Khapa here closely follows Kambala's commentary at SN 42b.

124. The term *bhuktā* does indeed mean "eating." I have not identified the source of this quote.

125. That is, a flesh-eating demon, a *sha za* or *piśāca*.

126. Padmavajra makes this argument in chapter 6 of the *Esoteric Accomplishment* (*Guhyasiddhi*). Tsong Khapa particularly refers to v. 13: "The equipoised one who is in union with his own tutelary deity should assume an intoxicated state, become silent, and wander like a goblin." (Samdhong and Dwivedi 1988, 40: *unmattarūpam āsthāya maunībhūtvā samāhitaḥ / svādhidaivatayo-gātmā paryaṭet tu piśācavat*).

127. Tsong Khapa here refers to the *caryānirdeśa* chapter (ch. 21) of SU, and he directly refers to vv. 13–14, which read as follows: "Or, a man who desires the practice named "the wind" should always wander about without friends, lonely and fixing his mind on one object. He who observes the vow of madness should, like a leaf moved (by the wind), roam about a graveyard, a place where there is only one *liṅga* column (*ekaliṅga*), a place where there is only one tree (*ekavṛkṣa*) or a forest" (Tsuda 1974, 305).

practice of "victory over the quarters,"[128] the practice of the central channel or *avadhūtī*,[129] and the practice of the observance of madness.[130] These can be categorized within the three [types of] practice, and are not additional [categories]. Since I have exhaustively commented on the other explanations elsewhere, I will not elaborate further. Instead, I will explain how the [next] three chapters show the elaborate [form of practice], and how the thirty-eighth [chapter] shows the other two [types of] practice.

3.3.3. 2.2.2. 5.2. The conceptually elaborate practices shown by three chapters

The second part has three sections: (1) the practice of the observances together with the offerings and sacrificial cakes, (2) the procedure of the inner fire sacrifice together with one clan, and (3) the characteristics of the messenger and provisional procedures for the attainment of heat or power.

3.3.3. 2.2.2. 5.2.1. The practice of the observances together with the offerings and sacrificial cakes

The first part has three sections: (1) the promise to explain, (2) the actual explanation, and (3) showing the name of the chapter.

3.3.3. 2.2.2. 5.2.1. 1. The promise to explain

Now, after the twenty-sixth [chapter], "I will explain" is applicable [here].[131] **The hero**'s, i.e., yogī's, **observances** such as the bone ornaments etc. are that in which one assumes the appearance of engaging with all of the clans of consorts (*mudrā*, *phyag rgya*). What is that hero like? He is **the adept of all yoginīs (27.1ab)**.

This is followed by two additional verses listing more practice places. None of these include "one's own home," contra Tsong Khapa's claim.

128. This is mentioned at ST 5.3, 106b; 5.4, 108b.

129. See ST 5.3, 106b.

130. See ST 5.4, 108b.

131. The text *bshad par bya/vakṣye* does not occur in any version of the text; Tsong Khapa seems to be arguing that it is implied here.

3.3.3. 2.2.2. 5.2.1. 2. The actual explanation

The second part has two sections: (1) the way of practicing the conduct and observances, and (2) the sacrificial procedure.

3.3.3. 2.2.2. 5.2.1. 2.1. The way of practicing the conduct and observances

The first part has three sections: (1) having sought the messenger, the way in which one conducts oneself toward her, (2) how the rites and observances should be practiced, and (3) the worship of the purities and its benefit.

3.3.3. 2.2.2. 5.2.1. 2.1.1. Having sought the messenger, the way in which one conducts oneself toward her

What is the method of attaining the yoginīs like? **Knowing the characteristic distinctions,** i.e. distinctive features, of the yoginīs, the yoginīs are attained. Why is this necessary? It is because one will rapidly engage the powers relying on the messenger.

What is the method of succeeding with the yoginīs? If one understands the previously explained **characteristic distinctions** of the yoginīs, one will succeed with the yoginīs. Why is this necessary? It is because relying on the messenger one will attain rapid engagement with the powers. Hence [the text] **one rapidly engages the powers (27.1cd)** occurs.

With respect to the method of seeking out the messenger, the yogī, **travelling from town to town** where people congregate, should **characterize,** that is, know, **the messenger** who lives there by means of her color, form, etc.[132] But is it difficult or easy to serve the messenger? **The messenger is like a sword blade.** Just as it is necessary to handle a sword blade fearlessly and with an unagitated mind, likewise one's sins will be **purified and merit augmented (27.2)** through **being very intimate with the messenger.** Thus, **the adept obtains power.**

Yet if one's service is deficient, not only will one attain no benefit, but the consequences will be very grave. The *Origin of Heruka* states:[133]

132. The Sanskrit text here, *grāme grāme vrajanti ca dūtayo* (Sugiki 2001, 127) indicates that it is the female messengers who travel, not the male yogī as Tsong Khapa states.

133. HA 6b: *rnal 'byor med par rnal 'byor 'chos / phyag rgya la ni bgrod 'gyur dang / ye shes*

If a fake yogī *sans* yoga
Has intercourse with a consort,
The gnostic art without gnosis,
There's no doubt he will go to hell.

It is essential that one understand the scriptural passages concerning the extreme retribution for acting in this fashion, lacking some of the characteristics of worldly supports.[134]

Practicing in reliance upon the messenger in this fashion, **even without** vocal **repetitions**, creation stage **meditation**, or outer **worship**, **one will succeed rapidly** (27.3), in this very life. **The adept engages in** inner **repetitions and** inner **worship** relying upon **the seal** (*mudrā, phyag rgya*). Aside from this, there is **no worship** that delights the **supreme** deity. Thus, this teaching is the **fixed**, i.e. immutable, [opinion] **of the treatises** (27.4) of the father and mother tantras, and through this knowledge, one who is **adept in the pleasures** on **the path** that depends on **the messenger** strives to achieve **power** (27.5ab).

The adept who is endowed with the spell consort's mantra and seal[135] **(27.5d)** and **who is well-equipoised (27.6a)** in Heruka's yoga **should always**, i.e., everyday, **eat**, i.e. drink, **the *charu* oblation**, i.e., ambrosia (27.5c). That is, one should eat and drink together with the messenger. He **should have intercourse with all** women of **classes** such as Akṣhobhya's and so forth, taking them as one class, without discrimination. One **should not discriminate (27.6b–d)**, [thinking] "this can be eaten," and "this cannot be eaten." Likewise, one should not discriminate with respect to whether or not [a woman] should be guarded against or slept with. **Since they** are **indivisible in their true nature** (27.7a), i.e., for that that reason, the differentiated classes of consorts, and the [question of] whether or not one should eat

med par ye shes tshul / dmyal bar 'gro bar the tshom med. Tsong Khapa reads *rnal 'byor chos* instead of *rnal 'byor 'chos*.

134. This translates *yul rten*, which here, I believe, refers to venerable or holy beings, who have qualities that are lacked by those who act in this fashion.

135. Tsong Khapa follows the Tibetan translations, all of which indicate mantra and seal (PM, SM: *rig sngags phyag rgyar yang dag ldan*; SL: *rig sngags phyag rgyas yang dag ldan*). The Sanskrit however, reads *vidyāmantrasamanvitaḥ*, lacking any mention of *mudrā*. See Gray 2012, 155, 336, 450, 528.

[with them], are truly inseparable. The great yogī who understands this, acts in accordance with this [realization].

With respect to the text **the messengers** [**have**] **two** [**means of achievement**] (**27.7b**), [Jayabhadra] Koṅkaṇapāda claimed that when one trains in the procedure of attaining the powers attained relying on the messenger, namely the two powers, the mundane and supramundane, it is just the yoga of Shrī Heruka practiced with the messenger that is alone supreme. Also, since this yoga at that time relates to the practice, i.e., accomplishment, of power through the excitation of the messenger, i.e., yoginī, it is supreme.[136] Laṅka [Jayabhadra] and Vīravajra also accord with this [explanation] and agree that the messengers have two means of achievement.[137]

The [text] **enjoyment** (**27.8**) means that the adept succeeds together with the messenger whom he loves.[138] When one is **endowed with** mantras through **the consecrations obtained from the lineage succession** of one holy **guru** to another (**27.9**), then one **speaks truly** to the messengers whom one should serve.[139] When one **is accustomed to union with** an outer yoginī

136. Tsong Khapa here paraphrases Jayabhadra's commentary. It reads as follows: "**The two means of achievement** refer to the means of achieving the mundane and supramundane powers. **While both** powers **are practiced, the messengers** [have] **only one;** the only one is Shrī Heruka's yoga; this indicates its superiority. Moreover, whoever has this single supreme yoga, practicing both powers, the messengers, that is yoginīs, are impelled by him, and are positioned in the means of achieving power" (Sugiki 2001, 127: *dvau sādhana iti laukikalokottarasiddhisādhanam ity arthaḥ / siddhau caramāṇasya eka eva hi dūtaya ity eka eva śrīherukayoga ity ādhikyaṁ darśayati / athavā siddhau caramāṇaḥ kaścit tasyaika eva yogavaras tadā tena dūtayo yoginyaḥ pracoditā bhavanti siddhisādhanasaṁnidhāv evaṁ saṁbandhaḥ*; cf. CP 58a).

137. Here again Tsong Khapa fails to recognize that Koṅkaṇapāda is in fact Laṅka Jayabhadra. Regarding Vīravajra, see SG 191a. In his PD commentary, he interprets the "two means of achievement" as reference to the secret and consort gnosis consecrations. See PD 406a.

138. Tsong Khapa here comments on the line *rang dga' nyid dang dngos grub ni* (PM, SM), which occurs only in the Tibetan translations. The SL translation preserves the variant reading *rab dga' nyid dang dngos grub nyid*. This is the only line in the PM and SM translations corresponding to verse 8 of the Sanskrit in my edition. See Gray 2012, 336, 451, 528.

139. That is, one is introduced to the *dūtī*s, the messenger or consort, during the consecration process. As Vīravajra indicates (PD 406a), they play key roles in the sexual rites of the secret and consort gnosis consecrations. They are plural because two are involved; the guru's consort in the secret consecration and an additional consort in the consort gnosis consecration.

who is like that, then **the** natural **gnosis** is perfected.[140] This **produces the cause (27.10abc)** of the Blessed Lord's gnosis, since Shrī Heruka is produced from that. This is explained in the commentaries.[141] Kambala explains that:[142]

> Through the realization of reality as inseparable, one should practice with the two messengers of perfected beauty for the sake of

140. Tsong Khapa here glosses the translation *legs rdzogs* as *yang dag par rdzogs pa*. Both are reasonable translations of the Sanskrit *saṁpūrṇa*, "perfect, complete."

141. Tsong Khapa here follows Jayabhadra's commentary quite closely; see Sugiki 2001, 127 and CP 58a; this commentary is repeated by Bhavyakīrti (BC 25b) and Vīravajra (SG 191a).

142. Tsong Khapa provides a somewhat abridged version of Kambala's commentary. Kambala's full commentary reads as follows, with text that is omitted by Tsong Khapa italicized, and readings that differ from his underlined: "Through that inseparable reality, **practice the two messengers** means that one should perfect the two consorts of perfected beauty for the sake of consecration. One is for the bestowal of the secret [consecration], and the second is for the sake of the consort gnosis [consecration]. *Thus, the tathāgata encouragement and, second, the permission of the mahāvajradhara encouragement are bestowed.* After that, a messenger is bestowed, and the master, the great spirit, practices for the sake of the great seal in the form of the observance. In this way, regarding *disclosure of the secret* obtained in the consecration through the process of the guru's oral instructions *that emerges from the esoteric seat that truly bestows the secret of all Tathāgatas*, it arises as the perfect body of gnosis taught by the yoginīs. One [who has attained this] is worthy of being venerated by all buddhas" (SN 42b2–5: *de nyid dbyer med de yis ni / pho nya mo gnyis bsgrub pa la / zhes bya ba ni dbang bskur ba'i don du rgyan thams cad yongs su rdzogs pa'i phyag rgya gnyis phun sum tshogs par bya ste / gcig ni gsang ba sbyin pa'i don du'o / gnyis pa ni shes rab ye shes kyi don du ste / 'di ltar de bzhin gshegs pa'i dbugs dbyung ba dang / gnyis pa rdo rje 'dzin pa chen po'i dbugs dbyung ba'i rjes su gnang ba byin la / de'i rjes su pho nya gcig pu sbyin pa ste / slob dpon bdag nyid chen po nyid kyis brtul zhugs gzugs kyi phyag rgya chen po'i don bsgrub par bya'o / 'di ltar de bzhin gshegs pa thams cad kyi gsang chen dam pa yang dag par sbyin pa gsang ba'i gnas las byung ba'i bla ma'i man ngag gi rim pas dbang bskur ba thob pagsang 'di ston pa ni rnal 'byor ma rnams kyis yang dag par gsungs pa'i ye shes yang dag rdzogs lus skyes zhes bya ba ji snyed pa'i sangs rgyas thams cad kyis phyag bya bar 'os pa'o zhes bya'o*; K 40b.5–41a.1: *abheyaṁ tattvaṁ tasya dūtaya dvau sādhana iti / abhiṣekārthaṁ sarvālaṁkāraṁ saṁpūrṇa dvau mudrā saṁpādayet / ekāṁ guhyadanārthe / dvitīyāṁ prajñājñānārthe / ekaṁ tathāgatāśvase dvītīyā vajradharīmātā / anujñā [d]attvā tadanta dūtīm ekāṁ dadyāt / vratarūpeṇa mahāmudrāsiddhyarthaṁ śiṣyam evaṁ mahātmanā / evaṁ sarvatathāgatarahasyaṁ satsaṁpradāyaṁ guhyapīṭha-vinirgatāṁ gurūpadeśakrameṇaiva prāptābhiṣekaṁ / aprakāśyam idaṁ guhya yoginībhiś ca samyaguktam / susaṁpūrṇaṁ jñānadehajaṁ / yāvat sarvabuddhair namaskṛtam iti*).

Note that the Sanskrit reads "non-disclosure" (*aprakāśyaṁ*) where the Tibetan reads the opposite, "disclosure" (*ston pa*). The Sanskrit also reads "the aim of the power of the great seal is to be taught by the great spirit" (*mahāmudrāsiddhyarthaṁ śiṣyam evaṁ mahātmanā*). The Tibetan seems to take the term *siddhi* in the compound as a verb.

consecration. One is for the bestowal of the secret consecration, and the second is for the sake of the consort gnosis consecration. Relying on these two, one is consecrated and given permission to undertake the practice. After that, the guru bestows a messenger, and the disciple who undertakes the practice, [now] a great spirit (*mahātmā*, *bdag nyid chen po*), practices in reliance on the messenger in accordance with the procedure of the accomplishment of the great seal in the form of the observance of assuming the appearance of Heruka. In this way, regarding the consecration that is obtained by means of the process of the guru's oral instructions, it arises in the body of perfect gnosis taught by the yoginīs. One [who has attained this] is worthy of being venerated by all buddhas.

He explains applying **the** three lines **messengers** [**have**] **two** etc. (**27.7b–d**) to the consecrations. The previous gurus explain that the two messengers are the womb-born and natural, and the solo messenger is the mantra-born.[143]

3.3.3. 2.2.2. 5.2.1. 2.1.2. How the rites and observances should be practiced

The second part has two sections: (1) how the rites should be practiced, and (2) how the observances should be practiced.

3.3.3. 2.2.2. 5.2.1. 2.1.2. 1. How the rites should be practiced

The yogī who undertakes the practice **arises at dawn** from the sphere of clear light. Being endowed with **the mind** that is **the nature** (**27.10d**)

143. Tsong Khapa here refers to Sachen's commentary, which reads as follows: "Regarding the two means of achieving the messenger when one serves the messenger who is like that, they are the womb-born and natural [types]. And one who has achieved those two first will succeed through the arousal of the mantra-born one. However, what messenger should a beginner adept serve? With respect to the supreme power, when one practices the procedure of achieving power through serving the mantra-born one, one serves the mantra-born messenger alone" (PG 339.3).

The three types of messenger are mentioned at CT 1.7. See Tsong Khapa's commentary on chapter 1, especially sections 3.2.3. 1.3 and 3.3.3. 2.1.1. 3.1.2, translated in Gray 2017, 66–68, 125–27.

of the adamantine mind (*thugs rdo rje*), which unites art and wisdom, he should meditate on the wheels of the mandala. With regard to **completing** donning the armors of the six heroes etc.[144] on **the body** (27.11a), it is explained that **putting into practice the body's places** (27.11c) indicates that one should don the armors. **Putting into practice the body's places** refers to well [placing] armor on the body.

According to Kambala, with respect to **one should put into practice the weapons that are extensions of the body and the body's places** (27.11bc), "extensions of the body" (*atyaṅgāni*) should be taken to be minor body parts (*nying lag*). The term *śāstrāṇi*[145] can designate both weapons or treatises; [here] it should be taken as treatises. Regarding putting into practice the minor body parts that are found on the body, one does so with bodily substances, namely the five ambrosias of seminal essence and so forth. One does this in order to avert all obstacles and to augment the two accumulations. Regarding "treatise," it indicates the treatises that shows the process of yoga. Putting them into practice, **the body is purified** (27.11d). This is via the placement of the seventeen etc. deities on the body, and body mandala meditation.[146]

144. Tsong Khapa comments on a line in the SM translation, *lus la thams cad byas nas ni*, which corresponds to the Sanskrit text, *sakalīkṛtya vigrahaṁ*. He mixes this with Jayabhadra's commentary, which reads as follows: "**One should put into practice . . . the body** is arming the body with the armors of the six heroes, etc." (Sugiki 2001, 127: *sakalīkṛtya vigrahaṁ śarīraṁ ṣaḍvīrādhikavacaiḥ kavacayitvā*).

145. Here I read *śastraṇi* as *śāstrāṇi*.

146. Tsong Khapa here closely paraphrases Kambala's commentary, which occurs here as follows: "**An extension of the body** is that which has passed from the body. They are the five ambrosias, seminal essence and so forth. One should put them into practice in order to destroy all obstacles, and to augment merit and gnosis. **The treatise** (*śāstraṁ*) indicates the treatise on yoga (*yogaśāstra*). 'Practice' (*ācaraṇa*) refers to conduct (*ācāra*). Regarding purifying the body, [it is done] by the deity yoga meditator" (K 41a.1–2: *atyaṅgāni śāstrāṇi dehasthāni samācared iti / aṅgād atikrāntam atyaṅgam / bodhicittāmṛtādipañcakā / sarvavignānā[ś]āya samācaret / puṇyajñānavṛddhaye / śāstraṁ yogaśāstrāya lakṣitam / ācaraṇaṁ ācāraḥ / pavitrīkṛtagātra[s] tu / devatāyogabhāvanayā*; SN 42b: *nying lag gis ni bstan bcos rnams / lus la gnas par kun tu spyad / ces bya ba yan lag shin tu dman pas na nying lag ste / byang chub kyi sems la sogs pa'i bdud rtsi lnga'o / bgegs thams cad bsal bar bya ba'i phyir ro / kun tu spyod pa dang bsod nams dang ye shes 'phel bar bya ba'i phyir ro / bstan bcos rnams ni rnal 'byor gyi bstan bcos kyi mtshan nyid yin la kun tu spyod pa rnams ni kun spyod do / dag byed byas pa lus dang ni / zhes bya ba ni lha'i rnal 'byor bsgom pas so*).

Note that Tsong Khapa differs from Kambala on the interpretation of the unusual term *atyaṅga*, which was rendered in Tibetan translation as *nying lag*, "minor part of the

The mantrī who is **always** protected in the manner previously explained **recites**, i.e., repeats, **mantra** (**27.12a**). Reciting and repeating the mantra, there is **yoga**, the concentration of great bliss. **The places** in which this arises are women. With respect to **the showing** them (**27.12b**), having shown the method of making the armor, one should confirm that one is armored. One **should not tread upon**, i.e., transgress, one who wears the previously explained **weapons** (**27.12c**), i.e., armors. That is, one should protect the commitments.

One who **has the** first **commitment should not** be angered by and **revile** (**27.12d**) the yogīs of the Saṁvara etc. If you become angry with the guru who bestowed the Chakrasaṁvara consecrations, [his or her] students, or the messenger, one will destroy in an instant the merit accrued from generating the spirit of awakening over ten million eons. Therefore, one **should not neglect to endeavor** (**27.13a**) to restrain anger toward such [persons]. This is the explanation of Kambala and Devagupta.[147]

Produce bliss via the method of the great seal **together with those** (**27.13b**) female committed ones (*dam tshig can ma*). Devagupta explains that **for the sake of liberation** means that one should maintain one's body, and for the sake of that body one should rely on the five ambrosias.[148] Regarding the statement **for the sake of that** (**27.13c**), three commentaries state that this should be done for one's own sake at the four junctions of the

---

body." This would be the proper translation of *pratyaṅga*. However, Kambala's gloss *aṅgād atikrāntaṁ* is almost certainly a gloss of *atyaṅga*, and not *pratyaṅga*.

147. Here again Tsong Khapa paraphrases Kambala's commentary, which reads as follows: *abhiyuktān iti abhidhānābhiṣiktasya guruśiṣyayoḥ dūtīṁ ca varalabdhā yasmāt / utpanna-bodhicittasya puṇyasambhārasaṁcayaḥ / kalpakoṭiśate[r a]pi tatkṣaṇād eva vi[na]śyati* (K 42a.3–5); *mngon par brtson las 'da' mi bya / zhes bya ba ni 'khor lo sdom par dbang bskur ba'i bla ma dang slob ma gnyis la brnyas pa mi bya ste / gang gi phyir pho nya mo'i bka' thob pa'i phyir / byang chub tu sems bskyed nas bsod nams kyi tshogs bskal pa du mar bsags pa yang de'i mod la 'joms par 'gyur ro* (SN 44a); *mngon par brtson zhes pa ni bde mchog gi rgyud 'dir bskur ba'i bla ma dang / slob ma dang pho nya ni gang gi phyir mchog thob pa yin pa'i phyir na de lta bu la ni byang chub tu sems bskyed cing bsod nams kyi tshogs bskal pa bye ba brgyar bsags pa can gyis kyang sdang bar byas na de'i skad cig nyid zad par 'gyur ro* (SS 115a).

Note that the Tibetan translation of Devagupta's commentary more closely matches the extant Sanskrit than the Tibetan translation of Kambala's commentary.

148. See SS 115a.

day, which is easy.[149] One should **undertake the practice of the commitments** (**27.13d**) of protection and eating.

Regarding **wandering**, it is said that one is **released** (**27.14ab**) as one wishes. It is explained that this means that it is certain that the yogī who wanders day and night is liberated from mistaken activities, and in this way is liberated as he pleases, that is, as desired.[150] Being **always**, i.e., continually, **naked**, that is without clothes and with one's hair down, one **should** worship the consort taking oneself as **black**-colored Heruka, and one's consort as **red**-colored Vajravārāhī (**27.14cd**).

3.3.3. 2.2.2. 5.2.1. 2.1.2. 2. How the observances should be practiced

The practitioner should assume the deity's attire by being **ornamented with a choker, a bracelet, an armlet, an earring, a sacred thread** (*yajñopavīta*), **a garland of** fresh **heads around his neck**, a twice-tied **girdle** made from the hair of executed thieves, and also with anklets bedecked with small bells that **produce a tinkling sound**[151] (**27.A1**).[152] **He has a crest of** piled-up **dreadlocks marked with** hanging **strips of** heroes' **cloth, and adorned with artificial hair,** real hair, **and so forth.** He has **a skull staff**, the skull of which is marked by a vajra, **and a *ḍamaru* drum**, and verbally **makes the sound *hūṁ*** (**27.A2**).

These [accoutrements] illustrate the conceptually elaborate practice and are the oral instructions of Nāropa. Regarding assuming the attire of deities

149. Tsong Khapa refers here to Jayabhadra's comment, which reads as follows: "**Undertaken for the sake of bliss and the sake of that** means that one who has yoga should do [this] always, day and night, at the four junctions of the day" (Sugiki 2001, 128: *ātmārthī ca tadarthī kṛtveti sadā yogavān apy aharniśaṁ catuḥsandhya, kuryād ity arthaḥ*; cf. CP 58b). This commentary is repeated by Bhavyakīrti (BC 26a) and Vīravajra (SG 191b).

The four junctions of the day are dawn, noon, dusk, and midnight.

150. Tsong Khapa here paraphrases and expands upon Jayabhadra's commentary, which reads here as follows: "As for **one engaged in wandering is released**, it is indeed certain that the wandering yogī is liberated as he pleases, that is, as desired" (Sugiki 2001, 128: *vai niścitam eva bhramaṇ yogī ceṣṭitaṁ mucyate yatheṣṭaṁ mukto bhavatīty arthaḥ*).

151. The Sanskrit preserved in Bhavabhaṭṭa's commentary reads *ghurghurā*, a "growling" sound (Pandey 2002, 492). The Tibetan translations, however, read *sil sil sgra sgrogs*, a "bell" or "tinkling sound."

152. 27.A1–A4 are four alternative verses only found in two of the Tibetan translations (PM and SM). This follows the Gray 2012 edition.

other than Heruka, **all** yogīs assume the attire of **the** twenty-four **heroes, and** all **yoginīs** the attire of the twenty-four heroines. They **are adorned,** i.e., protected, **with the three armors** (27.A3), namely, the armors of the heroes and heroines, and the great armor. Through this one should also know that yoginīs assume the attire of the twelve mothers and the principal female deity. This is also explained in the context of [passages] such as **stay together in the confluence of *soma*** (28.2d).

It seems that [this passage, which occurs] from **necklace** (27.A1a) up to **are adorned** (27.A3b), often does not occur at the end of the **black and red** [verse] (27.14d) and prior to **living being's body** (27.15a) in the translations of other commentaries. It does occur in the solo Mardo translation,[153] and also accords with Kambala's commentary.[154] It also occurs in this manner in the translation of Bhavabhaṭṭa's commentary.[155] It also appears to be implied by Durjayachandra's commentary.[156] There are also differences concerning the [verse 27.A3, regarding whether there are] three armors or two armors.[157] Bhava[bhaṭṭa] explains the three armors in terms of meditation on the triple wheel deities.[158] In a translation quoted elsewhere the two verses [beginning with] "heroes and heroines" (27.A3) occurs as "armors of

153. It occurs both in the solo Mardo (SM) and Mardo and Prajñākīrti (PM) translations.

154. Kambala only quotes the first word of this passage, laconically writing "**necklace**, etc. is clear" (K 42b.5: *kaṇṭhiketyādi spaṣṭa*).

155. Bhavabhaṭṭa quotes much of this passage, and provides the best, albeit partial, reading of the Sanskrit text of this passage. See Pandey 2002, 492.

156. Durjayachandra does in fact comment on this passage. See RG 292b. This passage appears to be a microform that was inserted into the text at some point circa 900 CE. It does not occur in older commentaries, such as Jayabhadra's, nor does it occur in the AU parallel passage. But it is attested by commentaries composed during the tenth century, such as those mentioned here, and occurs in two of the three Tibetan translations. It is somewhat problematic in that it calls for the wearing of a sacred thread, the wearing of which is specifically prohibited in the immediately following verse.

157. Both the PM and SM translations read "three armors," *go cha gsum*, and this reading is supported by Bhavabhaṭṭa, as Tsong Khapa indicates below (Gray 2012, 337, 529). Durjayachandra, however, reads two armors; see the passage translated below.

158. Bhavabhaṭṭa explains that: "**all heroes** refer to all of the heroes of the triple wheel, and their **yoginīs** are Prachaṇḍā, etc. This means that they should be visualized by the yogī. He is thus **adorned with the three armors,** for the three armors turn away Māra's weapons for those who abide in the triple wheel" (Pandey 2002, 492–93: *sarve vīrā yatra tatsarvavīraṁ cakratrayaṁ tasya yoginyaḥ pracaṇḍādayaḥ / etās tena yoginā bhāvayitavyā iti bhāvaḥ / ata eva sa kavacatrayabhūṣitam / tricakravartinyaḥ kavacatrayaṁ mārāśāstranirākaraṇāt*).

all heroes and yoginīs." This means that one is adorned with the two, the armor of the heroes and the armor of the heroines.[159] **Living being's body**[160] (27.15a) means wearing a tiger hide and elephant hide as one's lower and upper garments, [respectively].

One who desires and aspires to natural **bliss should arouse**, i.e., give rise to, that **bliss (27.15b)**, as is stated in the *Conduct*: "one who aspires to bliss should give rise to bliss."[161]

The sacred thread (*yajñopavīta*)—the *brahmasūtra*, which is said to be purifying in the texts of the *Vedas*—is **renounced.** The yoga of **depending upon Shrī Heruka is the** great **purity** (27.15cd). Does this mean that at that time one should also renounce insignia such as the necklace? It is explained that **as for having the five insignia** such as the necklace **bound (27.18cd)**,[162] **they should be in place**, i.e., should be employed, **at all times.**[163] While the sacred thread as well as the *brahmasūtra* that seems to occur elsewhere are

159. Tsong Khapa here paraphrases Durjayachandra's commentary, which reads as follows: comments that: "[Does one assume the attire of] him [i.e., Heruka] alone? The [text] **all heroes and yoginīs are adorned by the two armors** means that one is endowed with both armors, of the twenty-four heroes and heroines" (RG 292b: *de gcig pu yin nam zhe na / rnal 'byor ma bcas dpa' bo kun / go cha gnyis kyis rnam par brgyan / zhes bya ba la/ dpa' bo nyi shu rtsa bzhi dang dpa' mo de dag dang lhan cig go cha gnyis dang ldan pa zhes bya ba'i don to*).

160. This compound, *prāṇyaṅgavāsasāvāsaṁ*, is translated into Tibetan as *srog chags yan lag na bzar gyon* (PM, SM). The term *aṅga* was incorrectly translated into Tibetan as *yan lag*, "limb," rather than *lus*, "body." Tsong Khapa glosses *yan lag* as *lus*, correcting this mistake.

161. Tsong Khapa here quotes YS 15.3, which is in fact identical to CT 27.15. This line reads, in both texts, *sukhārthī cālayet sukham*. They differ primarily in their translations; *cālayet* is better translated in YS as "to give rise to," *bskyes* (Pandey 1998, 332) one of the meanings of the causative form of the verb, rather than *bskyod*, which better translates the non-causative forms of the verb.

162. Jayabhadra explains that "the five insignia are the necklace, crest jewel, earring, choker, and the sacred thread" (Sugiki 2001, 128: *pañcamudrā rucaka-śiroma[ṇ]i-kuṇḍala-kaṇṭhikā-yajñopavītāḥ*). These five are also listed in both PM and SL translations, with the addition of *thal ba*, "ash" (Gray 2012, 338, 451). This text is defective, however, in listing six items; it is not attested in any Sanskrit text, and it is likely an interpolation deriving from commentary such as Jayabhadra's.

163. Tsong Khapa here closely follows Butön's commentary. See NS 168a. His gloss of the verb *rnam par gnas* (*vyavasthita*) as *yang dag par spyad* is likely derived from Durjayachandra's (RG 293a) or Vīravajra's (PD 407b) commentaries, both of which contain this alternate translation or reading of the verb.

abandoned, they are not abandoned completely.[164] [The verse] from **by the adept** until **and ash** (27.A4) is not found in any commentaries, and since I have already explained [these insignia] with the exception of ash, there is no need [to further comment upon it.][165]

This enaction of the practice **should** also **always** be **displayed at night and concealed during the day** (27.16cd). Furthermore, **the** natural **gnosis** that is produced by **the ritual actions** of equipoise **should be well hidden** (27.17a). One's demeanor should be **calm**, and one's **fatigue should be restrained** (27.17b), that is, one should practice tirelessly. Although comments on these four [lines] from **night** (27.16c–17b) do not occur in other commentaries, they do occur in the four commentaries as well as Bhavabhaṭṭa's commentary.

3.3.3. 2.2.2. 5.2.1. 2.1.3. The worship of the purities and its benefit

The third part has two sections: (1) the worship of the purities, and (2) the benefit of doing so.

3.3.3. 2.2.2. 5.2.1. 2.1.3. 1. The worship of the purities

With respect to purification by the yoga of Heruka, one should **know** that **purity is threefold**. Moreover, Heruka **exists in the continuum of one's own** speech (27.17cd). **Disregard** good **social class**, such as brahmins etc., **and lack of social class** (28.18a), i.e., those of the lowest social class. One should renounce the practice of acknowledging them. Moreover, **one should also avoid tying up the hair in a crest, and so forth** (28.18b), including other worldly practices such as [wearing] crowns, ashes, dreadlocks, etc.

The first of **the** three **purities** is relying on **a messenger** (27.18c),

164. Tsong Khapa here attempted to resolve the contradiction caused by statement that the sacred thread should be worn, in v. 27.A1, and the prohibition against wearing one that follows in v. 27.15.

165. This verse, 27.A4 in my edition, is another variant verse that occurs only in the SM and PM translations. Since I did not translate it in my 2007 translation of the root text, I will do so here: "The adept strives for power. S/he is ornamented with a necklace, a bracelet, earrings, a crest jewel, a sacred thread and ash" (PM, SM: *sgrub pa po yis dngos grub brtson / mgul rgyan gdu bu rna rgyan dang / spyi bor nor bus rnam par brgyan / mchod phyir thogs dang thal ba dang*; Gray 2012, 338, 451).

because she is the source of the very precious bliss of all victors. The second is acknowledged to be *soma* (**27.18d**),[166] that is, the five ambrosias and alcohol.[167] It is taught that this is not intoxication. **Eating food**[168] **in one** bowl[169] with the consort **is said to be the third purity** (**27.19ab**). In this way, drinking *soma* and eating good food, and relying on the messenger via the method of expanding one's sensory spheres, one will augment one's concentration on bliss and emptiness. If one thus **gradually attains** the stage of **pristine purity, whence will the power** of the great seal **not arise** (**27.19**)? That is, it will arise from the three purities.

The powers attained by [mantra] **repetition and observances and so forth** (**27.21b**)—"and so forth" [here implying] by fire sacrifice, yantras, etc.—by means of the ***Compendium of Reality*** yoga tantra, **the *Network*,**[170] the ***Treasury of Secrets Tantra***,[171] the ***Glorious Primal Supreme*** yoga tantra (**27.20**), and the ***Adamantine Terror Tantra*** (**27.21a**)—**will be attained in an instant**, i.e., quickly, by **the mantrī through meditation** (**27.21cd**) that relies on the messenger in this enactment of the three purities. This shows the greatness of relying on the messenger. It is said that **he**, the yogī previously indicated, is a practitioner of **the purities of the pleasures of the path** (**27.22ab**) of the messenger, [which] concludes [this topic].

166. The term *soma* is translated in PM and SM as *zhi ba*, while the SL translation gives the better translation *zla ba*. Tsong Khapa glosses the former with the latter. See Gray 2012, 338, 451, 529.

167. Tsong Khapa here slightly expands upon Kambala's gloss of *soma* here, as ambrosia, namely, alcohol (K 42b.7: *somam amṛtaṁ / madyaṁ*, SN 44b: *zhi na ni bdud rtsi dang chang ngo*) Tsong Khapa follows the Tibetan translation, reading a conjunction between *amṛtaṁ* and *madyaṁ*, but I strongly suspect that the latter is a gloss of the former; it is treated as such in the translation of the same text in Devagupta's commentary (SS 116a: *zla ba ni bdud rtsi ste chang ngo*).

168. All of the Tibetan translations translate the Sanskrit *caruṁ*, a food oblation, as simply "food," *zas*.

169. Tsong Khapa glosses the Tibetan *gcig tu*, a translation of *ekatra*, "in one place," or, by extension, "together," as *snod gcig tu*, "in one vessel."

170. That is, the *Network of Ḍākinīs, Unification of all Buddhas Tantra* (*Sarvabuddhasamāyogaḍākinījālasaṁvara Tantra*) (JS), which is sometimes called the *sgyu ma bde mchog*.

171. The Sanskrit here reads *guhyatantreṣu*; Tsong Khapa follows Bhavabhaṭṭa (Pandey 2002, 494) and Butön (NS 169a) in identifying it with a tantra called the *Guhyakośa* (*gsang ba'i mdzod*). This may be an alternate name, or perhaps even the correct name, of the *Guhyagarbha* (*gsang ba'i snying po*).

3.3.3. 2.2.2. 5.2.1. 2.1.3. 2. The benefit of doing so

It is not possible to speak about **the expanse of the adept's good qualities** (**27.23a**), which exist on account of **the merit that derives from the** enactment of **the** three **purities** (**27.22cd**). Why is this not possible? How is it possible for one to speak of this? **One mouth** cannot speak that which cannot be stated by **one hundred thousand mouths** (**27.23b**). Lochen's translation reads "The expanse of the adept's good qualities cannot be stated by one who does not have one thousand mouths." On account of what does the adept possess such benefit? It is **the great gnosis of Shrī Heruka.** There is great benefit for the yogī who comes to have **all of the** virtuous **qualities**, such as the ten powers and so forth, which are **purified** of the afflictions (**27.23cd**).

The adept who non-dually unites **the water of bliss** (**27.24a**) that arises from the non-dual union of the adept and the messenger, that is, the non-duality of bliss and emptiness, **is purified** and **his sins are destroyed** (**27.24b**) **through contact**, that is, dependence, by contact with another's body and also **talk** (**27.24c**). If he is thereby **freed of all sins** (27.24d), how much more could be said of the yogī?[172] He who undertakes the practice of the purities is **a superior man** who is thus **free of all sins**, and whose **pure body**, i.e., [psycho-physical] continuum, **is faultless** (**27.25ab**). He **obtains the state of a tathāgata**, i.e., Vajradhara, **purified of all sins** (**27.25cd**), i.e., obscurations. Even if one has not yet achieved the supreme state here and now, **in life after life one is born in the tathāgata clan** purified of all sins, **and one becomes a king** who possesses **the teachings** (**27.26**) of mantric practice.

At this point Kambala's commentary has [the following] two lines that are unattested elsewhere: "Endowed with food, drink, and so forth, worship oneself as all buddhas and so forth."[173]

172. That is, he is completely liberated.

173. Tsong Khapa is correct in noting that this passage does not occur in other commentaries, although it is not clear that it is a quotation from the root text. It reads as follows: *tasmāt khānapānād[y]āyuktaṁ ātmānaṁ sarvabuddhādipujitaṁ* (K 43a.3); *de bas na/ bca' ba btung ba la sogs ldan / bdag nyid sangs rgyas kun sogs mchod / ces pa'o* (SN 45a). Since Kambala does not comment on it, it very well may be a quotation from another source.

3.3.3. 2.2.2. 5.2.1. 2.2. The sacrificial procedure

Always undertaking **the worship** of the purities **thus**, as previously explained, **one should offer sacrificial cakes** to the supramundane and mundane guests[174] **with a devotion**al intention (**27.27ab**). Why is this necessary? **The yogī should offer** sacrifice **in accordance with the ritual procedure** stated in the explanatory tantra[175] in order to achieve **his**, i.e., the adept's, **desired ritual action** (**27.27cd**). The *Origin of Saṁvara* states clearly that:[176]

> When one practices at the seats,
> The sacrifice of alcohol (*alibali*)[177]
> Is the highest among all rites,
> The mandala, fire sacrifice,
> Repetition, consecration,
> Pacification, enrichment,
> Controlling, expelling, killing,
> And the propitiation too
> Of the ghosts and the yakṣhiṇīs.

174. The "guests" (*mgron*) are the deities and spirits invoked to receive the offering. They are often classified into four types, including (1) the main deity, typically a buddha or bodhisattva, (2) Dharma protectors, (3) the "lords of the soil" (*sa bdag*), namely local spirits, and (4) sentient beings of the six realms of existence. See Beyer 1973, 217.

175. Tsong Khapa is almost certainly referring to the *balividhi* chapter of the *Origin of Saṁvara Tantra* (SU ch. 32), the first three verses of which he quotes below.

176. Here Tsong Khapa quotes the opening three verses of the *balividhi* chapter (ch. 32) of the *Origin of Saṁvara Tantra*, with the exception of the introductory opening two lines of the first verse. These verses read as follows: *maṇḍalaṁ homajāpaṁ ca pratiṣṭhā śāntipauṣṭikā /* 1 *vaśyoccāṭanamāraṇaṁ ca bhūtayakṣiṇīsādhanā / pīṭhasādhanakāle tu sarvakarmeṣu cottamam /* 2 *alibaliṁ vinā karma śīghraṁ siddhi na jāyate / balis tena praśasyante pūrvabuddhena bhāṣitam /* 3 (M 68b.3–5). The canonical Tibetan translation, which differs slightly from the version quoted by Tsong Khapa, reads as follows: */dkyil 'khor sbyin sreg bzlas pa dang / rab gnas dang ni zhi rgyas dang / dbang dang bskrad pa bsad pa dang / 'byung po gnod sbyin mo sgrub dang / gnas kyis sgrub pa'i dus dag ste / las rnams kun la mchog yin no / chang dang gtor ma med par ni / las rnams myur du 'grub mi 'gyur / des na gtor ma rab bsngags te / sngon gyi sangs rgyas kyis gsungs* (SU 307b).

177. The Sanskrit here, *alibaliṁ*, is translated into Tibetan as *myos byed gtor ma* in the translation quoted by Tsong Khapa, and *chang dang gtor ma* in the canonical translation. Both translations clearly read *ali* as "liquor," one of the numerous meanings of this term.

Without the liquor sacrifice,
The rites won't rapidly succeed.
Thus, the sacrifice spoken by
The previous Buddha is praised.

Regarding the time for [offering] sacrifice, in general it is [done] continuously, but in particular **one should** perform **the** sacrificial **worship quickly and energetically on the tenth day of the waning fortnight** and **on** the tenth day of **the waxing fortnight** (**27.28ab**). "Late night"[178] also indicates the time; it is explained that it should be offered at midnight.[179] The tenth day of the waxing and waning fortnights of the midwinter month[180] is particularly recommended; the *Conduct* states:[181]

Offer with faith on the tenth day
In the winter month and so forth.

The guests for the sacrifice is just illustrated by **Vajradevī**, which is like what is stated in the *Conduct* and the *Origin of Saṁvara*.[182] They also include the mandala deities and the guardians of the directions who live in the eight charnel grounds etc. Regarding the substance of the sacrifice, [the text states] **worship with liquor**, i.e., beer, **and meats** (**27.28cd**). Among the explanatory tantras, the preparation of the sacrifice is clear in the *Origin of Saṁvara*. Kambalāmbara's excellent elucidation of the intention that

178. Tsong Khapa appears to be quoting a commentary here; however, the text *'og gi mtshan mo* does not appear in the translations or extant commentaries. Indrabhūti's commentary indicates the time, but simply states that it occurs at night. See IC 78b.

179. Kambala's commentary, quoting v. 27–30, reads: "The sacrifice should be offered at midnight" (SN 45a: *mtshan mo phyed na gtor ma byin*; K 43a.6: *baliṁ dadyāt nisārdh[x]*).

180. This is the *puṣyamāsa* or *dgun zla 'bring po*. It is the eleventh month in the lunar calender, typically falling in December and/or January.

181. This text occurs at YS 10.9cd, as follows in Pandey's edition: *puṣyamāsādim ātmānaṁ daśamyāṁ pujya* bhaktitaḥ (1998, 96); *dgun zla 'bring po la sogs pa'I / tshes bcu la ni dad pas mchod* (1998, 281).

182. The parallel passage at YS 10.4ab repeats the same instruction as CT 27.28cd, on which Tsong Khapa is commenting here; see Pandey 1998, 92. Unlike these laconic texts, SU ch. 32 gives more detailed instructions regarding the worship of the mandala deities; see SU 308a–309b.

occurs here should be known from my commentary on Lūipa and my commentary on [his] meditation manual.[183]

Regarding the benefit of offering sacrifice, if **the man** who is an adept **worships** the two [types of] guests[184] by means sacrifice with **a devotional** intention, **Shrī Heruka** is **delighted** (**27.29ab**), i.e., pleased, with the adept. If he is pleased, he **confers** the supreme,[185] i.e., power, with **a contented mind, whereby** the adept **reaches the supreme**, i.e., glorious, **state**[186] **of being in their hands** (**27.29cd**). "One should offer sacrifice for the sake of the conferral of the supreme."[187] The *Conduct* states that:[188]

> Their worship by the devoted person
> Is thus the delight of Shrī Heruka.
> They confer boons with their minds contented,
> So, one's in the hands of those supreme ones.

183. Tsong Khapa here refers to Kambalāmbara's commentary on Lūipa's *Glorious Lord's Realization* (*Śrībhagavad-abhisamaya*), as well as two of his own commentaries on the same work, namely his *Wish-granting Cow, an Extensive Commentary on the Glorious Lord Chakrasaṁvara's Realization* (*bcom ldan 'das dpal 'khor lo bde mchog gi mngon par rtogs pa'i rgya cher bshad pa 'dod pa 'jo ba*) and his *Stages of the Rites for Reciting Lūipa's Glorious Chakrasaṁvara Realization* (*dpal 'khor lo bde mchog lūipa'i mngon rtogs ngag 'don gyi cho ga'i rim pa*).

184. That is, the supramundane and mundane guests, as discussed above.

185. Two of the Tibetan translations mistranslated the Sanskrit compound *varadāḥ* as "bestows the supreme," *mchog ni stsol* (PM, SM), while the SL translation simply reads *mchog dag*; *vara* here means "boon," not "supreme." See Gray 2012, 162, 340, 452, 530.

186. Tsong Khapa follows the Tibetan translatons in taking the adjective "supreme," *mchog*, as modifying the noun "state," *gnas* (PM, SL: *gnas mchog*; SM: *mchog gi gnas*). However, in the extent Sanskrit it declines with the third person plural pronoun and should thus be translated as "of those supreme ones" (*tāsāṁ karasthāni yato varāṇām*). See Gray 2012, 162, 340, 452, 530.

187. Tsong Khapa quotes a line here from an unnamed source. It appears to be a summary of the passage on which he is commenting here, but I have been unable to identify the source.

188. Tsong Khapa here quotes YS 10.11, which is simply a parallel text with CT 27.29. It reads as follows in Pandey's edition: *tāḥ pūjitā bhaktimato janasya śrīherukasyābhiratiṁ gatasya / saṁtoṣṭacittā varadā bhavanti teṣāṁ karasthāni yato dharaṇyām* (1998, 98); *de ni skye bo dang ldan rnams kyis mchod / he ru ka dpal mngon par dgyes gyur nas / kun tu dgyes pa'i mchog ni stsol 'gyur te/ gang phyir mchog ni de yi lag na gnas /* (1998, 282–83). Note that the text *dharaṇyām* is not supported by the translation; the reading *varāṇāṁ*, which occurs in the CT parallel passage, is almost certainly the correct reading.

How does one undertake union with one's deity at the time of sacrifice? **Should one offer sacrifice united** nondually **with Shrī Heruka**'s nature, **then the mothers are pleased** (27.30bcd). The *Origin of Saṁvara* also states that:[189]

> First, he who is endowed with the yoga
> Of the two-armed Saṁvara divine form
> Is protected by the two safeguards.
> The syllable *hūṁ* should be sounded, and
> One's body parts should be adorned
> By the twenty-four [sacred] sites.
> He instantly utters the mantra in
> Union with the instantaneous form.

The commentary explains that through the preliminary practice of union with two-armed Saṁvara, one recites that mantra of instantaneity, instantly purifying the aggregates, elements, and sense media, produce the two armors, visualize all of the twenty-four heroes and heroines and so forth in the twenty-four sites of one's body, and produce in front [of oneself] the mandala of fragrant [substances] etc. Worshipping the deity wheels there, one should offer sacrifice.[190] This procedure is excellent.

3.3.3. 2.2.2. 5.2.1. 3. Showing the name of the chapter

In the *Concise* ***Shrī Herukābhidhāna Tantra***, this is **the twenty-seventh chapter** on **the procedures of the conduct, observances, worship,**

189. Tsong Khapa here quotes the fourth and fifth verses of SU ch. 32, continuing where he left off earlier. It occurs as follows in the Sanskrit manuscript I consulted: *prathamaṁ devatākāraṁ dvibhujasaṁvarayogavān / rakṣādvayena saṁrakṣa hūṁkārapadanāditam / 4 caturviṁśatisthānena śarīragatrabhūṣiṇam / jhaṭityākārayogātmā jhaṭitā mantram uccaran / 5* (M 68b.5–69a.1); the Tibetan canonical translation, which differs somewhat from the translation quoted here, reads as follows: *dang por bde mchog phyag gnyis pa'i / lha yi rnam pa'i rnal 'byor ldan / srung ba gnyis kyis yang dag bsrung / hūṁ gi sgra ni bsgrag par bya / nyi shu rtsa bzhi'i gnas kyis ni / lus kyi yan lag brgyan par bya / skad cig rnam pa'i rnal 'byor gyis / skad cig gis ni gsang sngags brjod* (SU 307b–308a).

190. Tsong Khapa here summarizes the comments Ratnarakṣhita makes in his *The Lotus, a Commentary on the Glorious Origin of Saṁvara, King of Tantras* (*Śrīsaṁvarodaya-mahātantrarāja-padminī-nāma-pañjikā*), fol. 98a.

and sacrifice. This is the explanation of the twenty-seventh chapter in the *Illumination of the Hidden Meaning, A Detailed Exegesis of the Concise Saṁvara Tantra Called "The Chakrasaṁvara."*

Chapter 28

Chapter 28 Outline

3.3.3. 2.2.2. 5.2.2. The procedure of the inner fire sacrifice together with one clan

The second part, the procedure of the inner fire sacrifice together with one clan, has five sections: (1) the inner fire sacrifice along with sections on what should and should not be done, (2) heteropraxy and the one clan procedure, (3) showing other procedures of fire sacrifice, (4) the one clan procedure together with its benefit, and (5) showing the name of the chapter.

3.3.3. 2.2.2. 5.2.2. 1. The inner fire sacrifice, along with sections on what should and should not be done

The first part has two sections: (1) the procedure of inner fire sacrifice, and (2) showing the difference between appropriate and inappropriate actions.

3.3.3. 2.2.2. 5.2.2. 1.1. The procedure of inner fire sacrifice

"Moreover," occurring as "now" in the commentaries,[191] having shown the conduct, observances, etc. in the twenty-seventh [chapter], now the inner fire sacrifice and so forth are shown. Having been with the previously explained messenger, one is **worthy of worship**, meaning that one's reality or **nature is purified** due to undertaking the aim of unexcelled worship. **Nirvana** is the state of natural, supreme joy; **coming forth from** that, i.e., after the conclusion of that, applies to [the text] **one should worship the hero** (**28.1ab**) and yoginīs.

In this way, through the outer and secret worship one **worships oneself, and through that** one is **worshipped** as **a buddha. Buddha, etc.** (**28.1cd**) implies the worship of all bodhisattvas. **One should worship all heroes and yoginīs**, and all **inanimate** environments and **animate** [beings] (**28.2ab**), such as humans etc. They are worshipped visualized as Heruka, whose nature is great bliss. It seems that Lochen's translation lacks "**etc.**," which is good.[192]

Regarding **brothers** with whom one listens to the Dharma **and** "heroes," with respect to whom "companions" [also] occurs,[193] they have purified dispositions and practice yoga together. The term **and** [indicates that] they should **worship** (**28.2c**) the yoginīs. This is because one will not attain the

191. Tsong Khapa is commenting here on the text *gang yang*, an awkward translation of the Sanskrit *tataḥ*, which occurs in the PM and SM translations. The SL translation has the better translation *de nas*, as do commentaries such as Bhavabhaṭṭa's (Pandey 2002, 640), as noted. See Gray 2012, 163, 341, 452, 531.

192. Tsong Khapa here addresses the line 28.1d; all of the revised translations contain the text *sogs*.

193. Tsong Khapa is explaining the various translations of CT 28.2c; most of the Sanskrit sources indicate the compound *bhrātṛcārās*, "brothers' course," although Tsong Khapa prefers the reading preserved in the SL translation and Kambala's commentary, "brotherly companion," or "brothers and companions," *bhrātricārakaḥ*, *spun dang sdug* (see my translation of this passage below). The other Tibetan translations, however, read "brothers and heroes" (PM, SM: *spun dang dpa' bo*), a reading unattested elsewhere. See Gray 2012, 163, 341, 453, 531.

perfection of a yogī without worshipping them.[194] What are the "brothers" and so forth like? They are yogīs and yoginīs who **stay together in the confluence of** the activities of ***soma*** **(28.2d)**, of alcohol and great bliss. This shows the mandala of the yogīs and yoginīs who are equal in number to the deities. Their worship, by drinking *soma* and so forth, is the practice of the inner fire sacrifice. Assembling them and undertaking the extensive elaborations of song and song response etc. is undertaking the elaborate practice. Performing them setting aside these elaborations is the unelaborate practice.

3.3.3. 2.2.2. 5.2.2. 1.2. Showing the difference between appropriate and inappropriate actions

One should not disclose the gnosis of the great seal, **mantra and** the binding of **seals**, or the mandala or tantric feast (*gaṇacakra*, *tshogs kyi 'khor lo*), due to being overpowered by attachment to **brothers, sons,** etc., who **arise along with**, i.e., together with, oneself and all **happiness and suffering (28.3)**. Nor should they hear the adamantine songs (*vajragīta*, *rdo rje'i glu*). Likewise, it is said that they should not be revealed to those who deprecate commitments, repudiate the master, and harm beings. If they are revealed to them, they will go to hell. On account of that, the spirit of

194. Tsong Khapa here closely paraphrases Kambala's commentary. It reads as follows: "**Worship . . . brothers and companions** refers to disciples endowed with purified dispositions who are focused on the practice of a single yoga. The term **and** includes the yoginīs. This is because one will not be perfected without them" (K 46b.7–47a.1: *pūjayet bhrātricāraka iti saha śrāvakāḥ śuddhā[ś]ayasaṁpattyaḥ / ekayogakṛtaniścayāḥ / tuśabdāt yoginīnāṁ saṁgrahaḥ / yasmāt tābhir vinā na saṁpadyate tataḥ*; SN 48b–49a: *spun dang sdug pa'ang mchod par bya ste zhes bya ba ni lhan cig tu mnyam pa dang bsam pa dag pa dang nges par sbyor ba dang nges par sbyor ba dang gcig tu byas pa'o / 'ang gi sgras ni rnal 'byor ma nges par bzung ste / gang gi phyir de rnams ma gtogs par de'i phun sum tshogs par mi 'gyur ro*).

Note that the term *mnyam pa* in the Tibetan translation is almost certainly corrupt and should be read as *mnyan pa*.

awakening of the other beings with whom they associate is tarnished.[195] Another translation also has "harming [one's] mother and all [others]."[196]

Regarding **one should eat the purifying *charu* [oblation]**, it is explained that "having overpowered them, the unfit vessels, one should eat the *charu* together.[197] Devagupta states that "having done thus, one should always observe the commitments (28.4)."[198] Others say that the commitment is observed by eating purifying food.[199]

One should not give the mantra, i.e., the consecration and so forth, on account of greed etc., **to anyone whatsoever**, that is, kings and so forth. **The**

195. Tsong Khapa here closely paraphrases Kambala's commentary, which occurs as follows: "Regarding **along with one's brother or son**, the sons of masters who are commitment violators, repudiators of the master, and despoilers of all beings, due being overcome by attachment, are instructed in mantra and seal, shown the mandala and gaṇachakra, and [allowed to] listen to the adamantine songs, without having given rise to the spirit of awakening. On account of that they go to hell. This is because their spirit of awakening is tarnished through association with other beings" (K 47a.2–4: *bhrātṛputraikasārdham iti / snehava[ś]y[ā]d bodhicittotpādavinā mantramudrādeśanāt maṇḍalagaṇacakrayor darśanāt / vajragītaśravaṇāt / samayacchidrakaḥ / ācāryapratik-ṣepakaḥ dūṣakaḥ sarvasattvānā[ṁ] / tasmād ācāryaputrāḥ narakaṁ vrajanti / apare ca sattvāḥ saṁgamena tasya bodhicittamalinatvāt*; SN 49a: *spun dang bu dang lhan cig tu / zhes bya ba la brtse gdung gi byang chub tu sems bskyed pa ma gtogs par bya ste / sngags dang phyag rgya mchod cing dkyil 'khor dang tshogs kyi 'khor lo bstan pa dang rdo rje'i glu yang thos pas dam tshig la skur zhing slob dpon la smod dang / sems can thams cad sun 'byin par byed pa de'i phyir na rdo rje slob dpon gyi bu dmyal bar 'gro bar 'gyur zhing / de'i 'dus pa'i sems can gzhan yang byang chub kyi sems dri ma can du 'gyur ro*).

196. This line, *ma dang thams cad sun 'byin byed*, is not found in the PM or SM translations. A close variant, *ma dang thams cad spun ma yin*, does occur in the SL translation, which is likely the basis for this comment. See Gray 2012, 453.

197. Tsong Khapa again paraphrases, with slight elaboration, Kambala's commentary. A number of other commentators also follow Kambala's comments here, but none make the same elaborations as Tsong Khapa here. Kambala's commentary reads as follows: "Overpowering them, **one should eat the *caru* oblation** is relevant [here]" (K 47a.4: *tān parigrahya caruṁ bhakṣayed iti saṁbandhaḥ*; SN 49a: *de rnams yongs su gzung ba'i phyir zas la spyad par bya ba zhes bya bar sbyar ro*).

198. Tsong Khapa quotes Devagupta as follows: *de ltar byas na rtag tu dam tshig la spyod par 'gyur ro*. A close variant of this occurs in his commentary as follows: *de ltar na ni rtag tu dam tshig la spyod par 'gyur ro* (SS 121a.3).

199. Tsong Khapa here paraphrases Butön's commentary. Note, however, that all editions of Tsong Khapa's commentary read here *dad par byed pa'i zas*, which should be corrected to *dag par byed pa'i zas*, given the fact that the "food" (*zas*) or *caru* oblation is described as such (*pavitra, dag byed*) in the root text. Butön's commentary here reads *dag byed kyi zas* (NS 179a).

oral instructions should not be revealed (28.5ab). Lochen's translation has "the oral instructions should not be revealed."[200] Bhava[bhaṭṭa] explains that **nor should one destroy the oral instructions** means that one who has been solicited once should never bestow the consecration and so forth, due to avidity.[201]

In that case, to whom should they be given? It is said that **the oral instructions should be given appropriately to those** who have received consecration and **who abide by the commitments** (28.5cd). [The text also] states that **one should not, deluded by lust, abandon one's** committed **messenger and consort with another** desirable one (28.6ab). Someone explains that the path of the messenger suddenly purifies the afflictions and bestows vajradharahood in this very life. The fool who, desiring all powers, casts that aside and relies on other yogas, such as those of the disciples, the action and practice [tantras], and so forth, will have neither success nor happiness, like one who has lost a kingdom, since he lacks faith in the supreme path.[202]

200. This translation, *man ngag rnam par bstan mi bya*, appears as if it were based on a hypothetical Sanskrit text *upadeśaṁ na vidarśayet*. However, the extant Sanskrit actually reads *upadeśaṁ na vināśayet*, and two of the revised translations reflect this reading (SM: *man ngag rnam par gzhom mi bya*; SL: *man ngag rnam par nyams mi bya*). The PM translation preserves a reading that differs from both of the above variants (*man ngag nyams par sbyin mi bya*). See Gray 2012, 164, 341, 453, 531.

201. This passage occurs as follows in Bhavabhaṭṭa's commentary: *upadeśaṁ na vināśayed iti / sakṛd upayācito na tṛṣṇayā sekādikaṁ dadyāt /* (Pandey 2002, 499); */ man ngag rnam par nyams mi bya / zhes pa ni lan cig tsam gsol ba btab pa la sred pa'i dbang gis dbang bskur ba la sogs pa mi bya ba'o /* (2002, 645).

202. Tsong Khapa here abbreviates a longer explanation contained in Butön's commentary. (NS 179b). Butön, however, closely paraphrases the following passage in Kambala's commentary: "Regarding **messenger**, etc., her path is like a path, the path to awakening, which purifies the origination of endless afflictions, due to the adventitiousness of the afflictions, since it clears away mere confusion, like the sky [cleared of] clouds, fog, and smoke. One thus may become Vajradhara in this life. Should one deluded with lust for power renounce this and rely upon another yoga, be it the practice of the disciples or that which is taught in the action and practice tantras, etc., he will not have power or happiness, since he lacks the treasure of faith, like a man who has lost a kingdom" (K 47a.5–b.1: *dūtītyādi / mārgam iva mārgam bodhipathā / anantakleśotpādanaśodhinya / kleśā-nām āgantukatvāt / abhranīhāradhūmram ivākāśo bhramamātravikāśanāt / vajradharatva ihaiva janmani bhavet / tāṁ parityajya anyayogaṁ samāśrayet / śrāvakācārakriyācaryātantrādiṣu yathoditaṁ siddhikāmavimohitaḥ / na tasya siddhir na ca saukhyaṁ syāt / rājyabhraṣṭanarā iva / aśraddha[dha]natvāt*; SN 49a–b: *pho nya zhes bya ba la sogs lam dang 'dra bas lam ste / byang chub kyi lam mo / de yang mtha' yas pa'i nyon mong dang*

If that is so, how should it be done? [The text] states that if one **is always attached to,** relies passionately upon, **the messenger,** there is **liberation** (**28.6c**), i.e., one will be liberated.[203] Bhava[bhaṭṭa] quotes [the variant text] "[if] the messenger is always protected there is liberation," which means producing the protective armor for the messenger, i.e., the actual seal. Thence all [states of] possession are pacified. Moreover, by subjugating the messenger, not going to another is the protection of the messenger.[204] It is said that should one lack a well-educated consort, even if [one] has transgressed, then one should prepare and **enjoy** a fortunate woman.[205] One should endeavor to be accepted by a messenger who is "fortunate," i.e., committed, and who is has **"transgressed"** (**28.6d**), i.e., is powerful.

Regardless of whether or not one's actual seal is of great or lesser birth, if she does not have the perfect qualities of a messenger, she is of **lesser birth.** With respect to being **preoccupied** with her, the **reverential** (**28.7ab**) worship of her should be done since she has the complete qualities. But it should

---

skye ba sbyong ba ste / nyon mong pa glo bur pa nyid kyi phyir nam mkha' sprin dang khug rna dang du ba dang 'khrul pa tsam zhig bsal bas tshe 'di nyid la rdo rje 'dzin par 'gyur ro / de bas na de spangs nas rnal 'byor gzhan la brten par ni / nyan thos kyi spyod pa dang / kri ya dang spyod pa'i rgyud la sogs pa rnams su ji skad bshad pa'i dngos grub thams cad 'dod pa de dag rmong pas dngos grub med cing bde ba med par 'gyur ro / rgyal srid shor ba'i skyes bu bzhin / dad pa'i nor dang phral phyir ro).

203. Tsong Khapa here comments on the challenging line, *dūtīraktaḥ sadā mokṣaḥ.* Kambala unpacks it elegantly: "He who is attached to the messenger is liberated" (K 47b.1: *dūtīrakto yaḥ sa muktaḥ*).

204. Tsong Khapa here paraphrases the following passage in Bhavabhaṭṭa's commentary: *dūtīrakṣā sadā mokṣa iti / dūtyā bāhyāṅganāyā rakṣā kavacanam / tayā sarvagrahaṇapraśamaḥ / athavā vaśīkaraṇena dūtyā ananyagamitā kāryeti dūtirakṣā* (Pandey 2002, 500); *pho nya mo bsrung rtag thar pa/ zhes pa ni pho nya ni phyi rol gyi yan lag can no / bsrung ba ni go cha bya'o / de yis thams cad mngon par zhen pa zhi bar bya ba'o / yang na pho nya dbang du bya ste / gzhan la mi 'gro bar bya'o zhes pa ni pho nya srung ba'o* (2002, 646).

It should be noted that this variant reading, *dūtīrakṣā sadā mokṣaḥ*, is only found in Bhavabhaṭṭa's commentary. The AU parallel passage and Jayabhadra's and Kambala's commentaries read *dūtīraktā sadā mokṣaḥ.* See Gray 2012, 165.

205. Tsong Khapa here follows Jayabhadra, who wrote: "**Should enjoy [liberation], even if he has transgressed** means that, should she not be well educated, then one should prepare and enjoy a good and fortunate woman" (Sugiki 2001, 129: *atikramo 'pi bhojayed iti yady atiśayasuśikṣitā bhavet subhagā bhadrāṅganā tāṁ saṁskṛtya bhojayed ity arthaḥ*; CP 59b: *bda' ba yis kyang longs spyod bya / zhes bya ba ni shin tu legs par bslabs pa med na skal ba bzang por gyur ba de legs par sbyangs la longs spyad par bya'o*).

Note that I have followed the Tibetan reading of *shin tu legs par bslabs pa med na* rather than the Sanskrit *atiśayasuśikṣitā bhavet.*

not be done for that [reason] alone. According to Kambala, while it is not the case that one who has feted the messenger endowed with the [requisite] qualities should only, or just, do reverence, he should be equipoised, as he states, "She who lacks the aim of reverence desires sexual intercourse. Thus, one should embrace, obtaining the impassioned [woman]. Otherwise there will be no happiness."[206]

Those of lesser birth are of the vajra clan and so forth, and the term "and" implies the highest birth of the brahmin class etc. They should always be worshipped in the position of **a messenger** with an especially tender state of mind, overcome by extreme attachment, as if they were one's **mother, sister, daughter, and wife** (**28.7cd**). If one denigrates her, and practices **asceticism** with an inferior attitude, one will **destroy** all of one's perfections, and you will exhaust all of **the powers**, that is, virtues, accumulated in reliance on meditation on the mandala's **wheels** (**28.8ab**), in the manner previously explained. "Or thus the powers of the wheels" occurs in Devagupta's commentary, which is excellent.[207] If one impairs one's commitment in this fashion, the procedure for rising up from that, and the meditative practice (*sādhana*) and [mantra] repetition for the restoration of one's commitment is explained in Kambala's and Devagupta's commentaries.[208] In the manner of [the text] **one should draw forth together with the ultimate** (**28.8c**), one should not conceptualize in the rite of drawing forth soma together with the ultimate messenger.[209] If one enjoys food together with [her], one is

206. This passage does indeed occur in Kambala's commentary, as follows: "**Reverence should not be done** means those [women] who have the aim of reverence are eager for sexual intercourse. For that reason, one should embrace, obtaining the impassioned [woman]. Otherwise there will be no happiness" (K 47b.2–3: *satkāraṁ naiva kuryād iti / tataḥ satkārārthinyaḥ suratasaṁgamotsukāḥ / tasmād āliṅgayet / prāpyānurāgavatī / anyathā saukhyaṁ na syāt*; SN 49b: *bsnyen bkur kho na bya ba min / zhes bya ba la / bsnyen bkur gyi ni don can min / chags pas 'dus par dga' ba ste / de phyir 'khyud par rab tu bya / rjes su chags dang ldan pas 'thob / gzhan du bde bar mi 'gyur ro*).

Note that the Sanskrit *satkārārthinyaḥ* lacks the negative contained in the corresponding Tibetan text, *bsnyen bkur gyi ni don can min*. I followed the Tibetan reading in my translation in the main text, and the Sanskrit reading here in the note.

207. Tsong Khapa here comments on the translation of 28.8b contained in Devagupta's commentary, *'khor lo grub pa'ang de bzhin du'o* (SS 121b). Tsong Khapa's commentary closely follows Devagupta's here.

208. See SN 49b–51b, and SS 121b–23b.

209. Tsong Khapa here follows Jayabhadra, who wrote, "Regarding **one should draw forth together with the ultimate**, conceptual thought should not be produced in the

purified, since one has undertaken the performance of the commitment.[210] Many texts quote [this line] as "draw forth together with the ultimate and the lowly";[211] the ultimate and inferior [here] should be applied to the messenger. Regarding depending upon that sort of **fluid**,[212] it explained that this is **the determination (28.8d)** of the ultimate, or the determination of the buddhas, which is like that.[213] Kambala explains that the ultimate is the natural (*sahajā/lhan cig skyes ma*) [messenger], the middling is the womb-born (*kṣetrajā, zhing skyes ma*), and the lowly is the mantra-born (*mantrajā, sngags skyes ma*).[214] That which is drawn forth through union with them is the [fluid] that arises from all faculties inserted in the generative channel. That sort of fluid should be incited.[215] This is the meaning of the [alternate translation] "draw forth together with the ultimate, middling, and lowly."

---

procedure of drawing forth *soma*" (Sugiki 2001, 129: *ākarṣayec cottamaṁ sārdham iti somākarṣavidhau vikalpo na kartavyaḥ*).

210. Tsong Khapa appears to be following Butön here (NS 180b), who, in turn, is quoting the Tibetan translation of Jayabhadra's commentary (CP 59b). The extant Sanskrit, however, does not contain any text corresponding to this comment.

211. This textual variant for 28.8c, *mchog dang tha ma lhan cig 'gugs*, is not found in any of the revised translations, but is quoted in several commentaries, such as Jayabhadra's (CP 59b) and Bhavyakīrti's (BC 29b). Note that the Tibetan translation of Jayabhadra's commentary, the extant Sanskrit, quoted above, contains no text corresponding to the Tibetan *tha ma*, and thus matches the translation preserved in two of the revised translations (PM: *mchog la lhan cig dgug par bya*; SM: *mchog dang lhan cig dgug par bya*; Gray 2012, 342, 531). A third variant is preserved in the SL translation, "draw forth together with the ultimate, middling, and lowly" (*mchog dbus tha ma lhan cig 'gugs*; Gray 2012, 453); this reading is also found in Devagupta's commentary (SS 123b) and is implied by Kambala's (SN 51a–b). This is quoted and discussed by Tsong Khapa at the end of this section below.

212. As I noted in my translation of the root text (Gray 2007, 286, n. 17), in the context of this passage I translate the term *dravya/rdzas* as "fluid" rather than "substance," since it designates here, according to many of the commentators, sexual fluids generated by union with the messenger.

213. Tsong Khapa here paraphrases Bhavyakīrti's commentary, at BC 29b.

214. See Tsong Khapa's discussion of the three types of messenger in section 3.3.3. 2.1.1. 3.1.2 in chapter 1 of this work; see Gray 2017, 125–27.

215. Tsong Khapa summarizes a longer explanatory passage in Kambala's commentary; see SN 51b. The corresponding Sanskrit to this passage would have occurred on K fol. 49, which unfortunately is lost.

3.3.3. 2.2.2. 5.2.2. 2. Heteropraxy and the one clan procedure

The second part has two sections: (1) heteropraxy, and (2) the one clan procedure.

3.3.3. 2.2.2. 5.2.2. 2.1. Heteropraxy

[The text] states that [in] **the world** the yogī **always** engages in **heteropraxy**; briefly stated, the yogī is always heteropraxic. What is this heteropraxy like? When moving, one **advances with the left foot forward.** In actions involving the hand, one **proceeds with the left hand** forward, that is, one acts with it, indicating with it and so forth. One worships with the left hand, **showing respect** by employing the **left** hand (**28.9**). One **embraces** the consort **with the left** hand forward. **One presents libations** to the deities and **eats with the left** hand. Practicing this sort of sinister behavior[216] **does not destroy but fulfills** [this] **observance** (**28.10**).

At the end of an extensive elucidation of sinister behavior, the *Origin of Heruka* states:[217]

> I have said much about heteropraxy,
> And I have left unsaid a little bit
> On Shrī Heruka's heteropraxy.
> Its practitioner will achieve power
> From the left on the earth and underworld,
> Even without repetitions and vows.

216. My translation "sinister behavior," *vāmasamācāra/g.yon pa'i kun spyod*, is intended to evoke the original meaning of this term, namely, relating to the left-hand side. In the West as in India, the left side was seen to be inauspicious, hence terms relating to the left, like *sinister*, often had negative meanings. I do not think that is wise to try to avoid the use of such terms, for they were clearly used intentionally by the author(s) of this text, who recommend that the yogī cultivate what is clearly an unconventional code of conduct.

217. This passage occurs at the end of chapter 16, which treats this topic in depth. It differs slightly from the text as quoted by Tsong Khapa, which is: *g.yon pa'i kun spyod mang du gsungs pa'i mthar / cung zad gsungs dang ma gsungs pa / dpal ldan khrag 'thung g.yon pas spyod / sgrub po sa steng sa 'og na / bzlas dang brtul zhugs bral bas kyang / g.yon pas dngos grub 'gyur ba yin*. The canonical text occurs as follows: *g.yon pa'i thar pa'i mtshan nyid de / cung zad gsungs dang ma gsungs pa / dpal ldan khrag 'thung g.yon la spyod / sgrub pos sa stengs gnas nas ni / bzlas dang brtul zhugs bral byas kyang / g.yon pas dngos grub 'gyur ba yin* (HA 13a).

For what reason is sinister behavior praised as the means of achieving power? The very statement in the root tantra, the *Discourse Appendix*, and so forth that all animate and inanimate beings arise from the left is the reason for undertaking sinister behavior. The *Vajraḍāka* states that:[218]

> Arising from the left are all beings,
> The animate and the inanimate,
> So, one should eat and imbibe with the left.

The *Discourse Appendix* states:[219]

> Heteropraxy is wisdom,
> As a result, the right is art.

One should thus know that among the two, the left and the right, the left is said to be wisdom.

Regarding wisdom, all things, through the establishment by their own nature, are realities which are empty. There are two [types of] wisdom, that which is taken as the object of wisdom, and that which realizes the import of that. If you take it in terms of the first of those, it is establishing all functions of animate and inanimate beings, established by that reasoning. Since no functions whatsoever are suitable with respect to the establishment by their own nature, and since all activities are suitable with respect to the emptiness of things established by their own characteristics, it is said that all animate and inanimate beings arise from the left. And since the left is said to exist in women, all things arise from them, and all things arise from the white element that arises from the left channel. While it is not the case that

218. Tsong Khapa here quotes three lines corresponding to VD 1.49d–1.50b. They occur as follows: *vāmatarpaṇabhakṣaṇam / vāmodbhavaṁ jagat sarvaṁ sthāvarādy ā sajaṅgamam /* (Sugiki 2002, 91); *brtan pa dang ni g.yo ba yi / 'gro kun g.yon las byung bas na / g.yon gyis bzas zhing g.yon mchod bya* (VD 4a).

219. This passage occurs as follows in AU ch. 3: *g.yon pa'i spyod pa shes rab ste / g.yas pa de bzhin thabs yin no/* (AU 252a).

The Sanskrit text here reads: *vāmācāraṁ bhavet prajñā upāyaṁ tu dakṣiṇaṁ tathā* (H 9b.3–4; I 535b.2: *vātācāraṁ bhavet prajñā upāyaṁ dakṣiṇair na vā*; J 15.4: *vāmācāraṁ dakṣiṇāṁcārabhmaṁ prajñā upāyaṁ dakṣiṇaṁ na co*).

all things arise from the left hand, many tantras do state that everything arises from emptiness. Just as it is said,[220] "generation, destruction, and self-existence: these are just the gnosis of emptiness," it is the very spontaneous great bliss that inseparably produces bliss and emptiness. It is the agent that emits and reabsorbs the two pure and excellent habitat and inhabitant mandalas. Thus, the statement that all animate and inanimate beings arise from the left should be understood via both of these interpretive strategies.

Taken in this manner, the wisdom that is illustrated by the left is the accomplisher of all powers, which means that one performs heteropraxy because it brings together in the present time the auspicious coincidence that gives rise to the extraordinary gnosis of that path. This gnosis that perfectly comprehends the characteristics of reality with wisdom is common to the other vehicles and other classes of tantras as well. With the other paths, incalculable eons are needed to achieve awakening. Its attainment in this very life on this path is due to the meditation on reality by the spontaneous bliss that is the subjective supreme bliss, even though it is not distinctive with respect to objective reality. Since many of the messengers of the ḍākinīs delight in heteropraxy and are engaged by that activity, they are made happy by behavior that accords with heteropraxy.

3.3.3. 2.2.2. 5.2.2. 2.2. The one clan procedure

The adept's own activity is exertion in yoga, which is **practice** with **a committed clan**swoman. **One eats** and practices **together with** her. Practice with a committed one is also **practice in the five classes** of seal (consorts). Furthermore, the jewel (*ratna*) clan can also be subsumed into the immovable (*akṣobhya*) clan, so that they can be analyzed into **four classes** (**28.11**). They too can be subsumed into the three clans of body, speech, and mind, and those three into **the one clan** of Vajradhara, the great secret, **practice in** which is **revered** by **the successful yogī** (**28.12ab**), who accords with it.

220. Tsong Khapa does not indicate the source for this quotation.

3.3.3. 2.2.2. 5.2.2. 3. Showing other procedures of fire sacrifice

In order to vanquish those who would harm the three jewels and so forth, an array of ritual actions was taught. With the rites taught via the methods of undertaking fierce fire sacrifice, **one makes a triangular mandala (28.13a)** as a hearth and makes a fire with the requisites for violent fire sacrifice, namely mustard oil etc. Visualize that Khaṇḍarohā is inserted into one's right nostril and emerges from below. She holds an adamantine iron hook and a hooked knife. Visualize that the victim is summoned, naked and delirious, and is partitioned. Visualize that **the beef, horse meat, dog meat, and various others'** [meat] **(28.12cd)**, i.e., peacock meat and chicken meat is the victim's flesh. If one performs the fire sacrifice with the pride of a great fierce one, with the root mantra [augmented with] "Kill so and so!" **even the Buddha will be definitely destroyed (28.13b)**, i.e., will die. What need is there to speak of others when such an eminent one is mentioned?

Someone interpreted this in an inner and not an outer sense.[221] Others have done the opposite of that. Kambala seems to have explained both the inner and outer meanings, which is excellent.[222] Fearing prolixity, I will not write more about this.

3.3.3. 2.2.2. 5.2.2. 4. The one clan procedure together with its benefit

Just as the hero who is **furnished with** an outer yoginī well-instructed in **seals and mantra** is praised, so too is **the enjoyment** with the seal (consort), that is, **the hero (28.13cd)** who prepares the feast. **Shrī Heruka** is non-dual seminal essence, and his **emanation** is the yoga of becoming Heruka. **Service** means practicing with devotion to him. **All treatises** refer to other bad texts such as the *Veda*s etc. They are **abandoned,**[223] i.e., cast aside. If this service is **always retained** and the commitments **protected**, when one undertakes **all** desired **ritual actions (28.14)**, they are **accomplished** just

221. The "someone" here appears to be Sachen, who briefly discusses the text here before segueing to a discussion of the inner fire sacrifice. See PG 343.4 ff.

222. Tsong Khapa here summarizes Kambala's much longer presentation of this rite; Kambala gives much more information concerning its actual performance. See SN 52a–53b.

223. Tsong Khapa, naturally, follows the Tibetan translations, all of which here read *spangs*, "abandoned." All of the extant Sanskrit sources, however, read *vilakṣita*, "noted," which makes more sense in this context.

as one desires **without obstruction**. "Here they are not achieved **whatsoever**." In another translation it occurs as "For this there are no **others**."[224] Regarding the meaning of this, as previously explained it means that [this accomplishment] "does not occur in the awakening of the disciples and so forth."[225]

The adept, **together with his messenger**, who **is supreme**, i.e., utmost,[226] and **divine**, is **energetically (28.15)**, i.e., without laziness, motivated toward attaining power. Having found one like her, through **union** with her there will be the enjoyment of **impassioned sex**.[227] **The yogic fluid** is the seminal essence, the ambrosial alchemy that proceeds to omniscience. That which is **incited** by that is the conferral of the fruits of both special pleasure and liberation.

Once one has attained and meditated on **the guru's instructions**, if one cultivates awakening with constant joy and reverence, one will attain buddhahood in this very life. If a yogī has not attained it in this life due to insufficient zeal, he will acquire his desired **aims like the wealth giver (28.16)** until he attains awakening.

3.3.3. 2.2.2. 5.2.2. 5. Showing the name of the chapter

In the ***Concise Shrī Herukābhidhāna Tantra***, this is **the twenty-eighth chapter** on **the procedures of the inner fire sacrifice** of the enjoyment of

224. The former translation, *'dir ni 'gar yang 'grub ma yin*, occurs in the PM and SM translations, but doesn't make much sense, which is probably why Tsong Khapa quotes the alternate translation, *'dir ni gzhan dag 'gyur ma yin*, which makes more sense and accords with the extant Sanskrit. Tsong Khapa doesn't identify this translation, but I suspect it is the original unrevised Rinchen Zangpo translation. The SL translation preserves a close variant, *'dir ni gzhan du rtogs ma yin*. See Gray 2012, 343, 453, 532.

225. Tsong Khapa here quotes Kambala; see SN 55a. This is actually a gloss of the quoted text. A full translation of Kambala's comment would be "This yogī's [accomplishment] **is not achieved whatsoever** in the awakening of the disciples and so forth" (K 53a.4: *na kaścit pratipadyata iti śrāvakādibodhau tasya yoginaḥ*).

226. The Sanskrit here, *parā*, is translated as *mchog* in the translations of the root text, and *gzhan* in Kambala's commentary (SN 55a). Tsong Khapa here glosses the former term with the latter.

227. Tsong Khapa here glosses the prefix *anu/kun nas* from the word *anurakta/kun nas chags* as *shin tu* "extremely."

eating and drinking with the messenger, and of the worship of the messenger having taken all of the messengers' clans as **one clan** of Vajradhara. This is the explanation of the twenty-eighth chapter in the *Illumination of the Hidden Meaning, A Detailed Exegesis of the Concise Saṁvara Tantra Called "The Chakrasaṁvara."*

Chapter 29

Chapter 29 Outline

3.3.3. 2.2.2. 5.2.3. The characteristics of the messenger and procedure for the state of heat or power

The third part, the characteristics of the messenger and the procedure for the state of heat or power, has three sections: (1) the promise to explain, (2) the actual explanation, and (3) showing the name of the chapter.

3.3.3. 2.2.2. 5.2.3. 1. The promise to explain

Now, following the twenty-eighth [chapter], **one should know that which is taught**, i.e., which should be taught, **regarding the characteristics** that distinguish **the messengers**, from the characteristics previously explained. Why is this necessary? It is so that the yogī will **correctly discern** the characteristics of the messengers. If one knows this, **the ḍākinīs** will **abide** without transgressing **the commitments** (**29.1**) in order to benefit the adepts.

3.3.3. 2.2.2. 5.2.3. 2. The actual explanation

The second part has three sections: (1) the characteristics of the messenger, (2) the procedure of power, and (3) praise for Mahāyoga.

3.3.3. 2.2.2. 5.2.3. 2.1. The characteristics of the messenger

The previous [gurus] explain that if the adept knows and depends upon the commitment of the ḍākinīs, **in a moment they will see him as their brother, father, and their lord**, i.e., husband (**29.2ab**).[228] Regarding the method of finding and staying with a consort (*mudrā*), it is engaging in practice together with "father and likewise mother"[229] with a very affectionate attitude. With whom will they engage? It is with **their lord**, i.e., the yogī who has attained gnosis. "Seeing in a moment" is to perceive for as long as a moment the individual self-awareness of the nature of that gnosis through pure entry into the non-duality of bliss and emptiness.[230]

Her thick tongue and eyes are **tawny**,[231] and her **rough** limbs[232] and **hair** is also **tawny** (**29.2cd**). These four correspond to the four clans of consorts (*mudrā*). Kambala's commentary states the following regarding the first [of them]:[233]

228. Tsong Khapa here paraphrases Sachen's commentary on this verse. Here he wrote: "Regarding first displaying the signs of the messenger, those yoginīs who recognize them will, when the see the adept, will thus love him, for they will instantly see him as their charming brother, father, or lord, that is, husband" (PG 344.3: *dang po pho nya'i mtshan nyid bstan pa ni / ngo shes pa'i rnal 'byor ma de rnams kyis sgrub pa po mthong ba na / 'di ltar brtse zhing yid du 'ong ba ming po dang / pha dang / bdag po ste khyo nyid du skad cig gis mthong bar 'gyur ro*).

229. Tsong Khapa here quotes a variant reading of 29.2a, *pha 'am yang na ma dang ni*, which occurs only in Kambala's commentary, as follows: *mātaraṁ pitaraṁ vā* (K 53b.3), *ma dang pha* (SN 56a).

230. Tsong Khapa here glosses Kambala's commentary; see SN 56a.

231. Tsong Khapa follows the Tibetan translations in reading the adjective "tawny," *dmar ser* as applying to both her tongue and eyes. The Sanskrit, however, reads, *piṅgalākṣā*; since this adjective in is compound it can thus only modify *akṣā*, "eyes."

232. While the Sanskrit and Tibetan simply read "rough" (*karkaśī*, *rtsub*), Tsong Khapa glosses this as "rough limbs," *yan lag rtsub pa*, to enable him to read it as a list of four tawny body parts.

233. This is my translation from the Sanskrit and Tibetan texts of Kambala's commentary. K 53b.5–7: *sthūlāsyā sthūlapayodharā / tadanta hrasvā hrasvakeśī / madagandhā*

Her face is big, as are her breasts.
Yet she is short and her hair's short.
Her scent and swaying's intoxicating.
Taken together, she is known to be
Tall, and moreover to have a long face.
Her feet and her hands are likewise quite long.
She produces fluid that smells like sweetmeat.[234]
She is moon-like[235] with a long vagina,
And is evenly dusky with hard breasts.
Her body is small and her hair is fine;
Her breasts are small and her body hair's course.[236]
She's indolent,[237] has a prominent snout;[238]
Her neck's high but not excessively so.
Her beautiful form is like a white lotus,

---

madavihvalā / saṃhṛteti vikhyātā / dīrghā caiva dīrghavaktrā / dīrghapādakarā tathā / sā miṣṭagandhamadāvahā / dīrghayonyā śāśisaṃnibhā / samaśyāmā kharastanā / alpāṅgī alpakeśā ca yo[n]i kharā [r]oṃan / karā unnatā unnatagrīvā nātyantā / rūpyarūpā puṇḍarīkā / prasveda vahate nityaṃ sugandaṃ ca manoramam /mṛgākṣaṇā mṛgadṛṣṭi mṛgagrīvā mṛgodarī / mṛgarājakaṭiś caiva subhagā padmagandinī; SN 56a.1–3: *bzhin 'phel che zhing nu rgyas ma / gzhan yang thung zhing skra yang thung / glang chen dri bro dregs pa'am / mdor bsdus nas ni rab tu bshad / lus po ring zhing bzhin yang ring / de bzhin lag pa rkang pa'ang ring / nya yi dri bro khu ba 'bab / skye gnas ring zhing zla ba 'dra / mnyam zhing sngo bsangs nu ma mkhrang / yan lag chung zhing skra yang srab / skye gnas chung zhing skra yang rtsub / dal bar smra zhing sna mtho ma / mgrin pa ha cang ring ba min / gzugs mdzes pad ma dkar po 'dra / lus las rtag tu rdul 'byung ba / shin tu dri zhim yid 'phrog ma / mig dang lta stangs ri dags 'dra / ri dags mgrin pa ri dags lto / ri dags rgyal po'i rked pa can / skal bzang pad ma'i dri dang ldan.*

234. This translates the Sanskrit, *miṣṭagandha*. The Tibetan here reads *nya yi dri*, "smell of fish" (SN 56a.2).

235. This translates both the Sanskrit, *śāśisaṁnibhā*, and the accurate canonical translation, *zla ba 'dra* (SN 56a.2). Tsong Khapa, however, here quotes *zla ba 'bab*, which seems to be a conflation with the translation of *madāvahā* in the previous line, *khu ba 'bab.*

236. Tsong Khapa's quotation of this text reads *yan lag*, "body" or "limbs," here, rather than *skra* like the canonical translation. This interpolation is likely derived from Kambala's commentary that he quotes below.

237. This text, *dal bar smra*, does not occur in the Sanskrit here. However, it occurs again below, where it translates the Sanskrit *mantharā*.

238. The Tibetan here reads "nose," *sna*, but the Sanskrit reads *karā*, which does not mean "nose," but can designate the trunk of an elephant. This was likely used deliberatively to poetically emphasize the prominence of her nose.

Ever exuding a ravishing scent.
She has doe eyes, and she gives doe glances.
Her neck and her navel are both doe-like,
And she has the waist of the deer king too.
She is auspicious with a lotus scent.

Regarding the second [type of consort]:[239]

Both of her eyes are tawny, however,
Her feet are red and her hands are red too.
She is redolent with the jasmine scent,
And she delights in Buddhist assemblies.
A woman who always bestows power,
She's corpulent and tall[240] with swollen breasts.
Her hair moreover should be curly, and
She's indolent, with the gait of a goose,
Is not very tall and her face is round.
She's known for her pendulant navel folds.

Regarding the third [type of consort]:[241]

She is rough, having limbs that are rough too.
She is clever as well, just like Indra.

239. This is my translation from the Sanskrit and Tibetan texts of Kambala's commentary. K 53b.7–54a.2: *piṅgalākṣani . . . raktapādakarā tathā / mallikāgandinī saugatagoṣṭhīratā caiva / pramadā siddhidā sadā pīnonnatā pīnapayodharā / kuñcitāś ca bhavet keśāḥ manthārā haṁsagaminī / nātyuccā mukhaparimaṇḍalā [na]bhitrivalīmadhyāvalambinī sā jñeyā /*; SN 56a.3–5: *de yi mig ni dmar ser la / de bzhin lag pa rkang pa'ang dmar / mā li ka yi dri 'byung zhing / bde gshegs 'dus la dga' ba yi / bud med dngos grub ster bar byed / lus rgyas nu ma yang rgyas shing / skra ni 'khyil bar gyur pa dang / ngang pa'i 'gros can dal bar smra / shin tu ring min bzhin yang zlum / lte ba'i dbus su gnyer gsum ste / dbus nas 'phyang ba der shes bya.*

240. This translates the Sanskrit *pīnonnatā*; the Tibetan reads "with a stout body," *lus rgyas.*

241. The Sanskrit here reads: *karkāśī karkaśāṅgī kauśikī kuśalā* (K 54a.2); the Tibetan: *rtsub cing yan lag rtsub pa dang / lha sbyin lta bus gzhan la smod* (SN 56a.5).

Note that my translation of the second line follows the Sanskrit *kauśikī kuśalā.* The Tibetan reads here "she deprecates others as if she were Indra."

Regarding the fourth [type of consort]:[242]

> She has a mass of tawny colored hair,
> And her body is wan and is wasted.
> She is devoid of breasts just like a man.
> She burns with longing for the scent of rice,
> And is covered with the fragrance of rice.
> She always takes delight in alcohol.[243]
> Perfected in the commitments' practice,
> She closely attends to her mental state.
> She seeks out all scents, and especially
> Good scents, alcohol in particular.
> Excessively intoxicated,[244]
> She exudes copious sexual fluid.

These seals (*mudrā*) are companions who are **equal to all** yogīs, virtuous spiritual friends for the sake of the **accomplishment** of liberation (29.3a). **The twenty-four ḍākinīs bestow the fruits of enjoyment**, i.e., the supreme exalted state, **and liberation** (29.4ab) from attachment to things to that mantin who is **always intent upon [mantra] repetition and the observances**, who is **endowed with recollection** of the characteristics of the messengers, and who trains in yoga continuously and is **stationed**,[245] i.e., abides, in the commitments of gathering, eating, and protecting **together with the messenger, and so forth** (29.3bcd).

242. This is my translation from the Sanskrit and Tibetan texts. Differences from the text as quoted by Tsong Khapa are noted above. K 54a.2–3: *piṇḍapiṅgalakeśā vivarṇātasakṣitāṅgī pramivata pum iva stanarahitā śāligandharucā śālimodagandhāstarā / samayācarasaṁpannā āśayatatparā sugandhāśiṣṭā sarvagandhānugaminī madaviśe–ṣātisamāsada vihvalyā śukrabahulā*; SN 56a.5–7: *skra ni 'khyil zhing kham par gnas / mdog ngan yan lag rtsub pa dang / skyes pa lta bur nu ma spangs / sā la lta bu'i dri yang bro / 'od 'bar sā la'i dris byugs la / rtag tu chang la dga' ba ste / dam tshig spyod pa phun sum tshogs / bsam pa rtogs la nan tan byed / khyad par can gyi dri zhim pa / chang gi rjes su 'gro ba ste / chang gi khyad par dag dang ni / chang gis shin tu myos pa dang / de bzhin khu ba mang du.*

243. This line is omitted in the extant Sanskrit.

244. This translates the Tibetan *chang gis shin tu myos pa dang*; the Sanskrit here is corrupt.

245. For some reason Tsong Khapa treats the noun *go 'phang*, which translates the Sanskrit *pada*, as a verb here.

3.3.3. 2.2.2. 5.2.3. 2.2. The procedure of power

Meditate on Heruka's mandala wheels, and **always repeat the** definitive and interpretable **root mantras.** That is **the means of achieving all desired aims (29.4cd)**, and it **pacifies all** obstructing **devils.** All power **arises** from this **mantra**, i.e., are attained by one who is very well trained. What are they? **Everything mobile**, i.e., the inhabitants, and **immobile**, the habitat, namely **the triple world**—the underworld, surface world, and celestial pure buddhalands—are **the gift of the fruits** of enjoyment and liberation through **the yogic play** (**29.5**) of experiential uniformity in the reality of Vajradhara.

The adept who is **endowed with the mantra** that protects the mind **and the consort is entirely focused on** the attainment of the supreme **power.** But **the mantra devoid of** union with **the consort** will yield no power for **the embodied** (**29.6**), i.e., the adepts, meaning that power will be very hard to attain. Therefore, **through constant practice** in the application of mantra and the consort (*mudrā*), should one endeavor for however long it takes to attain **the exercises of heat**, that is, the powers of destroying and benefitting, **one will be awakened (29.7ab)** regardless of whether one has attained them or not. One should practice having attained heat. Moreover:

> The first is wisdom that's heated,
> While the second should be smoky.
> In the third is quavering light,[246]
> And in the fourth a lamp-like flame.
> The fifth is perpetual light,
> Just like a sky without a cloud.[247]

246. This translates the Tibetan *gsum pa la ni 'od 'khrug 'byung*; the Sanskrit here is defective.

247. Tsong Khapa quotes Kambala's commentary here. K 54b.5–6: *prathamam uṣmāyate prajñā dvitīye dhūmravatī bhavet / tṛtīye tyajati spalimāni / caturthe dīpavat jvalam / pañcamaṁ tu sadālokam / nirabhra. . . .* The remainder of this verse is lost due to ms. damage. SN 57a.1–2 reads: *dang po shes rab dro ba ste / gnyis pa du ba ldan par 'gyur / gsum pa la ni 'od 'khrug 'byung / bzhi pa mar me ltar 'bar ba / lnga pa rtag tu snang ba ni / sprin med pa yi nam mkha' bzhin.*

The four—heat, peak, endurance and the supreme phenomenon—are as explained in the *Abhidharmasamuccaya* and *Ornament of the Universal Vehicle Sutras*.[248]

3.3.3. 2.2.2. 5.2.3. 2.3. Praise for Mahāyoga

The third part has two sections: (1) the consequences of hating and rejecting Mahāyoga, and (2) the benefits of establishing oneself in Mahāyoga.

3.3.3. 2.2.2. 5.2.3. 2.3.1. The consequences of hating and rejecting Mahāyoga

Those confused ones who, due to consorting with sinners, harm by **disparaging the great yoga** (*mahāyoga*) of Shrī Heruka **that is the means of achieving all desired aims (29.7cd)** in this very life will go to Avīci Hell. After being released from there, they will also be born from **one hundred dog wombs.** And when they are reborn as humans, they **will be born among the chaṇḍālas (29.8ab)**, that is, in a wretched social class.

For example, **if someone** who desires **butter were to churn water with** great **confidence (29.8cd), butter would not be produced, only physical pain (29.9ab)**, i.e., suffering. Likewise, those who reject this yoga and **resort to other yogas due to the motive of [earning] a livelihood (29.10ab)**, in the end, here and elsewhere, **uphold or even revere them in error and in vain (29.9cd)**.

3.3.3. 2.2.2. 5.2.3. 2.3.2. The benefits of establishing oneself in Mahāyoga

The heroes, i.e., adepts, **uphold** the supreme **great yoga** of Shrī Heruka; **one should select the land in which** they **dwell** as the land of heroes, **even if it is in a land of chaṇḍālas and barbarians (29.10c–11b)**. Since **I**, Heruka, **always exist,** i.e., reside, in that land **in order to benefit the sentient beings (29.11cd)** of that land, their relatives should by all means also worship me.

248. Tsong Khapa explains the term "heat," *uṣman* in a variety of ways. He alludes to Bhavabhaṭṭa's interpretation of it in terms of the mundane powers, as well as Jayabhadra's connection of it to the "heat" that is the first of the four "aids to penetration" (*nirvedabhāgiya*) of the Path of Application (*prayogamārga*) described by Asaṅga/Maitreyanātha in the *Ornament of the Universal Vehicle Sutras*. Regarding this see Gray 2007, 290, n. 8.

3.3.3. 2.2.2. 5.2.3. 3. Showing the name of the chapter

In the *Concise* ***Shrī Herukābhidhāna Tantra***, this is **the twenty-ninth chapter** on showing **the characteristics of the messenger and the procedure** that is the means of generating **the power** of heat. This is the explanation of the twenty-ninth chapter in the *Illumination of the Hidden Meaning, A Detailed Exegesis of the Concise Saṁvara Tantra Called "The Chakrasaṁvara."*

Chapter 30

Chapter 30 Outline

3.3.3. 2.2.2. 6. Selecting the protective mantra that removes obstacles

The sixth part, selecting the protective mantra that removes obstacles, has three sections: (1) the promise to explain, (2) the promised import explained, and (3) showing the name of the chapter.

3.3.3. 2.2.2. 6.1. The promise to explain

Now, following the twenty-ninth [chapter], one should know as well from the selection of Heruka's mantra the realization of the Shumbha mantra. Moreover, it is **the chart** of vowels and consonants **that is very hard to obtain** by the master of another tantra. Regarding the need [for this], **there is rapid perfection of the power** of pacifying obstacles **through mere knowledge** (**30.1**) of the selection of this mantra by an adept.

3.3.3. 2.2.2. 6.2. The promised import explained

The second part has three sections: (1) performing ground cleansing etc. and selecting the mantra, (2) the greatness of the selected [mantra] and its procedure, and (3) arranging the four mantras in a series and showing them.

3.3.3. 2.2.2. 6.2.1. Performing ground cleansing etc. and selecting the mantr

The first part has four sections: (1) assembling the basis on which the mantra is selected, (2) showing the yoga by which one selects, (3) placing the basis from which one selects, and (4) the actual method of mantra selection.

3.3.3. 2.2.2. 6.2.1. 1. Assembling the basis on which the mantra is selected

The piece of ground on which the mantra is selected must be a **level** surface free of highs or lows, and **pleasing, anointed with sandalwood** extract. On that **perfumed** ground scattered **flowers** are **arranged** as a carpet (**30.2**). The mantra is selected on ground that is dense with **rows of lamps** and made **pleasant** with **the fragrance** of good **incense** (**30.3ab**).

3.3.3. 2.2.2. 6.2.1. 2. Showing the yoga by which one selects

As [the text] states, the mantra selector, **having done everything** that needs to be done by **oneself** (**30.3c**), should select the mantra. As the *Origin of Saṁvara* states:[249]

249. This text occurs in SU ch. 27, as follows: *sngags pas tsa ru'i bza' ba spyad / de bzhin*

The mantrin should prepare the oblation,
And then he should drink the ambrosia down.
Through self-exceeding deity yoga,
Give the preliminary sacrifice.
United with all of the ḍākinīs,
The master is very well equipoised.

Through union with Heruka one first offers the sacrificial cakes (*bali*, *gtor ma*), then one should from the start be equipoised in the concentration of being united with all of the heroes and ḍākinīs. Immediately after that one should select the mantra having also **undertaken the binding of the directions** (**30.3d**). The binding of the directions involves placement of the adamantine ground, fence, cage, and canopy, as well as the net of arrows and fire mountains.

3.3.3. 2.2.2. 6.2.1. 3. Placing the basis from which one selects

Then, after binding the directions, one should draw on the ground a shape like **a bound kettledrum**. Surrounded by eight lines in each of the directions, make a seven by seven chart, which has forty-nine squares. After the chart is finished, it is en**circled** by the **ninth line** (**30.4ab**), that is, it is in the center of that. Since the four commentaries state that one should make the chart on the kettledrum-like shape,[250] this means that while the bound kettledrum-like shape should serve as the foundation for making the chart, it should not be taken as the shape of the chart itself. The shape that is surrounded by the nine circular lines is the kettledrum, [the size of] a bucket, which appears to be bound as if wound with binding.

Write down in the forty-nine squares are the **letters**, i.e. consonants, and the **class**, the vowels. The very well **equipoised** master **should place** (**30.4cd**) them, from *a* up to *ha*. The *Vajraḍāka* states:[251]

---

bdud rtsi btung bar spyad / rang gi lhag pa'i lhar sbyor bas / sngon du gtor ma sbyin bya ste / mkha' 'gro ma kun mnyam sbyor bas / slob dpon legs par mnyam bzhag pas (SU 300a.5–6).

250. Jayabhadra, for example, commented as follows: "**Then, having made the kettledrum binding**, means that one should draw the shape of a kettledrum with a forty-nine-square [grid]" (Sugiki 2001, 130: *murajabandhaṁ tataḥ kṛtveti murajākāraṁ ekonapañcāśat-koṣṭhayuktaṁ likhet ity arthaḥ*; see CP 60b).

251. This passage occurs in VD ch. 8 as follows: *dbus kyi re'u mig stong pa la / ka ṣa zhes bya*

One should draw the syllable *kṣha*
In the void of the central square.

Therefore, in the central void [square] draw *kṣha*.

3.3.3. 2.2.2. 6.2.1. 4. The actual method of mantra selection

The fourth part has three sections: (1) summary of mantra selection (2) the definitive meaning of the basis of selection and the summary, and (3) detailed exegesis of mantra selection.

3.3.3. 2.2.2. 6.2.1. 4.1. Summary of mantra selection

One should select the hero, i.e., the mantra, which **achieves all desired aims** (**30.5ab**) from among the vowels and consonants positioned in the kettledrum figure. The term "hero" is used in reference to the mantra due to the inseparability of the mantra and the deity.

How is it selected? **The adept** selects **having entered into the calculation of these** (**30.6a**) forty-nine letters, that is, of their squares, **through the normal order** for the vowels, **and the reverse order** for the **letters** (**30.5cd**), i.e., consonants. As the *Origin of Saṁvara* states:[252]

Lord of secrets, the mantra should be known
By arranging it in a clockwise way,
Beginning with the letter *a* and so forth,
And concluding with the syllable *ha*.

Since it states that both the vowels and consonants are arranged in a clockwise manner, it does not mean that the vowels are arranged clockwise and the consonants counterclockwise, in the normal and reverse orders,

---

yi ger ni / gnas pa'i pa ni bri bar bya (VD 21a.3–4). Tsong Khapa quotes it as follows: *dbus kyi re'u mig stong pa la / ka ṣa zhes bya'i yi ger ni / gnas pa yi ni bri bar bya.*

252. This passage occurs in SU ch. 27 as follows: *a sogs yi ge nas brtsams te / yi ge ha yi bar du sngags / g.yas skor rnam par sbyar bar ni / gsang ba'i bdag pos shes par gyis* (SU 300a.7–b.1). It is quoted by Tsong Khapa as follows: *dang po a yig nas brtsams te / ha yig rnam pa'i bar du sngags / g.yas skor rnam pa'i sbyor ba yis / shes par bya'o gsang ba'i bdag.*

respectively. Therefore, with respect to the normal and reverse orders, one should take [the former] as the method of mantra selection.

3.3.3. 2.2.2. 6.2.1. 4.2. The definitive meaning of the basis of selection and the summary

Here Kambala and Devagupta wrote an explanation of the definitive meaning from [the line] **then, having made the bound kettledrum** (30.4a) up to [the line] **having entered into the calculation of these** (30.6a).[253] The three syllables of *muraja*,[254] the equivalent term of "kettledrum," "are the three bodies through the distinctions of body, speech, and mind."[255] Regarding taking these three syllables as body, speech, and mind, *oṁ* is taken to be body, *āḥ* as speech, and *hūṁ* as mind. These three can be assigned, respectively, to the emanation body, communal enjoyment body, and reality body. Kambala wrote:[256]

> The eight lines should be affixed,
> And thoroughly wound with wind.
> The ninth abides in the middle.

Since Devagupta explains the round central line in terms of wind, this means that wind is the ninth line that is surrounded by the eight lines, which is their basis.[257] That is, the mantra of the three seed syllables and wind are inseparably united. Regarding:[258]

253. This is indeed the case, and as indicated Tsong Khapa here relies on their commentaries, which he paraphrases in this section. See SN 57a–b and SS 130b–31a.

254. Tsong Khapa transliterates this term as *mu ra dze*. Devagupta's commentary gives the incorrect transliteration *mu raṁ dzaṁ* (SS 130b.7). Butön gives the correct transliteration, *mu ra dza* (NS 193b.3).

255. SN 57b.1: *rdza rnga zhes bya'i yi ge gsum / sku gsum thugs kyi dbye bas gsum mo*. The extant Sanskrit is a bit more laconic: *muraj[e]ty akṣaraṁ trikāyābhedya* (K 55a.4).

256. SN 57b.1: *rlung gis shin tu bskor ba yis / ri mo brgyad la yang dag brten / ri mo dgu pa dbus gnas pa*. The extant Sanskrit, which is a bit corrupt here, reads: *vāyunā suvartulaṁ / aṣṭatantraṁ (aṣṭarekhāḥ?) samādhitya navamaṁ madhyavartī syāt* (K 55a.4–5).

257. Here Tsong Khapa paraphrases Devagupta's commentary; see SS 130b.7.

258. Here Tsong Khapa quotes two lines from Kambala's commentary, namely, *stong pa'i rnam pa dri med dgod / ā li kā li mnyam rgyas bya* (SN 57b.1); *śūnyatākāranirmala-prakaraṁ ālikālisamākīrṇaṁ* (K 55a.5).

The stainless expanse, form of emptiness,
Is strewn over with vowels and consonants.

This will be explained below. Regarding:[259]

Consisting of the four joys, it's
The unbeatable Dharma drum.

There are two drums, the Buddha's Dharma drum and the unbeatable drum of the heart within the body. That has the nature of the four joys, i.e., possesses the source of the four joys. The vowels and consonants, which are equally stainless with respect to each of the letters, should be strewn on the chart that has the form of emptiness; that is, the chart should be filled with them. Hence it is said:[260]

The sacred teachings in twelve divisions
Are fulfilled by the Dharma syllables.

This illustrates the perfected teaching by the great drum of the Dharma of the Dharmic syllables of the twelve branches of scripture that are the essence of the vowels and consonants. Since the root of all such speech acts is the wind that exists in the indestructible [drop] in the heart, it is the basis of all of the letters of the forty-nine squares. The letter *kṣha* in the center illustrates the indestructible [drop]. With respect to the earlier explanation of the syllables of the term *muraja*, since the meaning of the name is explained here, it is particularly important. Thus:[261]

Included in the summation of that,
Depending on the selflessness of things.

259. Here Tsong Khapa quotes two lines from Kambala's commentary, namely, *dga' ba bzhi yi rang bzhin can / chos kyi rna chen mi shigs pa* (SN 57b.1–2); *caturānandamayaṁ dharmabherī anāhataṁ* (K 55a.5).

260. Here Tsong Khapa quotes two lines from Kambala's commentary, namely, *gsung rab yan lag bcu gnyis pa / chos kyi yi ge yongs rdzogs pa* (SN 57b.2); *dvādaśāṅgapravacanaṁ dharmākṣa-* (K 55a.5; the remaining syllables on line 6 are illegible).

261. Here Tsong Khapa quotes two lines from Kambala's commentary, namely, *de nas grangs kyi nang song bas / chos bdag med pa yang dag bsten* (SN 57b.2); *etat saṅkhyāntargataṁ dharmanairātmyaniḥśritaṁ* (K 55a.6).

Just as Devagupta explains that the selection from within, that is, between, their summation is the emptiness of things,[262] the selection of the mantra from amongst the vowels and consonants is therefore the selection of the gnosis of selflessness that is the essence of the vowels and consonants of the twelve branches of scripture. Hence:[263]

> The celebrated four-faced one
> Tears asunder the four māras.

The *Origin of Heruka* states:

> These mantras of the four-faced one
> Have not arisen, nor will they arise.[264]

This reference to the Shumbha mantra[265] as the mantra of the four-faced one indicates that it is well known as the mantra of the four-faced one.

The definitive meaning of the conquest of the māras by the utterance of this selected mantra is that uttering it eradicates the inner demons by means of the gnosis of the inseparability of bliss and emptiness that extracts the essence of scripture. Regarding the meaning of:

> One should radiate riding wind
> And draw together the three realms,
> Knowing well wind's reality.[266]

262. See SS 131a.1.

263. Here Tsong Khapa quotes two lines from Kambala's commentary, namely, *zhal bzhi par ni rnam par grags / bdud bzhi rnam par 'joms pa'o* (SN 57b.2–3); *caturmukhaṁ tu vikhyātaṁ caturmāravidārakaṁ* (K 55a.6).

264. This translates Tsong Khapa's version of the text, *zhal bzhi pa yi sngags 'di dag / ma byung 'byung bar mi 'gyur ro*. It occurs as follows in the Kangyur: *bzhi pa yi ni sngags 'di dag / ma byung 'byung bar mi 'gyur ro* (HA 4a.2).

265. Tsong Khapa refers to this as the *sumbhani* mantra. However, **sumbhani* mixes the names of two Asura, Shumbha and Nishumbha, whose names are stated in the first of the mantras coded below.

266. Here Tsong Khapa quotes three lines from Kambala's commentary, namely, *rlung la zhon nas spro byed cing / khams gsum pa ni yang dag sdud / rlung gi de nyid shin tu rig* (SN 57b.3); *sphared vāyusamārohyaṁ saṁharec ca tridhātukaṁ vāyusutatvavit* (K 55a.6).

Devagupta explained, "as for radiation and contraction when repeating the syllables of the mantra,[267] through being mounted on wind, one should know the entire three realms as the reality of wind."[268] Radiating and contracting while repeating the Shumbha mantra, knowing that the reality of wind is the root of the three realms, is engaging in the adamantine repetition that fixates upon wind. This applies to the previous explanation of the inseparability of wind and the three syllables. Regarding the meaning of:

> Sounds, both signified and signifying,
> That arise from the vowels and consonants,
> By means of both with and against the grain,
> Are regarded as being like echoes.[269]

If one applies the two to the subject matter, that is, the meaning of with and against the grain, there is the descending progression of the four joys and the ascending retrogression of the four joys. These two emerge from the commingled red and white elements that are illustrated by the vowels and consonants. If one applies it to the discourse, the arrangement of the vowels and consonants is a reflection of the two, the insubstantial vowels and consonants. This illustrates the realization that all speech is like echoes. If one summarizes the meaning of this, the essence of scripture is the union of the two aims of selflessness and the natural great bliss of the four joys that is drawn forth through the practice of adamantine repetition of the three, the arousal, entry and abiding of wind from the indestructible [drop] of the heart.

This explanation in terms of the definitive meaning of mantra selection having arranged the vowels and consonants in the shape of a bound kettle-

267. The Tibetan here reads "form of the mantra," *sngags gi gzugs*. I suspect that this is the result of the misreading of the Sanskrit *mantrākṣara* or *mantrakāra*, "syllables of the mantra," as *mantrākāra*.

268. *sngags kyi gzugs rnams bzlas pa'i dus na rnam par 'phro ba dang bsdu ba ni rlung la mnyam du zhon pas khams gsum ma lus pa rlung gi de kho na nyid du rig par bya'o* (SS 131a.2).

269. Here Tsong Khapa quotes four lines from Kambala's commentary, namely, *rim bzhin 'byung dang rim min pa'i / ā li kā li las byung ba / rjod dang brjod bya'i yi ge ste / sgra brnyan lta bu'i rnam rtog* (SN 57b.3); *anuloma[vilomena] ālikālisamudbhūtā vācyavācakākṣarāḥ prati[śrud i]va bodhitā* (K 55a.6–7).

drum is the explanation by means of Kambala's oral instruction. It seems to be the explanation that captivates the scholars.

3.3.3. 2.2.2. 6.2.1. 4.3. Detailed exegesis of mantra selection

The third part has four sections: (1) selecting the mantra's first line, (2) selecting the mantra's second line, (3) selecting the mantra's third line, and (4) selecting the mantra's fourth line along with the first and final syllables.

3.3.3. 2.2.2. 6.2.1. 4.3.1. Selecting the mantra's first line

The two lines "the virtuous sage, having undertaken" do not occur in the other translation or in the commentaries.[270] In the *Discourse Appendix* it also occurs in the manner of the root tantra:[271]

> Entering the calculation of this,
> The sage should take the thirty-second square. (**30.6ab**)

It seems to lack the first line, which is good.[272]

Since the sages are seven in number, **the thirty-second square** counting from *ka*, namely *s*, from the class that is the count from that sage, i.e., from the consonants, **is taken** (**30.6b**). Since it is **distinguished by the fifth** vowel counting from *a*, namely short *u*, hence it is *su*. **Half of a hundred** is fifty, and **half of** that is the twenty-fifth. Counting from *ka* the twenty-fifth **is taken** to be *m*. It is distinguished by the twenty-fourth, *bha*, which is affixed

270. Tsong Khapa appears to be drawing attention to a discrepancy among the Tibetan translations. The extant Sanskrit of verse 6, in both CT and AU, has only three lines, namely: *etat saṁkhyāntargataṁ muneḥ koṣṭhakā dvātriṁśati saṁgṛhya / pañcamena tu bheditaṁ* (Gray 2012, 173). The PM and SM revised translations translate this with four lines, and the line Tsong Khapa quotes, *dge ba thub par byas nas ni*, occurs only in these translations; it is omitted in the "other" SL revised translation. I am not sure what is the second line to which Tsong Khapa refers. The other lines are attested in the Sanskrit and in commentaries such as Kambala's.

271. This text occurs as follows: *etat saṁkhyāntargataṁ muneḥ koṣṭhakā dvātriṁśati saṁgṛhya /* (Gray 2012, 173); *thub pa de lta'i grangs 'gyur las / re'u mig sum cu gnyis pa blang* (AU 355b.7–56a.1).

272. By first line I presume that Tsong Khapa means the line that he quoted above. It is actually the second line in the PM and SM translations that contain it.

to the *m*. Taking **the thirty-sixth square** counting from *a*, namely *n*, it is **distinguished**, i.e., made distinctive, **by the third** vowel (30.7), *i*, thus *ni*. Then **take the thirty-second** counting from *k*, namely *s*, **it is distinguished by the fifth** vowel, *u*, hence *su*. **Taking the twenty-fifth,** *m*, after that, **it is linked**, i.e., affixed, **to the twenty-fourth,** *bha* (30.8). **Take** as well **the thirty-third** counting from *k*, namely *h*. **The fifteenth square** counting from *a* is *aṁ*, and since this implies the utterance of the *a* vowel, since it is endowed with an *o* vowel after the drop on *ha*, hence *haṁ mo*. It is **endowed with the fifth** vowel, *u*, hence *huṁ mo*. This is **the first line** of the mantra, **which is held to be the supreme of the magnificent** (30.9).

3.3.3. 2.2.2. 6.2.1. 4.3.2. Selecting the mantra's second line

Counting from *a*, take **the nineteenth square,** *g*, **is endowed with the son of fire,** *r*, and **is distinguished by the third square** of the vowels (30.11), short *i*, hence *gri*. **The seed** that is **eighth** counting **from** *y* of the **semivowel class** is *h*, which has **the thirty-sixth square** counting from *a*, namely *n*. That is, the *n* is affixed to *h*. Moreover, joining these **syllables,** *grihṇa*,[273] **is the means of achieving all desired aims** (30.12).

Taking the self-arisen, *h*, **it is conjoined with the fifth** from, i.e., from within, the square, namely *u*, hence *hu*. Connected to its crown is **a drop** and crescent, yielding *hūṁ*.[274] This line of the mantra, **the second line, which is called the means of achieving all aims, is stated** (30.13).

3.3.3. 2.2.2. 6.2.1. 4.3.3. Selecting the mantra's third line

The nineteenth square from *a* is *g*. It **is distinguished by the twenty-seventh** from *k*, namely *r*, hence *gr*. **The third** of the vowels, *i*, is **conjoined** with that, thus *gri* (30.14). Although a certain Tibetan claims that, when one selects the [syllable] *gri* of the second and third lines, having selected the application of *i* to *r*, once that is selected there is the application of *ṛ* to

273. There are some inconsistencies in the coding of this mantra; text codes *grihna*, while the mantra actually reads *gṛhṇa*, with the retroflex vowel and retroflex nasal. Tsong Khapa here corrects the latter mistake.

274. The text here incorrectly codes *huṁ* rather than *hūṁ*. Tsong Khapa again corrects this without commenting on the mistake.

g in the majority of Indian texts. So, one should know to apply the *ṛ* vowel to *g*.[275] However, in the root text itself *r* and *i* are selected individually, and since it is thus stated even in the commentaries, my previous comments in chapter five are good.[276]

Taking the thirty-third counting from *k*, namely *h*, it is linked to **the second** of the vowel squares, long *ā*, and **it is endowed with the** twentieth from *k*, namely *n*. That is, it is affixed to *h*. This syllable is constituted as **magnificent and supreme** (30.15). In regard to this Laṅka [Jayabhadra] stated, "By virtue of *ra* and *ha*, the letter *na* which exists below the term *griha* changes to *ṇa*."[277] Since he explains that it the *n* changes to *ṇ* by virtue of the *r* before it and the intervening *h*, the *n* should be reversed;[278] this should likewise be done in the second line as well.

The twenty-first letter from *k*, namely *p*, and **the twenty-sixth**, *y*, are **likewise** selected. **The one who is well-equipoised** in the Heruka's pride **should select the word** *grihṇāpaya* which is **repeated twice** (30.16). **Next, take the first** by **reversing** the **order** of the consonants, namely *h*. "**From the square**" (*re'u mig las ni, koṣṭhakāt*) means "from within the square." Since *kṣha* is placed in the center it comes after *ha*. Regarding the explanation that *ha* is selected as the first square in the fourth line of the mantra it is explained as the reverse order of the consonants, since the order of

275. Tsong Khapa here paraphrases Butön's commentary at NS 194a.5. However, Tsong Khapa's comments here are better preserved, as several vowel markers appear to be missing in the print of the NS commentary I consulted. Tsong Khapa represents his comments as follows: *ra la i zhugs pa btus nas / btus zin pa na ga la ṛ zhugs pa rgya dpe phal che ba la 'byung bas / ga la dbyangs kyi ṛ zhugs par shes par bya'o*; the following text is preserved at NS 194a.5: *ra la a zhugs pa btus nas / btus zin pa ga la dbyangs ṛa zhugs pa / rgya dpe phal che la 'byung ste.*

276. As noted below in the context of chapter 5, Tsong Khapa is correct that the text codes the syllable *gri* here, even though *gṛ* is etymologically correct, as Butön seems to recognize. These phonemes were commonly confused, likely because the retroflex vowels were no longer used in the colloquial speech of the time. Interestingly, the Tibetan translation of Kambala's commentary correctly transliterates the second and third lines as follows: *oṁ gṛhṇa gṛhṇa hum hūṁ phat / oṁ gṛhṇāpaya gṛhṇāpaya hum hūṁ phat /* (SN 57b.4). However, these phonemes are confused in the extant Sanskrit manuscript, where these lines occur as follows: *oṁ grihna 2 hūṁ phat / oṁ gṛhnāpaya 2 hūṁ phat* (K 55a.7–b.1).

277. Jayabhadra refers here to the internal sandhi rule concerning the transformation of the dental nasal *na* to retroflex nasal *ṇa*; see CP 61a. The Sanskrit text here is corrupt; cf. Sugiki 2001, 131.

278. In Tibetan orthography, the retroflex letter *ṇa* is represented by reversing the letter *na*.

the consonants is reversed, and since the consonants are otherwise mainly selected from below. By that logic one should know that the selection of vowels occurs mainly in the forward order.

The fourth of the vowels is long *ī*, and at **the end** of that is *u*. Since the *h* **is endowed with that** thence there is *hu*. Likewise, *hu* gets the drop from the back of *aṁ*, **the fifteenth** vowel (30.17). **The third line** of the mantra **is spoken for the sake of** achieving **the morality** that attains the sublime states,[279] **wealth**, i.e., riches or enjoyment, the basis for **desire, and liberation**, the ultimate good (**30.18ab**). In addition to the four, morality and so forth, it is said that there are the fruits of the four classes [of tantra].[280]

3.3.3. 2.2.2. 6.2.1. 4.3.4. Selecting the mantra's fourth line along with the first and final syllables

Take the seed of the second square of the vowels, long *ā*, **the thirty-sixth square** (**30.18cd**), *na*, and likewise **the twenty-sixth** counting from *k*, namely *ya*, as well as **the thirty-third** from *a*, *h*. Since [the latter] has **the thirteenth square** from *a*, that is *o*, hence *ho* (**30.19**). **The adept** takes *bha*, **the tenth square** counting up from *ha* **via the reverse order** of the consonants. **The nineteenth from the square** is *ga* (30.20), **and likewise the twenty-ninth square** is *b*, **which is linked to the second square** from *a*, long *ā*. Since **it is adorned with a sound** (*nāda*) **and a drop** (**30.21**),[281] hence *vāṁ*. **Next the seed of water,**[282] *va*, and **once again the eighth** from *k*, that is *j*, **are taken up**. It is **distinguished by the son of fire,** *ra*, meaning that it is affixed to *j*. In the *Origin of Heruka*, the terms *bhagavān* and *vajra*

279. That is, the three higher rebirth destinations.

280. This statement is made by Butön, who glosses these four as the fruits of the four classes. See NS 194b.6.

281. Tsong Khapa here comments on the line as preserved in the SM commentary, *sgra dang thig les rnam par brgyan* (Gray 2012, 535). The other two translations preserve the reading "adorned with a drop above" (PM *steng du thig les rnam par brgyan*, Gray 2012, 349; SL *steng du thig les brgyan par bya*, Gray 2012, 456), which matches the extant Sanskrit, *bindunā ūrdhabhūṣitaṁ* (Gray 2012, 177).

282. It should be noted that the text "the seed of water," (SL: *cho bo yi sa bon*; SM: *chu yi sa bon*) is found in both of Sumatikīrti's revised translations. The canonical translation, however, reads "lord of the Earth," (PM: *sa bdag*), a reading that is also found in the extant Sanskrit texts, *pārthivaṁ*. See Gray 2012, 177, 349, 456, 535.

are not selected, and *vidyārāja* is selected [instead].[283] **The syllable *hūṁ***[284] **is affixed to the end** [of the mantra] (30.22).

This is **the mantra called the conquest of the triple world**, that is, [conquest of] the three, Brahmā, Viṣhṇu, and Īshvara, which **is ornamented with four lines.** For each of the four lines, ***oṁ* illumines all**, i.e., is affixed to front, **and the syllables *huṁ phaṭ* are affixed to the end** of each line (30.23). The tops of these *huṁ* [syllables] lack cresent marks, but they all have drops. Since these join the previously [indicated] *huṁ*, each [line] has two *huṁ*s and a *phaṭ*.

3.3.3. 2.2.2. 6.2.2. The greatness of the selected [mantra] and its procedure

The second part has two sections: (1) the mantra's greatness, and (2) the mantra's procedure.

3.3.3. 2.2.2. 6.2.2. 1. The mantra's greatness

The spells are the deities, and their king is **the universal monarch** Syllable Hūṁ (*hūṁkāra*). **This mantra** of Shumbha **has not** previously **occurred, nor will it occur** again later. In what other [sources] has it not occurred? It is not found **in the *Compendium of Reality*** root tantra, the *Glorious **Primal Supreme*** intertextual tantra, the *Network*,[285] or in the ***Adamantine Terror** Tantra* (30.24). This means that the previously explained definitive meaning of the basis of the selection of the Shumbha mantra and the selected mantra's recitation does not occur in those tantras. The word "wheel" does not occur in the other translations or in *Discourse Appendix*.[286]

While "in the *[Adamantine] Terror*" is what is connected to [the text]

283. See SU 250b.2.

284. This reading is found in all three of the Tibetan translations of this work. The extant Sanskrit, however, reads "the syllables *hūṁ phaṭ* is affixed to the end," *hūṁ-phaṭ-kārāntayojitā* (Gray 2012, 178).

285. That is, JS, the *Network of Ḍākinīs, Unification of all Buddhas Tantra* (*Sarvabuddha-samāyogaḍākinījālasaṁvara Tantra*).

286. Tsong Khapa here is referring to the line in the SM translation, *bde mchog 'khor lo 'jigs byed du* (Gray 2012, 535). The term *'khor lo* does not occur in the other two translations (Gray 2012, 349, 456) or the AU translation (AU 356b.3), all of which read *rdo rje* instead.

"has not occurred," there is the explanation that those tantras are endowed with the four fierce ones through the four lines of the mantra, but this is not the [actual] meaning [of this line].[287]

3.3.3. 2.2.2. 6.2.2. 2. The mantra's procedure

Regarding **endowed with the four fierce ones**, while the three commentaries state that the four fierce ones are not mentioned by name in the four [lines of the] mantra,[288] however, it seems that Durjayachandra's explanation is excellent; he quotes the explanation in the sixtieth chapter of the *Discourse Appendix* that the Syllable Hūṁ (*hūṁkāra*), with eight faces and sixteen hands in the middle of a lotus, is surrounded by those four, namely Desire King, Blue Jewel, Great Strength, and Immovable.[289]

In Kambala's commentary there occurs the following:

287. Tsong Khapa here is referring to Butön's explanation that: "This mantra exists in the *Compendium of Reality*, the *Glorious Primal Supreme*, the *Saṁvara* and *Adamantine Terror* tantras in the manner of **the eight forms**, that is, the eight worldly protector or the eight forms of earth, water, fire, wind, moon, sun, Yama, and Yakṣha, instantaneously, through being **endowed with the four fierce ones** whose names are mentioned in the four lines of the mantra" (NS 195a.4–5: *de kho na nyid bsdus pa dang / dpal mchog dang po dang / bde mchog dang / rdo rje 'jigs byed kyi rgyud rnams su sngags kyi tshig bzhis mtshan ma smos pa'i khro bo bzhi dang yang dag ldan pas skad cig gis ni / sku brgyad de / 'jig rten skyong ba brgyad dam / sa chu me rlung zla nyi gshin rje gnod sbyin gyi sku brgyad kyi tshul du sngags 'di gnas par 'gyur ro*).

288. See CP 61b.1 and SG 195a.2. Bhavyakīrti follows Jayabhadra's commentary closely, but the translation of his commentary omits the negative particle *ma*, seemingly suggesting that he argues that they are mentioned by name in the mantra (see BC 29b.1), but this is almost certainly a mistranslation of the Sanskrit, given the fact that the negative particle *a* in Jayabhadra's commentary is elided due to *sandhi*, a fact that the translators of Bhavyakīrti's commentary apparently failed to recognize. The Sanskrit text here reads: *catuḥkrodhasamāyuktam iti mantrasya catvāri padāni catuḥkrodharājāno 'nirdiṣṭābhidhānā ucyante* (Sugiki 2001, 132).

289. Tsong Khapa here very concisely summaries the description of Hūṁkāra and the four fierce ones found at AU 60.29–45 (in my forthcoming edition; see AU 356b–57a), large portions of which are quoted by Durjayachandra (see RG 298b.7–99a.7). There is considerable divergence concerning the names of these deities, however. The names given in AU are Desire Diamond (*ṭakkivajra*), Indigo Diamond (*nīlavajra*), Moving Diamond (*calavajra*), Immovable Diamond (*acalavajra*). See J fol. 287, and AU 357a.3. However, Durjayachandra quotes their names as *'dod pa'i rgyal po dbyig sngon dang / stobs po che dang mi g.yo mgon /* (RG 299a.5–6). Tsong Khapa follows this reading closely, but instead of *dbyig sngon*, "Blue Jewel," his commentary reads *dbyug sngon*, "Blue Mace," which is apparently a corrupt reading of Durjayachandra's text.

In order to protect the mandala,
All of the wicked ones are demolished,
Well endowed with the four fierce ones,
He assumes the eight forms in an instant (30.25).[290]

Regarding the meaning of the third line [of this verse], there is a Syllable Hūṁ (*hūṁkara*) like this stated in the fourth chapter of the *Discourse Appendix*.[291] Regarding the explanation that a protective retinue of ten fierce ones surrounds him, I discuss this at length in my commentary on Lūipa's meditation manual.[292]

Regarding "he assumes the eight forms in an instant," Kambala explains that "instantaneously" means that by reciting each of the mantra's four lines one radiates, in twos, the eight gate and quarter guardians, who then summon the obstacle spirits.[293] [Kambalāmbara's explanation of this mantra in his] commentary on Lūipa's meditation manual is not the same as what Kambala wrote.[294] Durjayachandra, quoting the line "is complete with the eight forms,"[295] explains that he is complete with the eight messengers who abide in the commitment wheel.[296] Two commentaries quote this text as[297]

290. This text is a close variant of CT 30.25 and is actually Kambala's quotation of the root text. It occurs as follows: *dkyil 'khor bsrung ba'i don du ni / gdug pa thams cad nges gnon pas / khro bo bzhi dang yang dag ldan / skad cig gis ni sku brgyad 'gyur* (SN 57b.5); *maṇḍalasya tu rakṣārthaṁ sarvaduṣṭaniniśumbhanam / catuḥkrodhasamopeta aṣṭamūrtir bhavet kṣaṇāt / iti* (K 55b.1–2).

291. AU ch. 4 features a detailed visualization of Vajrasattva, also identified in the text as Vajrahūṁkāra, who radiates the eight fierce ones, who are listed by name and described in this text. See AU 254a, 254b as well as my forthcoming translation of this text.

292. That is, his massive *Wish-granting Cow* (*bcom ldan 'das dpal 'khor lo bde mchog gi mngon par rtogs pa'i rgya cher bshad pa 'dod pa 'jo ba*).

293. See SN 57b.5–6.

294. Tsong Khapa here points to differences in the interpretation of this mantra between Kambala's (SN) root tantra and Kambalāmbara's (Q 4661) *Commentary on the Realization of Shrī Chakrasaṁvara*.

295. This is the standard version of this line found in the majority of sources. See Gray 2012, 178.

296. Durjayachandra wrote that: "Regarding **complete with the eight forms**, the eight forms indicate the messengers who abide in the commitment wheel, from Yamadāhī up to Yamamathanī" (RG 299b.2: *gzugs ni brgyad po yang dag ldan / zhes bya la / gzugs brgyad ni gshin rje sreg ma la sogs pa nas / gshin rje 'joms ma'i mthar thug pa dam tshig 'khor lor gnas pa'i pho nya mor bstan to*).

297. Tsong Khapa here cites a variant translation of the Sanskrit *aṣṭamūrtisamanvitaṁ*

"Regarding being endowed with the eight forms," and while this may be explained as the four [lines of the] mantra existing in the mode of the eight forms, namely the four elements, the sun, moon, Yama and Yakṣha, the previous two [explanations] are better.

[Syllable Hūṁ] creates the four fierce ones and the eight forms as well as, for the sake of protection, the mandala of the Syllable Hūṁ that is "blissful," i.e., the essence of great bliss. "His mandala" also occurs.[298]

Just by obtaining this destruction of all of the wicked ones, the wicked ones **will undoubtedly**, i.e., without a doubt, **die.** From your own body enter the body of the consort (*shes rab, prajñā*). Entering your own body again, if you **utter** this mantra with oneself **in union with the wheels, one will give rise**, without obstruction, **to the fruit of all powers** (30.26).

3.3.3. 2.2.2. 6.2.3. Arranging the four mantras in a series and showing them

oṁ sumbha nisumbha huṁ huṁ phaṭ
oṁ grihṇa grihṇa huṁ huṁ phaṭ
oṁ grihṇāpaya grihṇāpaya huṁ huṁ phaṭ
oṁ anayahobhagavāṁ vajra huṁ huṁ phaṭ[299]

3.3.3. 2.2.2. 6.3. Showing the name of the chapter

In the *Concise* ***Shrī Herukābhidhāna Tantra***, this is **the thirtieth chapter** on **the procedure of selecting the** four-line **mantra** from the arrangement of vowels and consonants in **a bound kettledrum**-like shape. This is the explanation of the thirtieth chapter in the *Illumination of the Hidden Meaning, A Detailed Exegesis of the Concise Saṁvara Tantra Called "The Chakrasaṁvara."*

(Sugiki 2001, 132), namely *sku brgyad dang ni bcas pa ru*, found in the Tibetan translations of Jayabhadra and Bhavyakīrti's commentaries. See CP 61b.1 and BC 29b.1.

298. Here Tsong Khapa discusses two variant translations of CT 30.25c, which reads in Sanskrit either as *maṇḍalasya tu rakṣārthaṁ* or *maṇḍalaṁ tasya rakṣārthaṁ* (Gray 2012, 179). The second variant Tsong Khapa lists, *de'i dkyil 'khor* occurs in the PM translation and is clearly a translation of the second Sanskrit reading (2012, 347). The first variant, *bde ba'i dkyil 'khor* is found only in the SM translation and is unattested elsewhere (2012, 535).

299. Tsong Khapa's version of this mantra differs slightly from what is found in the Sanskit manuscripts and the Tibetan translations. See Gray 2012 for a complete account of these variant readings.

Chapter 31

Chapter 31 Outline

3.3.3. 2.2.2. 7. The detailed exegesis of the food commitments

The seventh part, the detailed exegesis of the food commitments, has three sections: (1) the chapter on the procedure of the hand signs, (2) the chapter on the procedures of the achievement of the sacrificial victim and zombie, and the creation stage, and (3) the chapter on the secret and reverential worship.

3.3.3. 2.2.2. 7.1. The chapter on the procedure of the hand signs

The first part has four sections: (1) explanation of the scope of engagement of heteropraxy, (2) detailed exegesis of heteropraxy, (3) acting to hide and disclose this method, and (4) showing the name of the chapter.

3.3.3. 2.2.2. 7.1.1. Explanation of the scope of engagement of heteropraxy

Then, following the thirtieth [chapter], the thirty-first should be explained. It is the nondeceptive explanation of **the destruction of all,**

namely fire sacrifice and so forth **with the great meat**, i.e., human flesh, which **arises from the vajra**. It is explained as well that these are performed by means of gnosis of the inseparability of the vajra, namely the concentration of the body of Vajradhara that arises from that. This human flesh fire sacrifice is described as **the dreadful destroyer of**, i.e., has the power [to destroy], the life force of **all the cruel ones** (**31.1**).

Is human flesh alone what is needed? In the same manner as human flesh, the cruel ones are destroyed even if one offers fierce **fire sacrifices and sacrificial offerings** to the deities **with the meats of dogs, pigs,** or chickens **that have copper [colored] crests as well.** However, here the power is greater from human flesh. In order to perform these three[300] one is primarily engaged in heteropraxy.

If in doing thus one does so having realized the natural clear light **without consideration** (**31.2**) of suitability or unsuitability,[301] **one will attain all** of the great powers of the sword and so forth **without exception**, and the state of awakening in which there are no more powers [to be attained]. One will also **subdue all of the kingdoms** (**31.3ab**) of a universal monarch or a lord who protects the world. It is held that these meats do not arise from one killing them oneself.[302]

300. The root text here mentions three actions, the actions of eating, fire sacrifice, and sacrificial offerings (*bhakṣahomabalikriyā*). Tsong Khapa only mentions the latter two ritual actions, but presumably he is referring to all three here.

301. Tsong Khapa here expands upon Kambala's brief comment: "**Without hesitation** means from the natural clear light" (K 57a.5: *avicāra iti prakṛtiprabhāśvaratvāt*; SN 59b.3: *rtog dang bral bas bya zhes bya ba ni rang gi rang bzhin gyis 'od gsal ba'i phyir*).

302. It is not clear if Tsong Khapa here advocates the outer sacrifice of the flesh of living beings without killing them oneself, or an inner, visualized sacrifice that doesn't actually employ flesh at all. I suspect the latter is the case since that came to be the standard Tibetan Buddhist ritual practice. This clearly is the import of a passage in Kambala's commentary that appears to be Tsong Khapa's source here. The passage reads: "Just by injuring beings one will not obtain accomplishment with the consort. The mind that is free of conceptions is famed as the hearth. Kindling the fire of discrimination, one should offer all conceptions as a sacrifice made of rice. What horrible person would offer meat and human flesh? No killing of beings will arise by drinking various alcoholic drinks" (K 57a.6–7: *sattvāpakāramātreṇa mudrāsiddhi na labhyate / avikalpaṁ yac cittaṁ kuṇḍaśabdena kīrtitam / vivekāgniṁ prajvālya juhuyāt samastaṁ tu vikalpa baliśālijaṁ / dyūt* (?) *kiṁ janajugupsita / sattvaprāṇāṁ na saṁbhavaṁ nānāmadhupānataḥ*; SN 59b.4–5: *sems can gnod pa tsam gyis ni / phyag rgya'i dngos grub thob mi 'gyur / rnam par mi rtog sems gang zhig / thab khung sgra ni rab tu grag / rnam dben me ni rab sbal la / ma lus rnam par rtog pa yis /*

"The three such as the conch and so forth of the *Vedas* are purifiers. The skull should not be held since it is impure." In response to this, if **conch, mother-of-pearl, and pearl**, i.e., **the tripartite cause, arise from (31.3cd)** non-virtuous actions, yet are praised as "purifiers," **who would disparage the** human **skull (31.4b)**, saying it is not a purifier, since it comes from the body that is very hard to attain, and is produced from a great store of merit? It should not be disparaged.[303]

Why is the human body supreme? It is said that "since it is the distinctive place for attaining the liberation of the reality body, and the gnosis of great bliss, the human support is supreme."[304] And if it arises from the tripartite cause here, it is **of the body of the gnosis of reality (31.4a)**. In the manner of "by arising from the tripartite cause of conch, mother-of-pearl, and pearl," is relevant to "by arising from the cause[305] of the three of pearl [etc.]."[306] In another translation [these lines] occur as "conch, mother-of-pearl, and pearl are the tripartite cause."[307]

Bhavyakīrti states that that there is no difference in cause with respect to [the statement that] conch etc. are purifiers while the skull is not, since it seems that [they all] arise from the cause of the aggregates etc.[308] While

---

sha dang sha chen sbyin sreg bya / skye bos smad ba gang ce'ang rung / srog chags yan lag las byung dang / sna tshogs chang ni btung bar bya).

303. Tsong Khapa here points out the absurdity of labeling human skulls impure, and conch shells etc. pure, given the fact that the latter typically derives from the killing of a living being. Durjayachandra makes a similar point; see RG 300a.4–5.

304. Sachen makes a similar point at PG 347.4–48.1, but Tsong Khapa is not directly quoting Sachen here.

305. Tsong Khapa here glosses *rgyu mtshan*, the Tibetan translation in this context for the Sanskrit *nimitta*, "cause," with *rgyu*, also meaning cause. This gloss reflects a subtlety that cannot easily be expressed in English.

306. Here Tsong Khapa simply partially restates and glosses the translation found in both the PM and SM translations.

307. This is the reading of the SL translation. Tsong Khapa quotes it as: *dung dang nya phyis mu tig ste / gsum char rgyu mtshan byung yin no.* It occurs as follows in the extant SL translation: *dung dang mu tig nya phyis te / gsum char rgyu mtshan byung yin na* (Gray 2012, 457).

308. See BC 30b.5–6.

Vīravajra also explains that the cause is the same as flesh,[309] the system of Kambala is better.[310]

Since the human skull also serves as a purifier, **the hero**-lord **has a garland of** dry and wet human **skulls.** His head **is adorned with a half moon** (**31.4cd**). It is said that even **the hero's** skull piece **arises from the hero** (**31.5a**) Heruka, in the same way that the full moon emerges from the form of the waxing half-moon.

3.3.3. 2.2.2. 7.1.2. Detailed exegesis of heteropraxy

The second part has two sections: (1) heteropraxy in general, and (2) worship with the left hand in particular.

3.3.3. 2.2.2. 7.1.2. 1. Heteropraxy in general

It is explained that **the five signs** are the five goddesses, Vajravārāhī and so forth, and that one should rely, i.e., meditate, upon the five skulls of the dreadlock crest.[311] This means that one should meditate upon the five dried skulls that are the essence of the five goddesses. Moreover, the signs of the five fingers, should be displayed to one who has the commitments of eating, drinking, and so forth, **with the adept's left hand** (31.5bc) that achieves power with the gestures (*phyag rgya*), from the perspective of what is shown below.

309. See SG 195a.5.

310. Kambala likewise views these supposedly auspicious implements as arising from sinful actions. He notes, "Regarding **the cause, it** is from non-virtuous karma that they **arise**" (K 57b.1: *nimittam akuśalakarmaṇaḥ / tena saṁbhavā iti*; SN 59b.6–7: *rgyu ni las mi dge ba rnams te de las yang dag par byung ba'o*).

311. Tsong Khapa here paraphrases Jayabhadra's commentary, which reads: "Regarding **should display the five signs**, by the usage of the word "sign" here the five goddesses, Vajravārāhī, etc., are related. This means that one should display and visualize the five goddesses on the five skulls that adorn one's dreadlock crest" (Sugiki 2001, 132: *cchommakān darśayet pañceti atra cchommakaśabdenopacārād vajravārāhyādyāḥ pañca devatyaḥ kathitāḥ jaṭāmakuṭamaṇḍiteṣu pañcasu kapāleṣu pañcadevatīṁ darśayed dhyāyed ity arthaḥ*; CP 61b.3–4: *brda ni lnga po bstan pa dag / ces bya ba 'dir brda'i sgra ni rdo rje phag mo la sogs pa lha mo lnga la bya ba yin te / ral pa dang cod pan brgyan pa'i thod pa chen po lnga lha mo lngar bstan cing bsgom par bya'o zhes bya ba'i don to*).

Note that Tsong Khapa's commentary reads "rely," *brten pa*, in place of the term "display," *bstan/darśayet* we find in Jayabhadra's commentary.

The reason for this is that the left hand **is the abode of the heroes** and heroines such as Vajrasattva. Since **all beings of the triple world**, including the **animate** inhabitants and **inanimate** habitat, **are born from the left** (**31.6**), one should thus practice from the left. Kambala wrote, "the left is wisdom, namely the truth of the lack of intrinsic reality. If you ask about that in conventional terms, it is characterized as the non-dual reality of things."[312] Bhavyakīrti takes **all animate and inanimate** in terms of the emptiness of intrinsic reality, stating "empty phenomena arise from phenomena that are truly empty," as if quoting Nāgārjuna.[313] His commentary also has an alternative explanation, stating that the left refers to women.[314] I have previously explained this at length.[315]

3.3.3. 2.2.2. 7.1.2. 2. Worship with the left hand in particular

Now, regarding the performance of hand worship, what deities are placed on the fingers and so forth of the left hand? **Vajrasattva abides** by the "big one" or "tree," that is, on the thumb.[316] **Vairochana likewise** abides **by the creeper**, i.e., the index finger. If [the line] "in the manner of the ritual form," which is not found in the other translations, seems to occur, the deities are also placed on the remaining [fingers] in the same manner as the ritual form for placing the deities on those two fingers.[317] **Padmanartaka**, that is, [Padma]narteshvara, is **at the chief** (**31.7**), i.e., the middle finger. **The hero** Heruka, who is **the bestower of all powers, abides in the receptacle**,[318] i.e.,

312. See SN 60a.3–4. The Sanskrit here is corrupt; see K 57b.4–5.

313. See BC 31a.4. Bhavyakīrti does not indicate the source of this quotation; it is not a quote from the *Mūlamadhyamakakārika*.

314. More precisely, he states that the "left is an outer woman." BC 31a.4: *g.yon pa ni phyi rol bud med do.*

315. See section 3.3.3. 2.2.2. 5.2.2. 2.1 in chapter 28 above.

316. "Big one," *sbom po*, is the translation found in the SM commentary, while *sdong po* is an accurate translation of the extant Sanskrit, *tarave*. The PM and SL translations give the interpretive translation *mthe por/'the bor*, "on the thumb," based upon the commentarial tradition. See Gray 2012, 181, 352, 457, 536.

317. This line, *cho ga'i rnam pa de lta bur*, is only found in the PM translation, and only in two of the Kangyur recensions I consulted. The majority of recensions read *go cha'i rnam pa de lta bur.* See Gray 2012, 352.

318. The Tibetan in the PM and SM translations read *brtan par*, "in/on/by the receptacle/

the ring finger. **The last one**, i.e., the little finger, **has the unbearable**[319] form of **Ākāshagarbha**, i.e., Vajrasūrya (**31.8**). In Rinchen Zangpo's translation the five [fingers], thumb and so forth, are called by their own names.[320] **The surface of the fingernails pressed together is the abode of Hayagrīva**, i.e., the supreme steed. The arrangement **of all** of these **heroes** on **the left hand is the reason** (**31.9**) why it is with the left hand that signs are displayed and food offered.

Vīravajra explains that one should visualize a five-petalled, four-colored lotus **on the palm of** one's left **hand**. On its anthers, i.e., in its center, the two, **Shrī Heruka and** his lady **Vārāhī**, are **united**, thus producing supreme **bliss** (**31.10ab**). Visualize Yāminī on the front [petal], Mohinī on the left, Saṁchālinī on the right, and Saṁtrāsanī on the back, and Chāṇḍalī "desiring equipoise" in the northeast quarter.[321] Bhavyakīrti and Laṅka [Jayabhadra] place Trāsanī on the right [petal] and Saṁchālinī on the back one.[322]

One should definitely ascertain, i.e., visualize, the twelve deities or the triple wheel deity host **on the back** (**31.10c**) of the left hand as well, just as a reflection appears in a mirror. **They**, i.e., the deities, **are placed on the hand**. In **the union of all loving**, i.e., agreeable, yoginīs, one **should worship the supreme**, i.e., most excellent, **hero by means of the rules of ritual** (**31.11**) with **the five types of signs** (**31.10d**) of hand worship and the five ambrosias, namely feces and so forth. The visualization of the four elements of the left hand as the four [goddesses], **Lochanā** etc. is indicated by the four lines beginning with "**earth**" (**31.12**). Bhavyakīrti and Laṅka [Jayabhadra] state that Lochanā etc. should be taken to be the four [essence yoginīs], Ḍākinī and so forth.[323] Therefore, Lochanā, Māmakī, Pāṇḍarā and Tārā

basis." The Sanskrit, however, reads *dhārāyāṁ*, "in/on/by the current/stream." See Gray 2012, 181, 352, 536.

319. Tsong Khapa here gives the reading *mi bzad*, "unbearable," found in the SL and SM translations. The PM translation reads *mi zad*, "inexhaustible," which is closer to the Sanskrit reading *avyayaḥ*, "imperishable." See Gray 2012, 181, 352, 457, 536.

320. That is, the translation is an interpretive one, rather than a literal one. The SL translation retains this feature of the original Lochen translation.

321. Tsong Khapa here summarizes Vīravajra's longer description of this visualization; see SG 195b.6–7.

322. See BC 31a.7, CP 62a.1, and Sugiki 2001, 132.

323. The four goddesses associated with the four great elements are not part of the

are, respectively, Ḍākinī, Rūpiṇī, Khaṇḍarohā, and Lāmā, and they should be visualized as the reality of the four [elements], earth, etc. While Vīravajra explains that[324] "the four, Rūpiṇī, etc., are implied through the mention of Lochanā and so forth," the system of the previous two is better.

The void, that is, the space element, **is** visualized as **Chumbikā**, "Kisser." She is explained to be Vajravārāhī. Furthermore, this goddess is also Prajñā**pāramitā. In the middle** is the realm of empty space, which **is** also **the abode** in which **all heroes** play. **The sage invites them to the back** (31.13) is explained to mean that the deities who are placed on the hand come there in the manner of a reflection appearing on the back of the hand. [The alternate reading] "should ascertain on the back" is explained as having the same meaning.[325] The arrangement of hand worship should be known from my detailed presentation in my extensive commentary on Lūipa's meditation manual.[326]

3.3.3. 2.2.2. 7.1.3. Acting to hide and disclose this method

This secret should not be disclosed to unsuitable vessels; **it should be zealously concealed. The hero**es of Chakrasaṁvara and so forth **employ signs** and worship **in this manner**, i.e., with the substance, the five ambrosias and so forth, placed in a "great conch" human skull for hand worship. When they enjoy food, they **commence**, i.e., enjoy the food **in one** vessel, without dividing it into separate vessels. By doing this, they [form] **the network of the ḍākinīs united with all heroes**, which is Chakrasaṁvara, the principal of all hosts.

Chakrasaṁvara mandala. To resolve this problem Bhavyakīrti and Jayabhadra equate them to the four essence yoginīs. See BC 31b.2, CP 62a.3–4, and Sugiki 2001, 132.

324. See SG 196a.3.

325. The Sanskrit here reads *pṛṣṭhe tu visarjayet*, "should commit to the back," which the three revised translations render as "invite to the back," *rgyab tu gshegs su gsol*. Here Tsong Khapa mentions an alternate translation, *rgyab tu nges byas*, variants of which are found in the commentaries of Bhavyakīrti, Jayabhadra, and Vīravajra (BC 31a.7, CP 62a.1: *rgyab tu shin tu nges byas te*; SG 196a.1–2: *rgyab tu nges par bya*).

326. This is his *Wish-granting Cow* (*bcom ldan 'das dpal 'khor lo bde mchog gi mngon par rtogs pa'i rgya cher bshad pa 'dod pa 'jo ba*).

3.3.3. 2.2.2. 7.1.4. Showing the name of the chapter

In the *Concise* ***Shrī Herukābhidhāna Tantra***, this is **the thirty-first chapter** on **the procedure of** engaging with **the signs** that depend upon **the hand** when engaging **in the rites of eating, fire sacrifice, and sacrificial offerings.** This is the explanation of the thirty-first chapter in the *Illumination of the Hidden Meaning, A Detailed Exegesis of the Concise Saṁvara Tantra Called "The Chakrasaṁvara."*

Chapter 32

Chapter 32 Outline

3.3.3. 2.2.2. 7.2. The chapter on the procedures of the achievement of the sacrificial victim and zombie, and the creation stage
3.3.3. 2.2.2. 7.2.1. The promise to explain
3.3.3. 2.2.2. 7.2.2. The promised import explained
3.3.3. 2.2.2. 7.2.2. 1. The achievement of the sacrificial victim for the sake of fire sacrifice
3.3.3. 2.2.2. 7.2.2. 2. The achievement of the zombie for the sake of great power
3.3.3. 2.2.2. 7.2.2. 3. Showing the yoga of the creation stage that is essential for all of them
3.3.3. 2.2.2. 7.2.2. 3.1. Creation of the habitat
3.3.3. 2.2.2. 7.2.2. 3.2. Creation of the inhabitant deities
3.3.3. 2.2.2. 7.2.3. Showing the name of the chapter

3.3.3. 2.2.2. 7.2. The chapter on the procedures of the achievement of the sacrificial victim and zombie, and the creation stage

The second part, the chapter on the procedures of the achievement of the sacrificial victim and zombie, and the creation stage, has three sections: (1) the promise to explain, (2) the promised import explained, and (3) showing the name of the chapter.

3.3.3. 2.2.2. 7.2.1. The promise to explain

Then, after the thirty-first [chapter], **I will explain** [something] **other** than hand worship.[327] What is this? There is the sacrificial victim that is the cause of eating, **feasting** by those who enjoy it, and the gathering of

327. Here Tsong Khapa glosses the Tibetan text *de nas gzhan yang*, which opens the first

them is a **fellowship. Through** knowledge of **the correct application** of appropriate deity yoga and so forth, one will **rapidly**, i.e., in this very life, **engage in power** (32.1).[328]

3.3.3. 2.2.2. 7.2.2. The promised import explained

The second part has three sections: (1) the achievement of the sacrificial victim for the sake of fire sacrifice etc., (2) the achievement of the zombie for the sake of great power, and (3) showing the yoga of the creation stage that is essential for all of them.

3.3.3. 2.2.2. 7.2.2. 1. The achievement of the sacrificial victim for the sake of fire sacrifice

The adept, via the aforementioned procedure, summons, i.e., achieves, without himself causing harm, the flesh of **sacrificial victims** (**32.2ab**), namely the five, the donkey and so forth, which are purified as the five buddhas.[329] It is stated that "aforementioned" refers to the demonstration in chapter fourteen of the indications of the seven lived one, by which one will recognize the seven lived one. Or, one might obtain ordinary flesh that is not depleted by disease and free of abscesses and leprosy. Or, later the signs are displayed when the mandala of the host is made in the seats, subsidiary seats, and so forth, with the rite of displaying hand signs that was previously [discussed].[330]

One will also succeed with one that has five claws in the same manner as one succeeds relying upon seven-lived sacrificial victims. In accordance with the explanation in the two commentaries that "those with five claws are

---

verse of this chapter. This is a translation of the Sanskrit *ataḥ paraṁ*, "henceforth," but here he treats *de nas* and *gzhan yang* as separate terms.

328. Here Tsong Khapa closely follows Butön's commentary (NS 203a), which in turn is based on Bhavyakīrti's. Bhavyakīrti glosses *samyak* as *śobhanaṁ*, and *vidhānaṁ* as *devatāyogādi*. See Pandey 2002, 519.

329. Tsong Khapa here paraphrases Kambala's comment, namely "**The sacrificial victim** is the donkey and so forth, purified as the five buddhas" (K 59a.4: *paśum iti kharādayaḥ pañcabuddhaviśuddhyā*).

330. Tsong Khapa here closely paraphases Kambala's commentary; see SN 61b.6–7 and K 59a.6.

the dog, cat, rabbit, etc.," **the sacrificial victims** have five claws.[331] Vīravajra explains that[332] "[the sacrificial victims] have claws and are five; namely, the tortoise, camel, dog, jackal, and horse are the five."

Someone states that "the equivalent term of 'horse' (*rta*) in an Indian text is 'claw' (*sen mo*), the meaning of that is the 'five clawed ones.'"[333] However, this does not conform to [the root text's] statement "**the sacrificial victims are thus five** (32.2c)." Regarding "the five clawed ones" (*sder mo can lnga*), since "those with five claws" (*sen mo lnga pa*) occurs in the commentaries, it is necessary to take this as "the five clawed ones." From [the root text] **the donkey, tortoise, the man, camel, jackal, and horse, and so forth** (**32.2d**) the bull is implied as well. The flesh of **these sacrificial victims in the mandala that is the means of attaining** mundane **power** is a **limb of**, i.e., support for, **success** (**32.3ab**).

While donkeys and so forth are cattle *qua* sacrificial victims, why are humans called cattle?[334] The equivalent term to "cattle" can also designate

331. Jayabhadra's comment occurs as follows: "those with five claws are the dog, cat, rabbit, etc.; these are the five clawed species" (CP 62a.6: *pañcanakhāḥ śvānamārjāraśaśādayaḥ pañcana-khajātīyāḥ* [Sugiki 2001, 133]; *sen mo lnga rnams ni khyi dang / byi la dang / ri bong la sogs pa rnams te / sen mo lnga'i rigs so*); see also BC 31b.3.

332. Tsong Khapa omits a portion of Vīravajra's commentary that make it seem as if he is incorrectly stating the horses have claws. His full commentary occurs as follows: "What are the sacrificial victims? Those with claws are the cat, rabbit, and so forth. The tortoise, camel, dog, jackal, and horse are the five. Thus, are the sacrificial victims and clawed species" (SG 196a7–b.2: *phyugs gang zhes pa la / sder mo ni byi la dang ri bong la sogs pa'o / lnga ni rus sbal dang rnga mlo dang khyi dang ce spyang dang rta dang lnga ste / de ltar phyugs sder mo can gyi rigs te*).

333. Butön makes this comment at NS 203b.3. It appears that Butön is trying to explain away the issue of the "clawed ones," since some of the animals listed have hoofs rather than claws. But I am not sure exactly what his point is; the Sanskrit term for horse used in the root text is *haya*, while the term "claw" used in Jayabhadra's commentary is the unrelated term *nakha*.

334. At issue here is the term in the root text, *paśu*, which literally means "that which is tethered," hence domestic or sacrificial animals, although humans were included in the list of "five sacrificial animals" in vedic texts such as the *Śatapatha Brāhmaṇa*, which clearly are the source of this concept of five sacrificial victims. Regarding this see Gray 2007, 300, n. 2. The term *paśu* is translated as the Tibetan term *phyugs*, meaning "cattle" or domesticated animals.

"holy" or "supreme."[335] Thus it is said that **from among the** ordinary **species**, the human **is the best** sacrificial victim among **the species,** because they are endowed with all of the good qualities praised as supports for attainment on the path. **From among the four-footed**, the donkey and so forth, **the elephant** is the best (**32.3d**). **From among the winged**, crows and so forth, **the goose** is best. With respect to the line [beginning with] **lower animals** etc., the reading occurs "from among the quadrupeds there is the turtle king." It is explained that the turtle king is a jeweled serpent.[336] Someone explained that among the aquatic animals the turtle is king, i.e., the principal one.[337] These [creatures' supremacy is indicated by] the above statement regarding "supreme" as a synonym for "sacrificial victim."

The gods are Brahmā, Viṣhṇu, and Shiva (*īśvara, dbang phyug*). Someone explains that by making inner and outer fire sacrifices with mantra and the flesh of the five sacrificial victims, their mouths tremble, that is, they are brought into one's control.[338] Someone [else] explained, quoting [the line] **the movement of the mouths of the gods** (**32.3d**), that by goats, water buffalos, and chickens, and by the play of various forms, the faces of the gods, that is, the titans, are made to move.[339] The translation "from/due to

335. I am not sure what source Tsong Khapa is depending upon here. The term *paśu* can designate the soul of the adept vis-à-vis Shiva in a Shaiva context, which may be what inspired this comment.

336. Tsong Khapa quotes a variant reading of 32.3c, *byol song rnams las rus sbal rgyal*, quoted in Vīravajra's commentary. See SG 196b.2–3. He then summarizes Vīravajra's explanation of this line.

337. Butön states this at NS 204a.5.

338. Butön states this at NS 204a.6–7.

339. Tsong Khapa here refers to Bhavabhaṭṭa's commentary, although his understanding of it differs from mine. In my reading of this passage, it seems that Bhavabhaṭṭa is referring to the gods causing the mouths of various animals moving, apparently indicating that they are favored sacrificial victims. His comments read as follows: "As for **those whose mouths are moved by the gods**, it is the goat, water buffalo, and chicken whose mouths are moved, i.e., their mouths are caused to move, referring to the goat, and so forth. By whom are their mouths caused to move? The gods, titans, and so forth, play by means of diverse forms" (Pandey 2002, 520: *devānāṁ mukhacālanam iti chāgalo mahiṣaḥ kukkuṭāś ceti mukham cālayatīti mukhacālanaṁ chāgalādayaḥ / keṣāṁ mukhacālanam ityāha dīvyanti nānārūpeneti devā dānavādayaḥ*).

This uncertainty is a product of the Sanskrit line itself, *devānāṁ mukhacālanam*, which is quite obscure. Tsong Khapa also quoted a translation of this line, *lha rnams kyi ni kha g.yo ba*, which is found in a minority of editions of this text in the Tengyur. The correct

the gods" (*lha rnams las*) does not occur in the other two translations and commentaries.[340]

The types of flesh are the kinds previously stated. The flesh of **these sacrificial victims** is enjoyed in the tantric feast **in the mandala that is the means of achieving** mundane **power** (**32.5ab**). By **feasting, fire sacrifice, and** making **sacrifices** (**32.6a**) to the gods with the flesh of **the crow, heron, swan,**[341] **the twice-born the prime minister**, i.e., the parrot, **curlew,**[342] **the crane,**[343] **and the kādamba goose** (**32.5cd**), one will **achieve** one's **desired power** (**32.6b**). The listing of the **jackal** among the birds is a translation error [made] from a corrupt text, and Bhavabhaṭṭa's commentary also lacks it.[344]

3.3.3. 2.2.2. 7.2.2. 2. The achievement of the zombie for the sake of great power

The adept who has received signs of attainment having repeated one hundred thousand times the Shumbha mantra, the root mantra, or the essence mantra should find the corpse of one who was strangled or some other suitable corpse that is unblemished, not decomposed, and attractive. On the eighth or fourteenth day of the dark fortnight, the adept should sit facing east gazing at the heart of the supine corpse with its head to the east, positioned in the center of a mandala on a mountain peak or in a charnel

---

reading, *lha rnams kyis ni kha g.yo ba* (Pandey 2002, 700), which is found in the majority of Tengyur editions, correctly reads *devānāṁ* as instrumental rather than genitive, reflecting the fact that in later Sanskrit the genitive case was often used in place of the instrumental case.

340. The translation of *devānāṁ* as *lha rnams las* is found in both the PM and SM translations. The SL translation has the ambiguous reading *lha rnams*. In the other commentaries that address this line the term is translated as *lha rnams kyi* (CP 62a.7, SG 196b.3).

341. Tsong Khapa here reads *bzhad*, which can mean a swan. The Sanskrit here is *jambuka*, "jackal," which is accurately translated in the Tibetan translations as *lce spyang* (PM, SL) and *ce spyang* (SM). See Gray 2012, 183, 354, 458, 537.

342. Tsong Khapa gives the Tibetan translation, *khrung khrung* or "crane," for the Sanskrit term *krauñca*, "curlew."

343. Tsong Khapa gives the Tibetan translation *ri skegs* for the Sanskrit term *sārasa*, which can designate the crane or swan.

344. Tsong Khapa is correct in noting that the jackal in anomalous in this list. However, it does occur in the extant Sanskrit as well, so it is not a translation error as he suggests.

ground. **The confident**, i.e., fearless, one **desiring** power,[345] **should sacrifice** with faith **up to as many as one hundred and eight** or eight hundred **times with the** Shumbha or essence **mantras, offering into the mouth of the corpse** (32.7) the fire offering substances of **a porridge of black dog** or cow **milk, black** *māṣha*,[346] i.e., **lentils, and black rice** (32.6cd).

Having done thus, **the dead person**, i.e., corpse, **stands up and questions the adept, saying "What should I do?** (32.8ab)"[347] Since it seems that "dead person" (*yi dwags*) and "corpse" (*ro*) have a common equivalent term, [i.e., Skt. *preta*], some translate it as "corpse" and some as "dead person."[348] Then, paying the fee[349] to him, ask for one's desired aim, saying, "Ho, great hero! Excellent! I, Vajrasattva, have accomplished well the observances. Please grant me the power of excellent bliss." Thence he will **bestow one** suitable **power** (32.9c) from among the following powers, namely the powers of **the underworld**, i.e., of entering subterranean cavities, **rising**, travelling in the atmosphere, and mastery of **the sword**. The word **or** implies mastery of **the wheel** and so forth. [Also included are the powers of] **destroying**, i.e., subduing evil doers, **benefiting** (32.8cd), mastery of **the pill**, seeing subterranean **treasure** through the application of eye **ointment**, **swift-footedness** through wooden shoes and so forth, or **the alchemy** (32.9ab) of maintaining life for an eon. [The word] **also** implies other powers as well. The statement after [the list of the powers]—that it is certain that [the power will] **not go otherwise** than (32.9d) to oneself—should be taken to mean that there is no uncertainty. This means that it will not come about that a suitable accomplishment is not given.

345. The text *'dod pa* is found in the PM and SM translations, but not in the SL translation or extant Sanskrit.

346. Tsong Khapa transliterates this term as *ma sha*.

347. Tsong Khapa follows the PM and SM translation, both of which contain the line *sgrub po de la 'dri byed de*, interpreting the very terse Tibetan translation here, *ci bgyi*, as a question. However, this line is omitted in the Sanskrit and the SL translation, and the extant Sanskrit, *kiṁkaro 'haṁ* is actually a statement, "I am [your] servant." The Tibetan *ci bgyi* is thus a translation of the Sanskrit noun *kiṁkaraḥ* and should not be read as an interrogative pronoun and verb.

348. Tsong Khapa is correct; the Sanskrit term *preta*, "dead person," is translated in the PM and SM translations as *yi dwags/yi dags*, and in the SL translation as *ro*.

349. Tsong Khapa closely follows Kambala's description of zombie practice (at SN 62a–b), but it should be noted that Kambala calls for offering water to the corpse here, rather than a fee. See SN 62b.4.

Having **invoked** the yoginīs of the three wheels, who are **the messengers above** who range in space and the messengers **below** who range on the earth and in the underworld, there is **no doubt regarding this the** ***Chakrasaṁvara Tantra*** (**32.10ab**) that they will convey one to their place and teach one their arts.

If one desires to know in more detail about the achievement of the zombie, one can know via Kambala and Devagupta's commentaries as well as the [*Twofold*] *Commentary* [by Tathāgatarakṣhita].

3.3.3. 2.2.2. 7.2.2. 3. Showing the yoga of the creation stage that is essential for all of them

The third part has two sections: (1) the creation of the habitat, and (2) the creation of the inhabitant deities.

3.3.3. 2.2.2. 7.2.2. 3.1. Creation of the habitat

Regarding the four lines beginning with "cattle pen" (**32.10cd–11ab**), in another text [there is the following alternate reading], "**the ash of cattle** dung, and likewise the remainder and **a dried head**, that which is arises from **the great conch**, and that which is made with **turtle**."[350] Regarding the meaning of this, Koṅkana, Bhavyakīrti, Laṅka [Jayabhadra], and Vīravajra do not connect it to the creation of the stacked-up elements and Mount Sumeru.[351] The first, [Koṅkana Jayabhadra, states,] "Take a broken, dried human skull and make a great conch."[352] The second, [Bhavyakīrti

350. The first two lines that Tsong Khapa quotes here are also quoted by Bhavabhaṭṭa; see Pandey 2002, 705. The Sanskrit *mahāśaṁkhamayaṁ* is mistranslated in the PM translation as *bde ba chen po'i ngo bor bya*, an error corrected in the SM translation, which reads *dung chen po yi rang bzhin bya*; see Gray 2012, 355, 538.

351. These commentaries only briefly address these lines and do not discuss at all their relevance to visualization practice. Koṅkana and Laṅka are both place names are connected by the same person, Jayabhadra. Tsong Khapa apparently takes them as separate individuals; his citation of the former is via Bhavyakīrti's commentary. The additional commentator who could also be added to this list is Bhavabhaṭṭa. This connection is made, as Tsong Khapa discusses below, by Kambala and Devagupta.

352. Tsong Khapa here appears to quote an alternate translation of Jayabhadra's commentary that is much closer to the Sanskrit original than the canonical translation. The Sanskrit here reads: *śuṣkam akhaṇḍaṁ naraśiro gṛhītvā mahāśaṅkhaṁ kuryāt* (Sugiki 2001,

states,] "Take cow or water buffalo bones and make a rosary for the various ritual actions,"[353] while the third, [Koṅkana Jayabhadra, states,][354] "Take an unbroken, dried skull and make a great conch, or take **turtle** to be a skull." The fourth, [Vīravajra], states: "Take a dried human skull and make great bliss. **Turtle** should be taken to mean a skull."[355]

The other two masters also state that "**the cattle pen** is earth, **ash** water, the **dried head** fire, and **thence** or the weapon wind, and **the great conch**, Sumeru, which should be taken to be the essence of the great mountain,"[356] which has the same meaning. In the same manner that "cattle pen" etc. occurs here, this and the four lines are similar to the Ghaṇṭapāda's five deity [system], and there are also three similar lines in Kṛiṣhṇāchārya's text.[357]

Furthermore, if one explains this as applied to the stacked-up elements below the habitat mandala, "cattle pen" is as stated in [Nāgārjuna's] *Crushing the Categories*: "speech, a quarter of the compass, the earth, a light ray, a diamond, cattle, the eye, water, heaven: scholars thus limit the word "cow"

---

133). Tsong Khapa quotes this as *mi mgo'i dum bu skam po blangs la / dung chen po bya'o*, which differs only in reading **khaṇḍaṁ* rather than *akhaṇḍaṁ*. This is actually a summary of Bhavyakīrti's quote, which he attributes to Koṅkana. See BC 31b.6. The canonical translation here reads *chag grugs med pa blangs la dung chen po bya ba'am* (CP 62b.4), correctly translating *akhaṇḍa* but failing to translate *śuṣkam* and *naraśiro*.

353. Bhavyakīrti comments: *skal ldan grags pa ni 'di dang ma he la sogs pa gang yang rungs pa'i rus pa blangs pa las kyi dbang las phreng ba bya'o zhes 'dod do* (BC 31b.7).

354. As noted above, this is an alternate translation of Jayabhadra's comment; see CP 62b.4.

355. Vīravajra comments: *mgo ba skam zhes pa ni dum bu med pa'i mi'i mgo skam blangs nas bde chen po byed do / rus sbal ni thod pa'o* (SG 197a.4).

356. Tsong Khapa here did not directly quote Kambala or Devagupta's commentaries, but rather compiled a list based upon them both. The commentaries here read as follows: *mgo'i sgra ni sa'o / thal ba ni chu'o / mgo bo skam zhes bya ba ni me'o / mtshon cha zhes bya ba ni rlung ste / de dag ni 'byung ba chen po bzhi'i dkyil 'khor ro / ri chen po'i ngo bor bya zhes bya ba'i rgyal po lhun po'o* (SN 62b.7–63a.1); *lci ba zhes pa'i sgra ni sa'o / thal ba zhes pa ni chu'o / mgo bo skam zhes pa ni me'o / de bzhin zhes pa ni rlung du shes par bya'o / de dag gi 'byung ba chen po bzhi'i bkyil 'khor du dgongs so / dung chen po las byung bas bya zhes pa ni / ri bo chen po las byung bya* (SS 137a.7–b.1).

Note that the term "weapon," *mtshon cha/śāstra*, occurs in Kambala's commentary but not not elsewhere; Devagupta instead correlates the word "thence," *de bzhin/tataḥ*, to wind.

357. Kṛiṣhṇāchārya quotes these lines in his *Meditation Manual on the Shrī Chakrasaṁvara* (*Śrīcakrasaṁvarasādhana*); see fols. 272b.7–73a.1.

(*gau*) to nine meanings."[358] The word "cow" (*gau*) designates cattle or cows and bulls, but here it is "earth" as it also designates the earth. With respect to where the flowers and so forth are placed, they "float above," i.e., on water.[359] That which dries completely is fire. That which moves within the channels is wind.

Next, the equivalent term of "great conch" is *mahāśaṁkha*, and as both *śaṁsukha* and *saṁsukha* mean bliss, its meaning should be taken to be the nature of great bliss. The five complete awakenings can be taken to be illustrations of great bliss, and one should believe that the stacked-up elements and so forth are the reality of great bliss. While another commentary states that **that which is perfect of the turtle**[360] shows the creation stage of the egg-born deities,[361] [this line] is applied in the systems of Kṛiṣhṇāchārya and Ghaṇṭapāda only to the context of the generation of the habitat. The meaning of "or" (*yang na*) is said to be the meaning of the topic marker (*ni*), which means that one should visualize as well Mount Sumeru that is indicated by the term "turtle." [Kṛiṣhṇā]chārya also quotes the line "unbroken turtle" without the word "or."[362] As for there being no explanation here of the creation of the divine palace habitat, Sumatikīrti states that it is

358. This is an excerpt from a longer passage in this text, namely: "Furthermore, as it is evident that scholars of the world apply a signifier to many significands, they apply to many things the word *go*, and likewise the word *hari*. The various things to which the word *go* is applied include the following: speech, a quarter of the compass, the earth, a light ray, a diamond, cattle, the eye, water, heaven. Scholars thus limit the word go to nine meanings. Likewise, scholars understand the word hari [to refer to] Viṣhṇu, the lion, serpent, frog, the sun, moon, light, the monkey, tawny color, the parrot, Indra and nāgas." The *Crushing the Categories* (*Vaidalya-nāma-prakaraṇa*) fols. 106b–107a reads: *gzhan yang 'jig rten pa'i mkhas pa dag kyang rjod par byed pa dang brjod par bya ba du ma la sbyor ba mthong ba'i phyir ro / 'jig rten pa'i mkhas pa dag ni go sgra du ma la sbyor bar byed de / hari'i sgra yang de bzhin no / go sgra rnam pa du ma la 'jug pa ni 'di lta ste / ngag phyogs dang ni sa gzhi dang / 'od zer rdo rje phyugs dang mig / chu dang mtho ris don dgu la / mkhas pas go sgra nges gzung bya / ji ltar khyab 'jug seng ge glang po sbal / nyi zla 'od dang spre'u dang / ser skya ne tsho dbang po glu / mkhas pas harir shes par bya.*

359. Tsong Khapa here equates the text *steng lding*, found in the SM translation of line 32.10c where the Sanskrit reads *śeṣāḥ*, "residue," "remnants." See Gray 2012, 184, 538.

360. This translates the SM translation for line 32.11b; the Sanskrit here reads, "that which is unbroken of the turtle."

361. Kambala makes this claim; see SN 64b.3.

362. See his *Śrīcakrasaṁvarasādhana* fol. 273a.1.

"intended in the explanation of the previous second chapter."[363] Thus, by **this** meditation **accomplishment will be bestowed.**[364]

3.3.3. 2.2.2. 7.2.2. 3.2. Creation of the inhabitant deities

Kṛiṣhṇāchārya explains that **four hands** (32.12a) and so forth refer to the father deities, the causal vajrasattva and Heruka.[365] Kambala and Devagupta explain that [he is] the resultant Heruka that manifests by being aroused by song, and dissolves into the three-faced, six-armed Vajradhara together with his partner.[366] Bhavabhaṭṭa explains this in terms of deity yoga for accomplishing the zombie. Bhavabhaṭṭa explains that Heruka's main head is white, the left green, the back red and the right yellow, or, that all **four** of his **faces** are white, and his **four hands** hold a vajra, spear, skull and skull staff for the sake of accomplishing the zombie.[367] **Up to as many as one hundred thousand hands** (**32.12b**) implies that [the number of] hands and faces is not definite. So, one must rely on the esoteric instructions.

Regarding **body** color, the **great fierce one**[368] is **white.** Then, i.e., in that manner, **assuming a fierce form** (**32.12c**), his eyes **gaze at Vajravārāhī.** Vārāhī also assumes the white body **color** of her partner (*yab*), and has four arms, **holding weapons** (**32.13ab**), namely, a vajra and skull, in her hands. The hero partner **has a skull garland** on his head, and **his body is anointed with** charnel ground **ash** (**32.13cd**). **His dreadlocks** are bound in **a crest,** and he has **a lance** in his two right hands. His body is **adorned with insignia** such as a jewel on his crown. **His fangs jut out,** and he takes

363. This quote does not occur in the extant text of LA.

364. Tsong Khapa here glosses an additional line found in the SM translation, namely *'di de dngos grub sbyin 'gyur yin.* A variant of this line is found in the SL translation, *myur du dngos grub sbyin 'gyur yin.* It does not occur in the PM translation or the extant Sanskrit. See Gray 2012, 458, 538.

365. I have not been able to find this statement in Kṛiṣhṇāchārya's works. Interestingly, Sachen makes the same claim at PG 350.1.

366. See SS 139b.2–3.

367. See Pandey 2002, 706. Note that Bhavabhaṭṭa lists the colors of the four faces, but does not mention the alternative, that all four faces are white.

368. The term *khro bo che* occurs in all three Tibetan translations, but does not occur in the extant Sanskrit.

the great ghost, the lord of spirits, **as his seat** (**32.14**), together with the thirty-six deities.

The adept, knowing these deities, should visualize them with their mantras **at all times** (**32.15ab**), i.e., thrice [daily]. Bhavabhaṭṭa explains, regarding the hundred thousand hands, faces, and so forth, that there are vajras in all of the right hands, and lances in the left [hands], or skull staves and skulls. The faces are all white.[369] This is similar to the previous stacked-up elements visualization in Mardo's system. The "great conch" is taken as Mount Sumeru, and with the created divine palace the causal Vajradhara couple is generated from the five complete awakenings in Kṛiṣhṇāchārya's fashion, which is indicated by [the lines] **the four hands** (**32.12a**) up to **holding weapons** (**32.13b**). [The text] from **the hero has a skull garland** (**32.13c**) applies to the fruitive, womb-born Vajradhara. [The text] from "or" (**32.11b**) relates to the miraculous generation as is done in Lūipa's system. In this way it is said that it is necessary that the "great conch" is taken [to indicate] the simultaneous generation of the habitat and inhabitants from the five complete awakenings, and that the resultant Heruka is not visualized with a white body color. Durjayachandra applies it to the uncommon deity of the great zombie invocation,[370] and Bhavyakīrti etc. explain this in terms of a garland,[371] both of which are incorrect. It has been explained that[372] "This is clear since 'creation stage' is stated in the name of the chapter."

The adherents to Mal's tradition have also refuted [these positions] in this manner.[373] There is no application of this sort in Durjayachandra's commentary, and while Bhavabhaṭṭa applies it to the zombie invocation, he does not explain it in a way that is not shared with that [invocation]. There is thus

369. This instruction does not occur in the extant version of Bhavabhaṭṭa's commentary. Instead, he lists these implements, namely the vajra, lance, skull, and skull staff, as being held by his four hands. He also lists four different colors for his four faces. See Pandey 2002, 706.

370. Durjayachandra only briefly comments on these lines, taking them as part of the zombie invocation process. See RG 302a.6–7.

371. Bhavyakīrti discusses this creation stage passage as a garland of magical rituals. See BC 31b.7 ff.

372. I am not sure what source is being quoted here. I suspect that it is Mardo's lost commentary.

373. Tsong Khapa here in fact paraphrases portions of Sachen's commentary. See PG 350.2.

no contradiction between its application to the garland [of magical rites] etc. and the explanation in terms of the creation stage. Kṛiṣhṇāchārya's system does not indicate a boundary in the text with respect to the generation of the two Vajradharas, and this is very clear in his meditation manual.[374] It is not his intention that this is explained with reference to the red Vārāhī as well. Although Lūipa's system explains that they are miraculously born, this contradicts my claim in another context that they are egg-born. By the meditation on Heruka in accordance with the stages **thus** stated there one **will accomplish** all aims **of the particularly good qualities** (**32.15cd**).

3.3.3. 2.2.2. 7.2.3. Showing the name of the chapter

In the ***Concise Shrī Herukābhidhāna Tantra*** **is the thirty-second chapter** on **the procedures** of summoning the flesh **of the animal**, i.e., bird, donkey, etc., **sacrificial victims, the means of achieving the** great **zombie, and the creation stage** that is the prerequisite for those and so forth. This is the explanation of the thirty-second chapter in the *Illumination of the Hidden Meaning, A Detailed Exegesis of the Concise Saṁvara Tantra Called "The Chakrasaṁvara."*

374. That is, Kāṇha's *Śrīcakrasaṁvarasādhana* (Tōh. 1445).

Chapter 33

Chapter 33 Outline

3.3.3. 2.2.2. 7.3. The chapter on the secret and reverential worship

The third part, the chapter on the secret and reverential worship has three sections: (1) the promise to explain, (2) the promised import explained, and (3) showing the name of the chapter.

3.3.3. 2.2.2. 7.3.1. The promise to explain

Furthermore, after the thirty-second [chapter], **I will explain** the yoga of which there is none other that is greater among **all** applications, i.e., **yogas, for all adepts** (**33.1ab**). Another [translation] has:[375] "I will explain that which is absent in all [other] yogas for the adepts."

3.3.3. 2.2.2. 7.3.2. The promised import explained

The second part has three sections: (1) the reverential worship (2) the secret worship, and (3) the benefit of worship.

375. Tsong Khapa here quotes the SL translation of 33.1ab.

3.3.3. 2.2.2. 7.3.2. 1. The reverential worship

What is the yoga that is like that? **The food** to be enjoyed are medicines such as *gokudahana* etc.[376] **The eating** or feasting refers to yogurt, butter, honey, sugar, and sweetmeats (*laḍḍuka*), and so forth.[377] It is said to be a feast on many things such as yogurt. "Eating" thus should be changed to "feasting." **Fish** is Indian carp[378] and so forth. **Flesh** is goat flesh etc. **And so forth** means that one should accept whatever foods that one is able to obtain. These are suitable depending upon one's **ability (33.1cd)**, that is, one's wealth. **Even when the five** ambrosias **are not present** and one is unable to generate them, all **food** and drink should be visualized as the five ambrosias. It is said that one should **always**, i.e., continuously, **partake at night in** the requisites of **a feast**, an **extensive (33.2)** and excellent [spread] of food.[379] While one might also partake during the day, since the night is certain [for this activity, the root text] states **night**.

Kambala states, "Since it is the supreme method for accumulating great merit, one should undertake the host mandala, as Āryadeva stated in his *Lamp That Integrates the Practices*."[380] Devagupta also refers to the *Lamp*

376. Tsong Khapa here quotes Bhavabhaṭṭa's gloss of the Sanskrit, namely *bhakṣyaṁ gokudahanādi* (Pandey 2002, 524). Unfortunately, I have not been able to identify what *gokudahana* is. Tsong Khapa identifies it as a medicine, so I presume that it is some sort of medical substance.

377. Here again and in the remaining portion of this verse Tsong Khapa follows Bhavabhaṭṭa's commentary. See Pandey 2002, 524.

378. This is the *rohita* or Indian carp, *Labeo rohita*.

379. See Pandey 2002, 524, 710.

380. This translates Tsong Khapa's version of this quote, namely *bsod nams chen po gsog pa'i thabs mchog yin pas tshogs kyi dkyil 'khor brtsam par bya ste / 'phags pa lha'i zhal snga nas kyi spyod pa bsdus pa'i sgron ma las ji skad gsungs pa bzhin no.* The canonical translation reads: *bsod nams chen po sogs pa'i phyir ro / de bas tshogs kyi dkyil 'khor brtsam par bya ste / 'phags pa lha'i zhal snga nas kyi spyod pa bsdus pa'i sgron ma las / ji skad gsungs pa bzhin no* (SN 64b.7–65a.1).

The Sanskrit here is unfortunately somewhat corrupt. It reads: *mahāpuṇyopacadātvāt / tasmāt gaṇamaṇḍalam ārabhet / āryadeva-pādasya sūtramelācaraṇe yathā /* (K 62a.6–7). Kambala appears to be referring to Āryadeva's mention of the *gaṇamaṇḍala* in chapter 7 of the *Caryāmelāpakapradīpa*, as the site where the student presents the consort to the master at midnight. See Wedemeyer 2007, 254–55. This is not an exact quote from that passage, but Kambala appears to only be referring to this text, not quoting it precisely.

That Integrates the Practices, [stating that] one should make the host mandala in the manner stated in the *Lamp That Integrates the Practices.*[381]

Regarding **then the messenger should be bestowed** (**33.3a**), Durjayachandra explains that the messenger is bestowed by the guru to the disciple.[382] However Bhavyakīrti and so forth state that one should not eat [the feast] alone, but one should offer it to the yoginīs of good or bad clans. This means that one should prepare [the host mandala] in order to offer food to the messenger.[383]

3.3.3. 2.2.2. 7.3.2. 2. The secret worship

The adept, for the sake of worship amidst the host especially, **places the head in one's lap**, which means that the messenger, placed on one's left side, should be embraced with one's left hand, and should be **worshipped** through being **nondual**, i.e., in union with, **the hero** Heruka (**33.3bc**). Hence it states "placing the head in one's lap." Accordingly, it seems that there is a commonality between the Sanskrit equivalents to "placing the head in one's lap" and "embraced with the left," but their meanings diverged in Tibetan translation.[384] In Vīravajra's commentary [this line] occurs as:[385] "Placing the head embraced by one."

In accordance with the disciple "placing the head between the thighs of the lefty," the "lefty" (*g.yon pa*) is the messenger, and placing the head between her thighs means placing the head of the vajra in the lotus.

The messenger is one's **mother** or the other four [relatives] (**33.4ab**); I

381. See SS 139b.6–7.

382. See RG 302b.6.

383. See BC 33a.2. At issue here is the question of whether the messenger herself is the object of the act of offering, or its recipient. The Sanskrit, *dūtīṁ ca tato dadyāt,* supports the former reading of Durjayachandra and Āryadeva. However, Bhavyakīrti supports the latter reading.

384. Tsong Khapa is correct about the possible interpretations of this line, which in Sanskrit reads *svotsaṅge śiraḥ kṛtvā.* If we analyze *svotsaṅge* as a compound of the prefix *sva-* and *utsaṅga,* it should be noted that *utsaṅga* can mean "lap" or "embrace." The canonical translations interpreted it as meaning "lap," but, as Tsong Khapa notes below, Vīravajra's commentary followed the latter interpretation instead.

385. See SG 197b.2.

have already explained the significance of this.[386] When serving the messenger, should one serve her **thus in accordance with the rite**, that is, in the manner of visualizing oneself as Heruka and one's seal as Vajravārāhī, **one will be free of** habitual tendencies that **bind** one to the world (**33.4cd**).

From that secret worship of the messenger, that is, relying on that, one with his mind protected **accomplishes the mantra**, that is, nondual gnosis. How long is this done? [It is done] **until the end of the existence** of the afflictions (**33.5ab**). Devagupta quotes an [additional line] in this verse, namely "liberated from utmost bondage,"[387] meaning "until the habitual tendencies of bondage are exhausted."

How is the unmanifest Vajradhara attained? It is by **assuming the form of my master**, Vajradhara. By **accepting** inner and outer **worship** from **the adepts** (**33.5cd**) having assumed the form of the master, it will be as if Vajradhara were present. The *Direct Speech [of Mañjushrī]* likewise states:[388]

> For the sake of meaningful aims,
> I assume his form and accept
> Worship for the other adepts.
> Through this one's continuum's pleased,
> And cleansed of karmic defilements.

It seems to state that the guru of this vehicle even surpasses a buddha in the sphere of accumulating merit. Therefore, if one worships him, since it will be worship of Vajradhara, it will be worship of all victors.[389] Since it is shown that this is truly constant non-separation from this lord for his adepts, it is said that he is a "hero."

Have no doubt that the place, i.e., the abode, **of the hero** Heruka etc.

386. See section 3.3.3. 2.2.2. 4.2.2 in chapter 26 above.

387. See SS 140a.2.

388. Tsong Khapa here quotes Buddhashrījñāna's *Dvikramatattvabhāvana-nāma-mukhāgama.* It occurs as follows in the canonical text: *'di ni don ldan 'ga' zhig la / nga ni de yi lus gnas te / bsgrub pa gzhan la mchod pa len / de yis de mnyes rang gi rgyud / las kyi sgrib pa dag byed do* (15b.3).

Tsong Khapa's version of the text is slightly different, reading: *'di yi don ldan 'ga' zhig la / nga ni de yi lus gnas te / sgrub po gzhan la mchod pa len / de yis de mnyes rang gi rgyud / las kyi sgrib pa dag byed do.*

389. Tsong Khapa here paraphrases Bhavyakīrti's commentary; see BC 33a.

is indeed the consort (33.6ab) endowed with the defining characteristics. This shows that she is inseparably blessed by Heruka. Koṅkana [Jayabhadra] states that the [heroes'] place and the consort are the same.[390] Bhavyakīrti states these two separately; since it would be illogical to treat them as one, he explains that the "place" is food and drink, and he glosses the seal (*phyag rgya*) as "spell consort" (*rig ma*).[391] However, as Durjayachandra quotes [this passage as] "Have no doubt that the heroes' places are the seals," they are uncertain in one text.[392]

In this way Vajradhara abides in the body of the master and accepts the disciple's worship. Therefore, just as it is easy to complete the accumulations, since he abides as well in the consort one will quickly proceed on the path with his blessing. Thus, by being very **well equipoised** in the pride and supreme appearance that abandons attachment to ordinary appearances, **the adept** should worship himself and the consort with offerings of **song, dance, and so forth** (33.6cd).

So long as all embodied ones are not intent upon, i.e., do not take pleasure in, **knowledge of yoga** that inseparably unites skillful means and wisdom, **they roam through cyclic existence, overwhelmed by** physical **suffering** and **grief**, i.e., mental unhappiness (33.7). This means that with another path it will take a very long time to liberate oneself from cyclic existence and its habitual tendencies. Thus, due to that reason, **the adept should** be liberated quickly by **worshiping** himself and **the consort with all things.** Those who **desire to worship with offerings** are accepted by the distinctive messengers. By being **contemptuous** of them one **will burn** in hell (33.8).

Regarding showing that the messengers are common to the yoga tantras, **men**, i.e., yogīs, who practice **as taught in the yoga tantras** such as the *Compendium of Reality* and so forth take up a messenger such as the mother, sister, etc., who is **established** with the perfected characteristics of **the great seal** (*mahāmudrā*) that is the form of the deity, and draw the

390. Jayabhadra actually just quotes this line, and his only comment is glossing *mudrā* as "goddess." See Sugiki 2001, 133 and CP 63a.2.

391. See BC 33a.5–6.

392. I am not sure what Tsong Khapa's point is here. Durjayachandra's quotation of these lines, *dpa' bo rnams kyi gnas dag ni / phyag rgya dag tu the tshom med* (RG 303a.5), differs from the canonical translation only in portraying the consorts as plural, i.e., reading *phyag rgya dag tu* rather than *phyag rgya nyid du*, the reading of the canonical translations.

Chakrasaṁvara mandala at the isolated and pleasant assembly of all of the hosts of yogīs and yoginīs. Visualizing oneself in the form of the deity, then from sunset she **should be worshipped with great zeal** throughout the entire night. **Later,** after one enters the clear light by first practicing in this manner, one arises from the non-manifestation in the two clear lights, and **one should assume the heroism of the heroes** (33.9), that is, one manifests bodies of a buddha through the integration stage with the diamond-like concentration. One will exist adorned with all of the good qualities.

3.3.3. 2.2.2. 7.3.2. 3. The benefit of worship

Having relied upon the previously explained undertaking of service and secret worship, **the adept will attain without trouble**, i.e., suffering, all **ritual actions** for **any** power **whatsoever**, such as the power of **the underworld; arising** or travelling, i.e., travelling in the sky; **pacifying** disease, evil spirits and so forth; **enriching** one's lifespan, wisdom, and so forth; **subjugating** one's mother and so forth; **summoning** men and women; **killing** those who harm the [three] jewels etc.; **expelling** from a place; **and so forth**, [which implies] inflicting [someone] with madness and infectious disease, **and likewise inciting enmity** [among] loved ones,[393] **destroying and conferring benefit.** It is said that the equivalent term to "ritual action" (*las, karman*) in the first line is also that [of the same term in the line] "all ritual actions whatsoever."[394] In short, since **there is no doubt** (33.10–12), i.e., it is certain, that all powers will be attained by the adept who worships the consort, one should engage in her service and secret worship. The commitments of eating and worship have thus been explained extensively by the three, chapters thirty-one, thirty-two, and thirty-three.

393. Tsong Khapa here has the somewhat obscure text *mdza' ba dang dbye ba*, which seemingly should be read "affection and inciting enmity," which doesn't correspond to the root text, which here reads *jambhanastambhanaṁ caiva vidveṣe*, "even crushing and immobilizing, and likewise inciting enmity. . . ." However, Tsong Khapa here seems to be following Sachen's gloss of the Tibetan *dbye ba*, the translation of *vidveṣe*, namely *mdza' bo dang dbye ba*, "inciting enmity among loved one" (PG 351.3).

394. Tsong Khapa is referring to two lines in the Tibetan translation that both contain the term *las*. The first, which Tsong Khapa doesn't quote, is *las kyi dngos grub mchod par bya*, and the second is a variant reading of a line found in 33.12. This variant reading is found in Butön's commentary, which is Tsong Khapa's source for this observation. Butön, unlike Tsong Khapa, also quotes the first line. See NS 210a.7–b.1.

3.3.3. 2.2.2. 7.3.3. Showing the name of the chapter

In the *Concise* ***Shrī Herukābhidhāna Tantra***, this is **the thirty-third chapter** on **the secret worship** depending on the messenger and **the reverential worship** of eating and drinking. This is the explanation of the thirty-third chapter in the *Illumination of the Hidden Meaning, A Detailed Exegesis of the Concise Saṁvara Tantra Called "The Chakrasaṁvara."*

Chapter 34

Chapter 34 Outline

3.3.3. 2.2.2. 8. The detailed exegesis of the secret of the four [types of] worship
3.3.3. 2.2.2. 8.1. The chapter that shows the great seal
3.3.3. 2.2.2. 8.1.1. The promise to explain
3.3.3. 2.2.2. 8.1.2. The promised import explained
3.3.3. 2.2.2. 8.1.2. 1. Detailed exegesis of the import to be explained
3.3.3. 2.2.2. 8.1.2. 1.1. Explaining in terms of the interpretable meaning
3.3.3. 2.2.2. 8.1.2. 1.2. Explaining in terms of the definitive meaning
3.3.3. 2.2.2. 8.1.2. 1.2.1. The explanation that occurs in the oral instructions of previous gurus
3.3.3. 2.2.2. 8.1.2. 1.2.2. Kambala the Blanketed's explanation
3.3.3. 2.2.2. 8.1.2. 1.2.2. 1. The explanation in terms of the yoga of the drop
3.3.3. 2.2.2. 8.1.2. 1.2.2. 2. The explanation in terms of subtle yoga
3.3.3. 2.2.2. 8.1.2. 2. Summary of the explained import
3.3.3. 2.2.2. 8.1.3. Showing the name of the chapter

3.3.3. 2.2.2. 8. The detailed exegesis of the secret of the four [types of] worship

The eighth part, the detailed exegesis of the secret of the four [types of] worship, has four sections: (1) the chapter that shows the great seal, (2) the chapter that shows the reality seal, (3) the chapter that shows both the symbolic and actual seals through a single approach, and (4) the chapter on subjugating the actual seal (consort).

3.3.3. 2.2.2. 8.1. The chapter that shows the great seal

The first part has three sections: (1) the promise to explain, (2) the promised import explained, and (3) showing the name of the chapter.

3.3.3. 2.2.2. 8.1.1. The promise to explain

Next, after the thirty-third [chapter], I will explain the method whereby **any ritual action whatsoever**, that is, **the** previously explained **extensive procedure** for pacifying, enriching and so forth, of **the** essential Saṁvara **wheel of the ḍākinīs' network** of Prachaṇḍā etc., is **undoubtedly** achieved **by the adept rapidly** (34.1), i.e., without long delay.

Kambala quotes for the third line, "the means of achievement relying on one's mind," which he explains means that one finds in one's mind the means of achievement that relies upon the place of the central channel.[395] The previous gurus have stated that these four lines [indicate] that in order to meditate on the perfection stage one meditates extensively on the deity wheels, and having meditated on the deities prior to fire sacrifice, one undertakes fire sacrifice after one gathers them into oneself.[396]

3.3.3. 2.2.2. 8.1.2. The promised import explained

The second part has two sections: (1) detailed exegesis of the import to be explained and (2) the summary of the explained import.

3.3.3. 2.2.2. 8.1.2. 1. Detailed exegesis of the import to be explained

The first part has two sections: (1) explaining in terms of the interpretable meaning and (2) explaining in terms of the definitive meaning.

3.3.3. 2.2.2. 8.1.2. 1.1. Explaining in terms of the interpretable meaning

All of the heroes, Khaṇḍakapālin and so forth, **and the** twenty-four **ḍākinīs**, Prachaṇḍā and so forth, **should be placed** (*niyojayet*, *nges bar*

395. This translates Tsong Khapa's quotation of the line, *sgrub thabs yid la brten pa ste*, which accords with the canonical translation, *sgrub thabs yid la brten pa ste / a ba dhū tī'i gnas rnyed pa'i phyir ro* (SN 65a.6–7). The Sanskrit here is somewhat corrupt, reading: *sanaiva sādhayed iti / avadhūtapada prāptatvāt* (K 62b.5), which we might read as "**One should accomplish in one's mind**, because one has obtained the state of renunciation (*avadhūtapada*)." The term *avadhūtapada* may here mean the state of a yogī who has completely renounced worldly concerns.

396. See PG 352.1.

sbyor), i.e., set (*dgod*), **upon the lotus** of the navel,[397] that is, on its petals. The placement of the twenty-four heroes and heroines on three successive eight-petalled lotuses is explained in the *Vajraḍāka*.[398]

Both of **the eyebrows** indicate third eye of all deities. Just as there is an eye beneath each of the right and left eyebrows, an eye is also "inserted," i.e., **placed,**[399] **between**, i.e., amidst, the right and left eyebrows. This is **the point** of the *avadhūtī* (**34.2**), the upper end of the central channel. This is the intention of the five, Koṅkana [Jayabhadra] and so forth. It occurs as "One should likewise place the *avadhūtī* point between the eyebrows" in two commentaries.[400]

The yogī who has obtained the sign [of power], having brought himself into union with **the agitation**, i.e., impurity, **of the hero** Shrī Heruka, or **should sacrifice the oblation** of flesh with the concentration of having transformed into the ferocity of Shrī Heruka whose countenance agitates, i.e., mixes up, desire and anger, while some, being first endowed with the pride of oneself as a fierce one, satisfy themselves with the flesh however obtained. Then, after that, regarding eating in accordance with the rite, he should **offer** into **the mouth** of the wordly fire god (*agni*, *me lha*) **the five sacrifices**, i.e., oblations with the offering substances beef (*gaumāṁsa*) and blood (*rudhira*) **energetically** (**34.3**), unwavering from the divine pride.

In some of the translations "having desired" (*byas chags par*) occurs.[401]

397. Tsong Khapa here reads *lte ba'i padma*, "lotus of the navel." All three Tibetan translations, however, read *padma'i lte bar*, "on the corolla of the lotus." The Sanskrit, however, reads *puskareṣu*, "on the lotuses." See Gray 2012, 188, 359, 460, 540.

398. Tsong Khapa is referring to the description of the three eight-petalled lotuses, corresponding to the mandala's mind, speech, and body wheels, onto which the deity couples are placed. This is described in VD ch. 14, edited in Sugiki 2003. It is also described in other explanatory tantras such as AU.

399. Tsong Khapa glosses *gzhug*, a bad translation of the Sanskrit *nikṣipeta*, with *nges par bzhag*.

400. Tsong Khapa is quoting the following translation of that last half of v. 2: *a ba dhū tī'i gnas de bzhin / smin ma'i bar du nges par bzhag*. This is found in Jayabhadra's commentary as follows: *a wa dhū tī'i gnas de bzhin / smin ma'i bar du nges par bzhag* (CP 63a.5); Vīravajra's commentary quotes it as: *a wa dhū tī'i gnas de bzhin / smin ma'i bar du nges par gzhag* (SG 198a.4).

401. This translation of the first line of this verse is actually found in all of the extant translations of the root tantra itself. The PM translation reads *dpa' bo'i mchol bar byas chags par*, while the SM translation has the almost identical reading *dpa' bo mchol bar byas chags par*. SL has a variant translation *dpa' bo rme rtsegs chags byas la*, reading *chags byas la*

"Desired" (*chags pa*) does not occur in any of the commentaries or in Lochen's translation, although "having done" (*byas pa*) and "with the mouth" (*zhal gyis*) do occur in the commentaries.[402] If it seems that there should be [the term] "desired," [it means] that his visage mixes the sentiments of ferocity and desire, in the manner of Lochen's [translation], it "seems to become agitated and fierce."

And then, having offered the five sacrifices, one should **offer the nine sacrifices** of offering substances such as the five ambrosias etc. **in the fire blazing**[403] in the hearth, that is, the mouth of the mundane fire god. Having shown the sacrifice to the mundane fire god with these [lines], regarding offering sacrifice to the supramundane deity, **one should see**, i.e., visualize, him **there** in the dense light array, like **a fire-garlanded ocean** in the hearth. Another translation reads "then in the fire garlanded ocean," which accords with the commentaries.[404] How should it be visualized? One should visualize amidst that fire the mandala with four gates and a square divine palace as **the wheel**, the gates of **face in all directions** (34.4), i.e., in the four directions. [This] is the creation of the habitat.

Regarding the creation of the inhabitants, in the middle of an eight-petalled lotus, **there** within the divine palace, **is placed the four-faced lord of heroes, and the** twenty-four **heroes**, Khaṇḍakapālin (Broken Skull) and so forth, on their respective seats, the twenty four petals on the spokes of the [mandala's] three wheels, which is **the hero's abode**, and **the four messengers**, Ḍākinī and so forth, **on the** four **lotus petals** in the cardinal directions. One also places on the spokes the twenty-four [heroines], Prachaṇḍā, and so forth, who sport in great **bliss** through **nondual** union with all twenty-four **of the heroes**, who are not just solitary heroes (34.5). Through the example of them one should know that skulls or skulls with vases are

in place of *byas chags par*. None of these readings accord with the extant Sanskrit, which reads instead: *vīrocchuṣmamukhenāgnau*. See Gray 2012, 188, 359, 460, 540.

402. As noted above, "with the mouth," *–mukhena*, does occur in the extant Sanskrit.

403. Tsong Khapa here glosses the SM and SL translation of 34.4b, *de nas 'bar ba'i me la ni*. The PM translation reads *de nas 'bar ba'i byin za la*, which corresponds to the Sanskrit *jvalite ca hutāśane*, "in the blazing oblation eater." The term *hutāśana*, "oblation eater" naturally means fire. See Gray 2012, 359, 460, 540.

404. Tsong Khapa here refers to the SL translation, which reads *de nas 'bar phreng rgya mtshor ni*. See Gray 2012, 460.

placed on petals in the ordinal directions, and Crow Face (*kākāsyā*) and so forth are also placed at the gates and in the quarters.

The line [beginning with] "rite" (*cho ga*, **34.6a**) does not occur in the other translations and commentaries,[405] but if it does occur, it means that **Khaṇḍarohā** is **bestowed**, i.e., applied, with the form stated in accordance with the rite for achieving the ritual procedure. Khaṇḍarohā, who resides on the petal to the rear, is placed accordingly, and a second Khaṇḍarohā, who emerges **outside** from one's body, is applied to all ritual procedures. They should **reside**, that is, exist, in **their own forms**, which are white and so forth for each of the respective ritual procedures such as pacifying and so forth. Not only that, one should **view** the deities of **the wheels** (**34.6**) **in the center** of the hearth.

Regarding **making** these inhabitant **wheels radiant** (**34.7a**), this should be done as stated with respect to the white body color and so forth as well as one's own mood for the respective ritual procedure such as pacifying and so forth.[406] This is not the case just for the context of fire sacrifice, but also for the context of performing other ritual actions. Regarding the procedure of fire sacrifice, it should be known from my extensive instruction [on this topic] elsewhere. Fearing prolixity, I will not write about this here.

3.3.3. 2.2.2. 8.1.2. 1.2. Explaining in terms of the definitive meaning

Regarding the explanation of approximately one aspect of the definitive meaning of this in the *Vajraḍāka*, one should know this from its commentary. With respect to explanations of the other definitive meanings, there are two: (1) the explanation that occurs in the oral instructions of previous gurus and (2) Kambala the Blanketed's explanation.

405. Lines beginning with *cho ga* occur in all three of the extant translations.

406. That is, both the visualization of the deities and one's own inner mood must correspond to the ritual procedure undertaken. For pacifying, the deities would be visualized as white in color, and one would need to manifest a calm emotional state.

3.3.3. 2.2.2. 8.1.2. 1.2.1. The explanation that occurs in the oral instructions of previous gurus

Through the equipoise of the partners having visualized the means of achievement of this, one contemplates the experience of being pervaded by great bliss. The blissful spirit of awakening (*bde ba'i byang chub sems*) exists at the tip of the jewel like radiant white and red vowels and consonants. Having come up through the right nostril, proceeding from wheel of great bliss up until the wheel of the commitment, and through the beings of the three abodes appearing as manifestations of the mandala deities, one contemplates the experience of great bliss with all of them.

Through the experience of bliss, the heroes and heroines of the outer three abodes melt into the charnel grounds, and the charnel grounds melt and dissolve into the divine palace. Regarding the dissolution [of the divine palace] up until the four [essence yoginīs], Ḍākinī and so forth, this is the meaning of the two lines [beginning with] "all heroes" (**34.2ab**). They melt and enter into the left nostril of the four-faced [central deity]. Having entered the central channel between the eyebrows, the spirit of awakening descends and also pervades the four wheels; this is the meaning of the two lines [beginning with] "between the eyebrows" (**34.2cd**).

Then one visualizes oneself and Vārāhī melting into great bliss, the white drop becoming one with the red [drop] at the tip of the vajra and lotus. [This] is meditation on the actuality of great bliss. Regarding that co-emergence (*lhan skyes*), since he is devoid of conceptions of desire and so forth, the hero is "agitated," which is clarified as *utkaṭa*.[407] "Desire" (**34.3a**) is transforming into another, "offered" is becoming non-apparent, "beef" is earth

407. Tsong Khapa assumes here that the Tibetan *'chol ba*, in 34.3a, is a translation of the Sanskrit *utkaṭa*. This is a reasonable assumption, although the extant mss. here read *ucchuṣma*.

and so forth, the "five sacrifices" (**34.3c**) are the five aggregates, and the "blazing fire" is the fire-like co-emergence. "Offering the nine sacrifices" (**34.4a**) is making the five aggregates and four elements non-apparent. If one sees that one's mind is wavering from visualization of the drop in this manner, you should contemplate that very "fire-garlanded" (**34.4c**) radiant mass in the habitat and inhabitant mandala. With respect to considering the contemplation in this manner, the contemplative method is shown by the five lines beginning with "face in all directions" (**34.4d**).

If one contemplates in this manner with vehement exertion, you will see the signs of smoke and so forth within twenty-five days. In the interval between meditation sessions visualize the syllable *hūṁ* on a solar disk in one's heart, of oneself as Saṁvara with one face and two hands, ornamented with ornaments, through the yoga of radiating and drawing back light rays from the drop of bliss that transforms into the syllable *hūṁ*. By contemplating in this manner, one will see the five signs, and the visualization of the mandala will appear before one's eyes. Great bliss will manifest as well. This is meditation on the great seal, since it does not depend on the actual (*karmamudrā*) or symbolic (*samayamudrā*) seals, nor is it the reality seal (*dharmamudrā*) that takes a syllable as its basis.

[This] is the explanation.[408]

[The author] feels that it is necessary to establish one among the four seals by negating the other three. Regarding this it is stated in the explanation by Mar Chökyi Gyalpo[409] of Möndro in the system of the translator Mardo that:[410]

408. Tsong Khapa does not directly indicate whom he is quoting here, and I haven't been able to find the source of this commentary. In the explanation that follows, however, he seems to imply the source is Mardo, presumably Mardo's commentary on the root tantra which appears to have been lost.

409. Mar Chögyal or Mar Chökyi Gyalpo was evidently active during the 12th century.

410. Tsong Khapa identifies this work vaguely as the *dmar chos rgyal gyis bshad pa*. I am not aware that any works by this author have come to light.

> One's mind is fixed upon the condensed red and white drops as before, and, releasing the drop to its resonance (*nāda*), one apprehends the mind. With respect to that one also does not focus upon the fixed [mind] and resonance. One contemplates focusing one's attention on being devoid of all elaborations. Emerging from that one contemplates the wheel of the habitat and inhabitants. One should do thus three times in a single meditation session.

With respect to this, it seems that it does not accord with what is done in Nāropa's system. Whatever stage of condensation is actually done or not in that [system], one also absolutely reaches the contemplation of the clear light of the spontaneous bliss emptiness in dependence upon the other three seals from the juncture that gives rise to capability in the perfection stage, having stabilized the creation stage. Therefore, although the union of bliss and emptiness emerges at the limit of this stage of condensation, it thus cannot be differentiated from the contemplation of the other three seals. Since it seems that the emergence into the wheel of the deities is done in the creation stage, and since in this manner from then onward there is also perfection stage contemplation of the great seal, saying that this chapter teaches the perfection stage great seal contemplation are mere words.

This being so, the method of showing the perfection stage great seal in this chapter is via the capacity to generate the gnostic deity forms of the perfection stage. Moreover, the entry into clear light having relied on the stage of condensation of the final dissolution should be taken as the ultimate meaning of fire sacrifice and [the text] "all heroes" (**34.2a**) etc. Emerging from the mere wind mind of clear light as the wheels of the mandala should be taken as the ultimate meaning of the five lines [beginning with] "in all directions" (**34.4d**) etc.

Moreover, since the deity forms of the perfection stage are the great seal, it is good if one takes this chapter as showing the perfection stage great seal. Since the non-condensed drop and deity visualization are explained in terms of the creation stage, it does not seem that [Mardo's explanation], "if one sees that one's mind is wavering" and so forth, is appropriate. Even someone as lowly as the present person will see the profound instructions on condensing the wind of the right and left channels into the lower aperture of the central channel if he undertakes the stage of condensation in the previously [explained] manner and focuses upon the father and mother's melted red and white drop at the tip of the secret place.

3.3.3. 2.2.2. 8.1.2. 1.2.2. Kambala the Blanketed's explanation

The second part has two sections: (1) the explanation in terms of the yoga of the drop and (2) the explanation in terms of subtle yoga.

3.3.3. 2.2.2. 8.1.2. 1.2.2. 1. The explanation in terms of the yoga of the drop

All twenty-four of the heroes, Khaṇḍakapālin and so forth, are included in the twenty-four yoginīs, Prachaṇḍā, and so forth; in the context of [this] tantra the wisdom consorts (*shes rab ma*) are taken as primary. The yoginīs are also included in Vārāhī. And since Vārāhī is also said to be the drop of the navel, she is included in the fierce short *a*. Therefore, they are joined to, i.e., included within, that place of [the syllable] *a* in the center of the lotus of the emanation wheel.[411] Although his statement of and commentary on these two lines (**34.2ab**) are not clear, their meaning should be taken as being similar to what was stated by Durjayachandra.[412]

Kambala states that "It is the *avadhūtī* because it shakes the sin of discursive thought."[413] *Ava* is the sin of discursive thought, and *dhunoti*[414] means

411. Tsong Khapa here is commenting on Kambala's text, "**All heroes and yoginīs are united at the center of the lotus**. Regarding 'lotus of the navel,' it means that they are placed on the heart of the lotus of the navel." SN 65a.7: *dpa' bo kun dang rnal 'byor ma / padma'i lte bar nges par sbyar / zhes bya ba la lte ba ni lte ba'i padma'i snying po'i ste der nges par sbyar ba'o.*

The Sanskrit reading is somewhat different "**The ḍākinīs are placed upon the lotuses with all of the heroes** means they should be placed there in the navel of the lotus, that is, on the lotuses' pericarps." (K 62b.5: *sarvavīrasya ḍākinyaḥ puṣkareṣu niyojitam iti puṣkaranābhikamalakarṇikā tasmin tasmin niyojayet.*)

412. Kambala's commentary is not clear here with respect to this topic because he simply glosses the root text without going into any details concerning yogic practices. Tsong Khapa thus follows Durjayachandra's commentary instead. See RG 303b.4–6.

413. Tsong Khapa is quoting what appears to be a very bad translation of Kambala's commentary. It reads: *rnam par rtog pa'i sdig bskyod pas na a ba dhū tī'i ste* (SN 65a.7). See my translation of the Sanskrit in the footnote at the end of this paragraph.

414. Tsong Khapa's text here reads *dhū no tī*, which presumably is an attempt to give the 3rd person singular present form of the verb *dhū*, from which the terms *avadhūta* and *avadhūtī* derive. I have corrected this to *dhunoti.*

"shaking," i.e., removing, sin. It is called the *avadhūtī* since among the channels it is the lord of fire that has the form of blazing fire. The *dhūtī* is its site; it resides or exists there. It is said that through union with this, the site of the *dhūtī* is also for yogis.[415]

Where is the site of the *dhūtī*? It is between the two, left and right, eyebrows. Regarding what is positioned there, one conceives within the central channel a moon-like drop. Within, that is, encircling up to, the lotus at the edge of that moon and channel wheel are sixteen subsidiary channels.[416] As is stated:[417]

> The moon lotus at the eyebrow's juncture
> Is surrounded by the sixteen portions.
> Through union with art and with wisdom,
> It's said to be non-dually united.
> If you visualize that it is endowed
> With the first vowel it will quickly ignite.

The meaning of the two [lines beginning with "through union with] art and" is that through the union via blazing and trickling of both "art," which is the moon-like drop, and "wisdom," which is the letter *a* at the navel, there is said to be non-dual union (*saṁpuṭa*, *kha sbyar*). The [last] two [lines beginning with "with] the first" [indicate that] if you visualize the fury fire of the navel it will ignite. Through this exhalation of the upper aperture of the *dhūtī* between the eyebrows one should know as well the

415. The Sanskrit version of this section of Kambala's commentary reads: "It is the *avadhūtī* since discursive thought has been **shaken off**. The lord whose form is blazing fire is said to be the *avadhūtī*. Its **state** means that is the place in which it exists. It is said that through union with that one is thus a yogi" (K 62b.6–7: *avadhūtavikalpatvāt / avadhūtī jvaladagnirūpā tasyāḥ patiḥ / avadhūta ity ucyate / tasya padam pratiṣṭhā sthitir ity arthaḥ / tena yogāt yogī tathocyate*).

416. This section of Kambala's commentary reads, "Where is it? **Between the eyebrows.** The moon lotus is encircled by sixteen vowel forms" (SN 65b1–2: *gang du zhe na smin ma'i bar du zhes bya ba ste / zla ba dang padma'i bar du ā li'i ri mo bcu drug gis bskor ba'o*; K 62b7: *kasmin bruvo[r] madhya iti / indupadmasya madhye ṣoḍaśe staṁ? nuṣaṣṭhitaṁ?*).

417. The source for this quote is Durjayachandra's commentary, which in turn quotes another unnamed source. See RG 303b.7–304a.1.

stage of the seedless double vajra taught by Ghaṇṭapāda that is hidden in the root tantra.

That which rises up from the short *a* in the navel is the blazing fire. It is the "mouth" of the "hero" that is "agitated," i.e., disgusting.[418] Regarding sacrificing the five *homa* oblations there, one sacrifices the conceptions of the five sense faculties with the five meats illustrated by "beef" that are purified by the five tathāgatas, and of the five elements via the five ambrosias illustrated by "blood." Transforming the conception of each of those sets of five with the five aggregates and four elements yields sacrifices of five sets of nine. One thence gives the nine *homa* oblations.[419]

Regarding "then in the fire garlanded ocean" (**34.4c**), one sacrifices one's conceptions with the fiercely blazing fury fire. "Should see the wheel facing in all directions" means that the mantrin should see the wheel in that sacrifice. What is that wheel like? It is said that it is a mandala that faces everywhere, throughout the entire triple realm, and it is one's self-arisen personal deity. This shows one's emergence from clear light as the magical body personal deity, which is the means of engaging with any sentient being. One's mode of existence through union with one's personal deity is shown by the five lines [beginning with] "lord of heroes" etc. (**34.5a–6a**). One manifests as the magical body habitat and inhabitant mandala.[420]

418. This is based on Kambala's comment "**The hero's agitated mouth** is the agitated, i.e., disgusting, mouth of the lord" (SN 65b.2: *dpa' bo 'chol ba'i zhal du zhes bya ba la / 'chol ba ni 'jigs su rung ba ste bcom ldan 'das kyi zhal du'o*; K 62b.7: *vīrocchuṣmamukheti ucchuṣma b[ī]bhatsa bhagavato mukha*).

419. This is based on Kambala's comment: **The five homa oblations** are via purification with the five tathāgatas. **The nine homa oblations** mean that for each one you should offer up forty-five [oblations]. SN 65b.3: *bsreg bya lna zhes bya ni de bzhin gshegs pa lnga rnam par dag pa rnams kyis so / bsreg bya dgu zhes bya ba ni re re zhing ste / bzhi bcu rtsa lnga'i sbyin sreg ba'o zhes bya ba'i don to*; K 63a.1–2: *pañcahotaya iti pañcatathāgataviśuddhyā / navahotaya iti pratyekaṁ pañcacatvāriṁśati juhuyād ity arthaḥ.*

420.This is based on Kambala's comment: **The fire-garlanded ocean** is fiercely blazing. It is the mantrin who **should see**. What? **The wheel facing in all directions**, that is, one's self-arisen personal deity and the mandala of the entire triple realm. **Four faces** etc. mean with union with one's deity there is **the hero's abode**, i.e., one has a palace." K 63a.2: *jvālāmālārṇavam iti / depīpyamānam / paśyed iti mantrī / kiṁ tat cakraṁ sarvatomukham iti traidhātukam akhilamaṇḍalasvādhidevatasvayambhūḥ / caturmukham ityādi / svādhidevatayogena vīrālayam iti kuṭāgārasahitam.*

3.3.3. 2.2.2. 8.1.2. 1.2.2. 2. The explanation in terms of subtle yoga

Regarding showing the three wheels in terms of what is indicated by the two lines "these wheels" and so forth (**34.7ab**), they are explained with reference to **the accomplishment of all powers** (34.7c).[421] The visualization of these wheels of the mandala in the heart of the gnosis hero as **taught in the *Ocean of Spells*** (34.8a) will rapidly accomplish all powers. Regarding the method of visualizing the wheels, visualize in the heart of the gnosis hero a white lotus on which are the signs and hand emblems of whichever clan, and in the middle of that are the seed syllables of each clan, and within the drop of that,[422] are the seed syllables of each, *hūṁ* and so forth, from which manifests the mandala of the nature of great bliss, condensed in just an atom. From the light rays of gnosis that radiate thence the bodies of the various buddhas diffuse, and thence bless all beings with the commitments of the Vajraḍākas. If one meditates for a week with one's mind extremely stable by means of vase breathing, one will undoubtedly directly perceive shivering, shaking, settling, wavering, and ignition.[423]

While it is not clear where one visualizes the gnosis hero, since those who have the oral transmission of this system assert that it is visualized in the heart, it should be visualized within the central channel at the heart, and

421. This line is found in the extant Sanskrit sources but is omitted in all of the Tibetan translations. Tsong Khapa is quoting Kambala's quotation of this line as follows: *dngos grub thams cad sgrub byed yin* (SN 65b.7); *sarvasiddhiprasādhakaṁ* (K 63a.5).

422. That is, the *bindu* mark that indicates the *anusvāra* nasalization in the Sanskrit alphabet.

423. Tsong Khapa summarizes Kambala's commentary here; see SN 65b.7–66a.4. All but the last part of this passage is preserved in the extant Sanskrit, as follows: "As for **the accomplishment of all powers**, having visualized the lord of the triple realm mind palace within the drop of the symbolic seed syllable in the white lotus in the heart of the gnosis hero, there is the meditation of subtle yoga, having radiated of clouds of buddhas amidst the array of tens of millions of light rays, and having gathered them together through the yoga of the drop. In the sky-like expanse of the mandala that arises from *hūṁ* via the clan method and is included within the sign is the great abode of the Victor's jewels, the accumulation of subtle atoms of great bliss. One is self-established there as [Vajra]ḍāka, in the commitment of all beings." (K 63a.5–7: *sarvasiddhiprasādhakam iti jñānasattva-hṛdipuṇḍarīkacihnabījabindumadhyas tu traidhātukātmakaṁ cittaṁ kūṭālayaṁ dhyātvā raśmikoṭīsamākīrṇe buddhameghaspharaṇāvahaṁ binduyogasaṁhṛtya sūkṣmayogavi-bhāvanam / kulānukrama hūṁbhavaṁ cihnāntargatamaṇḍala-vyomaprabhāvist[ār]e jina-ratnamahālayaṁ mahāsukhasvasūkṣmaṁ par[am]āṇurūpaṁ saṁcayām aśeṣasattvasama-yaṁ ḍākasvapratiṣṭhitam*).

the vase breathing (*bum pa can*) should also be done in the heart. Therefore, with the two drops that are visualized as the syllable *a*, the actuality of white and red drops, within the central channel at the crown and navel, respectively, the life force is accumulated in the central channel in those places. The fire sacrifice (*sbyin sreg*, *homa*), which is the definitive meaning of the concept of "burning," enters into clear light. It is taught that one thence arises into the magical body. The meditation on the application and connection of the subtle yogic wind within the central channel at the heart **was taught in** the first chapter of **the *Ocean of Spells* *Tantra*** (**34.8ab**), and profoundly established by Kambala the Blanketed.[424] I have already explained in depth the definitive meaning of fire sacrifice [stated] in the *Kiss Tantra*.

3.3.3. 2.2.2. 8.1.2. 2. Summary of the explained import

Do not doubt that **that which was taught succinctly here** by **the hero** Heruka **in the manner** that the wheel was taught **in** the first chapter of great tantra (*mahātantra*) called the ***Ocean of Spells*** (**34.8ab**). While Laṅka [Jayabhadra] explains that the term **hero** is in the vocative case, it seems that it is better to explain it as [the instrumental] "by the hero," as is intended in the commentaries of Kambala and others.[425]

Having obtained the text of the mantra that is very difficult to attain, and which has the nature of **nondual union with the messenger, have no doubt that** he who exerts himself in repetition and visualization **will achieve** power (**34.8cd**). Bhavabhaṭṭa's comment that "equipoised with the messenger, one should make fire sacrifices"[426] accords with the context of the chapter's name.

424. As Tsong Khapa here indicates, he follows Kambala (SN 66a.4; K 63b.2) in indicating that this procedure was taught in the first chapter of the *Vidyārṇava*.

425. Jayabhadra does quote the text of 34.8, quoting here *vīra yathā* (Sugiki 2001, 134), which could be interpreted as vocative or nominative, but he does not actually explain the grammar of this verse. The Tibetan translator, however, interpreted it as vocative, translating it as *kye dpa' bo* (CP 63b.5), as Tsong Khapa quotes here. Kambala does not mention the term *vīra/dpa' bo* at all, so Tsong Khapa must be discerning his intention in some other manner. Bhavabhaṭṭa, however, does gloss *vīra* as *vīreṇa*, although the Tibetan translation of his commentary fails to communicate this grammatical gloss. See Pandey 2002, 529, 723.

426. This comment occurs as follows in Bhavabhaṭṭa's commentary: *dūtyā samāpanno*

3.3.3. 2.2.2. 8.1.3. Showing the name of the chapter

In the *Concise* ***Shrī Herukābhidhāna Tantra***, this is the chapter on **the fire sacrifice of the nondual messenger**. Regarding the meaning of the latter term,[427] Durjayachandra explains "messenger" in terms of meditation on the short *a* syllable that assembles all of the yoginīs.[428] Regarding the meaning of the former term, I have explained the definitive meaning of fire sacrifice. In addition to the definitive meaning, the interpretable meaning is said to be performing fire sacrifice in the manner of union with the messenger as Bhavabhaṭṭa [explained].[429]

This is **the thirty-fourth chapter** on **the procedure** of the rite of both the interpretable and definitive fire sacrifice. This is the explanation of the thirty-fourth chapter in the *Illumination of the Hidden Meaning, A Detailed Exegesis of the Concise Saṁvara Tantra Called "The Chakrasaṁvara."*

---

juhuyād (Pandey 2002, 529), *pho nya dang snyoms par zhugs pa la sbyin sreg bya'o* (2002, 723).

427. Tsong Khapa, following the Tibetan word order uses the expression "former term," *tshig snga ma*, which is the latter term in English translation.

428. See RG 303b.5–6.

429. See Pandey 2002, 529, 723.

Chapter 35

Chapter 35 Outline

3.3.3. 2.2.2. 8.2. The chapter that shows the reality seal

The second part, the chapter that shows the reality seal, has three sections: (1) the promise to explain, (2) the promised import explained, and (3) showing the name of the chapter.

3.3.3. 2.2.2. 8.2.1. The promise to explain

Now, after stating the thirty-fourth chapter, I will explain **the excellent and supreme** attainment of **ritual actions**. What is that ritual attainment like? It is **illustrated**, i.e., is known, in the manner of the uncorrupted scriptural tradition by means of **the succession** of the lineage from one guru to another. The mantrin whose **nature** is **united** to **the worship** that is **non-dual** with respect to both art and wisdom should **apply the corresponding** rite that is the means of achieving each of **the ritual actions (35.1)** such as pacifying etc. **I will explain successively the distinctions** by means of each ritual action, **the disclosure of these mantras that** have or will **yield success** of whatever rite (**35.2ab**).

3.3.3. 2.2.2. 8.2.2. The promised import explained

The second part has two sections: (1) explaining in terms of the interpretable meaning, and (2) explaining in terms of the definitive meaning.

3.3.3. 2.2.2. 8.2.2. 1. Explaining in terms of the interpretable meaning

The second part has two sections: (1) the method of repeating [the mantra], and (2) the method of achieving ritual actions with Khaṇḍarohā.

3.3.3. 2.2.2. 8.2.2. 1.1. The method of repeating [the mantra]

The term *varṇa* is translated by some as color, by some as syllable, and by some as class. Here the translation as "syllable" is acceptable.[430] This is because it occurs as "syllable" in the *Vajraḍāka*,[431] it is explained as "syllable" in the commentaries,[432] and Kambala also explains it as syllable.[433] In that way, **the syllables** are the sixteen vowels and thirty-three consonants. **The messengers** are the yoginīs, Prachaṇḍā, and so forth, who are the nature of the channels. By **and so forth** the twenty-four heroes are implied, while **the mantras** are theirs. [These terms] should be taken as explained in the *[Twofold] Commentary*, namely that "and so forth" implies the principal deity couple as well, and also their mantras.[434]

One should repeat those mantras knowing the distinctions of each of the ritual actions. Regarding the visualization accompanying repetition, when commencing the ritual of the destruction of an evil doer, visualize that **a**

430. It should be noted that the term *varṇa* was translated as *kha dog*, "color" in both the PM and SM translations (Gray 2012, 360, 540). This line is omitted in the SL translation. Tsong Khapa here is following Butön's commentary (NS 215b.6). Butön's commentary notes the ways the term was translated in the various commentaries, but it does not identify which meaning is correct here.

431. As Tsong Khapa indicates, *varṇa* is translated as *yi ge* in the VD parallel passage, which occurs at the opening of VD ch. 15; see VD 38a.1.

432. This is the case in some but not all of the commentaries. Bhavabhaṭṭa, for example, interprets the term as mantric syllables (see Pandey 2002, 530, 726), as does Tathāgatarakṣhita (UN 238a.3).

433. See SN 66a.7.

434. Tsong Khapa here paraphrases Tathāgatarakṣhita's comments at UN 238a.4.

knot is connected, **one to another**, of each of the mantra's syllables in the manner of well wound thread, such that they quickly enter **with the speed of** the nocking and firing of **an arrow**, that is, a bowshot, and that they **revolve (35.2cd)** in the manner of the buckets of a waterwheel, arising in quick succession from the mouths of both partners.

For pacification, the syllables of **the mantra**, which are **successively linked in** form of a garland, **are characterized by** loose, i.e., not rough, circulation, through **entry (35.3ab)**, i.e., by the process of entering through the region of one's mouth, and, being emitted again from the path of the vajra so as to enter into the lotus of the goddess, and then entering one's mouth from the mouth of the goddess.

For destruction, this is done in the manner of entry from one's mouth to the goddess's; it is simply that in particular. Just as [the lines] "for pacification it is loose, not rough" occur in many commentaries,[435] they also occur in another translation.[436] These two lines occurred in the text of the previous scholars. It is said by those who uphold the system of Mal that it did not occur in Sumati[kīrti]'s text.[437]

For enriching, **the garland of seed**, i.e., mantric, **syllables is taken**, meaning that it is repeated in the manner of [the syllables] being joined together, one after another. Regarding **then (35.3c)**, it means after the former syllable, then it is well joined to the latter syllable. This [line] is connected to enriching by Bhavabhaṭṭa.[438] Although no [statement] regarding controlling clearly occurs, those who uphold the system of Mal claim that one [visualizes] the circulation of [the mantra] in the form of a chain from one's mouth to the mouth of the [female] partner.[439] For each of the respective

435. It occurs as follows in Jayabhadra's commentary: "In pacification [rites] they are loose, not rough" (Sugiki 2001, 135: *śantau śithilāny aniṣṭhurāṇi*).

436. This text, *zhi ba la ni lhod pa ste / drag cing rtsub pa ma yin no*, only occurs in the SL translation. See Gray 2012, 461.

437. Tsong Khapa here is paraphrasing the following comment in Sachen's commentary: "For pacifying illness, etc., the mantra is circulated loosely, i.e., slowly. It is not repeated roughly. It is said that these latter two lines did occur in the Sanskrit texts of the previous masters, but did not occur in Lama Sumati[kīrti]'s text" (PG 355.1: *nad la sogs pa zhi ba la lhod pa ni / sngags dal gyis 'khor ba ste / drag cing rtsub par bzlas pa ma yin no zhes pa ste / tshig tha ma gnyis po de ni jo bo snga ma rnams kyi rgya dpe la yod pa / bla ma su ma ti'i dpe la med gsung ngo*).

438. See Pandey 2002, 531, 726–27.

439. See PG 355.2.

ritual actions, you should make the mantra have the corresponding color, white [for pacifying], and so forth.

For destruction, **the syllable *hūṁ*** should be **placed** before and **at the end (35.3d)** of the victim's name. [The writing] *"hūṁ* so-and-so die! *hūṁ*" (*hūṁ che ge mo mā ra ya hūṁ*) should be affixed before the *hūṁ hūṁ phaṭ*. Through doing this, **the victim will be restrained**, lacking the freedom to **proceed** even **one step (35.4ab)**; that is, he will die. Regarding **envelopment through the state of being enveloped (35.4c)**, for pacification [the name] is enveloped by two *oṁ* [syllables], i.e., *oṁ* so-and-so *svāhā oṁ* (*oṁ lha sbyin*[440] *svāhā oṁ*). In rites of destruction, before and after the victim's name there is envelopment by the vajra, that is, *hūṁ*; should it be **separated by the vajra (35.5a)**, i.e., *hūṁ*, successively as if **bound with an adamantine chain (35.4d)**, he will be destroyed.

In three commentaries there is the statement that the equivalent term to "bee" (*bung ba*) is **pacchika*, but as it is also an explanation that it should be translated as a bunch of feathers.[441] Therefore, one should visualize the uninterrupted circulation of the mantra from mouth to mouth, with no junction visible, as if surrounded by a bunch of **peacock feathers (35.5b)**.

3.3.3. 2.2.2. 8.2.2. 1.2. The method of achieving ritual actions with Khaṇḍarohā

If one desires at some time to summon a victim, one should augment [the mantra with] "*ja* Summon so-and-so! *jaḥ*" (*dza che ge mo ā karṣa ya dzaḥ*), and **one should summon** the victim **by just** holding aloft **the hook (35.5c)** of Khaṇḍarohā. Whenever one desires to **agitate** and disturb another's army and so forth, by repeating "Disturb so-and-so! *hūṁ*" (*che ge mo kṣo bha ya hūṁ*) and [visualizing] Khaṇḍarohā brandishing **a mace** in her hand,

440. The Tibetan *lha sbyin*, a translation of the Sanskrit *devadatta*, is a generic name, like the English "John Doe," meant to stand in for whomever's name the adept would want to use here. It thus means "so-and-so."

441. The Sanskrit here reads *picchaka*, which means a peacock tail feather or a bunch thereof, as Tsong Khapa correctly identifies below. However, in all of the Tibetan translations this term is mistranslated as "bee" (PM, SM: *bung ba*; SL: *ṣbrang bu*; Gray 2012, 361, 461, 541). Tsong Khapa here follows Butön's commentary; see NS 216b.1–2. Note that Butön's commentary doesn't give the incorrect transliteration *pacchika*; instead it reads *sicchaka*, which is almost certainly a corruption of the correct reading *picchika*, given the similarities between the Tibetan letters *pa* and *sa*.

the entire army and so forth will be agitated. Regarding **likewise** (**35.5d**), it means it is done by Khaṇḍarohā in the same manner as summoning.

If one repeats "*phaṭ* Eat so-and-so!" (*phaṭ che ge mo bha kṣa yaṁ*),[442] it is stated that he will be struck, i.e., **devoured**, just by Khaṇḍarohā brandishing **the vajra** (**35.6a**) in her hand. "Devoured by the vajra" occurs in the commentaries.[443] **For piercing** another's body, making a hole in it, and making it tremble, one should repeat "*phaṭ* Pierce so-and-so! *phaṭ*" (*phaṭ che ge mo be dha naṁ phaṭ*) and **employ** Khaṇḍarohā brandishing **an arrow** (**35.6a**).

For overcoming **untimely death**, visualize white Khaṇḍarohā brandishing **a skull staff in her limb** (**35.6cd**), i.e., left hand, and a thousand streams of ambrosia trickling from a white *hūṁ*, and repeat "*hūṁ* Let so-and-so live! *hūṁ*" (*hūṁ che ge mo dzi ba yā*[444] *hūṁ*). For all ritual accomplishments with Khaṇḍarohā, it is explained that one first should give **water offerings into the mouth** of Khaṇḍarohā by filling up **a skull bowl** with the five ambrosias. After that one should **apply the weapon** (**35.7**), the hook and so forth, to the limb of the victim.[445] [The text] from "envelopment" (**35.4c**) up to "should apply" (**35.7c**), except for the "piercing" line (**35.6b**), is also connected by Kṛiṣhṇāchārya to the causal Vajradhara-Heruka.

3.3.3. 2.2.2. 8.2.2. 2. Explaining in terms of the definitive meaning

Regarding Kambala's explanation of the definitive meaning of [the text] from "with the speed of an arrow" (**35.2b**) up to "devoured by the vajra" (**35.6a**), **the arrow** is wind, and through its **speed** going and coming cycles about. Furthermore, **interconnected** means a knot is formed or joined with **the mantra** of vowels and syllables when it goes hither and come thither.

442. The correct imperative reading, *bhakṣaya*, occurs in Bhavabhaṭṭa's commentary (Pandey 2002, 532). Tsong Khapa follows Butön in giving the incorrect transliteration *bha kṣa yaṁ* (NS 216b.5).

443. Tsong Khapa makes this comment because the Sanskrit *grasana* "devouring" is translated in the PM and SM translations as *'debs*, "strike" (Gray 2012, 361, 541). The correct translation, *bza'*, is found in the SL translation (Gray 2012, 461) and commentaries such as Bhavabhaṭṭa's (Pandey 2002, 729).

444. The correct transliteration should be *dzī ba ya* for the Sanskrit *jīvaya*. See Pandey 2002, 532.

445. Tsong Khapa here paraphrases Bhavabhaṭṭa's commentary. See Pandey 2002, 532, 730.

These vowels and consonants are **separated by** the regions of the navel, heart, throat, and crown, which means that they are placed in the four channel wheels. "Then," after **the placement** of the syllables in the four channel wheels, they are **taken** by **the seed**, i.e., vowel and consonant, **garland** into the left and right channels.[446] The *Vajraḍāka* states:[447]

> On both the left and the right sides,
> Write the twelve vowels by gazing up.
> Gazing down at *ka* and so forth,
> They increase on both of the sides;
> Thus, they are joined in the middle.

Regarding the four lines beginning with "[On both] the left and," when the two channels move on account of the wind from *ka*, they move onto the string of the twelve vowels. Since they follow after that string of vowels, the garland of *ka* etc. increases with *ka* etc. When the wind has entered from the two orifices, one should draw the garland of vowels and consonants facing down. One should know to gaze up at the movement due to wind, and gaze down at its entry within. This is explained in the commentary.[448] Regarding the last line, Kambala states that "[the two garlands of vowels and consonants] should be inserted into the middle of that."[449] This, moreover, means that the wind of the left and right [channels] is inserted into the central [channel].

Regarding will be **restrained** and the statement that "the two movements are bound,"[450] Durjayachandra, with his statement "**restraint** is restricting

446. Tsong Khapa here paraphrases Kambala's commentary; see SN 66b.1–2.

447. This passage occurs as follows at VD 38a.4–5: *g.yon dang g.yas kyi ngos gnyis su / dbyangs yig bcu gnyis steng bltas bris / ka sogs 'og tu bltas pa ni/ ngos gnyis dag tu spel ba ste / dbus su des ni sbyar bar bya.*

448. Tsong Khapa here paraphrases Bhavabhaṭṭa's commentary on the verses above. See VV 92a.2–5.

449. Kambala comments that "the two rows should be placed in the middle. paṅktidvaya madhyīkṛtāḥ" (K 64a.1); *phreng ba gnyis te de'i dbus su chud par bya'o* (SN 66b.3–4).

450. Tsong Khapa is referring to text quoted in the Kambala's commentary, namely "'The victim will be restrained;' in restraint there is the restriction of the two movements." (K 64a.2: *nirodhās tu bhavet sādhya iti nirodhe gatidvayavibandhaḥ*; SN 66b.4–5: *bsgrub bya 'gog par gyur na ni / 'gog pa ni rgyu ba gnyis rnam par bcings pa'o*).

coming and going,"[451] seems to be explaining in terms of inability to move the wind. That is accomplished, moreover, by the yogic power of pressing vital points on the body. This is relevant to all pressing of the body's vital points. Thus, one will succeed from the binding of the two winds; one will become accomplished. One will have the nature of great bliss that is uncontaminated, free of physical or objective reference.

Will not proceed one step means that there is no context for movement on account of wind. This is because the wind and mind itself of clear light naturally attain experiential uniformity, on account of the dissolution of the wind that moves conceptual thought.[452] Regarding **envelopment**, it is said that:[453]

> Envelopment and envelopment's state,
> Are proclaimed to be the moon and the sun,
> On the side of the left and of the right.
> The light-garlanded illuminator's
> Always positioned at the upper gate
> Via the adamantine chain binding.

As for the meaning of this, both the *lalanā* that exists to the left side of the central channel, and which is called "the moon," and the *rasanā* that exists to the right side of the central channel, and which is called "the sun," constitute the envelopment that encircles the central channel at each of channel wheels in the manner of an "adamantine chain," that is, an iron chain. "Envelopment's state" is the binding of the winds of these two [channels] in the central channel. The "light-garlanded illuminator" or sun that is "always positioned at the upper gate," i.e., facing upward in the navel, is the fury fire that, by ascending to the crown, is union in supreme bliss.

451. See RG 305a.5.

452. Tsong Khapa here expands upon Kambala's commentary; see SN 66b.5–6.

453. This is a quotation from Kambala's commentary, namely *saṁpuṭāṁ saṁpuṭībhāvaṁ candrasūryau tu vikhyāte / pārśve tu vāmadakṣiṇāṁ vajraśṛṅkhalabandhena ūrdhvadvāre sthīto nityaṁ bhāskaraṁ dīptimālinaṁ* (K 64a.3–4); *kha sbyor sbyar bar gyur pa ni / zla ba nyi mar rnam par bshad / g.yon dang g.yas kyi ngos gnyis su / rdo rje lu gu rgyud bcings pa / steng gi sgo ru rtag gnas pa'i / snang byed 'bar ba'i phreng ba can* (SN 66b.6–7).

As for explaining this in terms of union with the actual seal (consort), it is as stated in the *Vajraḍāka*:[454]

> The union of wisdom and art
> Is what is called envelopment.
> 'Tis said that both arms' embrace is
> The adamantine chain's binding.

There is **the separation** of the lotus of wisdom **by the vajra** of art; it circles, that is arouses, from outside to inside the lotus like a bee. **One should summon** all tathāgatas, that is, the spirit of awakening, **with the** noose, that is, **hook** of the passionate desire for the vajra to enter the lotus. One should **agitate** all channels with **the mace**, i.e., the vajra. As for "striking" or **devouring** with the vajra, there is enjoyment in the assembly of the tathāgatas, i.e., the spirit of awakening, at the tip of the vajra. [The following] is quoted in Kambala's commentary:[455]

> The lotus should be pierced by the vajra.
> Spread out, it's known as the honey maker.
> Moreover, it trembles through this coursing.
> One should insert the noose into the lotus,
> Via the nature of sexual bliss.
> Then all tathāgatas should be summoned
> By being hooked with exhilaration.
> The mace is thus renowned as the vajra,

454. VD 38a.7: *shes rab thabs kyi mnyam sbyor gyis / kha sbyor zhes byar brjod pa yin / lag gnyis kun tu 'khyud pa yin / rdo rje lu gu rgyud bcings brjod.* This verse is also quoted by Kambala as follows: *āliṅgana dvaukarābhyāṁ vajraśṛṅkhalam ucyate / prajñopāyasamāyaṁ saṁpuṭam ity abhidhīyate* (K 64a.4–5); cf. SN 66b.7.

455. This text occurs as follows in Kambala's commentary: *vajreṇa bhedayet padmaṁ picchakaṁ madhukartṛsmṛtam / bhrāmaṇacālanaṁ hy etat / suratānandasvabhāvena pāśa padmaṁ praveśayet / madanāṅkuśinaiva ākarṣayet sarvatathāgatān / akṣobhitākṣobhavajreṇa muṣalaṁ tat prakīrta / grasane melaka vajra* (K 64a.5–7); *rdo rje padma 'phyed ba ni / sgro chun sbrang rtsir byed par bshad / bskor bas 'di ni bskyod pa'o / bde dang dga' ba'i rang bzhin gyis / zhags pa padmar bcug pa ste / 'dod la chags pa'i lcags kyu yis / de bzhin gshegs pa thams cad dgug / mi 'khrug 'khrug byed rdo rje ste / de ni gtun shing rab tu grags / bza' ba rdo rje 'debs pa la / de bzhin gshegs pa 'dus pa'o* (SN 67a.1–2).
A similar, but not identical passage occurs in VD ch. 15. (VD 38b.1–2).

The unagitated agitator.
In devouring the vajra is struck;
This is the tathāgatas' assembly.

[This passage] shows, depending upon the *Vajraḍāka*, the fury fire of the four channel wheels and the perfection stage of the actual seal (consort). The previous lamas have also explained this chapter in terms of the definitive meaning. It is explained as having four stages in the manner of [Kāṇha's] *Ālicatuṣṭaya*. Regarding taking the placement of the syllables on the channels in terms of the reality seal, it is explained that the meditation on that is meditation on the reality seal. However, with respect to the reality seal, one should not engage in just the meditation focusing on the syllables; one should engage in the actual perfection stage that arises in dependence on that.

3.3.3. 2.2.2. 8.2.3. Showing the name of the chapter

In the *Concise* ***Shrī Herukābhidhāna Tantra***, this is **the thirty-fifth chapter** on **the ritual action** of **nondual** union **and the procedure of cheating death**, etc. This is the explanation of the thirty-fifth chapter in the *Illumination of the Hidden Meaning, A Detailed Exegesis of the Concise Saṁvara Tantra Called "The Chakrasaṁvara."*

Chapter 36

Chapter 36 Outline

3.3.3. 2.2.2. 8.3. The chapter that shows both the symbolic and actual seals through a single approach
3.3.3. 2.2.2. 8.3.1. The promise to explain
3.3.3. 2.2.2. 8.3.2. The promised import explained
3.3.3. 2.2.2. 8.3.2. 1. The worship of reality
3.3.3. 2.2.2. 8.3.2. 1.1. Worship depending on the two [types of] seals
3.3.3. 2.2.2. 8.3.2. 1.2. Explaining somewhat the classification of the four seals
3.3.3. 2.2.2. 8.3.2. 2. The procedure for ritual success depending on that
3.3.3. 2.2.2. 8.3.3. Showing the name of the chapter

3.3.3. 2.2.2. 8.3. The chapter that shows both the symbolic and actual seals through a single approach

The third part, the chapter that shows both the symbolic and actual seals through a single approach, has three sections: (1) the promise to explain, (2) the promised import explained, and (3) showing the name of the chapter.

3.3.3. 2.2.2. 8.3.1. The promise to explain

And then, after explaining about cheating untimely death, I will explain **the great worship** that depends upon the actual and gnostic **seal**. For what reason should one engage in the great worship of the seal? This is because the principal aim of **mantra** is nondual gnosis, and the syllables **laid down** in the two pure signs of that are also mantra. Having set them down, practicing its ritual actions **is famed as**, i.e., explained to be, the great worship. Since there is no doubt that with **this worship of the seal** one **will achieve power rapidly** (**36.1**), i.e., without long delay, those who desire power should rely upon this worship of the seal.

3.3.3. 2.2.2. 8.3.2. The promised import explained

The second part has two sections: (1) the worship of reality, and (2) the procedure for ritual success depending on that.

3.3.3. 2.2.2. 8.3.2. 1. The worship of reality

The second part has two sections: (1) worship depending on the two [types of] seals, and (2) explaining somewhat the classification of the four seals.

3.3.3. 2.2.2. 8.3.2. 1.1. Worship depending on the two [types of] seals

The mantra is applied to the two signs (36.2a) of the secret place that is taken in terms of the chief partners who are the gnostic seal, [or] oneself and the actual or symbolic seal [consort]. Kambala explains in his root tantra commentary that natural bliss is indicated by the generation by *hūṁ* that is the vajra and *āḥ* that is the lotus and by the *vaṁ* on the lotus stamens in the navel, and by the obstruction of the two apertures by *phaṭ*.[456] Also, with respect to that, a commentary on Lūipa's meditation manual explains that they are marked by a yellow syllable *vyā* on the tip of the red jewel that emerges from a red [syllable] *vyā*, and by a yellow syllable *dyā* on the tip of white lotus stamens that emerge from a white [syllable] *dyā*.[457]

This is evidently accomplished via two methods. The *Conduct of the Yoginīs* states:[458]

456. Tsong Khapa here paraphrases the following commentary by Kambala: "**The mantra is applied to the two signs** means that the vajra is always generated by the syllable *hūṁ*, and the syllable *āḥ* is the lotus. Through the syllable *vaṁ* is the stamen, and having obstructed the aperture with the syllable *phaṭ*, wisdom is illustrated" (SN 69b.1–2: *mtshan ma gnyis la sngags rab sbyar / zhes bya ba la yi ge hūṁ gis ni rtag tu rdo rje bskyed pa'o / yi ge a yis ni 'dab skyes so / yi ge baṁ gyis ni ze'u 'bru'o / phaṭ kyis ni bug bkag nas ye shes mtshon pa'o;* K 67a.2–3: *mantra saṁyojyetyādi / hūṁkārajanitaṁ kuliśaṁ / āḥkāreṇa paṅkajaṁ / vaṁkāra kiñjalkaṁ / phaṭ randhrā[x][x][x] jñānalakṣaṇaṁ*).

457. Tsong Khapa refers to comments in Prajñārakṣhita's *Glorious Realization, a Commentary [on Luipa's Chakrasaṁvara Sādhana]* (*Śrī-abhisamaya-nāma-pañjikā*), fol. 39b.6–7.

458. Tsong Khapa here quotes the first three lines of the *Yoginīsaṁcāra* 8.4, which occurs as follows: *adhiṣṭhayed yoginīvīraṁ mantrī dyākāraṁ saṁyojya ca nāsikāgre / vyākāraṁ*

The mantrin should establish the yoginīs's hero
Joining the syllable *dyā* to the nose's tip,
And laying down the *vyā* at the midst of the sign.

Regarding "the nose's tip," it is the tip of the lotus' nose, and the "sign" (*liṅga*) is the vajra. Regarding the "midst" (*varaṭaka, lte ba*), it is laid down at the tip in the middle of the jewel. Through these [explanations] one should also know the stage of the double vajra together with the seed stated by Ghaṇṭapā that is hidden in the root tantra.

The ḍākinī, Vajravārāhī, **and the hero are non-dually** (**36.2b**) united. **Moreover, with the essences** (**36.3a**) means laying down both the partners' essence and quintessence mantras, regarding which the *Conduct* states:[459]

In the navel, heart, and on the forehead,
Consecrate with the mantra assembly.
And the hero should consecrate
On both the tongue and the forehead
As well as in the navel and the heart,
With the yoginī Buddhaḍākinī.
The yoginī and hero are nondual.

[Tathāgatarakṣhita's] commentary explains that two lines that [begin with] "[In the] navel" [indicate] mantric consecration in the four places of the principal lady, while the [four lines] from "navel" up to "should consecrate"

---

vinyasya ca liṅgavaraṭake (Pandey 1998, 78); *sngags pas dpa' bo rnal 'byor ma byin brlab / yi ge dyā ni sna rtser yang dag sbyar / byā ni mtshan gyi lte bar rnam par dgod* (Pandey 1998, 262).

459. This translates the text as quoted by Tsong Khapa, namely: */lte ba snying kha kha dang dpral ba ru / sngags kyi tshogs dang bcas pas byin gyis brlab / lte ba snying khar rnal 'byor ma / sangs rgyas mkha' 'gro ma yis te / lce dang spyi bo gnyis su ni / dpa' bos byin gyis brlab par bya / rnal 'byor ma dang dpa' gnyis med.*

The canonical translation differs in reading: *a ba dhū tī gnyis kyis dpa' byin brlab* rather than *lce dang spyi bo gnyis su ni / dpa' bos byin gyis brlab par bya*. It occurs as follows: *lte ba snying ga kha dang dpral ba ru / sngags kyi tshogs dang bcas pas byin gyis brlab / lte ba snying gar tag tu rnal 'byor ma / sangs rgyas mkha' 'gro ma yi sngags kyis ni / a ba dhū tī gnyis kyis dpa' byin brlab / rnal 'byor ma dang dpa' bo gnyis med yin* (Pandey 1998, 263–64).

The Sanskrit, 8.4d–5d in the Pandey ed., is quite distinct, reading: *mukhādike mantra-gaṇena sārdham / 4; adhiṣṭhayen nābhau hṛdi ca yoginīṁ buddhaḍākinīm / jihvāva-dhūtīdvaye vīraṁ yoginī-vīram advayam /* 5 (Pandey 1998, 78–79).

[i.e., lines three through six of the translated passage above, indicate] mantric consecration in the four places of the father.[460] In the manner of the [alternate translation] "tongue and central channel," the tongue refers to the throat, which is also like the mouth.[461] Regarding the *dhūtī*, its upper orifice is between the eyebrows.

The father's navel is consecrated with the yoginī's, that is, mother's, essence, and the heart is consecrated with the buddhaḍākinī mantra. The tongue and crown are consecrated by the father's essence and quintessence [mantras]; Mardo's translation [here] is excellent.[462] **The mantrin should be endowed with the ḍākinī** Vārāhī, and the mantras **as well** should be placed in the four places. Bhavyakīrti and so forth quote [this text] as:[463] "**The mantrin should be endowed with the ḍākinī, and with the essences as well (36.3ab).**"

After doing thus, **the wise one**, through his skill in the rite of equipoise, **churns** in the lotus of **the yoginī (36.3c)**, that is, of the actual or symbolic seal [consort], and performs reality worship. By assuming **a purified** divine **body** free of ordinary dualistic perception, **as desired (36.3d)**, the yogī will accord with the clan of his own seal. Having obtained any suitable seal (consort) from among those previously explained, who are like one's mother, daughter, etc. and who have the discipline of protecting well the commitments, and relying on her, one should perform **the worship** ceremonies **of the hero** Heruka, and **energetically perform** all **ritual actions (36.4ab)**, pacification and so forth. This shows that one will rapidly attain those powers performed in reliance upon the seal.

Regarding meditation in reliance on the two seals, since it is the intention of Nāropa that this applies to the perfection stage and not to the creation stage, the meditation relying on the actual seal is the meditation depending upon the insertion of the life force into the central channel by means of that

460. See Pandey 1998, 78–79, 263–64.

461. Tsong Khapa here is apparently referring to an alternate translation corresponding to the extant Sanskrit, *jihvāvadhūtīdvaye*. He is likely referring to Tathāgatarakṣhita's commentary, which comments on *lce* and then *avadhūtī*, evidently glossing this compound.

462. As I noted above, the translation of YS 8.5c that Tsong Khapa quotes above, *lce dang spyi bo gnyis su ni*, differs from the canonical translation. It appears that Tsong Khapa is identifying this source as an alternate translation by Mardo, which was not accepted into the Kangyur collections.

463. See BC 35a.7.

condition. If one is skillful in undertaking the trio of inserting, stabilizing, and dissolving the wind in the central channel having previously meditated in reliance on the gnostic seal, being able to condense the life force in the central channel in reliance on the symbolic seal and understanding in that context is the essential aim.

3.3.3. 2.2.2. 8.3.2. 1.2. Explaining somewhat the classification of the four seals

It is said that the thirty-fourth and thirty-fifth [chapters] showed the great seal and reality seal, and that this chapter, beginning here, distinguishes the four seals via the method of indicating the symbolic and actual seals. The explanatory tantra states:[464]

> Therefore, one should unify the four seals
> Via the generation of gnosis.

Regarding the meaning of this, the *Sheaf of Esoteric Instructions* explains that there are two sets of four seals in the context of the two stages [of practice].[465]

Regarding the four seals of the creation stage, the actual seal is meditation on the form of the goddess who is desired solely as the outer wisdom consort. The reality seal is the syllable *hūṁ* and so forth that are visualized in the body. The symbolic seal is radiation, recollection and so forth of the assembled wheels of the perfected mandala from the seed syllables etc. The great seal is visualizing oneself in the form of the principal deity.

Regarding the placement of the four seals of the perfection stage in the context of the path from the two [stages], the outer wisdom consort is the actual seal because she bestows joy through the actions of embracing and so forth. The inner wisdom consort, the central channel, is the reality seal. The result of these seals, of the spirit of awakening of great bliss, is the great seal. The manifestation of the various deities is the symbolic seal. As for their placement with respect to the result, the emanation body is the actual

464. This quote occurs in the kalpa 2, section 2 of the *Kiss Tantra* as follows: *de phyir ye shes skyed pa yi / phyag rgya bzhi ni sbyar bar bya* (ST 87a.4).

465. See AM 80a.

seal, the reality body is the reality seal, the communal enjoyment body is the great seal, and the body of great bliss, the spirit of awakening of bliss and emptiness, is the symbolic seal. This is the explanation of the nature of each one of the sets of four seals.[466] The previous lamas' distinguishing between the actual and symbolic seals accords with Ghaṇṭapāda. As there are great differences with respect to the other two seals, they should be known from my explanation in the *Five Stages of Chakrasaṁvara*.[467]

3.3.3. 2.2.2. 8.3.2. 2. The procedure for ritual success depending on that

The mantrin, through the method of delighting in whomever **he wishes** from among all of the mandala deities of the tantric feast, **should divide** (**36.4a**), i.e., apportion, the feast substances to each of them. When attending to the seal (consort), **one should unite in an inverted** [manner] (**36.4b**), with the yoginī positioned on top like a man. Why is it necessary to do this? It is **for the aim**, i.e., aims, **of destroying** the afflictions **and benefiting** sentient beings (**36.5a**).

Action is the characteristics of the concentration of the purified self-awareness of the tathāgatas, and **meditation on the actuality** (**36.5b**) of this is meditation avoiding all perverse diversions. **Reality** refers to the five clans, and regarding its divisions, one regards the eye and so forth as Mohavajra and so forth, which purify the eye and so forth that **divides with divisions** (**36.5c**). This should be **applied to the paths**, i.e., the sense objects, **of the channels** (**36.5d**), the channels of the eye and so forth.

Regarding **the aim of the application**, through awareness of the clear light that is the reality of cyclic existence in the objects from the perspective of hero's channel, one is united with the actuality of those sense powers and objects. Or, moreover, one is unified having become aware of the non-duality of the sense powers and objects and one's magical nature. As for **executing** (**36.6a**) the ritual action, Bhavyakīrti and so forth explain that the mantra, distinguished by means of the distinctions of each ritual action,

466. Tsong Khapa here summarizes Abhayākara's explanation at AM 80a–81a.

467. That is, Tsong Khapa's *Exegesis that is the Eye that Sees the Hidden Meaning Stated in the Saṁvara Five Stages* (*bde mchog rim lnga'i bshad pa sbas don lta ba'i mig rnam par 'byed pa*), his commentary on Ghaṇṭapā's *Five Stages of Shrī Chakrasaṁvara* (*Śrīcakrasaṁvarapañcakrama*) (Tōh. 1433).

is applied in the channel of the vajra and lotus, i.e., in the path of the channel.[468] The ritual action is accomplished through the method of cycling the mantra between the two secret places.

While the line ". . . as externally" does not occur in the translations of Lochen, Mal, or in [Mardo's] dual translations, it occurs just as was stated, that "it should be connected to the commentaries of Kambala and Devagupta,"[469] even though it does not occur in the other commentaries.

What is the method of union with the actuality of clear light or union with the magical in enjoyment of the sense object by the sense power? There are two methods of union, (1) relying on the blazing of great bliss when one experiences sense objects with one's inner eye etc. in the same manner that one (2) draws forth great bliss relying on an external seal (consort). Lama Mardo explains that this is for the sake of also succeeding in reliance upon the inner symbolic seal in the same way that one succeeds in reliance upon the external actual seal (consort).

Regarding the **aim of the application**, i.e., yoga, for achieving power, if it is the case that **through this** reliance on the two seals **one will swiftly subdue** via the methods of destroying and benefitting **the gods, titans, and men** (**36.6**), what need is there to mention any others?

3.3.3. 2.2.2. 8.3.3. Showing the name of the chapter

In the *Concise Shrī Herukābhidhāna Tantra*, this is **the thirty-sixth chapter** on **the procedure of reality worship** in reliance on the two seals and **achieving** the ritual actions of pacifying and so forth. This is the explanation of the thirty-sixth chapter in the *Illumination of the Hidden Meaning, A Detailed Exegesis of the Concise Saṁvara Tantra Called "The Chakrasaṁvara."*

468. Tsong Khapa paraphrases Bhavyakīrti's commentary at BC 64b.7–65a.1.

469. Tsong Khapa is quoting a commentary here, and it is almost certainly Mardo's lost commentary, since he refers to it in his explanation below. He is right that this line occurs in the PM translation only as well as Kambala's and Devagupta's commentary. It occurs as follows in Kambala's commentary, "internally in the same manner as externally," *yathā bāhyaṁ tathādhyātmaṁ* (K 67b.1); *ji ltar phyi rol de bzhin nang* (SN 69b.6–7); cf. SS 146a.1–2.

Chapter 37

Chapter 37 Outline

3.3.3. 2.2.2. 8.4. The chapter on subjugating the actual seal (consort)

The fourth part, the chapter on subjugating the actual seal (consort), has three sections: (1) the promise to explain, (2) the promised import explained, and (3) showing the name of the chapter.

3.3.3. 2.2.2. 8.4.1. The promise to explain

Now I will explain aside from (37.1a) that which was previously explained. What is this? As Bhavyakīrti and so forth state it is **the method of overpowering the body** (37.1b), the form or body being the person such as a woman, and the procedure for overpowering that is to control them. It is that which will be explained.[470] It is vanquished, the body of the victim being vanquished with the divine medicine mantra.[471] "Overpowering"

470. See BC 35b.5.

471. Tsong Khapa here quotes a comment in Kambala's commentary, namely *tshar gcod ces bya na ni / sman bzang po dang bcas pa'i sngags kyi tshar gcod pa'o* (SN 70a.1); *visrjya*

means subjugating all women who are deceitful, roguish, and wicked.[472] The adept, together with them, enjoys the five sensual pleasures.

3.3.3. 2.2.2. 8.4.2. The promised import explained

The second part has two sections: (1) the worship of reality, and (2) the procedure for ritual success depending on that.

3.3.3. 2.2.2. 8.3.2. 1. The worship of reality

The first part has three sections: (1) subjugating the victim relying upon food, (2) subjugating the victim relying upon fire sacrifice, and (3) showing praise for the subjugation procedure.

3.3.3. 2.2.2. 8.3.2. 1.1. Subjugating the victim relying upon food"

The [text] **interconnected** and so forth (**37.1c** ff.) is said to be a means of accomplishing the performance of a ritual procedure. The interconnection is external and internal. **The** twenty-four **ḍākinīs** are **the mantras** since they correspond to the mantras.[473] It is explained that **applied to each one of the ḍākinīs** (**37.1d**) means that you assemble, i.e., visualize, both their placement in the outer mandala and their placement in the inner body mandala.[474] Bhavyakīrti etc. [explain that] both root mantras of the partners are united, i.e., brought together. This means that the ḍākinīs are united with the [female] partner's root mantra.[475]

---

divyauṣadhīmantra (K 67b.2). Note that *tshar gcod* is not a very good translation of *visṛjya*, which in this case means "to utter," i.e., utter or recite the mantra.

472. Tsong Khapa here closely paraphrases Kambala's commentary, which reads *gnon pa zhes bya ba ni bud med thams cad mnan pa ste sgyu can dang g.yo can dang gdul dka' ba ma lus pa dang lhan cig tu bsgrub pa'o* (SN 70a.1); *ākranteti ākramya sarvaṇārīṁ śaṭhāṁ dhūrtāṁ duśca[r]itāṁ* (K 67b.3).

473. That is, each of the twenty-four ḍākinīs has a corresponding mantra. Apparently, it is these mantras that are employed here.

474. Tsong Khapa here refers to Kambala's commentary at SN 70a.3.

475. Bhavyakīrti (at BC 35b.6) simply quotes Jayabhadra's comment that "**intertwined mantras** mean that both root mantras are combined" (Sugiki 2001, 136: *ayonyavalitā mantrā ity ubhayor mūlamantrāv ekīkṛtya*).

One should thus recite the two mantras in four daily session for seven days, and **eat** and swallow **food** such as butter, and then **vomit** into a skull bowl **at the conclusion of the** mantra **repetition.** After completing [this process] for **seven nights**, i.e., days, by **applying**, i.e., presenting that food as **food and drink** (37.2) to any victim such as a woman etc., **have no doubt** that this victim **will be under one's power for as long as one lives.** Eating **tawny butter** or **drinking** clarified butter over the previously stated period of days, **it should be vomited at the conclusion of the repetition** (37.3), and **one should anoint one's own face** with that vomitus. If the butter that is anointed is applied to, presented as food or drink, **should one be angered** the victim **shall always be brought under one's control** just **through looking** (37.4) at the object of the practice.

Regarding another [rite] that is especially similar to the first, blend the filth of one's body with red **sesame oil** and red **rice flour**, and **smear** one's body with it. **The mantrin should make a pastry** from a lump of rice [flour dough] cooked in oil. If it is **used**, i.e., given, **as food** (37.5), **that victim will always be in one's power for as long as one lives, so long as one does not relinquish** this **ritual** application (**37.6ab**).

Regarding **black sesame seeds along with black mustard seeds,** it is **eaten and regurgitated** (**37.6cd**) with black mustard seeds. **Pulverize** this **together with kuṣhṭha root discharged from the anus** seven times, "that which grows on the hand (*karaja*, *lag skyes*)" i.e., fingernails, **intestinal worms** that emerge from the anus, and with **one's own blood**, and **mix** this with *sva*, i.e., one's own, *śukra*, i.e., semen (37.7) **Should it be used as an unguent with food, drink, eye ointment, or clothing, have no doubt that** he or she **will be in one's power for as long as one lives** (37.8) through this application. This should also be done after [mantra] repetition as previously explained.

3.3.3. 2.2.2. 8.4.2. 2. Subjugating the victim relying upon fire sacrifice

On a hearth for the various rites of subjugation or for all rites **beef is anointed with blood.** If one calls out the name[s] of the victim over seven days and make each time one hundred **oblations** in four sessions, **from that moment on the deities** who are the victims **comes under one's power.** The word **or** [indicates] that **should** the victim **not come** before one, **it will die** (37.9).

Create Heruka together with his retinue amidst the hearth, and **imagining** oneself as Heruka positioned **before him**, for the ritual application **the sage, having offered the sacrificial cake** with beef and blood **at the end** of the previously described **sacrifice, will, after seven nights**, i.e., days, **achieve the summoning in an instant of the triple world** (37.10).

Kambala explains that one should visualize in the hearth of the navel within the lotus the deity, who is the size of the thumb or a grain of barley, with a red body color, one face, and two arms, positioned on a solar disk, and manifesting as a vision of light. If you summon the victim with breath and burn him or her in the fire of the navel, the victim will be subjugated.[476]

3.3.3. 2.2.2. 8.4.2. 3. Showing praise for the subjugation procedure

This subjugation of the actual seal (consort) through **the characteristics of the** yogī's **commitments and conduct, difficult to obtain in the three worlds**, i.e., the subterranean, terrestrial, and celestial, **should always be zealously concealed** from unworthy recipients **with the hidden** practice of **one's own mantra** (37.11).

Even if it is bestowed to **the unfortunate, they will not apprehend the** profound **hidden meaning**, nor will they have faith in it. Even if is **attained** by those of lesser fortune, they will not succeed. This exceptional method will not even **be seen** by those of lesser fortune, just like a precious jewel placed in the hand of a blind person. With respect to those whose fortune is not inferior, the profound meanings hidden in the tantra will **be attained**

476. Tsong Khapa here relates and glosses the following comment of Kambala: "**Beef**, etc., indicates the inner oblation. In the fire pit of the navel, amidst the lotus is the deity, who appears [the size of] the joint of the thumb, with two arms and a red complexion, resting on a solar disk, appearing as a vision of light, and measured as just the length of a grain of barley. [The victim] is summoned by breath and burned through the mental state entering into visualization (*dhyāna*, *bsam gtan*); this is both subjugation and summoning" (K 67b.7–68a.2: *gomāṁseti ādhyātmahomam / nabher agnikhada caiva padmamadhye tu devatam / aṅguṣṭhe parva sādṛṣyaṁ dvibhuja raktavaktraṁ sūryamaṇḍalam avaṣṭabhya jyotirāloka-saṁsthitam / yavamātrapramāṇitam / śvāsākarśamiśritam / tatdhyānagata-cetasā / vaśyā-karṣaṇam eva*; *ba lang sha zhes bya ba la sogs pa ni nang gi sbyin sreg ste/ lte ba'i thab khung nyid du ni / padma yi ni dbus su lha / mthe bo'i tshigs tshad tsam du blta / phyag gnyis sku mdog dmar ba la / nyi ma'i stan la bzhugs pa ni / 'od kyi snang bas legs gnas pas / yang na nas kyi tshad tsom la / dbugs kyis bkug ste bsreg par bya / de yi bsam gtan chud sems gyis / dbang dang dgug pa nyid du 'gyur* (SN 70b.6–7).

by adepts whose previously accrued **merit is trifling**, i.e., who are not superior, **on account of my**, i.e., the guru who is not different from Heruka, **being pleased** (37.12). Since they are attained [these adepts] will succeed.

3.3.3. 2.2.2. 8.4.3. Showing the name of the chapter

In the *Concise Shrī Herukābhidhāna Tantra*, this is **the thirty-seventh chapter** on **the procedure of inner subjugation**—but the principal name is imputed in the manner of Kambala the Blanketed's statement that it is subjugation via inner oblations.[477] This is the explanation of the thirty-seventh chapter in the *Illumination of the Hidden Meaning, A Detailed Exegesis of the Concise Saṁvara Tantra Called "The Chakrasaṁvara."*

477. Kambala doesn't comment on the chapter title itself, although he does state this in his commentary on 37.9, which is quoted above.

Chapter 38

Chapter 38 Outline

3.3.3. 2.2.2. 9. The detailed exegesis the two remaining [modes of] conduct

The ninth part, the detailed exegesis the two remaining [modes of] conduct, has three sections: (1) the promise to explain, (2) the promised import explained, and (3) showing the name of the chapter.

3.3.3. 2.2.2. 9.1. The promise to explain

Next, i.e., after explaining the disclosure of the subjugation of the seal (consort), I will explain that which is concealed, **the attainment** of the placement in the inner and outer bodies **according to** the explanation of what are **the** physical and verbal **signs and the physical characteristics of the** yoga of **the** twenty-four **ḍākinīs** such as Prachaṇḍā, as well as **the physical distinctions** upon which one meditates as **the hero (38.1)** Heruka, and the distinctions of the twenty-four inner sites, and the body color and [number of] faces and hands of the deity hosts placed therein. Another translation has "I will explain according to. . . ."[478]

3.3.3. 2.2.2. 9.2. The promised import explained

The second part has two sections: (1) showing the commitment to protect the performance of conduct etc., and (2) showing conduct performance together with the locations.

3.3.3. 2.2.2. 9.2.1. Showing the commitment to protect the performance of conduct etc.

The first part has two sections: (1) showing the commitments that pertain to what the yogī should not do, and (2) showing the commitments that pertain to what should be done.

3.3.3. 2.2.2. 9.2.1. 1. Showing the commitments that pertain to what the yogī should not do

Regarding the commitment for secrecy, one should write in a thoroughly secret manner, and should **not write** openly regarding the forms of Vārāhī and so forth, as illustrated by the **lord of heroes** (**38.2a**), i.e., Heruka, and that what one has written should be concealed. Thus, the explanatory tantra states:[479]

> If scriptures and divinities' paintings
> Are seen by any unfortunate ones,
> There will be no achievement in this life,
> Nor will there be in the next life's domain.

478. Tsong Khapa refers to the SL translation, which concludes the first verse with the line *de bzhin du ni bshad par bya* (Gray 2012, 462). Tsong Khapa here follows the SM translation, which reads: *de bzhin du ni 'grub 'gyur ba* (Gray 2012, 543). The PM translation has yet another reading, which he doesn't mention, namely *grub par gyur pa de grub 'gyur* (Gray 2012, 365). The extant Sanskrit omits the final *pada*.

479. This verse occurs in the *Kiss Tantra* section 9.3, as follows: *glegs bam dang ni bris sku nyid / gal te skal ba med mthong na / skye ba 'dir ni 'grub mi 'gyur / 'jig rten pha rol spyod yul min* (ST 154a.7).

This is also stated very earnestly in the *Vajra Rosary* explanatory tantra.[480] It will take a great deal of time for those who show the paintings of divinities to unworthy recipients etc. to achieve power. Therefore, one should endeavor to guard against this very imminent [danger].

Three commentaries quote [line 38.2a] as "the lord of heroes does not speak," and comment "the lord does not see those who transgress the commitments."[481] Regarding this tantra **not being recited in front of anyone** (**38.2b**), i.e., those who have not received the consecration and who do not guard the commitments, this path should also not be explained to them. Regarding **the heteropraxy** of this tantra, one should adhere to it with great **secrecy** (**38.2c**). Bhavabhaṭṭa quotes [this line] as "heteropraxy is well-concealed." While it is clear that this relates to both that and the term "adept" (*sgrub pa po*, *sādhaka*), here Bhavabhaṭṭa's commentary is superior.[482]

If one recites madly the mantra of the ḍākinīs or the scripture **that is characterized by secrecy**, then I, Heruka, **do not look upon**, i.e., consider with kindness, **him**, i.e., one who is like that (**38.3**). Later, with respect to the alternate perspective, [the tantra] states: "**I will favor him who protects the tantra—which is the awesome teaching of Shrī Heruka (38.7ab).**" Therefore, it is not just reciting the mantra in a non-secret fashion that is at issue here. It is undertaking any disclosure of a secret to an unworthy recipient without protecting this commitment in general, and without protecting that which should be concealed in particular.

480. This occurs in chapter 9 of the *Vajra Rosary Tantra* (*Śrīvajramālābhidhānamahāyogatantra-sarva-tantrahṛdayarahasyavibhaṅga*, Tōh. 445), fol. 219b.

481. The line quotation and commentary occur in Bhavyakīrti's commentary as follows: *dpa' bo'i dbang phyug mi dgongs zhes bya ba ni dam tshig las 'da' bar byed pa la bcom ldan 'das kyis mi gzigs so zhes bya ba'o don to* (BC 36a.3). This commentary is repeated by Vīravajra (SG 201a.2). The comments originate in Jayabhadra's commentary, the translation for which contains the correct translation for likhati/lipyate. It occurs as follows: *na ca lipyate vīreśvara iti samayācāralaṅghakaṁ na paśyati bhagavān ity arthaḥ* (Sugiki 2001, 136); *dpa' bo'i dbang phyug mi bri'o / zhes bya ba ni dam tshig las 'da' bar byed pa la bcom ldan 'das mi gzigs zhes bya ba'o don to* (CP 65b.1).

482. Tsong Khapa is referring here to two different readings of 38.2c. The Sanskrit mss. read *vāmācāras tu sādhakaḥ*, a reading matched by two of the Tibetan translations (PM, SM: *g.yon pa'i kun spyod sgrub pa pos*; Gray 2012, 195, 365, 543). Bhavabhaṭṭa quotes an alternate reading, *vāmācārasugopitaṁ*, *g.yon pa'i kun spyod sgrub legs sbas pa* (Pandey 2002, 538, 743). This reading is also found in the SL translation (Gray 2012, 462).

It is not just that one is not considered with kindness. **This bad natured one** who lacks any observance of the commitments **will be eaten by many thousands of ḍākinīs. Have no doubt that** he is **a commitment killer**, i.e., destroyer, is one who engages in evil actions prohibited by Vajradhara, who has accumulated sins such as being **the slayer of a brahmin** (38.4), i.e., buddha. **This** self-**deceived bad natured one** who is **a fool** with respect to the karmic consequences of **wicked** and transgressive **conduct—I**, Heruka, **will not rescue him when he is being devoured by the** malicious **yoginīs** (38.5). The *Secret Moon Drop* states:[483]

> Those who aspire to mantric achievement
> Should endeavor to guard the commitments.
> The mantric adept who does otherwise
> Will not succeed in mantra and so forth.
> If one prays for the commitments' [renewal],
> Even the gods will not assent to this.
> In this life one will have great misery,
> And in the afterlife, there will be hell.
> This is what is attained by the foolish
> Who transgress the practice of commitments.
> In this way, moreover, disciples who
> Are feebleminded will gain suffering,
> And the goal of mantra will not ripen.
> For the gods' great bliss is never granted
> To disciples who lack the commitments.

Regarding the meaning of "even the gods," in the manner of Jñānabodhi's statement:[484]

483. This passage occurs in chapter 5 of the *Śrīcandraguhyatilaka-nāma-mahātantrarāja*, as follows: *sngags kyi dngos grub don 'dod pas / dam tshig bsrung la brtson par bya / gzhan du byas na sngags mkhan gyi / sngags la sogs pa'i don mi 'grub / lha rnams kyang ni dam tshig gi / gsol yang bzhes su mi gnang ste / 'jig rten 'di ru sdug bsngal che / 'jig rten pha rol dmyal ba'i rnams / dam tshig spyod pa 'das pas so / rmongs pa'i bdag nyid des 'thob bo / slob ma de yang de bzhin du / blo zhan sdug bsngal 'thob 'gyur te / des na sngags kyi don mi smin / lha rnams kyi ni mchog tu bde / dam tshig med pa'i slob ma la / nam yang sbyin par mi 'gyur ro/* (280b.3–5).

484. This quotation occurs in Jñānabodhi's *Summary on Commitments for Beginners*

They will not accept offerings
Of incense, flowers, and so forth.

If one has transgressed the commitments, even if one offers worship to the buddhas and bodhisattvas it will not be accepted. It is extremely important that the mantrin understands these statements and endeavors to protect the commitments.

Amidst the secret ones, i.e., the practitioners of secret mantra, **that adept** who has not protected the commitments is like **cattle**, i.e., is extremely stupid. He who scorns and **harms the guru and the commitments** is one **who has fallen from the world** of disciples who are embraced by the compassion of **the buddhas** (**38.6**), meaning that they have departed from within that [realm].

3.3.3. 2.2.2. 9.2.1. 2. Showing the commitments that pertain to what should be done

The *Tantra of Shrī Heruka* is difficult to see,[485] i.e., if it is seen by those who do not understand reality. The yogī **who** well **protects**, i.e., guards, the commitments of generating fear will be one whose **attractive face**, i.e., mouth, is well regarded by the heroes **with the company of the ḍākinīs**, i.e., heroines. It seems that one should take *mukhā* in terms of the latter of its two [meanings], face and mouth.[486] **I**, Heruka, **favor him** (**38.7**) who protects the commitments.

The ḍākinīs always delight in the adept who **honors the guru** with devotion and **who treats** the secret place **sincerely**. All **accomplishments will arise for**, i.e., be granted to, **him** (**38.8**). Lochen translated [lines 38.8bc]

(*Prathamakarmasamayasūtrasaṁgraha*; Tōh. 3726) as follows: *spos dang me tog la sogs pa / phul yang bzhes par mi 'gyur te* (D fol. 52a.5–6).

485. This text in Sanskrit reads *tantraṁ śrīherukaghoradarśanaṁ*, which I translate as "the tantra that is the awesome teaching of Shrī Heruka." The canonical Tibetan translation, however, reads *he ru ka dpal lta dka' i rgyud*, "the tantra of Shrī Heruka that is difficult to see." Tsong Khapa, naturally, comments here on the Tibetan translation.

486. The Sanskrit term *mukha* can mean face or mouth. However, here the Sanskrit does not read *mukha*, but rather its synonym *ānana*, in the compound *śubhānanaṁ*, translated into Tibetan as *dge gdong*.

as "the ḍākinīs always delight in the adept who protects the secret."[487] Regarding these accomplishments, **the adept becomes the hero**, i.e., Heruka himself, **the commander flying through the triple world** and the sky. **The adept** who succeeds correctly having **desired** to attain the state of **being a hero becomes worthy of worship everywhere** (38.9).

That one who protects the commitments delights in engaging in **the yoga** of inseparable art and wisdom, and **he knows the** genuine **lineage tradition**[488] having been granted it by the guru. On the other hand, it seems to have been quoted as "knows the thoroughfare," and Koṅkana-pāda and so forth state that it means experiencing all of the bliss that one can pursue, i.e., enjoy, in the triple world.[489]

If one's **master and the** divine form of the **hero**, Heruka, are **seen** by **the adept who upholds Shrī Heruka's observances** (38.10), i.e., who protects that textual tradition, one **should utter with rapture those mantras** that occur below. Regarding the way of being enraptured, one is delighted through the condition of just seeing, that is, by **seeing** the master and **seeing** the divine form. Regarding what mantra is recited, one **should utter seven times the** eight-line [mantra], the **supreme** portion of **the hero** Heruka's **root mantra**. Mardo states that[490] "if you lack the time to do this, you will succeed even with one [recitation]." One **recites the supreme** eight-line

487. This translation, *gsang ba srung ba'i sgrub po la*, is closer to the extant Sanskrit, *gūhayanti ca sādhakaḥ*, "adepts keep secret," than the canonical translation, *gsong por byed pa'i sgrub pa po*.

488. This translation follows the Tibetan translation, *yang dag sbyin pa'ang rig par 'gyur*, which Tsong Khapa follows here. The Sanskrit reads *saṁpradāyaṁ ca vindati*. The verb was evidently read (incorrectly or creatively) as deriving from the verb *vid* "to know" rather than than "find, obtain, acquire, possess," which is the actual meaning of the form *vindati*.

489. Tsong Khapa here quotes an alternate version of this text and commentary that he attributes to Koṅkana Jayabhadra. He relates this as follows: *yang dag 'gro ba rig par 'gyur / zhes 'don pa ltar na khams gsum na 'gro ba ste spyod pa'i bde ba kun nyams su myong bar 'gyur ro / kong ka na pa sogs bzhed do*. The source of this comment is Jayabhadra, who wrote "**has the lineage tradition** means that one experiences that bliss that exists in the triple world" (Sugiki 2001, 136: *saṁpradāyaṁ ca vindatīti trailokye yat sukhaṁ tad anubhavitīty arthaḥ*). However, the translation of this commentary correctly translates *saṁpradāyaṁ* as *yang dag sbyin* rather than *yang dag 'gro* (CP 65b.1–2: *yang dag rab sbyin ba rig par 'gyur / zhes bya ba ni khams gsum gyi bde ba gang yin pa de myong bar 'gyur ro zhes bya ba'i don to*). The source for this quote is Bhavyakīrti's commentary, which contains the incorrect translation of *saṁpradāyaṁ* (BC 36a.3–4: *yang dag 'gro ba'ang rig par 'gyur / zhes bya ba ni khams gsum gyi bde ba gang yin pa de myong bar 'gyur ro zhes koṅka na'i zhal snga nas bzhed do*).

490. Here Tsong Khapa is evidently quoting Mardo's lost commentary on this text.

mantra, distinguished by the utterance of **the syllable *hūṁ*** at the end **and so forth**, i.e., two *hūṁ* and *phaṭ*, and ***oṁ*** (**38.11**) at the beginning.

Then, **bowing down with zeal, all the buddhas**, and, by **and so forth**, the bodhisattvas, **are worshipped. Have no doubt that** by acting in this manner, that one will **sport with the great hero** (**38.12**), i.e., Heruka. Furthermore, **in the heart of that** adept is **Vajravārāhī. Residing with me**, Heruka, **the** twenty-four **heroes, the** twenty-four **yoginīs** and twelve heroines, he is empowered. The adept, **by seeing** him or herself and whichever sentient being simultaneously as **living beings who are** well-born, i.e., course in bliss, accumulates a vast amount of **merit** (**38.13**).

3.3.3. 2.2.2. 9.2.2. Showing conduct performance together with the locations

The yogī endowed with the commitments in this manner who desires to undertake the conduct and worship should undertake the conduct and worship in those sorts of places, namely **everywhere, on the banks of rivers, the ocean, and ponds, on mountains, and likewise at crossroads** and on the banks of **waterholes**, pools, **and wells, and in empty houses and in** town **alleys**. If this is done, **the ḍākinīs** (**38.14**) **stay to look passionately** (**38.15a**), i.e., with desire, that is, they look at him with affection.

The great hero, that is, the adept, **plays at ease**, i.e., fearlessly, **in the company of those** (**38.16bc**) who abide **in the** dreadful **charnel ground of great terror**, namely the yoginīs who **range in space and likewise in the underworld**, and, illustrated by those two, the yoginīs who range on earth, **and also many zombies** (**38.15**) **with dreadful forms and great mighty ones** (**38.16a**).

In secret places, that is, isolated places, such as **in a hollow** or **a cave, in these** previously explained **regions**, i.e, **places, the** distinctive **yoginīs and the men** who are adept in **mystery**, i.e., one's practice companions, **sport with the adept upon the earth** (**38.17**).

With respect to the uncontrived [conduct], it is said that: "by reducing the contrivances of activity in the contrived conduct there is the uncontrived."[491] With regard to that it is explained in the *Lamp That Integrates the*

491. I have not been able to locate the source of this quotation. Tsong Khapa, however, is addressing here Sumatikīrti's claim that this chapter illustrates the uncontrived and extremely uncontrived conduct. Butön also addresses this issue, and points to chapter 21 of the *Origin of Saṁvara* and chapters 3 and 5 of the fifth section of the *Kiss Tantra* for more discussion of these topics. See NS 228a.4–5.

Practices that there are the three, extensive, condensed, and middling [modes of] the uncontrived, of engaging in the conduct of gathering and practicing with the yogīs and yoginīs who are equal in number to the mandala deities, or with four or five yoginīs who are actual seal (consorts), or assembling one, as well as the extremely uncontrived conduct that is undertaking the conduct of Bhusuku, relying upon a gnostic or symbolic seal.[492] Regarding the method of undertaking the conduct, it is done as indicated by Kambala the Blanketed with respect to the *[Lamp That] Integrates the Practices*.[493] In this chapter it is largely stated in terms of the powerful yoginīs.

3.3.3. 2.2.2. 9.3. Showing the name of the chapter

In the *Concise* ***Shrī Herukābhidhāna Tantra***, this is **the thirty-eighth chapter** on **the procedure of the place** wherein is the attainment of conduct relying upon the powerful yoginīs **and** the attainment by **heroes**, i.e., the adept, of **the secret** attainment of the path. This is the explanation of the thirty-eighth chapter in the *Illumination of the Hidden Meaning, A Detailed Exegesis of the Concise Saṁvara Tantra Called "The Chakrasaṁvara."*

492. These topics are covered in chapters 10 and 11 of the *Caryāmelāpakapradīpa*, on the topics of the uncontrived and extremely uncontrived modes of conduct. See Wedemeyer 2007, 307–31.

493. Tsong Khapa here refers to references to the *Lamp That Integrates the Practices* that Kambalāmbara makes in his *Commentary on the Realization of Shrī Chakrasaṁvara* (Q 4661).

Chapter 39

Chapter 39 Outline

3.3.3. 2.2.2. 10. Examining the signs of the attainment of power

The tenth part, examining the signs of the attainment of power, has three sections: (1) the chapter on vision and "*ha ha*" laughter, (2) the chapter on subjugating the five classes and serving the great seal, (3) the chapter on the placement of the mandala of twenty-four syllables, and (4) the chapter on the laughter mantra and the cause of the ḍākinīs' forms.

3.3.3. 2.2.2. 10.1. The chapter on vision and "*ha ha*" laughter

The first part has three sections: (1) the promise to explain, (2) the promised import explained, and (3) showing the name of the chapter.

3.3.3. 2.2.2. 10.1.1. The promise to explain

Now, after explaining the play of the play of the yoginī and adept on earth, I will explain the bestowal of **the vision of the eightfold laughter mantra.**

3.3.3. 2.2.2. 10.1.2. The promised import explained

The second part has three sections: (1) the method of giving rise to vision through laughter, (2) showing the consequence of fear when [they] are seen, and (3) showing the benefit of not being afraid when [they] are seen.

3.3.3. 2.2.2. 10.1.2. 1. The method of giving rise to vision through laughter

The adept who is **a great yogī** due to attaining firmness in yoga, at the time of undertaking conduct should go to a charnel ground etc. and regard all things as false and illusory, and one should **laugh**, repeat verbally, **the eightfold** laughter **mantra**, which has eight parts. Regarding the necessity for doing this, having made the eight laughs, **then, on account of this** cause, **have no doubt** that the ḍākinīs **bestow the vision** of their own forms **for** him (**39.1**), i.e., the adept.

Regarding the eightfold laughter, according to many commentaries it consists of portions of the [male] partner's root mantra, namely the following set of eight [groups of syllables]: *kili kili sili sili hili hili dhili dhili.* It is also explained as the eight [syllables] of the [female] partner, namely *ha ha hi hi huḥ u huṁ huṁ.*[494] The previous lamas have explained that it is the six, *ha ha* etc., and the eight, *he he* etc.[495]

3.3.3. 2.2.2. 10.1.2. 2. Showing the consequence of fear when [they] are seen

When seen in this manner, **the ḍākinīs** cry out **the many kinds of awesome sounds**, which are unendurable and terrifying. **If the hero**, i.e., adept, **is frightened** by those cries, he will not attain power since he **flees** hither and thither due to being **scared** (**39.2**), that is, not at ease.

494. Both of these explanations were originally made by Jayabhadra, who wrote: "**should turn to the fourfold laughter** refers to four portions of the hero's root mantra, *kili kili sili sili cili cili dhili dhili*, and *hā hā he he ho ho hūṁ hūṁ* of the Ḍākinī's root mantra" (Sugiki 2001, 136: *hāsyaṁ caturvidhaṁ nyased iti vīramūlamantrasya caturvidham / kili kili sili sili cili cili dhili dhili / ḍākinīmūlamantrasya / hā hā he he ho ho hūṁ hūṁ iti*).

This explanation is repeated by other commentators such as Bhavabhaṭṭa. See Pandey 2002, 542.

495. Previous lamas such as Sachen and Butön explain the mantra as eightfold following the Indian tradition. See, for example, PG 361.3 and NS 228b.4. I have not found any commentators who explain that the mantra is sixfold.

3.3.3. 2.2.2. 10.1.2. 3. Showing the benefit of not being afraid when [they] are seen

If the hero, i.e., adept, **is not frightened** at the sight of them, **then held by the left hand** by them **he will be led by them to their abode and be together with the ḍākinīs** (39.3), **and he will always play** and sport with them. **One will go to state of the Land of Bliss**, that is, the state of accomplishing the power of the great seal, which is great bliss. **Through** great **devotion and** great **desire**, i.e., great zeal, **for Shrī Heruka, one is conducted to the state** of **going to the space** (39.4) for achieving that,[496] namely, the place of practice. **For the adept who has a mantric**, i.e., gnostic, **body, there is no old age, death** and so forth **in cyclic existence** (39.5). In this chapter is a demonstration that examines the signs of power through the indications of fear and fearlessness from the perspective of the eightfold laughter mantra.

3.3.3. 2.2.2. 10.1.3. Showing the name of the chapter

In the ***Concise Shrī Herukābhidhāna Tantra***, this is **the thirty-ninth chapter** on **the procedure of vision** in which the ḍākinīs display their forms **and "*ha ha*" laughter.** This is the explanation of the thirty-ninth chapter in the *Illumination of the Hidden Meaning, A Detailed Exegesis of the Concise Saṁvara Tantra Called "The Chakrasaṁvara."*

496. Tsong Khapa here glosses the Tibetan *mkha' la 'gro ba'i gnas*, which is a translation of the Sanskrit *khecarīpada*.

Chapter 40

Chapter 40 Outline

3.3.3. 2.2.2. 10.2. The chapter on subjugating the five classes and serving the great seal

The second part, subjugating the five classes and serving the great seal, has three sections: (1) the promise to explain, (2) the promised import explained, and (3) showing the name of the chapter.

3.3.3. 2.2.2. 10.2.1. The promise to explain

Since we have arrived the occasion of explaining the fortieth chapter, **now I will explain**. What will be explained? It will explain **abiding by the procedure of** Heruka's **yoga** and **the subjugation of** people who are **mortals** etc. by the appropriate fire sacrifice [undertaken] by **the hero who has repeated** Heruka's yoga and **the** eight-line **mantra** (40.1).

3.3.3. 2.2.2. 10.2.2. The promised import explained

The second part has three sections: (1) outer and inner fire sacrifice, (2) the number relative to each [type of] victim, and (3) the benefit doing so.

3.3.3. 2.2.2. 10.2.2. 1. Outer and inner fire sacrifice

One prepares **a lamp,**[497] that is, flesh, since it illuminates accomplishment. In the Lochen and Mardo solo translations there are "intoxicants" (*smyo byed*), while the dual translation and Mal have [the variant spelling] (*myos byed*). If we explain here in accordance with the latter, it means **with intoxicants**, namely, beer, **together with the flesh of fish. The lord of heroes** together with his retinue, **due to the adept's** (40.2) dedication to the performance of inner and outer fire sacrifices for subjugation in three sessions [per day] over **seven days in all circumstances, grants**, that is, bestows, **the great power** of **subjugating** those who are to be subjugated.

Regarding **night**, in accordance with [the statement] "the yoginī is said to be the night,"[498] one should **perform fire sacrifice** (40.3a) being equipoised with the yoginī. One thus engages in both outer and inner fire sacrifice. One should also perform the inner fire sacrifice of enjoying food and drink.

3.3.3. 2.2.2. 10.2.2. 2. The number relative to each [type of] victim

If one prepares subjugation fire sacrifices **at the three divisions of the day consisting** of, i.e., having, **one hundred and eight fire sacrifices** (40.3b–d) [in each session], **within seven days one will subjugate a king together with his army. With half** of one hundred and eight, i.e., fifty-four, one [subjugates] **a great hero**, i.e., a town chieftain, **and with half of that**—fifty-four, hence twenty-seven—**a minister** (40.4) [is subjugated]. **Through**

497. Tsong Khapa comments on the Tibetan translation *sgron ma*, which usually means "lamp." However, in this case it is an unusual translation of the Sanskrit *piśitam*, which means butchered flesh or dressed meat. The Tibetan translation appears to be an obscure translation based upon the root meaning of *piśita*, deriving from √*piś*, "hew, carve, prepare, make ready," and the meaning of the Tibetan verb *sgron*, "to set, lay out."

498. Tsong Khapa quotes this line *rnal 'byor ma ni mtshan mor brjod* without indicating the source. What appears to be a slightly different translation of the same line, *rnal 'byor ma ni mtshan mor bshad*, is quoted in Vṛddhakāyastha's commentary on the *Kiss Tantra*, the *Very Clear Commentary on the Kiss [Tantra]* (*Suviśada-saṁpuṭaṭīkā*) (Tōh. 1190), fol. 14a.3. This text also quotes the line without indicating the source. It does so in the context of commenting upon a similar line in the *Kiss of the Four Yoginīs Tantra* (*Caturyoginīsaṁpuṭatantra*), namely, "It's said the day's the lord Vajrin, and the night's the wisdom consort" (Tōh. 376, 45b.4: *nyin mo bcom ldan rdo rje can / mtshan mo shes rab tu ni brjod*).

the process of making **fire sacrifice thirty-two** [times], **a vassal lord**, i.e., regional lord etc., is subjugated.

For a brahmin, one should sacrifice twenty [times] in three daily sessions **over seven days** (40.5). **Likewise,** one should do **seven fire sacrifices for kṣhatriyas, five fire sacrifices for a vaishya, three fire sacrifices for a shūdra, and one fire sacrifice for the lowest,**[499] chaṇḍāla and so forth (40.6). Thus [the text reads] **the hero through the stages of the social classes for one month**, but as this does not accord with all of the previous [statements] of seven days, it is as occurs in the Indian text and the commentary, "resorting to a single session."[500] So, the partners resorting to a single session or seat, **the adept equipped with mantra will summon all beings** (40.7) of the five classes, such as brahmins and so forth.

3.3.3. 2.2.2. 10.2.2. 3. The benefit doing so

If **the hero,** i.e., the adept, adheres to the procedure for subjugating whichever victim he **desires** to subjugate, **depending upon** sensuous pleasures such as sights, sounds, and so forth, with **the previous procedure**, that is, with the preliminaries of deity yoga and fire sacrifice, he **will attain** the subjugation. **He will be like a lord of love on earth**, that is, like Maheshvara, and will have **the glory** of merit, and will be born with the **great fortune** of an [attractive] form and so forth. **Have no doubt that the adept will be pleasing to the ḍākinīs** (40.8).

In this chapter are ritual practices for subjugating and so forth when one has reached stability in the perfection stage. Examining whether they are accomplished or not within seven days, it is seems that they are accomplished, this reveals an indication that one will rapidly attain the power of the great seal. The past sages intended that one examine thus once one has reached stability in the creation stage as well.

499. The Sanskrit reads *antyaja*, "outcaste," while the Tibetan reads *tha ma*, "lowest, last," evidently reading *antya*.

500. Tsong Khapa here refers to the text *zla ba gcig tu*. While the Sanskrit for this verse is lost, Bhavabhaṭṭa's commentary, to which Tsong Khapa refers, points to an alternate reading. Bhavabhaṭṭa reads, "**Resorting to a single session** means that one has resorted to Shrī Heruka" (Pandey 2002, 545: *ekam āsanam āśritya iti śrīherukam āśritaḥ*).

The Tibetan translation *zla ba gcig tu* may be a misreading of the Sanskrit *ekam āsanam*.

3.3.3. 2.2.2. 10.2.3. Showing the name of the chapter

In the *Concise* ***Shrī Herukābhidhāna Tantra*****,** this is **the fortieth chapter** on **subjugating the five social classes** such as the kṣhatriya and so forth and the five classes of seals, and, depending on that, cultivating **the great seal.** This is the explanation of the fortieth chapter in the *Illumination of the Hidden Meaning, A Detailed Exegesis of the Concise Saṁvara Tantra Called "The Chakrasaṁvara."*

Chapter 41

Chapter 41 Outline

3.3.3. 2.2.2. 10.3. The chapter on the placement of the mandala of twenty-four syllables

The third part, the chapter on the placement of the mandala of twenty-four syllables, has three sections: (1) the promise to explain, (2) the promised import explained, and (3) showing the name of the chapter.

3.3.3. 2.2.2. 10.3.1. The promise to explain

Now, having explained the fortieth chapter, I will explain **the accomplishment of the excellent, supreme ritual action by** the adept who **knows** (**41.1ab**) the mantric yoga that reveals the accomplishment of all powers for those who reside in the perfection stage. Even though this can also be achieved by those on the creation stage, here it is the perfection stage practitioner who examines the signs of achieving the supreme power. Therefore, in three commentaries it is applied to the perfection stage practitioner.[501] It is said that the mantric attainment that is secret and difficult to obtain should be known by one, that is, that [practitioner], from the explanatory and appendix tantras as well as from the guru's mouth.[502]

3.3.3. 2.2.2. 10.3.2. The promised import explained

The second part has two sections: (1) classifying the ritual actions to be achieved, and (2) showing the cause of their achievement.

3.3.3. 2.2.2. 10.3.2. 1. Classifying the ritual actions to be achieved

Regarding the ritual actions that are to be achieved, there are **twelve great ritual actions** (41.3c). The two, **subjugating** and **summoning**, should be counted as one. There is also **dividing** loved ones. **Killing** and **expelling** should be counted as two. **And so forth** (41.1cd) implies pacifying and enriching; these two should be individually undertaken. There are also the three, mentally **befogging**, **immobilizing**, and **stupefying**, which is rendering someone senseless. The four—**staking**, **stealing** the capacity for **speech**, rendering someone **mute**, and making ears deaf, and eyes **blind** (41.2)—immobilize the sense powers, and should be taken as one. **Causing impotence** and **changing** into various **shapes** amount to twelve in the system of the previous gurus.

It seems that in the system of Bhavyakīrti and so forth that there are twelve by counting subjugating and summoning as one, counting killing and expelling as one, and counting stealing speech and making mute as one.[503] In this context it is explained that one accomplishes the ritual action

501. Vīravajra defines the "adept" as a perfection stage practitioner (PD 432a). Bhavyakīrti explains that this chapter "shows the attainment of all powers of the perfected yogī" (*rdzogs pa'i rnal 'byor pa'i dngos grub thams cad grub par ston pa yin no*, BC 36b.1), which could be interpreted as referring to a perfection stage practitioner. I haven't found a third commentator who addresses this issue.

502. Tsong Khapa here paraphrases Butön's commentary. See NS 230b.1.

503. Bhavyakīrti specifically calls for counting the pair of subjugating and summoning

relying upon a magical diagram (*yantra, 'khrul 'khor*) with the mantra of the four-faced one and so forth. Fearing prolixity, I will not write further about this.

3.3.3. 2.2.2. 10.3.2. 2. Showing the cause of their achievement

The second part has two sections: (1) the concise exposition and (2) the detailed exposition.

3.3.3. 2.2.2. 10.3.2. 2.1. The concise exposition

Regarding **the adept always achieves these twelve great ritual actions (41.3cd), have no doubt that the adept achieves** the desired power **through recollection** (**41.4ab**). This is intended with respect to superior individuals. Success with magical diagrams correlates to middling and inferior [individuals].

3.3.3. 2.2.2. 10.3.2. 2.2. The detailed exposition

The second part has three sections: (1) showing in detail the sites with the ḍākinīs, (2) recognizing the chief among the sites, and (3) showing protection by means of meditation and worship.

3.3.3. 2.2.2. 10.3.2. 2.2.1. Showing in detail the sites with the ḍākinīs

What are these procedures for obtaining power through recollection only? **The seats** of the land of Jambhudvīpa are **the superior**, i.e., best, of **all** lands. **And so forth** implies [the remaining types of sites], from the subsidiary seats to the subsidiary charnel grounds. **The ḍākinīs** of the twenty-four lands **pervade all** of the lands (**41.4cd**).

Who are these ḍākinīs? **They are born in land after land**, such as Pullīramalaya and so forth, and each of **their** immeasurable **places of birth** (*yoni, skye gnas*) is **endowed with the gnosis** of great bliss. It is the ocean of the ultimate spirit of awakening.

---

and the pair of killing and expelling as one, respectively, but he does not mention the final pair, of stealing speech and rendering mute. See BC 36b.2.

Who is born from that? The twenty-four **ḍākinīs** who are shown to be the essence of the twenty-four realms of the adamantine body. They are Prachaṇḍā, and so forth, who taken together are the **mistresses of the mandala** that is **adamantine** (41.5), meaning it has the nature of gnosis of nonduality. In short, the ḍākinīs who bestow the accomplishment of the ritual actions through mere recollection are Prachaṇḍā, and so forth. Regarding their bestowal of the powers of pacifying and so forth through mere recollection, one should know this to be a sign that the supreme power will be quickly attained.

3.3.3. 2.2.2. 10.3.2. 2.2.2. Recognizing the chief among the sites

The second part has three sections: (1) showing the twenty-four sites, (2) the way to engage with the blessings of the yoginīs there, and (3) those who are included with the yoginīs.

3.3.3. 2.2.2. 10.3.2. 2.2.2. 1. Showing the Twenty-Four Sites

Just as I indicated that the order of the twenty-four yoginīs in chapter four was reversed, here too I will show that the twenty-four sites were reversed. [They are:] **Kulutā, Maru,** that is, the land of sorrow,[504] **the land of Sindhu, Nagara, Suvarṇadvīpa, Saurāṣhṭra, Gṛihadevatā** (41.6), **Pretapurī, Himālaya, Kāñchi, the land of Lampāka, Kaliṅga, Koshala, Trishakuni, Oḍra** (41.7), **Kāmarūpa, Mālava, Devīkoṭa, Rāmeshvara, Godāvarī, Arbuda, Oḍḍiyāna, Jālandhara, and Pullīramalaya.** It begins with the body wheel and concludes with the mind wheel. **And so forth** (41.8) implies the final [types of sites], namely villages, subsidiary villages, and so forth, which yields thirty-two sites. These lands that are the residences of the twenty-four mistresses are also the residences of the twenty-four heroes.

504. Tsong Khapa here seems to be referring to a translation of the place name *marudeśa* in Kambala's commentary (K 70a.2) as *mya ngan yul* (SN 72b.1), evidently based on the root meaning of the term *maru*, "desert" or "wasteland."

3.3.3. 2.2.2. 10.3.2. 2.2.2. 2. The way to engage with the blessings of the yoginīs there

All of these **girls of these** twenty-four **sites are yoginīs who are nondual,** equipoised, **with the heroes,** Khaṇḍakapālin and so forth, **have** the ability to transform into many different **forms** just as they **desire.** Why should these twenty-four yoginīs be placed in the mandala? Since one visualizes these twenty-four yoginīs in the outer and body mandalas, they quickly depart **with the power of the mind** (**41.9**), i.e., as if with the power of mind, and bestow blessings upon the adept. By visualizing them, one will swiftly encounter the heroines who reside in the distinctive sites, and in relying upon them one will rapidly and effortlessly progress along the path.

3.3.3. 2.2.2. 10.3.2. 2.2.2. 3. Those who are included with the yoginīs

Regarding Nāropā's oral instructions and the two translators' way of explaining [verse 41.10], from **six yoginīs** up to **mistresses,** the six yoginīs are Lāma, Rūpikā, Sabālikā, Parāvṛittā, Aihikī and Anivartikā.[505] They are included among the yoginīs who reside in the twenty-four sites. How are they included? It is Mahāvīryā who resides in **Kulutā**, the northeast section of the body wheel. **In the land of Maru are the six mothers,** the chief of whom is Chakravartinī, [in the] northwest of the [body] wheel. It is Mahābalā who resides **in the land of Sindhu,** the southwest [of the body wheel]. **The clan mistress in Nagara** (**41.10**) is Suvīrā who resides there, in the southeast [section of the body wheel]. The four females who occupy the ordinal directions of the body wheel are included among those who have the nature of the lāmās.

Residing **in Lampāka** and Suvarṇadvīpa is Chakravarmiṇī, of the south of the [body] wheel, and **the clan goddesses are in Saurāṣhṭra,** the chief of them being Shauṇḍinī to the west, Khaṇḍarohā to the north who resides in **Mahākāla**[506] Gṛihadevatā, and Chakravegā to the east in **Pretapurī.**

505. These are six of a list of seven ḍākinīs listed earlier, at 17.3. The ḍākinī from this list that is excluded here is Chumbikā.

506. Tsong Khapa's text here reads *ka tya che gri ha de ba tar.* The text *gri ha de ba tar* is a translation of Gṛihadevatā. The text *ka tya che,* however, derives from the SM translation of 41.11cd, which reads: *ka tya che pre ta pu ra / mkha' 'gro gzugs can ma ru bcas.*

The text *ka tya che* appears to be a transliteration from the Sanskrit, and surviving

Regarding **ḍākinīs together with Rūpinī** (41.11), those who reside in the body wheel's cardinal directions are included among those who have Rūpinī's self-nature.

Residing **at the Himālaya mountain** is Khagānanā, of the speech wheel's northeast [section]. Residing at **Kāñchi** is Hayakarṇā of [the speech wheel's] northwest [section]. Residing at **Pañchāla**[507] is Subhadrā of [the speech wheel's] southwest [section]. Residing at **Kaliṅga** are **the household goddesses**[508] (41.12) **who uphold the observance** (41.13a), namely Shyāmādevī of [the speech wheel's] southeast [section]. Those of the speech wheel's ordinal directions are subsumed under **Sabālikā**. Mal states that they are subsumed under Parāvṛittā.

The carnivore who dwells **in Koshala** is Surābhakṣhī in the south. **The vajraḍākinī** residing in **Pretapurī** and Oḍra is Mahābhairavā in the north. Airāvatī in the east resides **in Sthūleshvara** and Kāmarūpa, and Vāyuvegā in the west resides in **Trishakuni**. These four who reside in the cardinal directions of the speech wheel and subsumbed under **Khaṇḍarohā** (41.13) and Parāvṛittā.

Prachaṇḍā in the east of the mind wheel resides at **Pullīramalaya. Likewise** [implies] Prabhāvatī in the west who resides in Oḍḍiyāna, Mahānāsā in the south who resides in Arbuda, and Chaṇḍākṣhī in the north who resides in Jālandhara of the gold mountain. These four [goddesses] of the mind wheel's cardinal directions **are born in the chaṇḍāla caste**, that is, are subsumed under Aihikī. **Twenty-one thousand women** (41.14) means that each of the yoginīs of those sites also has a retinue to that extent.

Regarding the **other additional** ones, Drumacchāyā in the northeast resides in Mālava, Laṅkeshvarī in the northwest resides in Devīkoṭa, Kharvarī in the southwest resides in Rāmeshvara, Vīramatī in the southeast resides in Godāvarī. These four [goddesses] of the mind wheel's ordinal directions are subsumed under Anivartikā. **The great churner** is

Sanskrit texts reads *pretapuryāṁ mahākāla ḍākinī saha rūpiṇī*; evidently it is a transliteration of *mahākāla*, perhaps a faulty reading, since the graph *tya* looks quite similar to *la* in many scripts.

507. Tsong Khapa represents this site with the unusual transliteration *pañtsa la li pa ka*. The translations all give the simple transliteration *pañtsa la*.

508. The Sanskrit here reads *gṛhadevatā*, one of the names of the twenty-four sites. The Tibetan translations read it as "household goddess" instead (SM: *khyim lha mo*; PM: *khyim gyi lha mo*; SL: *khyim gyi lha mor*).

Vajravārāhī; **Shrī Heruka** is hers. If **the lady** is Vārāhī, subsumed under her are the four [essence yoginīs,] Ḍākinī, and so forth, and the eight [doorkeepers], Kākāsyā and so forth. Therefore, all thirty-six of the **yoginīs** (**41.15**) are subsumed under Vārāhī. There is no difference between her and the Blessed Lord.

It is explained that **all** three **worlds**, the heavens, earth, and underworld, **are pervaded by these ḍākinīs** and so forth, namely the aerial, terrestrial, and subterranean ones.[509] There are two among the claims made by other scholars mentioned by Bhavyakīrti.[510] Regarding Koṅkanapāda [Jayabhadra]'s claim, **the six yoginīs** are the six heroines of the [female] partner's armor.[511] **The mothers** residing in the land of Maru, who are all of those eight doorkeepers, delude the evil ones. **The lāmās** of the land of Sindhu are the fierce yoginīs who belong to their clan. **Clan mistress** refers to the [four] Ḍākinī [etc.] Regarding **Beauty** (*rūpinī*), they are beauties distinct from Chumbikā and so forth. Regarding **Pañchāla**, the land of "taking the five,"[512] it refers to a particular accomplished site aside from seats and subsidiary seats. **And so forth** simply implies something not stated. At length, there are twenty-one thousand accomplished yoginīs. With the exception of just these [comments] this is similar to Laṅka [Jayabhadra] and Vīravajra's [comments] as well.[513]

509. Tsong Khapa here summarizes Butön's more extensive comments on this text. Butön wrote: "**All worlds, the animate** sentient beings and **the inanimate** aerial, terrestrial, and subterranean habitats, the heavens, earth, and underworld, and the sentient beings by means of their natures—body, speech, and mind—**are pervaded by these twenty-four ḍākinīs**" (NS 244b.7–45a.1: *mkha' 'gro ma nyi shu rtsa bzhi po 'dis rgyu ba sems can dang / mi rgyu ba snod dang bcas pa'i sa 'og sa steng sa bla'i 'jig rten dang / 'gro ba sems can kun ni / 'di'i sku gsung thugs kyi rang bzhin gyis khyab bo*).

510. Bhavyakīrti discusses at length the identities of the yoginīs mentioned in this chapter. See BC 36b–37a.

511. That is, the six goddesses associated with Vajravārāhī's armor mantra, discussed in chapter 8 above.

512. Tsong Khapa here provides an alliterative etymology for the place name Pañchāla.

513. Tsong Khapa here is refers to Bhavyakīrti's summary of Jayabhadra's commentary, at BC 36b.6–37a.2. As noted previously, Tsong Khapa does not realize that the name mentioned by Bhavyakīrti, Koṅkanapāda, refers to Laṅka Jayabhadra. This text occurs in Jayabhadra's commentary as follows: "**The six yoginīs** are Vajravārāhī and so forth ending with Chaṇḍikā. **The mothers** are Kākāsyā and so forth. **The lāmās** are the fierce yoginīs who belong to the lāmā [clan]. **Clan mistress** refers to the four ḍākinīs. **Mahākāla** refers to Mahābhairava, and **with the ḍākinīs** is instrumental in the sense of accompaniment.

Lochen translates [two lines as] "In the **Mahākatya* and Pretapurī (*yi dwags yul*) is Mahākālā (*nag mo che*)," and, with respect to [an alternate translation of] Pretapurī (*yi dwags grong*), is "the cannibals are in Pretapurī (*yi dwags grong*)."[514] As for mentioning the claim of Shrī Oḍḍiyāna-pāda,[515] fearing prolixity I will not write further.

The ladies of the mandala are **the twenty-four ḍākinīs. These** twenty-four **pervade**, i.e., move through, **everything,** namely **the animate**, i.e., **all beings**, and **inanimate triple world** (**41.16a–c**) habitat.

3.3.3. 2.2.2. 10.3.2. 2.2.3. Showing protection by means of meditation and worship

This commitment of the ḍākinīs, which should not be transgressed, is the ḍākinīs' **meditation** with respect to outer and inner bodies **emanated** (**41.16de**) via concentration. **Any** ritual action **whatsoever**, pacification and so forth, **is brought to completion, i.e., accomplished, on the surface of the earth** through repetition and so forth by means of **the meditative states and so forth** of the two stages. The adept should undertake secret conduct being **equipoised** in concentration and sky-clad or **naked at night** (**41.17**). If the thus qualified person **worships** the **self-emergent one with offerings of gesture and dance**, which is the art of **pleasing the heroes** and any woman, **left wise,** as **all yoginīs,** this is the method by which **everything**

With whom are they accompanied? It is the beauties (*rūpiṇayaḥ*). The term *rūpiṇī* refers to other beauties, meaning that they should be considered as being accompanied by beauties who exist separately from the beauties Chumbikā, Sabālikā, and so forth. **Pañchāla** is an accomplished place aside from the seats, subsidiary seats, and so forth. **And so forth** implies others than are unstated. At length, there are twenty-one thousand accomplished yoginīs who wander everywhere in diverse forms" (Sugiki 2001, 137: *ṣaḍ yoginyo vajravārāhādicaṇḍikāntāḥ / mātaraḥ kākāsyādyāḥ / lāmās tv iti lāmājātīyā ugrayoginyaḥ / kulanāyikā ḍākinyaś catasraḥ / mahākālo mahābhairavaḥ / ḍākinībhir iti sahārthe tṛtīyā / kiṁbhūtābhiḥ saha, rūpiṇyaḥ / rūpiṇīty anyā rūpiṇyaś cumbikāsa[b]ālikāpra-bhṛtayaḥ pṛthagbhūtāḥ saha rūpiṇībhir iti draṣṭavyāḥ / pañcāla iti*).

514. As noted above, Rinchen Zangpo has the unusual partial translation/transcription *ka tya che* where the extant Sanskrit reads *mahākāla*. Tsong Khapa appears to be commenting here on two alternate translations for Pretapurī found in this text. The second line, *yi dwags grong du sha chen za*, is unattested elsewhere.

515. Tsong Khapa refers here to Kambala, who reputedly hailed from Oḍḍiyāna.

is achieved without exception, i.e., all powers. Once should engage in **the worship of** the wisdom consort who is of **the left** (**41.18**).

3.3.3. 2.2.2. 10.3.3. Showing the name of the chapter

In the *Concise* ***Shrī Herukābhidhāna Tantra***, this is **the forty-first chapter** on **the procedure of laying down the** heroes' **mandala** in the twenty-four sites that are illustrated by **the twenty-four syllables**, such as *pu*, *ja*, and so forth. This is the explanation of the forty-first chapter in the *Illumination of the Hidden Meaning, A Detailed Exegesis of the Concise Saṁvara Tantra Called "The Chakrasaṁvara."*

Chapter 42

Chapter 42 Outline

3.3.3. 2.2.2. 10.4. The chapter on the laughter mantra and the cause of the ḍākinīs' forms
3.3.3. 2.2.2. 10.4.1. The promise to explain
3.3.3. 2.2.2. 10.4.2. The actual explanation
3.3.3. 2.2.2. 10.4.2. 1. The first exegetical method
3.3.3. 2.2.2. 10.4.2. 1.1. The method of laughter
3.3.3. 2.2.2. 10.4.2. 1.2. The signs of laughter together with the remainder
3.3.3. 2.2.2. 10.4.2. 2. The second exegetical method
3.3.3. 2.2.2. 10.4.3. Showing the name of the chapter

3.3.3. 2.2.2. 10.4. The chapter on the laughter mantra and the cause of the ḍākinīs' forms

The fourth part, the chapter on the laughter mantra and the cause of the ḍākinīs' forms, has three sections: (1) the promise to explain, (2) the actual explanation, and (3) showing the name of the chapter.

3.3.3. 2.2.2. 10.4.1. The promise to explain

"**Then,** having explained the forty-first chapter, I will explain the forty-second chapter"—this is implied by the force of the word "then."[516]

516. In other words, this chapter really has no introduction, aside from the single word "then," *tataḥ, de nas*; Tsong Khapa proposes the hypothetical introduction that it implies.

3.3.3. 2.2.2. 10.4.2. The actual explanation

The second part has two sections: (1) the first exegetical method and (2) the second exegetical method.

3.3.3. 2.2.2. 10.4.2. 1. The first exegetical method

The first part has two sections: (1) the method of laughter and (2) the signs of laughter together with the remainder.

3.3.3. 2.2.2. 10.4.2. 1.1. The method of laughter

Regarding clarifying here the disclosure of the eightfold laughter in chapter thirty-nine, **the hero**, i.e., adept, having found a girl with beautiful eyes,[517] and **having drunk** with his vajra **the flower water** that naturally arises through union with her, **should recollect** laughter with **this mantra**, *ha ha* and so forth, and smile. **The adept**, being equipoised **with the seal (consort)**, should always laugh in this manner with the eightfold mantra. Furthermore, **at night he should eat meat** (**42.1**) together with wine. [The line] **thrice [enchanted] with this mantra** is quoted in Kambala's commentary; should one, equipoised, repeat three times the mantra "Oṁ Impassioned with All Vajras, purify all comestibles, Having the Secret Vajra Svāhā" (*oṁ sarvavajrakāmini sarvabhakṣaṁ śodhaya guhyavajriṇi svāhā*),[518] one will rapidly attain the power of great bliss.

The drinking by oneself of the spirit of awakening that streams in this manner, abiding in the lotus, and making an **offering** (**42.2**) to that seal (consort), one should **touch**, i.e., join the vajra to, that great place of the supreme lotus, with the intention that one attain power, and one should **laugh**, chanting the eightfold mantra.

Regarding **the great lady** and the "mantra of alcoholic intoxication,"[519]

517. This expression, "girl with beautiful eyes," *bu mo mig bzang ma*, is often used in reference to nonhuman *yakṣhī* girls.

518. This mantra occurs in Kambala's commentary as *oṁ sarvavajrakāmini sarvabhakṣaṁ śodhaya guhyaṁ vajriṇi svāhā* (K 70b.1). It occurs as follows in Tsong Khapa's commentary: *oṁ sarvavajrakāmini sarvabhakṣa śodhaya guhyavajrini svāhā*.

519. This, apparently, is a mantra related by Bhavabhaṭṭa, "Oṁ May Bliss be Produced

the translation "great clanswoman" (*mahākulī, rigs ldan chen mo*),[520] who possesses the mantra and is intoxicated with vital essence (*bcud*), is excellent. This means that one's seal (consort), who is taken to be a great clanswoman, is intoxicated by the vital essence that is the descent of the spirit of awakening. Why is this? It is because all tathāgatas are assembled in the adept's body mandala, and likewise, all goddesses likewise are assembled in the body mandala of one's seal (consort) whom one visualizes as Sparshavajrī. One should worship that very consort (*phya rgya mo*).

What is Sparshavajrī like? [This is indicated] in the line **truthful and chaste . . . at the beginning and end** and **assembled with glances, laughter, and signs.** Therefore, the seal who glances with the eye is an actual seal. She is **haughty**, i.e., endowed with majesty, and **renowned** for **glancing** (**42.3**) at the adept with her left eye. Relying upon her who is renowned for conferring great bliss to the adept, one will achieve great gnosis through the gateway of the eightfold laughter with this. Should one **at night or** likewise **during the day** meditate **making laughter with this** union with the seal, i.e., inserting one's mind into that, indications or signs of the attainment of the supreme great seal will arise.

3.3.3. 2.2.2. 10.4.2. 1.2. The signs of laughter together with the remainder

In what way do the signs that are **the essence of form and action** that direct one toward the supreme power exist? The command is **listen, hero.** (**42.4**), that is, Vajrapāṇi. This pill was stated by the hero himself in chapter twelve; [in that context] the hero is Heruka. Here **hero** and **listen** were stated to Vajrapāṇi, as Kambala explains.[521] Regarding the signs that are **the essence of form and action**, Kambala explains that they are the eight superhuman powers.[522] The superhuman powers, in the *Lamp That Integrates the*

Hūṁ" (*oṁ astu sukhāvahaṁ hūṁ*). He also quotes a variant, "Oṁ Bliss Production Hūṁ" (*oṁ sukhāvahaṁ hūṁ*; Pandey 2002, 551).

520. The extant Sanskrit sources here attest two variants, *mahākālī* and *mahākulī*. The latter reading is attested in Bhavabhaṭṭa's commentary (Pandey 2002, 551), and it is what Tsong Khapa refers to here. The Tibetan translations all read "great lady" (*gtso mo che*), which does not correspond to any of the Sanskrit readings.

521. Kambala wrote, "The Blessed Lord said, 'Listen, Vajrapāṇi!'" (K 70b.4–5: *śṛṇu vajrapāṇe ity āha bhagavān*; SN 73a.2).

522. What Kambala actually states is that "This in that [context] is the secret sign of the

Practices, are: "Subtle form, light touch, omnipresence, attaining [things], as well as illumination, firmness, mastery [over self and others], and terminating desire."[523]

Regarding the meaning of that, since it seems the previous Tibetan [masters] do not appear to have explained the eight superhuman powers,[524] one should apply the explanation of Avalokitavrata.[525] With respect to that, one is masterfully "subtle" in the creation and destruction of sentient beings, and "light" in the creation and destruction of wealth. One attains mastery in the creation and destruction of both [beings and things]. This means that the yogī has the ability to both emanate and recollect them. As for the latter [powers, this is also] illustrated by "attaining [things]" (*saṁprāpti*, *yang dag thob*). Worship with all things is shown by the "illumination" or radiance that overcomes others with brilliance. "Mastery" is having the power to harm or benefit sentient beings. Mastering desire with respect to virtue is what is meant by having "desire." Being able to attain whatever one desires to obtain is abiding in one's desire, and that is shown by "firmness." Showing many different forms to others is "form," and that and "omnipresence" and "mastery" are the secret of form.

As the *Lamp That Integrates [the Practices]* states, "the threefold prac-

---

hero oriented toward power" (K 70b.5: *siddhyabhimukhavīrasya tatredaṁ guhyanimittaṁ*; SN 73a.2: *dngos grub mngon du phyogs pa'i dpa' bo'i gsang ba'i mtshan ma ni 'di dag ste*). It is Tsong Khapa who equates this with the eight superhuman powers, the *aṣṭaguṇaiśvarya*.

523. Tsong Khapa here is most likely quoting Kambala who quotes this verse (K 70b.5: *sūkṣmarūpa[ṁ] laghusparśaṁ vyāptisaṁprāptim eva / prakāśaṁ caiva sthairyavaśitvaṁ kāmāvasānikam iti*; SN 73a.2–3: *gzugs phra ba dang reg pa spang ba dang / rab tu snang ban yid brtan pa dang dbang du gyur pa dang 'dod dgur gyur pa zhes bya'o*). However, as Tsong Khapa knew, this verse also occurs in the *Caryāmelāpakapradīpa*. See Wedemeyer 2007, 493. This apparently is a list of the *aṣṭaguṇaiśvarya*, which is also mentioned in the latter text, but not enumerated, at the beginning of chapter 9 (Wedemeyer 2007, 277). Wedemeyer translates the verse as a list of seven rather than eight items (2007, 326), but according to Tsong Khapa it is evidently a list of the *aṣṭaguṇaiśvarya*.

524. Tsong Khapa is correct that the previous masters do not appear to have commented on this. Butön quotes Kambala's commentary but does not explain this list in terms of the eight superhuman powers (NS 248a.4–5). Sachen has an entirely different explanation of this passage of the root text, commenting on the "five secrets of form" and the "five secrets of action." See PG 365.2.4–5.

525. *Avalokitavrata, or *spyan ras gzigs brtul zhugs*, is the author of one work preserved in the Tengyur, the *Commentary on the Lamp of Wisdom* (*shes rab sgron ma rgya cher 'grel pa*, or the *Prajñāpradīpaṭīkā*; Tōh. 3859).

tice will give to the signs of attaining the power of the great seal for those who train in it for a fortnight, month, or six months, and these are the signs."[526] This means that there will be signs for the supreme power within six months. When one has attained these eight superhuman powers, one will not be afflicted by hunger or thirst, and defecation and urination will cease.

Observing without distinction all of these [signs] and dreams, **tears** always **arise** from that yogī's two eyes. Here there is no refuge from cyclic existence for those who cannot endure suffering, and who do not think even for a moment on "Alas, all of these sentient beings," and on the ultimate method of liberation from cyclic existence. One gives rise to fierce compassion for those who shake and tremble due to fear of birth, old age, sickness, and death.

Through the arising, that is, trickling, of blissful ambrosia depending upon the lotus of the wisdom (consort), **her body hair** simultaneously **stands on end due to devotion.** By thinking "Since it is difficult to destroy, I should **pass over,** i.e, transcend, the cyclic existence of the triple world[527] which is like a **vajra,**" one acts like a man with the wisdom (consort). It occurs as "should pass over" in Kambala's commentary, and it is explained thus in what appears to be a good translation in Devagupta's commentary.[528]

The wisdom (consort) being **thus naked,** one sits, gazing upon her breasts, armpits, calves, and lotus, and rubbing them with one's hands, one should **worship** (**42.5**) through the method of union. One should experience in this manner **the sequence** of the blissful savors **of** all **hosts** of sense powers

526. This passage in the *Caryāmelāpakapradīpa* occurs immediately before the list of eight signs quoted and discussed above. See Wedemeyer 2007, 493, 652.

527. Tsong Khapa here follows the Tibetan translation of Kambala's commentary, which reads "three realms," *khams gsum* (SN 73a.6). The Sanskrit, however, reads "triple world," *trailokya* (K 71a.1).

528. Tsong Khapa here reports *'gom par bya*, which is a good translation of the Sanskrit preserved in Kambala's commentary, namely *laṅghanaṁ kuryāt* (K 71a.1) However, the canonical translation of this commentary reads "not passing over," *'gom mi byed* (SN 73a.5). The canonical translation of Devagupta's commentary has the faulty translation "should visualize," *bsgom par bya* (SS 150a.3). Since Tsong Khapa quotes a good translation and seem to attribute it to the latter text, I presume that he was working either from an alternate translation, or perhaps a better, less corrupt version of what became the canonical translation.

of all **seal** (consorts) who are **the passionate ladies. Exhalation** means as Kambala stated, namely "moving via the winds of the wisdom [consort]."[529]

The wind of the messenger's central channel is inserted into the gate of the "art" (male consort)'s central channel, and thereby becomes a causal factor; this is a very profound essential point for the descent of the spirit of awakening. For great understanding it is essential to know about this in detail depending upon the *Vajraḍāka* explanatory tantra.

Regarding **exhortation**, it is physical trembling due to the descent of the spirit of awakening. **Laughter** is the wisdom (consort) overcome with the body of laughter.[530] **Erotic dance**[531] is engaging the wisdom (consort) by means of dance steps. **Marvelous** (**42.6**) is doing what is miraculous for ordinary individuals. This means that having done thus, one should exult in this manner **before the entirety of those who are**, i.e., before all of, the yoginīs. Moreover, one should exult **recollecting the laughter mantra** with **the seal** (consort). **The eightfold laughter** mantra is ***ha hā he hai ho hau*** ***haṁ haḥ***; one should exult with these eight syllables. These explanations occur in Kambala's commentary and are clarified and supplemented in Devagupta's commentary.[532]

3.3.3. 2.2.2. 10.4.2. 2. The second exegetical method

Bhavyakīrti and so forth[533] [explain] **flower water** as previously [indicated], that **the mantra** (**42.1**) is the root mantra or the seven-syllable [quintessence mantra], **offering thus** (**42.2**) is offering to those who abide in the three wheels, and state **great black one** (*mahākālī*) in place of "great lady." The meaning of this is stated to be Vajravārāhī, and that one should visual-

529. Kambala's commentary here occurs as follows: *recakair iti carat prajñāvāyubhiḥ* (K 71a.2); *dbugs 'byin zhes bya ba ni shes rab kyi rlung rnams kyis dbab pa'o* (SN 73a.7).

530. Tsong Khapa here is expanding slightly one of Kambala's cryptic comments. It is "**With laughter** (pl.) means with bodies overcome by laughter" (K 71a.2: *hāsyair iti hāsyamūrtikrāntaiḥ*; SN 73a.7: *dgod dang zhes bya ba ni dgod pa'i lus mnan pa'o*).

531. This is a translation of the Tibetan *sgeg gar*, which in turn is a translation of the Sanskit *tāṇḍava*, which I earlier translated as "ecstatic frenzy" (Gray 2007, 341). It evidently was a form of dance with wild and erotic characteristics.

532. Tsong Khapa does indeed rely on these commentaries, as noted above.

533. Here Tsong Khapa paraphrases Bhavyakīrti's commentary (BC 38b), which in turn closely follows here Jayabhadra's commentary. See Sugiki 2001, 138, and CP 66b.

ize the actual seal (consort) as her. **Beginning** and so forth means that the seal (consort) comes under one's control from the beginning to the end.

Since **laughter** is the seal (consort), one causes satisfaction through laughter and play, primarily, on account of being sealed by her display of a **haughty glance.**[534] She is **renowned** (42.3) as a goddess who has haughty laughter. **Laughter** is just a synecdoche that is connected to the whole which is the bliss of great sexual pleasure, which **should be produced at night or during the day.**[535]

Regarding **of form and action** (42.4) and so forth, this shows the unprecedented form and actions of the goddesses who are achieved by a glance of the adept. There is always the display of the action and reaction, namely, the dance and so forth, which is the action of the goddess.[536] **With the vajra** (42.5) and so forth is the adept's action.[537] **Exhortation** and so forth is exhaling without movement of wind. **Erotic** (42.6) refers to a type

534. This is a close paraphrase of Jayabhadra's comment, namely: *hāsa eva mudrā / līlapradhānahāsena saṁtoṣakarī tayā mudraṇāt / dṛṣṭaḥ saṁdarśito garva ātmā yayā sā dṛṣṭagarvā* (Sugiki 2001, 138); *bzhad pa nyid phyag rgya yin pas na rol cing dgod pa gtso bor gyur pas dga' bar byed pa ste / phyag rgya des so / lta ba'i snyems pa yang dag par ston cing snyems pas mthong pas mthong ba ni snyems pa'o* (CP 66b.3).

535. Cf. Jayabhadra's commentary: *hāsyam ity upalakṣanaparam / sarvaṁ eva mahāsuratasukhaṁ rātrāv ahani vā kuryād iti saṁbandhaḥ* (Sugiki 2001, 138); *bzhad pa ni nye bar mtshon pa tsam ste / rab tu dga' ba'i bde ba thams cad kyang mtshan mo'am nyin mo bya'o zhes bya bar sbyar ro /* (CP 66b.4).

536. Tsong Khapa's commentary here reads *rtag tu zhes sogs te*, which appears to be based on the canonical translation of Bhavyakīrti's commentary, which here is faulty. It reads: *de'i las dang las kyi lan bstan pa ni rtag tu zhes bya ba la sogs pa yin te / lha mo'i bya ba ni . . .* (BC 38b.5). This text is a quotation from Jayabhadra's commentary, which here reads, "One displays her actions and reactions, namely, her dance and so forth; this is the action of the goddess" (Sugiki 2001, 138: *tatkarma pratikarma ca darśayati / nṛtyetyādi devatīkriyā*). The translator of Bhavyakīrti's commentary confused *nṛtya* with *nityaṁ*, and also incorrectly assessed sentence boundaries. It is correctly translated in the canonical translation of Jayabhadra's commentary, as follows: *de'i las dang las kyi lan bstan pa ni gar dang zhes bya ba la sogs pa yin te lha mo'i bya ba'o /* (CP 66b.5). Here I am following the more accurate reading in Jayabhadra's commentary.

537. As above I follow here the correct sentence boundaries in Jayabhadra's commentary; Tsong Khapa here follows the defective reading in Bhavyakīrti's commentary, i.e., *rdo rje la ni zhes bya la sogs pa yin no / sgrub pa po'i bya ba ni . . .* (BC 38b.5–6). Jayabhadra's commentary reads here, "**Not mounting with the vajra** is the adept's action" (Sugiki 2001, 138: *vajrasyālaṅghanam ityādi sādhakakriyā*; CP 66b.5–6: *rdo rje la ni zhes bya la sogs pa ni sgrub pa po'i bya ba'o*).

of dance. **All** are those for whom the adept's action is performed.[538] [This is] the explanation.

The ladies who govern **all** among the messengers serve as the **ultimate** in **love** (42.7) or passion. One states ***ha hā***[539] **in their vicinity**; this is done by the the adept in the presence of the distinctive messengers. Those who **weep** and produce **tears always**, that is, for as long as they are with the adept, are praised. **One becomes the love of those** messengers through weeping, tearing, and the repetition of the eightfold laughter. Having **well-deployed meditative concentration**, i.e., deity yoga, **and mantra** (42.8) repetition, the yoginī who is one's spell consort (*rig ma*) is well subjugated.

One will experience **the bristling** of one's **body hair** and natural **bliss in conjuction with the ladies,** the heroines such as Prachaṇḍā, and **heroes,** Khaṇḍakapālin and so forth. In the manner of **one should not pass over the vajra**, one's vajra should not pass from entry into the lotus. This means that **the left is fixed** (42.9) by the yoginīs.

3.3.3. 2.2.2. 10.4.3. Showing the name of the chapter

In the *Concise* ***Shrī Herukābhidhāna Tantra***, this is **the forty-second chapter** on **the procedure of the** eightfold **laughter mantra and the magic of the ḍākinīs' forms,**[540] that is, the emanation of the forms of Prachaṇḍā, and so forth. This is the explanation of the forty-second chapter in the *Illumination of the Hidden Meaning, A Detailed Exegesis of the Concise Saṁvara Tantra Called "The Chakrasaṁvara."*

538. Tsong Khapa ends this passage with the quotation indicator *zhes*. As noted above, here he closely paraphases, but does not directly quote, Bhavyakīrti's commentary, which in turn is based almost entirely on Jayabhadra's commentary.

539. Tsong Khapa follows the SM translation in reading *ha hā* here; the PM translation and extant Sanskrit reads *hā hā*, while SL reads *ha ha*. See Gray 2012, 205, 376, 467, 548.

540. Tsong Khapa's commentary here reads *mkha' 'gro ma'i gzugs kyi rgyu*, following the SM translation. A better reading is preserved in the PM translation, namely *mkha' 'gro ma'i gzugs kyi rgyu ma'i* (PM), with *sgyu ma* corresponding to *–māyā*. See Gray 2012, 376, 548.

Chapter 43

Chapter 43 Outline

3.3.3. 2.2.2. 11. Showing other methods for the attainment of mundane powers

The eleventh part, showing other methods for the attainment of mundane powers, has five sections: (1) ritual success with the father's quintessence and armor [mantras], (2) ritual success relying on the heroine's armor and five *ha* [syllables], (3) success with the buddhaḍākinī mantra and continual performance of deity visualization, (4) detailed exposition of the examination of the seven-lived one, and (5) ritual success with the mother's essence mantra.

3.3.3. 2.2.2. 11.1. Ritual success with the father's quintessence and armor

The first part has two sections: (1) success relying upon the father's quintessence and (2) success relying upon his and the mother's armor.

3.3.3. 2.2.2. 11.1.1. Success relying upon the father's quintessence

The first part has three sections: (1) the promise to explain, (2) the promised explanation of the meaning, and (3) showing the name of the chapter.

3.3.3. 2.2.2. 11.1.1. 1. The promise to explain

Now, having explained the forty-second chapter, **I will explain** the method of **glancing** (*gzigs*) with the eye (*spyan ras kyis*)[541] so that adepts will be accepted by the yoginīs. Why is the yoginīs' method of glancing with the eye explained? It is because, if the yoginī glances with her eye, the adept, regarded as among **men who are the hero** Khaṇḍakapālin and so forth, becomes **nondually** equipoised with the yoginī Prachaṇḍā, and so forth.

At what sort of adept does she glance with her eye? She glances with her eye at him who **knows the procedure of classifying** the seats, such as the seat of Pullīra[malaya] etc., subsidiary seats, and so forth, that is, the outer mandala, and who knows how to visualize the inner body mandala, and who, knowing that, **always,** i.e., at all times, **delights in meditation** (43.1) upon them. Through this one encounters the supreme messengers and progresses on the path. This shows the necessity for knowing unerringly the spiritual discipline (*sādhana, sgrub thabs*) of this tradition and meditating continually upon it. It is essential to gain great certainty in this [practice].

541. The Sanskrit here reads *avalokanaṁ*, "glancing, seeing, beholding." This was accurately translated as *gzigs pa* in the SL translation, but erroneously translated as *spyan ras gzigs*, i.e., Avalokiteshvara, in the PM and SM translations. Tsong Khapa here glosses that translation, making clear that it is not a reference to the great bodhisattva.

3.3.3. 2.2.2. 11.1.1. 2. The promised explanation of the meaning

The second part has five sections: (1) places in which they glance, (2) naked worship, (3) the mantra that protects against obstacles, (4) ritual success relying on the attainment of mantric power, and (5) techniques for achieving ritual power.

3.3.3. 2.2.2. 11.1.1. 2.1. Places in which they glance

Abiding at what sort of place can one be seen by a yoginī? **The ḍākinī sees** with a compassionate eye **even from a far** land, just as flocks of geese gather at a lotus pond, those who abide **at crossroads, in** their own **houses, at the abodes of heroes**, that is, directional guardians (*phyogs skyong, dikpāla*) and so forth, **or on mountains**, as well as those who **abide in** the proper protection of **the commitments** (43.2) concerning eating, protection, and service. This is because the yoginīs are overwhelmed with compassion for a disciple who is a worthy vessel. The understanding of [the second half of verse two as] "the ḍākinī sees, even from afar . . . in the place of the commitments" is excellent.[542]

3.3.3. 2.2.2. 11.1.1. 2.2. Naked worship

The yogin, being free of clothes, becomes naked, and as he worships **the seal consort** (*phyag rgya mo*), this is **naked worship. One is liberated through the** very **ritual action** of worship. As is said, "one is liberated through the very ritual action of worship with the naked seal (consort)."[543]

542. Tsong Khapa here appears to be quoting the translation of the latter half of 43.2 in the Tibetan translation of Kambala's commentary. The text occurs as follows in the canonical translation: *dam tshig la gnas mkha' 'gro ma / ring bo nas kyang gzigs par 'gyur* (SN 73b.5–6). Tsong Khapa's quote is almost identical to this, reading: *dam tshig gnas la mkha' 'gro ma / ring bo nas kyang gzigs par 'gyur*. The three canonical translations of these lines differ considerably from this; see Gray 2012, 377, 467, 538.

543. Tsong Khapa is quoting Kambala's commentary as it occurs in the canonical translation, namely: *phyag rgya gcer bu mchod pa yi / las nyid kyis ni yongs su grol* (SN 73b.6–7). The extant Sanskrit is slightly different here, with no equivalent to *mchod pa*. It reads, "They are liberated through ritual action with the naked seal [consort]"; *nagna-mudrāyāḥ karmataḥ parimucyante* (K 71b.1).

One is covered with clothing[544] of tiger hide, i.e., a lower garment. The word "**or**" indicates that one may be naked, and **other** that bone ornaments are positioned on one's limbs. The yogin **should not be covered by accoutrements for his desires** (43.3), just as the lotus, uncovered by water, is not injured by the scorching of the sun. As the *Vajra Rosary Tantra* states:[545]

Having undertaken the negations,
And renouncing doing and not doing
One is not covered by phenomena,
Like the lotus uncovered by mud.

"Not covered" does not mean that one does not give rise to affliction in one's mental continuum. This is because this path takes the affliction of passion as the path. It thus means that the negative consequence for the affliction of that time is not covered by the fault of leading one to the lower realms. Since "phenomena" are stated, there is a need to destroy (*zhig*) the many decisive views of reality that are insufficient simply with respect to the capacity to hold on, without discharge, to the spirit of awakening.

The Great Brahmin [Saraha] critiques[546] the one who just attains bliss in the non-emission of the spirit of awakening in the union of the two faculties. Without the cause of union [of that bliss] with emptiness, that is the knowledge of emptiness as the nature of all things in cyclic existence and cessation (*nirvāṇa*), [bliss] does not in any way undermine the mistaken knowledge of the conception of intrinsic reality that is the root of existence. Moreover, to the extent that one cultivates bliss in that manner, one proceeds to increase further the attachment that is drawn forth from the conception of intrinsic reality. It is as if one possessed by thirst and lust conceives illusory water and enters it. He praises, from the perspective of

544. Tsong Khapa follows the canonical PM translation, *gos nyid kyis bkab pa'am gzhan*. The Sanskrit here reads *prakṣipyāmbaraṁ anyat*, "casting away clothing or other [garb]."

545. This translates the text in the canonical translation, *dgag pa dag kyang byed pas na / bya dang bya min rnam spangs te / padma la ni 'dam gyis bzhin / ngo ba nyid ces gos mi 'gyur* (*Vajra Rosary Tantra*, Tōh. 445, D *rgyud 'bum* vol. ca, 265a.6). Tsong Khapa quotes this verse as follows: *dkag pa dag kyang byed pas na / bya dang bya min rnam spangs te / padma la ni 'dam gyis bzhin / ngo ba nyid shes gos mi 'gyur.*

546. In what follows Tsong Khapa provides a commentary on the verses from Saraha's *Treasury of Songs* (*Dohakoṣagīti*), which he quotes below.

the rapid path, those who have the ability to unite bliss and emptiness as previously explained, as lacking that method, there will be no rapid attainment as a buddha who fulfills the hopes of the beings of the three worlds. Saraha stated:[547]

> One who seeks bliss in sexual union,[548]
> Not knowing the nature of anything,
> Thus thirsts, as if racing to a mirage,
> He thirsts and dies; does he taste sky water?
> He frolics in the very rapture that
> Exists between the vajra and lotus.
> Why? It has no capacity for truth,[549]
> So how could it fulfill the three worlds' hopes?

Thus [the root text] states that, being naked and adorned with a hide robe, the one with hair let down should commence with all ritual actions for delighting the seal consort in the manner of the treatises on love (*kāma-śāstra*). Furthermore, the one who is naked with **his hair let down**, being devoted to her, will accomplish all ritual actions, or **will commence all ritual actions (43.4ab)** such as those for teaching and consecration. The

547. This is passage occurs in Saraha's *Treasury of Songs* (*Dohakoṣagīti*) 76a.2–3 as follows: *ma lus rang bzhin mi shes pas / kun du ru yi skabs su bde chen sgrub pa ni / ji ltar skom pas smig rgyu'i chu snyegs bzhin / skom nas 'chi yang nam mkha'i chu rnyed dam / rdo rje padma gnyis kyi bar gnas pa / bde ba gang gis rnam par rol pa yin / ci ste de bden nus pa med pas na / sa gsum re ba gang gis rdzogs par 'gyur*. It is quoted by Tsong Khapa as follows: *ma lus rang bzhin gang gis mi shes pa / kun tu ru yi skabs su bde chen sgrub pa ni / ji ltar skom pas smig rgyu chu snyeg pa bzhin / skom nas 'chi yang nam mkha'i chu rnyed dam / rdo rje padma gnyis kyi bar gnas pa / bde ba gang gis rnam par rol ba ni / ci ste de bde bsten nus pa med pas na / sa gsum re ba gang gis rdzogs par 'gyur*. For alternate translations and explanations of these verses, see Jackson 2004, 105, 107 and Schaeffer 2005, 166.

548. The text reads "at the occasion of Kunduru," *kun du ru yi skabs su*. The term *kunduru* refers either to a tree, Boswellia thurifera, which exudes a fragrant resinous sap, or the resin derived therefrom. It is usually interpreted in this context as a reference to sexual union; see Schaeffer 2005, 166.

549. This translates the canonical translation's version of this line, *ci ste de bden nus pa med pas na*. Tsong Khapa quotes here instead, "Why? It cannot cultivate bliss," *ci ste bde bsten nus pa med pas na*.

[text] "topknot" (*gtsor gyur*) does not occur in the other two translations and does also not occur in the commentaries.[550]

3.3.3. 2.2.2. 11.1.1. 2.3. The mantra that protects against obstacles

Will obstacles arise in the performance of the ritual action of naked equipoise? With respect to "commencing in all ritual actions," one does this having guarded [against them] through the application of the [male] partner's **root mantra** and likewise **others**, i.e., the mantra of **the four**-faced one,[551] to the [vajra] wall, net, that is, tent, canopy, and arrow net, and [the application of] the mantras of the net of fire to **the binding of the directions (43.4cd)**.

Do naked **worship** and so forth **without being seen**; that is, if one is not seen **even by the hosts of gods in heaven (43.5ab)**, what need is there to mention [being seen] by humans? As it is translated by the Great Translator as "Do worship without being seen even by the hosts of gods in heaven," and as [this translation] also occurs in Devagupta's commentary, it is excellent.[552]

3.3.3. 2.2.2. 11.1.1. 2.4. Ritual success relying on the attainment of mantric power

The fourth part has two sections: (1) methods for gaining particular mantric powers and (2) methods for success in rites relying upon them.

550. The PM and SM translations translate the Sanskrit *muktaśikho bhūtvā* as *skra grol gtsor gyur pas.* The SL translations gives the simpler and more accurate translation *sgra ni grol 'gyur ba.* I presume that the original Rinchen Zangpo translation accorded with the latter, making thus two translations that omit *gtsor.* While *gtsor* is a translation of *śikha*, *skra grol gtsor* is a cumbersome, confusing, and redundant translation, as Tsong Khapa recognizes. See Gray 2012, 206, 377, 467, 549.

551. That is, the mantra also known as the Shumbha mantra, discussed in chapter 30 above.

552. Tsong Khapa's quotation from Lochen's translation, *lha yul lha yi tshogs kyis kyang / ma mthong bar ni mchod pa gyis*, is very similar to the text preserved in the PM and SM translations (see Gray 2012, 377–78, 549), but quite distinct from the text preserved in the SL translation, namely "Doing worship, one will not be seen even by the hosts of gods and titans" (Gray 2012, 468: *lha dang lha min tshogs kyis kyang / mchod byed gang gis ma mthong bar*). Devagupta's canonical commentary does not preserve this exact translation. Instead, it contains a gloss similar to Tsong Khapa's, reading, "This means that, if it is unseen by the gods, what need is there to speak of humans?" (SS 151a.2–3: *lha rnams kyis kyang mi mthong na / mi rnams kyis lta ci zhig smos zhes pa'i don to*).

3.3.3. 2.2.2. 11.1.1. 2.4.1. Methods for gaining particular mantric powers

If one's **cupped hands are filled with flowers**, and one enchants them with the mantra and **tosses them up** into the sky, if all of them are **flying** (**43.5cd**), i.e., remain in the sky, such that **not** even one of **those flowers falls** to the ground, and the flowers **are not seen fallen to the ground, then** one will be able to undertake all ritual actions. **One will subjugate** a land and the countless [beings] who dwell **in particular on that** land, i.e., the residents who characterize it, as illustrated by **the thousand** (**43.6**) ḍākinīs.

One will summon the lady of speech, that is, divine girls such as Sarasvatī, **and the power of speech**, that is, the eloquent one, the guru of the gods Bṛihaspati, as well as others illustrated by those [examples], such as Mahādeva. **One will know the speech of a god with** [another] **god** (*lha dang lha*), a repetitive expression indicating multiplicity, that is the language of all of them, and one will know **as well the course of the heavenly bodies.** [The text] **gradually** (**43.7**) and so forth does not occur in the commentaries.[553] If it seems to be valid, it means that the [divine] languages are known without their order being confused.

3.3.3. 2.2.2. 11.1.1. 2.4.2. Methods for success in rites relying upon them

The second part has three sections: (1) ritual success in invisibility and tree summoning, (2) ritual success in dream interpretation and the descent of the divinatory image, and (3) ritual success in the pacification of illness etc.

3.3.3. 2.2.2. 11.1.1. 2.4.2. 1. Ritual success in invisibility and tree summoning

If one always recalls the seven-syllable **quintessence** (**43.9a**) through intimacy with **the essence in towns** (*grong grong*), which is a repetitive expression implying many towns (*grong mang*), and likewise in isolated **forests, cities, and crossroads**, and at **a solitary tree**, that is, a tree not

553. Tsong Khapa refers to the line in the line *go rims ji lta ba bzhin tu* in the SM translation, and the variant *rim pa ji lta bzhin du'o* in the PM translation. The extant Sanskrit, which is incomplete here, has no equivalent to this line, nor is it quoted in the commentaries, which is not surprising given its lack of semantic content. See Gray 2012, 378, 549.

struck by the shadow of another tree, namely a tree not encroached upon by another tree, not even by its shadow, in **the house of a hero,** i.e., a temple of a field protector (*zhing skyong, kṣetrapāla*), **on a mountain peak or at a sign**, i.e., *liṅga*, **of Mahādeva** (43.8), and if one repeats them from the perspective of achieving invisibility, since one is **not seen by gods and men**, one achieves invisibility. Since they are achieved if one practices in those previously explained **places, the adept always stays in these** (43.9) regions, namely towns and so forth.

Visualize oneself as Shrī Heruka, in whose heart are **the seven syllables** of the quintessence, **red colored, manifesting** on a six petalled lotus, and if one visualizes red mantra [syllables] spread out **at the top of a tree** like a swarm of bees, the seven syllables inseparably mixed, the tree trunk will **bow down**, i.e., fall down. Regarding whether or not one visualizes the syllables at the "tree base" (*shing drung*) or root of the tree,[554] Bhavabhaṭṭa explains that one visualizes the seven syllables on the top.[555] Regarding "grounds" (*sa rnams*), it occurs as "mountain" (*sa 'dzin*).[556] It is said that this means a stony mountain,[557] and if you take it thus, even they fall down, **not otherwise** (43.10).

3.3.3. 2.2.2. 11.1.1. 2.4.2. 2. Ritual success in dream interpretation and the descent of the divinatory image

Visualize a six petalled red lotus in the heart of **one's body** appearing as Heruka, and **place** each of the seven syllables of the quintessence on the petals and navel of that [lotus]. Having made **a grass mat on ground** that has been anointed with the five ambrosias beneath, **one should recline on it. One repeats the mantra** that includes **the seven syllables** to a count of **one hundred and eight** (43.11), and [one visualizes] it spreading out from oneself to the circle of ḍākinīs and mixing with the triple world. It reenters

554. This variant is found in the SM translation. The other two translations read "at the tree top," *shing rtser*. See Gray 2012, 378, 468, 549.

555. See Pandey 2002, 556, 791.

556. The PM and SM translation reads *sa rnams* here, while the SL translation reads *sa 'dzin*, which is a better translation of the Sanskit *bhūdhara*. See Gray 2012, 208, 378, 468, 549.

557. Tsong Khapa refers to Bhavabhaṭṭa's gloss, *bhūdharān śilāśailān* (Pandey 2002, 556).

one's left nostril. It is said that if one reclines in the manner of going to sleep, **all of the deeds one desires** in one's mind **will be revealed in one's dream** (**43.12ab**).[558]

In the *Twofold Commentary*, [Tathāgatarakṣhita] explains that one should "visualize successively the wheels of the mandala **in one's body**, and **recline on a grass mat** anointed with the five ambrosias. By reclining while repeating the mantra one hundred and eight times, they will be revealed by the yoginī in a dream."[559] Vīravajra explains that "**place in one's body** means that one places the white colored seven syllables on lunar disks at one's crown, forehead, two eyes, mouth, shoulders and heart."[560] Bhavabhaṭṭa claims that **place in one's body** means that the six syllables, beginning with *oṁ*, are placed on the eyes, ears, nose, tongue, body and mind, with *huṁ* placed on the mind, after which *phaṭ* is placed.[561]

Since this dream ritual is easy to perform, of great importance, and as it occurs in the oral instructions of the various great adepts, if one understands it completely, even if [the sign] does not occur in one [performance],

558. Tsong Khapa here summarizes Kambala's commentary, which reads as follows: "**Placing in one's body**, that is, the wheel, **one should recline** according to the rite, having repeated [the mantra] one hundred and eight time **on a grass mat on the ground** that has been anointed with the five ambrosias. It emanates to the circle of ḍākinīs, mixes with the triple world, and reabsorbed" (K 71b.6–7: *ātmakāye tu vinyasya cakraṁ pañcāmṛtopaliptabhūmau kuśāstaraṁ / aṣṭottaraśataṁ japtvā vidhivat śayet / ḍākinīcakraspharāvahaṁ / trailokyena saha miśritam praviśanta*; SM 74a.6–7: *bdag gi lus la rnam bkod de / zhes bya ba ni 'khor lo ste bdud rtsi lngas sa gzhi byugs la ku sha bting ste brgya rtsa brgyad bzlas brjod byas la cho ga bzhin du nyal na mkha' 'gro ma'i 'khor lo spros nas / 'jig rten gsum dang lhan cig 'dres shing rnam par zhugs te*).

559. Tsong Khapa provides a summary of Tathāgatarakṣhita's somewhat longer commentary, which occurs as follows: *rang gi lus la dkyil 'khor gyi 'khor lo rim pa ji bzhin du bsgom pa'i khongs su gtogs par byas la bdud rtsi lngas byugs pa'i ku sha'i stan gyi steng du nye bar 'dug ste / yi ge bdun pa'i sngags brgya rtsa brgyad yongs su bzlas te / de nyid nyal du bcug pas ston par 'gyur te / rnal 'byor mas zhes lhag ma'o / yid la 'dod pa ston par 'gyur te* (UN 243b.4–6)

560. This passage occurs at SG 203a3.4, as follows: *rang gi lus la rnam bkod de / zhes pa ni spyi bo dang dpral ba dang mig gnyis dang kha dang phrag pa dang snying gar zla ba'i dkyil 'khor mdog dkar ba'i yi ge bdun gyi bdag nyid dgod par bya'o.*

561. Tsong Khapa paraphrases and elaborates on Bhavabhaṭṭa's commentary, which simply states that *phaṭ* is placed on the mind. It reads as follows: *ātmakāye tv iti / cakṣuḥśrotaghrāṇajihvākāyamanassu ṣaḍakṣarāṇi manasi [ca] phaṭkāraṁ vinyasya* (Pandey 2002, 556); *bdag gi lus la zhes pa ni / mig dang / rna dang / sna dang / lce dang / lus dang / yid rnams su yi ge drug go/ yi la ni phaṭ bkod nas* (2002, 792).

one can proceed since it is permissible to produce another sign. The oral instructions of a previous lama state the following:[562]

> Repeat the mantra one hundred and eight times over sand from a river bank and *kuśa* grass and scatter the five ambrosias over them. Sit atop the sand in a clean place and imagine the wheel in one's heart. Repeat the mantra through the yoga of [visualizing that] the mantra one is repeating emanates from one's mouth, eyes, ears, and nose, pervades sentient beings, and is recollected. One reclines with one's right side down, as stated.

Regarding the manner in which one's mind's desires is revealed in a dream, everything—that is **all deeds**, namely **untimely death, destruction, or annihilation,** or **any other** (**43.12cd**) of the various things to be done or not done, as previously explained—are revealed by a yoginī in a dream. Three commentaries explain first line beginning with **untimely** such that death that is not timely is destroyed, i.e., eliminated, and that **annihilation** is increased.[563] If one sees a sign of untimely death etc. by showing the method [with the text] "do thus for this,"[564] one undertakes the elimination of untimely death and so forth.

Regarding showing what should be done or not done in the descent of the divinatory image through the power of the deity **in the same manner**

562. The source of this quote is unclear to me; it may be Mardo's lost commentary, or perhaps a *man ngag* text attributed to him or Sachen. The opening portion of this passage, concerning the enchanting of river sand and *kuśa* grass, is found in Sachen's commentary, but the closing portion does not occur there.

563. Tsong Khapa appears to be summarizing these commentaries in a very oblique manner. Jayabhadra's commentary makes these points, reading: "**Destruction of untimely death and annihilation** means that untimely death is eliminated and one's lifespan is increased, and a 'lost being' (*naṣṭasattvaṁ*) is brought back" (Sugiki 2001, 138: *apamṛtyuhataṁ naṣṭaṁ tathaiva cety āyur vardhate mṛtyum apaharati naṣṭasattvaṁ ānayatīty arthaḥ*; see also CP 67a.2–3, but note that the Tib. trans. here is incomplete). Vīravajra's commentary reads: "**Destruction of untimely death and annihilation** means that one's lifespan is increased and death is annihilated, or sentient beings are annihilated, i.e., killed" (SG 203a.4: *dus min 'chi dang bcom dang nyams / zhes pa ni tshe 'phel ba dang 'chi ban yams pa ste / sems can nyams shing 'chi ba yang zhes pa'i don to*). Bhavyakīrti has a shorter gloss of these terms at BC 39a.2–3.

564. Tsong Khapa quotes here the text *'di la 'di ltar gyis*, although I do not know what source he is quoting; this text does not occur in any of the translations of the root text.

as predictions are revealed in dreams by a deity, one enchants by **repeating** one hundred and eight times with **the** quintessence **mantra** at an unestablished time, i.e, in the evening, over a beautiful, blindfolded, young virgin girl or boy. It will be revealed at dawn. Lamps should blaze in the house, and one should worship paintings and images [of the deity] with pots filled scented water. Displaying **a sword, water, one's thumb, a lamp, or a mirror,** the adept, continuously endowed **with the yoga of oneself** as Shrī Heruka, **causes the descent of the divinatory image (43.13)**. Having **visualized** Shrī Heruka and having **repeated** the quintessence **seven times**, the deity's power **will reveal the auspicious**, i.e., what is suitable to do, **and the inauspicious (43.14ab)**, i.e., what is unsuitable to do.

Alternatively, rub one's thumb with sesame oil and anoint it with fingernail paint, i.e., lacquer resin. If you show it to the virgin boy or girl, he or she will say who is carrying wealth. The descent of the divinatory image to the thumb can also reveal destruction, annihilation and so forth.[565]

3.3.3. 2.2.2. 11.1.1. 2.4.2. 3. Ritual success in the pacification of illness etc.

The third part, ritual success in the pacification of illness etc., has five sections: (1) pacifying illness relying upon mantra and a wheel, (2) fire sacrifice for subjugation, along with the options, (3) showing the different colors for the different ritual actions, (4) methods for destroying poison, plague, etc., and (5) victory in gambling and fighting, and additional matters.

3.3.3. 2.2.2. 11.1.1. 2.4.2. 3.1. Pacifying illness relying upon mantra and a wheel

Now, having explained the descent of the divinatory image, there is the explanation of ritual success through **the division** via dissimilarity by **setting down** on a wheel [the syllables of] **the hero** Heruka's **seven-syllable** quintessence **mantra (43.14cd)**. Regarding this, one mentally **visualizes** the actual placement or writing of the syllables *haṁ* etc. of the quintessence **within a solar mandala**. Visualizing the disease within that, **repeat** the quintessence with an augment **one thousand times**. If you visualize

565. In this and the preceding paragraph Tsong Khapa closely paraphrases Kambala's commentary. See SN 74a.7–b.2.

the mantra's syllables as **crystalline** on one's hand, and **you display this to** the patient **afflicted by disease** (43.15), **have no doubt the disease will be broken** just by the sight of one's hand. In this context many commentaries explain it that if one visualizes the patient's consciousness as pure crystal the size of his or her thumb in his or her heart, he or she **will be free of disease**, and this is established by the text as well.[566]

Visualize a lunar disk that is like **the moon** of **the autumnal** (43.16) season and **arrange** it such that **the center** and cardinal directions **form five** squares; and including the ordinal directions there is a nine square [three by three] chart. Place *oṁ* in its center, *hrīḥ* to the east, *ha* to the south, *ha* to the west, *huṁ* in the north, and *huṁ* is also in the middle, and four *phaṭ* [syllables] in the ordinal directions, or four *pha* [syllables] excluding the [letter] *ṭ*. **The syllables appear crystalline** white, and the illnesses are completely eliminated within the radiant wheel. Visualize the wheel that exists within the patient on one's **left hand** (43.17) and place it on the head of one afflicted by animate or inanimate poisons. If you visualize that there is no poison throughout his or her body due to the flow of nectar from that [hand], she or he will be free of poison. Likewise, **have no doubt that all diseases** include those [caused by] animate and inanimate poisons indicated by the words **fever, astral spirits** and so forth, and tumors and so forth indicated by the words **epilepsy and severe pain**, and those **caused by the consumption of the poisons** of **leprosy** (43.18), fangs, and so forth, as well as all other diseases aside from them.

Having visualized one's left hand on which is placed the seven syllables in the shape of the moon, one can do this revealing it to the one afflicted by disease or not. If you visualize that the syllables of the mantra arise in the form of ambrosial light and **disperse throughout**, i.e., pervade, **the**

566. Jayabhadra comments here as follows: "Should one produce in the his or her heart the consciousness which is blazingly radiant **like crystal, the size of the thumb**, then she or he will be healthy" (Sugiki 2001, 139: *taddhṛdaye 'ṅguṣṭhamātraṁ spaṭikanirmalaṁ jvaladbhāsurākāraṁ vijñānam ā[r]abhet sustho bhavati*; CP 67a.4: *de nyid kyi snying gar mthe bo tsam gyi tshad la shel ltar dang ba'i 'od zer 'bar ba dang bcas pa'i rnam shes pa'i rang bzhin bsams na nad med par 'gyur ro*).

Note that I read *ārabhet* rather than *ālabhet*, following an alternate reading in one of the manuscripts. See Gray 2007, 346, n. 23. See also similar comments in the commentaries by Bhavabhaṭṭa (Pandey 2002, 557) and Vīravajra (PD 438a).

ten directions (**43.19ab**), east and so forth, the poisons and so forth are eliminated.

3.3.3. 2.2.2. 11.1.1. 2.4.2. 3.2. Fire sacrifice for dominion, along with the options

The time for fire sacrifice is **at night**, and **the place** is **secret**, that is, isolated. Although [the Sanskrit] *go* can have many meanings, here it means **cow**. *Māṁsa* means **flesh**. It is **pulverized with the three sweets** (**43.19cd**), namely molasses, honey, and sugar. **Should** one who **knows** the method of performing fire sacrifice with **the seven-syllable mantra** and the offering substances saturated with those three [sweets] **perform eight thousand fire sacrifices** in a hearth for all of the rites of dominion, **in the morning the mantrin will obtain a thousand measures of gold** (**43.20**).

Through ten thousand fire sacrifices, one obtains an excellent, i.e., superior, **country**. **Moreover**, regarding another rite accomplished with fire sacrifice, **have no doubt that a king of mantra generates**, i.e., brings forth, that aim which he **contemplates**, pacifying and so forth, when repeating the quintessence **in whichever** of the previously explained **places** (**43.21**).

A Tibetan explains,[567] "Having thought, every morning, 'I will be born in whichever place I want to be born,' if one repeats the quintessence one hundred and eight every day, one will be born in whichever place one desires," but this is makes no sense, since it seems to indicate that there are approaches involving either doing or not doing fire sacrifice in order to achieve ritual actions.[568]

3.3.3. 2.2.2. 11.1.1. 2.4.2. 3.3. Showing the different colors for the different ritual actions

Regarding making **white** the color of mandala deities, fire deity, mantra, garments, and offering materials such as flowers, [by so doing] one

567. I have not been able to identify the source of this quotation; it may be Mardo's lost commentary.

568. Tsong Khapa seems to be objecting to the fact that this commentary does not entail the practice of fire sacrifice, and just repetition, in order to attain a desired end. In his understanding, the text here is describing a fire sacrifice of dominion, and not a practice involving just mantra repetition.

accomplishes rites for **the pacification** of illness, astral spirits, and so forth. By taking **black** as the color for these [things], **one kills instantly** (**43.22**), i.e., quickly. One should understand that expelling and causing dissension is also implied by that. By making them **red one subjugates** one's victim **and** also **summons** him or her **immediately. By** taking **yellow** as the color of the deities and so forth, **all** of an enemy's army etc. are **subdued.** This explanation of the distinctions of each color for a respective rite **is the fixed opinion of the teaching** from the tantras.

As for showing who is subdued implied by [the text] **all are subdued, with yellow** as the color of deities and so forth, the enemy's **army is subdued,** and his **boats** on the water, **the war machines** made by the enemy, and **the elephants** and so forth **are subdued** (**43.23**), that is, immobilized.

Just by contemplating in one's mind these [things] as the color **white,** the cause of untimely death is also pacified, **the dead are revived,** that is, they are liberated from that [state of death]. **One who has** the disease of poison **afflicted by** the poison of the fangs of **one hundred great serpents is also quickly revived** (**43.24**), i.e., liberated from that [affliction].

3.3.3. 2.2.2. 11.1.1. 2.4.2. 3.4. Methods for destroying poison, plague, etc.

The adept, **seeing those who are unconscious due to poison, rouses** them from unconsciousness through the method of rousing from unconsciousness. Those afflicted by **fevers** of one day and so forth, **astral spirits** such as Rahu, and the astral spirit of **epilepsy,** [their afflictions] **are destroyed,**[569] that is, broken, by **seeing** the wheel written on **the hand** (**43.25**) of the mantrin.

3.3.3. 2.2.2. 11.1.1. 2.4.2. 3.5. Victory in gambling and fighting, and additional matters

If, **while** engaging in **gambling,** i.e., throwing dice, and **fighting, one makes a fist** with the hand that has the quintessence and **always mentally repeats** the quintessence mantra with an augment, **so long as one does not relax one's fist** (**43.26**), **everything one** desires to **undertake will be**

569. Tsong Khapa follows the reading in the SM translation, *'jig par 'gyur.* The PM and SL translation read *'jigs par 'gyur,* "are terrified." The Sanskrit for this verse is lost, unfortunately.

accomplished, i.e., one will accomplish them. **Even if one's enemy wields a weapon in his hand, so long as one does not relax one's fist** (43.27), **the weapon will not be able to strike.** Kambala explains with regard to this ritual application the following:[570]

> Draw the wheel on the left hand with realgar or turmeric or on a copper plate with the augment "block all weapons[571] at so-and-so's body," and repeat the mantra one thousand times, wiping the face and inserting it into the vajra water. If one then takes it up, repeats the manta, and inserts it into one's fist, one will not be injured by a weapon so long as one does not relax one's fist. Having obstructed them, place a medicinal stone in the mouth of a corpse and then take it out. If you draw this wheel without facing west, you will win in dice just through this drawing.

Furthermore, it is excellent that [the word] **thus** occurs, since [it indicates that] **all deeds**—the paralyzation of the body and speech of other enemies in addition to the previously explained subjugation of armies—**are**

570. Tsong Khapa here quotes Kambala's commentary, but also elaborates upon it. It occurs as follows: "Drawing this wheel on the left hand with realgar or turmeric, or likewise inscribing it on a copper plate, repeat [the mantra] one thousand [times] enveloping [the augment] 'block all weapons at so-and-so's body,' and insert it into the adamantine fist. Then one should recall the king of mantras. So long as one does not relax one's fist, even if one's enemy wields a weapon in his hand, the weapon will be blocked, so long as one does not relax one's fist. With this one will be victorious in battle and victorious in dice. Having obstructed them, place the wheel in the mouth of a corpse and then take it out. If you draw this wheel without facing west, you will win in dice just through this drawing" (K 72b.1–2: *haritāla haridrayā vā vāmahast[a] [i]daṁ saṁlikhya cakraṁ / athavā tāmrapatre tathaiva ca saṁlikhya cakraṁ / amukasyāṅge sarvaśāstraṁ nivārayet / sahasraṁ japya veṣṭayitvā vajrahaste prakṣipyet / mantrarājaṁ tataḥ smaret / muṣṭiṁ yāvan na muñcati / udyatāyudhahastena vairiṇā bhavante yadi / nivārayaty āśu sarvāṇi muṣṭiṁ yāvan na muñcati / eva teṣu jayo bhavati*; SN 75a.1–4: *ldong ros sam yung bas lag pa g.yon pa la 'khor lo 'di dag bris pa'am / yang na zangs ma gligs pa la 'khor lo bris la / che ge mo'i lus la mtshon cha thams cad zlog shig ces bya ba dang / sngags lan stong bzlas nas bcings nas rdo rje khu tshur gyi nang du bcug ste / de nas gsang sngags rgyal po dran / ji srid khu tshur ma grol bar / dgra bo gal te lag na ni / mtshon cha 'phyar bar byed pa yang / ji srid khu tshur ma grol bar / mtshon cha gtong bar mi nus so / 'di yis g.yul las bdag rgyal zhing / rgyan po 'gyed las bdag rgyal 'gyur / yang 'gegs nas shi ba'i khar 'khor lo bcug nas de nas bslang te/ des rang gi kha nub phyogs ma yin par bltas la / 'di bris pa tsam gyis rgyan po las rgyal bar 'gyur ro*).

571. Here I follow Kambala's text; Tsong Khapa quotes here "block all wheels," which makes less sense.

accomplished, that is, will be accomplished, in the previously explained manner, that is, with a fist having applied the wheel to one's hand.

The oral instruction is that the mantrin should arrange **leaves, flowers, fruit, betel nut, and** likewise **food** (**43.29ab**) as well as the quintessence in a three-by-three chart on a wheel on a lunar disk on one's left hand. She or he should visualize ambrosia trickling from that and pervading everything, and s/he should enjoy it.[572] It should be performed in this manner.

3.3.3. 2.2.2. 11.1.1. 2.5. Techniques for achieving ritual power

The method for attaining the power to accomplish the previously explained rites, staying in the previously explained sites, **first** there **is the union**, i.e., practice of yoga that is **physical**, of the body. This perfects one in the form of Shrī Chakrasaṁvara. **The second** is mentally visualizing the goddess Vārāhī. It appears that the equivalent term to "**is power**" (**43.29**; *nus pa yin*) is "of the mind" (*yid kyi yin*).[573] Regarding **the third is speech**, Tathāgatarakṣhita explained that:[574]

> one will attain all ritual actions through repetition of the mantra having progressively perfected [oneself] through preliminary acceptance having worshipped and praised so as to encounter [the goddesses] from Ḍākinī up to Yamadāḍhī.

This means that having previously habituated oneself to the spiritual discipline of [mantra] repetition and so forth, one will later accomplish the ritual actions. **The fourth is not objectified** does not occur in the commentaries or Lochen's translation. In the system of those who have it, it is explained

572. Tsong Khapa here paraphrases Vīravajra's commentary; see SG 203b.2.

573. The Sanskrit equivalent to the Tibetan *nus pa* here is *śaktikaḥ*, a term that Bhavabhaṭṭa glosses as *śaktimān*, "possessing power, mighty." (Pandey 2002, 559). Numerous commentaries gloss *nus pa* as *yid kyi nus pa*, "power of the mind." See SG 203b.4.

574. This passage occurs in Tathāgatarakṣhita's commentary: *gsum pa ni mkha' 'gro ma la sogs pa nas gshin rje 'joms ma la thug par mchod pa dang / bstod pa nas bzung ba sngon du 'gro bas rim pa ji lta ba bzhin du rdzogs par byas nas sngags kyi bzlas pa las thams cad 'grub par 'gyur ro zhes pa'i don to* (UN 244b.3–4). Tsong Khapa quotes this passage as follows: *gsum pa dag ni ngag nyid de zhes pa ni mkha' 'gro ma nas gshin rje brtan ma la thug par mchod pa dang bstod pa nas gzung ba sngon du 'gro bas / rim pa ji lta ba bzhin du rdzogs par byas nas sngags kyi bzlas pa las thams cad 'grub par 'gyur ro.*

that it means that it is none other than the three yogas of body, speech, and mind.[575]

If one undertakes the ritual actions once one has practiced in the previously explained manner, **they will be achieved by the king of mantras** quintessence. What will be attained? **Have no doubt** that one will achieve here the powers that exist **imputed to,** i.e., connected with, **the seashore** of the four outer directions along with those illustrated by **the earth and trees. One will be able to** alternately, with **a curse** or mere word, harm or **benefit the animate** inhabitant beings **and the inanimate** vessel world **of the three realms** (43.30–31).

3.3.3. 2.2.2. 11.1.1. 3. Showing the name of the chapter

In the ***Concise Shrī Herukābhidhāna Tantra,*** this is **the forty-third chapter** on **the procedure of accomplishing the ritual actions** from the perspective of **the quintessence.** This is the explanation of the forty-third chapter in the *Illumination of the Hidden Meaning, A Detailed Exegesis of the Concise Saṁvara Tantra Called "The Chakrasaṁvara."*

575. Tsong Khapa here follows Butön, who simply notes that there is no Sanskrit equivalent and that it is omitted in all of the commentaries (NS 253b.4). Sachen comments upon it, but has a different commentary, writing, "The fourth person, the unobjectified, succeeds spontaneously through repetition of the seven-syllable king of mantras by means of the first, second, or third" (PG 368.2: *gang zag bzhi pas ni dmigs med ni gcig gam gnyis sam gsum gyis nges pa med par sngags kyi rgyal po yi ge bdun bzlas pas 'grub par 'gyur ro*). I have not found the source for the explanation Tsong Khapa summarizes here.

Chapter 44

Chapter 44 Outline

3.3.3. 2.2.2. 11.2. Success relying upon his and the mother's armor

The second part, success relying upon his and the mother's armor, has three sections: (1) the promise to explain, (2) the promised explanation of the meaning, and (3) showing the name of the chapter.

3.3.3. 2.2.2. 11.2.1. The promise to explain

Now, having explained the forty-third chapter, one should connect "I will explain" to **the ritual action of accomplishing,** i.e., subjugating, **the messenger, which once begun, will be quickly achieved by those who are endowed with the seven-syllable mantra** (44.1) of the six yoginīs armor, having relied upon the messenger who is an actual seal (*las rgya'i pho nya mo*).

3.3.3. 2.2.2. 11.1.2. 2. The promised explanation of the meaning

The second part has three sections: (1) the rite of summoning from the perspective of dominion, (2) the rite of suppression and subsequent release, and (3) the rite of maddening and subsequent release.

3.3.3. 2.2.2. 11.1.2. 2.1. The rite of summoning from the perspective of dominion

The first part has two sections: (1) summoning relying on a wheel and (2) summoning relying on fire sacrifice.

3.3.3. 2.2.2. 11.1.2. 2.1.1. Summoning relying on a wheel

Draw a six petalled multicolored lotus in the center of a six spoked **wheel in the middle**, i.e., on the palm, **of one's left hand. Set down** *oṁ* in the center of that [lotus] and *hriḥ ḥa ha huṁ huṁ phaṭ* on the petals. On the wheel's six spokes set down **the six** [syllables of] the mantra of **the yoginīs'** armors, *oṁ vaṁ* etc., which are colored according to the ritual action, augmented with the victim's name.

[The text] **the procedure of the seven-syllable** [mantra] and **six yoginīs abide** (44.2) should be understood as it occurs in Durjayachandra's commentary, namely:

> Set seven syllables amidst the hand.
> Six yoginīs abide on the six spokes.[576]

One should set down the six yoginīs in the middle of one's hand, as the wheel wherein the six abide by means of the procedure of the seven-syllable [mantra].

Repeat [the mantra] with the wheel on one's left hand and with an **impelling** augment with [the victim's] name and **visualize that** the victim is drawn forth apprehended in **his** own **form** through the emanation of light rays in the form of hooks from the mantra. Just as one **repeats** the seven-syllable **king of mantras** from one's mouth, the victim to whom **one's hand** is **shown** (44.3) **will be summoned** (44.4a).

576. Tsong Khapa here quotes a variant reading for 44.2ab quotes by Durjayachandra as follows: *lag dbus yi ge bdun dgod bya / rnal 'byor ma drug rtsibs drug gnas* (RG 311b.2). The canonical (PM) translation reads "Place the six yoginīs according to the rite of the seven syllables," *yi ge bdun pa'i cho ga yis / rnal 'byor ma drug rnam par dgod.*

3.3.3. 2.2.2. 11.1.2. 2.1.2. Summoning relying on fire sacrifice

Mix together red sandalwood dust or **powder and likewise black mustard seeds and salt** with **the earth of the victim's footprint** (44.4b-d) and **examine** it carefully. **Knead it with both hands,** displayed for a month and a day, and draw the wheel of **the** six **yoginīs** armors on a hearth. **Sacrifice** it, **reducing it to ash in a chaṇḍāla fire or a charnel ground fire at night** (44.5), with the yoginīs' mantra and impelling augment.

Then you should make an image of the **victim** in the ash, draw the wheel on birch bark and put it on his heart. Position it **facing** oneself, putting "summon the maddened victim" on the image, **and commence with this yoga** of repeating the mantra with the name augment. **As soon as one repeats [the mantra] one hundred times** (44.6), **he will be summoned with that,** have no doubt. **His very self as well as his wealth and the retinue** of him on whom this rite of summoning **is performed will be brought under one's control. This ritual application will succeed** (44.7), **I do not say otherwise** (44.8a), it is never otherwise.

3.3.3. 2.2.2. 11.1.2. 2.2. The rite of suppression and subsequent release

Taking that very powder, that is, the previously explained powdered mixture of red sandalwood etc., **burn it with powdered iron.** Then **wrap it in charnel ground cloth** (44.8b–d) on which is written the name of the victim. **Repeat** the augmented mantra **seven times and dig the earth to the depth of eight inches at a crossroad.** Repeat the mantra **together with the name of one's enemy,** that is, **the victim whose name one states. Hiding it there** (44.9) in the excavated earth, he **will be quickly overcome,** i.e., will be paralyzed.

If you desire to restore him, remove the wheel from the ground, and **enchant that very powder** that is within the wheel with the mantra and a liberating augment. By **energetically washing** the wheel **with pure milk,** that paralyzed one **will be restored** (44.10). **Have no doubt that** the restoration will be **achieved** (44.11a).

3.3.3. 2.2.2. 11.1.2. 2.3. The rite of maddening and subsequent release

Take this previously explained fourfold **powder together with the intoxicants** that are taken to be **five,** namely the root, stem, leaves, flowers and fruit of the datura plant. **Bind it**, i.e., wrap it, with **charnel ground cloth**, that is, a corpse cloth on which is **written** (44.11b–d) the previously explained wheel together with **the name of one's enemy** as an augment. **If one repeats** the mantra together with the victim's name augment **one hundred times and hides it** burying it in the earth **in a charnel ground, then the victim will become insane** (44.12) immediately.

If you desire to restore him, **by taking it out he is released. Take** the wheel **out** from under the earth **and wash it energetically with** pure **cow's milk, and he will be revived—have no doubt** the revival **will be achieved** (44.13). It was taught thus as was the case previously.

3.3.3. 2.2.2. 11.1.2. 3. Showing the name of the chapter

In the *Concise* ***Shrī Herukābhidhāna Tantra***, this is **the forty-fourth chapter** on **the procedure of** accomplishing **ritual actions** with **the six yoginīs' seven-syllable** armor and quintessence [mantras]. This is the explanation of the forty-fourth chapter in the *Illumination of the Hidden Meaning, A Detailed Exegesis of the Concise Saṁvara Tantra Called "The Chakrasaṁvara."*

Chapter 45

Chapter 45 Outline

3.3.3. 2.2.2. 11.2. Ritual success relying on the heroine's armor and five *ha* [syllables]

The second part, ritual success relying on the heroine's armor and five *ha* [syllables], has two sections: (1) procedures for achieving the heroine's armor and the power of speech, and (2) ritual success relying on the five *ha* [syllables].

3.3.3. 2.2.2. 11.2.1. Procedures for achieving the heroine's armor and the power of speech

The first part has three sections: (1) the promise to explain, (2) the promised explanation of the meaning, and (3) showing the name of the chapter.

3.3.3. 2.2.2. 11.2.1. 1. The promise to explain

Next, having explained the forty-fourth chapter, regarding **the excellent and supreme ritual action** that is the best among those explained [herein], the performance of the ritual action relying upon **achieving the** distinctive **powers of speech** (**45.1ab**) will be explained.

3.3.3. 2.2.2. 11.2.1. 2. The promised import explained

The second part has four sections: (1) the method for achieving the power of speech, (2) success in multiple rites of summoning relying on that, (3) achieving the power of speech relying on other methods, and (4) having obtained that, achieving many different rites with speech.

3.3.3. 2.2.2. 11.2.1. 2.1. The method for achieving the power of speech

Regarding **the oleander** (*karavīra*) [plant], it has been said that since a pebble-sized quantity can kill a horse, it is called "horsebane."[577] Its flowers come in red and also white and blue [colors].[578] **Assemble one hundred and eight red flowers** (**45.1cd**) of that [plant] **and rinse them thoroughly with cow's milk. Enchant** them **one hundred times** (**45.2**) with the heroine's armor mantra. **Hit the head of the penis** (*liṅga, ling ga*) **with a flower** as **each** one is being **enchanted** in this manner. **The one well-equipoised** in deity yoga **should do thus,** drinking and washing with the milk, **for a week** (**45.3**).

577. The oleander plant (*Nerium oleander*), called *karavīra* in Sanskrit, was also known as "horsebane" (*aśvamāra* or *aśvaghna, rta gsod*), due to its poisonous nature. Jayabhadra gives the Sanskrit *aśvamāra* and glosses it as *karavīra*, although the extant mss. read the latter here. See Sugiki 2001, 139 and CP 67b.1. This is repeated by Vīravajra at SG 204a.1.

578. The Tibetan *nag po* here likely designates the color blue, which may be a possible color for oleander flowers.

After seven days have passed one should fast for three days. On **the eleventh day, take** those **flowers** and string them on [strips of] oleander bark. **Go to** the bank of **a great river** where it empties into the ocean, worship the yoginī's wheel, **and cast** the flowers into the river **one by one** (45.4). **One should apply an enchantment to each** and all of these flowers **successively.** When **the final flower** is cast **in the river, if it is carried upstream** (45.5), and if one **grasps** the flower **together with** a palmful of **water and drinks** the flower with the water **without touching it with one's teeth,** then the adept **will attain this power of speech divulged in the secret tantra** (45.6) canon.

3.3.3. 2.2.2. 11.2.1. 2.2. Success in multiple rites of summoning relying on that

The second part has three sections: (1) summoning in reliance on binding the vulva seal, (2) summoning in reliance on fire sacrifice, and (3) ritual success relying on the oleander flower.

3.3.3. 2.2.2. 11.2.1. 2.2.1. Summoning in reliance on binding the vulva seal

After achieving the power of speech, regarding **the vulva seal** (*yonimudrā, skye gnas kyi phyag rgya*), Durjayachandra explains that it is: "a triangle that is white like the autumnal moon, outside of which is a multicolored lotus in space."[579] This is actually the reality-source seal (*dharmodayamudrā, chos 'byung gi phyag rgya*). Bhavabhaṭṭa explains, "Make the vajra handclasp in the couch position. Join tips of the two middle fingers to the tips of two thumbs and extend the two index fingers, connecting them: this is the vulva seal."[580] In other commentaries, **binding the vulva seal** is

579. This is Durjayachandra's commentary as reported by Tsong Khapa. The canonical version reads as follows: "**Binding the vulva seal,** namely a triangle that is white like an autumnal cloud, outside of which is a multicolored lotus in space" (RG 312a.1–2: *nam mkha'i dbus su sna tshogs padma de'i phyi rol du ston ka'i sprin ltar dkar ba'i zur gsum skye gnas kyi phyag rgya bcings te*).

580. The commentary occurs in Bhavabhaṭṭa's commentary. Note that the extant versions of Bhavabhaṭṭa's commentary give an alternate name for this *mudrā*, the *yoginīyogamudrā*. Tsong Khapa's commentary quotes it as providing the standard name, *skye gnas kyi phyag rgya*. It occurs as follows: *yoginīyogamudrāṁ paryaṅkaṁ baddhvā vajrabandhaṁ kṛtvā madhyamādvayamukhenāṅguṣṭhadvayamukhe yojayed ity yoginīyo-gamudreti*

explained as union with an external spell consort (*phyi'i rig ma*);[581] it is accomplished relying on both dependence upon binding the reality-source seal (*dharmodayamudrā*) and a spell consort (*rig ma*).

Binding that reality-source seal, **the mantrin should repeat** the summoning mantra along with an augment **one hundred and eight** times, **facing** the direction of **the victim**'s image. The wheel is **positioned**, i.e., placed, **on the abdomen** of **the victim**'s image (**45.7**) **in the manner** of a visualized image **positioned by one's mind. The wise one**, that is the adept, **in three sessions should** press the channel with the thumb of his left hand and **move** the channel of the secret place with his **little finger**; it is explained that this is the way of forming the image and so forth.[582]

If one does thus, even [if one] has great sin as illustrated by **brahmin-slayer, after seven days Shakra, and so forth**, [indicating] Īshvara etc. **will be summoned** (**45.8**). This implies that those types of people who have embarked upon this vehicle even though they have previously committed great sins attain the distinctive ability to eliminate sin.

Regarding an explanation of that in which one makes an image of the previously explained victim, **make an image of the victim** who is to be summoned in the earth of the victim's footprint **with red sandalwood powder. Anoint the form** of that image with **the three spices**, i.e., ginger, long pepper (*pipli*), and black pepper, and furthermore this form is **also smeared with beeswax** (**45.9**). Other commentaries explain that "one should make

---

kecit / (Pandey 2002, 565; *rnal 'byor ma'i rnal 'byor gyi phyag rgya ni skyil krung bcas la rdo rje bcings par byas nas gung mo gnyis kyi kha dang mthe bong gnyis kha sbyar nas mdzub mo gnyis sgreng ste / phan tshun sbyar ba ni rnal 'byor ma'i rnal 'byor gyi phyag rgya zhes kha cig zer ro* (2002, 815–16).

581. This comment was made by Jayabhadra, who wrote, "**Binding the vulva seal** is uniting with an external woman" (Sugiki 2001, 139; *yonimudrāṁ baddhveti bāhyāṅganāsaṁpuṭībhūtvā*; CP 67b.1: *skye gnas rgya bcings pa zhes bya ba ni phyi'i lha mo dang kha sbyor gyi sbyor ba bya ba'o*). This commentary is repeated by Bhavyakīrti (BC 39b.1) and Vīravajra (SG 204a.1).

582. Tsong Khapa here follows Kambala's commentary, which here reads: "Draw on the channel in her vulva; it can also be visualized in the penis. The wise one should press the channel with the thumb of the fist of the left hand and move the little finger in three sessions" (SN 75b.7–76a.1: *de'i skye gnas nas skud pa dbyung ngo / yang na ling gar yang bsams la / lag pa g.yon pa'i khu tshur gyi mthe bos skud pa mnan la / blo ldan thun gsum mthe'u chung bskyod*). The Sanskrit for this occurs on K fol. 74a, which unfortunately is not readable.

the image from beeswax and smear it with red sandalwood powder and the three spices."[583] It is explained that the wheel is to be placed on its navel.[584]

The adept pierces it with a copper needle in the secret place, i.e., in the vulva for females and the penis for males. Place a thread in its track and move that thread with one's little finger. The *Twofold Commentary* [states], namely, that the partners unite before the image, one repeats the mantra with an augment, and after that, up until **mind positioned on that** (45.8a), [there is] **the little finger**, which is said to be the vajra, the root at the end of the left one, meaning that one should move it with one's mind in three sessions.[585] If one explains in this manner, it means that at the conclusion of one's mind being focused on repetition, and at the conclusion of the vajra of the secret place enjoying the "left one," the woman, one stimulates the channel of the secret place, called the "root" or "lower one" with the little finger. Once this is done, one creates the intention with one's mind to arouse the lotus of the victim at the three junctures of the day. That [work] also states, "Through this the yogī adept will fulfill all passionate [desires]."[586] By doing

583. This comment was made by Jayabhadra, who wrote: "Regarding **smear with beeswax**, it is applicable here that one should make the image with beeswax and smear it with red sandalwood powder and with the three spices" (Sugiki 2001, 139: *sikthakena pralepayed ity atra sikthakena prakṛtiṁ kṛtvā raktacandanadhūlibhis trikaṭukena pralepayed iti yojanīyam*; CP 67b.1–2: *sbra tshil gyis kyang rab tu byug / ces bya ba ni / 'dir sbra tshil las gzugs brnyan byas la / tsanda na dmar po'i phye ma dang tsha ba gsum gyi lde gus byug / ces bya ba sbyar*).

This commentary is repeated by Bhavyakīrti (BC 39b.1–2) and Vīravajra (SG 204a.2). This seems like a more plausible recipe for a figurine that is to be pierced by needles.

584. This comment is made by Tathāgatarakṣhita. See UN 246a.2–3.

585. Tsong Khapa paraphrases Tathāgatarakṣhita's commentary here; the passage reads as follows: *bsgrub bya'i gzugs brnyan gyi mdun du las kyi lhag ma dang lhan cig tu kha sbyor du byas la bsgrub bya'i ming brten pa'i sngags brgya rtsa brgyad bzlas par bya'o zhes pa'i don to / de'i rjes thogs su mthe'u chung zhes bya ba la sogs pa ni de la yid kyi gnas zhes pa'i mthar te / rdo rjes g.yon pa'i mthar rtsa ba'i sgrar brjod do / de yid kyi thun gsum du bskyed par bya'o zhes dgongs so*. My translation follows Tsong Khapa's paraphrase, which occurs as follows: *bshad sbyar las gzugs brnyan gyi mdun du yab yum kha sbyar du byas te / sngags spel tshig dang bcas pa bzla la / de'i rjes su mthe'u chung zhes bya ba la sogs pa ni/ de la yid kyis gnas zhes pa'i mthar te / rdo rjes g.yon pa'i mthar rtsa ba'i sgrar brjod do / de yid kyis thun gsum du bskyod par bya'o zhes 'chad pa ltar na* (UN 245.4–5).

586. Tsong Khapa quotes Tathāgatarakṣhita again. The passage quoted reads: *'di ni rnal 'byor pa sgrub pa pos chags pa can gyi thams cad rdzogs par 'gyur ba bstan pa yin no* (UN 246a.5).

thus, the victim will fulfill all of one's passionate desires, which means that he or she will be in one's power for a long time. Bhavabhaṭṭa explains:[587]

> Regarding **little finger**, insert into the navel of the image made from the earth of the victim's footprint, etc., a sheet of paper on which is written a mantra garland with the syllables of the six yoginīs' armor mantra along with the augment. **Should move** means should repeat that mantra, namely that you repeat it placing your mind on it in three sessions in front of the image.

The wise one, in applying the ritual action, **should heat** that previously explained image without melting the beeswax **with smokeless acacia charcoal for seven days** (45.10), **enchanting it one hundred times** in each session. Once one has enchanted it by doing thus, one can "come before **the king**,"[588] that is **summon** him **along with his vassal lord**, high minister, **and harem** (45.11).

Write the wheel of the armor **mantra** as previously explained, **adding the name of the king together with his court, on a leaf of birch bark**. "Ghost" is **a corpse**, and its **lac** is a resin that is painted on nails. *Ro tsa na* (*rocanā*) is a concretion. It should be written by one who is equipoised, i.e., has an unwavering mind, with ink made from these two things,[589] and placed on the navel of the victim's image. Then **repeat** (45.12) the mantra augmented

587. This is a translation of Tsong Khapa's slightly abridged version of Bhavabhaṭṭa's commentary; the canonical version of the commentary occurs as follows: *kaniṣṭhāṁ ṣaḍyoginīṣaḍ[a]kṣaramālāṁ savidarbhāṁ yantragatāṁ kṛtvā sādhyapādadhūlyādikṛtā-yāḥ sādhyapratikṛterudare nikṣiptām / cālayej japet / kiṃbhūto japed ity āha sādhyasya pratikṛtigatasyābhimukhaḥ / trisandhyaṁ tanmanaḥsthitaḥ śakrādivaśam ānayet /* (Pandey 2002, 565); *mthe'u chung ni rnal 'byor ma drug gi yi ge drug gi phreng ba spel ba dang bcas pa shog bur rtogs par byas la / bsgrub bya'i rkang rjes kyi rdul la sogs pa las byas pa'i gzugs brnyan gyi lto bar bcug ste / bskyod pa ni bzlas par bya'o / ci lta bur gyur pas bzlas zhes pa la gsungs te / bsgrub bya'i gzugs brnyan gtogs pa la mngon du phyogs te / thun mtshams gsum de yid la gnas pas brgya byin la sogs pa 'gugs par byed do* (2002, 816).

588. Tsong Khapa here glosses the canonical translation, "come before the king," *mi'i bdag po mdun na 'don*, which has no equivalent in the Sanskrit, and which simply includes the king in the list of those summoned.

589. That is, the lac and concretion of a corpse. The text being commented upon is *pretālaktarocanayā likhet* (45.12c), which the SM translation renders as *yi dags sen rtsi ro tsa nas / mnyam par bzhag ste bris nas ni*. The canonical PM translation, like the Sanskrit, omits *mnyam par bzhag ste*, but also omits any equivalent to *pretālakta*. It reads: *gi wang dag gis bris nas ni*. See Gray 2012, 215, 386, 553–54.

with the name of the victim one hundred times for a week, **facing his** image, and **burn**, i.e., warm, that image **on a** smokeless **fire of acacia wood. It is** also **said that for the sake of success** in the rite of summoning it should be scorched **over a fire of charnel ground** charcoal or ash. If **the beeswax** of the image **does not melt** (45.13) **while being heated**, once one has repeated the mantra one hundred and eight times for a week, ordinary **kings along with**, i.e., also including, **a universal monarch, are summoned** (45.14ab).

3.3.3. 2.2.2. 11.2.1. 2.2.2. Summoning in reliance on fire sacrifice

Dust from the victim's feet and also red sandalwood (45.14cd) **and** "burnt **charnel ground ash**"—Mal's translation reads "burnt charnel ground ash,"[590] which is excellent—**the adept compounds** these substances, and with them makes an image of the one to be summoned. Then **warm** that image **vigorously over a smokeless acacia wood fire** (45.15). Place the two previously indicated wheels on **both hands**, and **grind that powder**, grate the image to powder and **immolate it. One will succeed** by **immolating it as soon as** the summoning is to be achieved.

The two lines [beginning with] **having taken that powder** do not occur in either the dual translation or in the other two translations; [my explanation thus] accords with the *Twofold Commentary*.[591] As they seem to occur, **having taken that powder**, i.e., image, **bury it** in a charnel ground, holding one's breath **without wavering and without exhaling** (45.16); this is the system of not immolating it. If this is done, one will see that the victim **is stupefied**, as if **rendered senseless, beguiled** so he or she knows nothing, and **afflicted**, i.e., tormented by suffering. **He or she will come with the speed of the wind and throw herself down before the adept** (45.17).

3.3.3. 2.2.2. 11.2.1. 2.2.3. Ritual success relying on the oleander flower

Thus, having explained fire sacrifice, regarding **messenger . . . by the ritual action**, go to the burning ground, to the cremation site of a man, together

590. Tsong Khapa quotes Mal Lotsawa's translation as *dur khrod thal bar bsregs pa rnams*, which is close to the extant SL translation.

591. The next two lines, *rdul de blangs nas ma yengs par / dbugs mi 'byin par sbas na ni*, actually occur in all three of the extant translations, but is not commented upon by Tathāgatarakṣhita.

with a woman. Calling out the woman's name, she will be made to **accept** (**45.18**) the thrice [made] command, "My bidding will always be done by you!"[592]

Taking a measure of the complete upper **arm**[593] or about two and a half hands of length **of a moist oleander shoot** (**45.19**), **cast it into a blazing funeral fire. Quickly seize** that shoot **before it is consumed** (**45.20**), and **repeat wisdom's**, i.e., the heroine's, armor **mantra seven times.** If you circumambulate left-wise, i.e., counterclockwise, repeating "So-and-so come here!" or "Bring such-and-such boy or girl here!" **in a moment**, as soon as one circumambulates, **a comely man or woman will come with the speed of the wind** (**45.21**). Both this [augment] "So-and-so come here!" and the previous "Die, woman!" are to be appended [to the mantra].[594]

3.3.3. 2.2.2. 11.2.1. 2.3. Achieving the power of speech relying on other methods

A red oleander flower, enchanted one hundred times and taken up **during the Puṣhya conjunction, is smeared with concretion by the adept. The flower is placed in** intoxicating **water** (**45.22**) and enchanted one hundred and eight times. **Entering into a river, positioned in the water up to one's navel,** it should be **enchanted thus one thousand times.** After that, a practice companion should **position**, i.e., place, [the flower] with flawless anthers etc. in **one's**, i.e., the adept's, **cupped hands** (**45.23**), and should spread the flower's petals. Regarding *phyir klags*, since it also occurs as "full" (*legs bkang*),[595] **both of one's** [cupped] **hands are filled** with the flower by

592. Tsong Khapa here follows Kambala's commentary. See SN 76a.2.

593. The Sanskrit here reads *bāhupramaṇataḥ*, a "forearm's measure," which was translated into Tibetan as *dpung pa'i tshad mnyam*, an "upper arm measure."

594. Here Tsong Khapa is making a cryptic reference to a verse in this chapter that he really did not explain, 45.18, which appears to refer to human sacrifice. I translated it as: "She should be made into a sacrificial victim or a messenger. Thus, indeed is a messenger captured by means of the ritual action" (Gray 2007, 356). Kambala lists the augments added to the mantra in both instances. See SN 76a.2–3.

595. The Sanskrit, *saṁpūrṇa*, is clearly translated as *legs bkang* in the SL translation, and obscurely translated as *phyer brlags* in the PM translation, and *phyer glags*. Tsong Khapa quotes it as *phyir klags*, and there are many spelling variants in the different print and manuscript editions of these texts, evidently due to the obscurity of this translation. Regarding this, see Gray 2012, 388, n. 3268; 55, nn. 706, 707.

one's practice companion, and one **should drink it together with water** without [the flower] contacting one's teeth. **Then**, after drinking it, that **adept will obtain the power of speech** (45.24) through which all ritual actions are accomplished with just speech.

Devagupta quotes [a variant of 45.23c], "positioned in the vulva," and since this seems to be the intention of Kambala as well,[596] it should not occur as "positioned in both of one's hands." If it is as they [indicate], then it is said that during a solar eclipse the red flower is positioned in the union of the two "birth places" (*skye gnas*), that is, the two secret places. It appears that it is drunk with the water when the sun and moon come out, liberated from the planet [Rāhu].

3.3.3. 2.2.2. 11.2.1. 2.4. Having obtained that, achieving many different rites with speech

The fourth part has two sections: (1) rites of summoning and destroying, and (2) explaining the rite of summoning in particular.

3.3.3. 2.2.2. 11.2.1. 2.4.1. Rites of summoning and destroying

Regarding the necessity for achieving the power of speech, **the king or queen will be summoned with one's** summoning **mind** if you say his or her name and say "Summon!" By speaking thus, **titans and men** along with **the gods will be instantly brought into one's power** (45.25). **One may kill them with the words** "Kill such-and-such" with a **fervent** intent. One can cause them to remain with affection or **hostility** and also **expel** them. In short, **the adept can subjugate with just a word** (45.26).[597]

With the words, "Immobilize such-and-such!" **one may** "suppress"

596. Kambala's commentary here quotes only part of the line as follows: "**Positioned in** means positioned in union in the vulva" (SN 76a.3: *dbus gnas zhes bya ni skye gnas kha sbyar ba'i dbus su gnas pa'o*; K 73b.2: *saṁstitam iti yonisaṁpuṭamadhyasthitam*). As Tsong Khapa notes, Devagupta quotes the alternate reading of 45.23c, and then repeats Kambala's commentary. It occurs as follows: *skye gnas dbus nas me tog de / zhes pa la dbus gnas zhes pa ni/ skye gnas gnyis kha sbyar ba'i dbus na yang dag par gnas pa'o* (SS 153b.2–3).

597. Tsong Khapa follows the Tibetan translations in reading hostility (*dbye ba*), expelling (*bskrad pa*) and subjugation (*tshar gcod pa*) as the magical operations to be accomplished here. The Sanskrit, on the other hand, reads controlling (*vaśa*) rather than hostility, but agrees with the latter two, with *uccāṭana* and *nigraha*, respectively.

(*gnon*), that is, **immobilize,**[598] **rivers, vehicles, war machines,**[599] **the ocean, elephants, horses, and likewise clouds, people,** that is men, while the word **or** [indicates] women and **even birds** (45.27). In short, having contemplated **with one's mind, with a word one can do everything,** i.e., one can do **whatever** ritual action **one desires** (**45.28ab**) in one's mind. This is the force that accomplishes the power of speech.

3.3.3. 2.2.2. 11.2.1. 2.4.2. Explaining the rite of summoning in particular

The application of summoning a victim will be explained; **bewitching,** i.e., intoxicating, **all women** (**45.28cd**) is just an example. As for showing this, **take a red oleander blossom** while one is fervent. **Having enchanted it one hundred**[600] **times with the spell,** i.e., the heroine's armor mantra, **place it in the vulva** (45.29) of the seal. As for the meaning of that, that flower is that which is **put in,** that is, inserted into, **the secret place** of the seal who is **united with** the outer actual seal (consort) (*phyi'i las rgya*). **The mantrin who has the yoga of nondual gnosis should repeat** the armor mantra with the name augment **one hundred and one times** (45.30). **The adept should take one flower from among those** flowers **in the vulva. She who is struck by the flower will come into one's power at the moment** (45.31) she is struck.

Regarding the manner in which she comes into one's power, through the magical force of being struck by the flower, that victim **faints and is rendered senseless,** i.e., unconscious, **under the power of another,** that is, the adept, lacking autonomy in the functioning of **all of her limbs and joints.** With respect to her previous state of mind, **her confidence is thwarted,** i.e., overturned. Regarding **her coming under one's power instantly** (45.32), it is **a power** achieved through **confidence** in the application of mantra. It is the rite of action that is **done without fail** (45.33), i.e., that bears fruit when undertaken.

598. Tsong Khapa glosses the verb *gnon* with *rengs*, which is a better translation for the Sanskrit verb *stambhayet*.

599. The term *yantra*, *'khrul 'khor*, "device," in this context refers to war machines or siege engines.

600. The PM and SM translations read *brgya*, "one hundred." However, the Sanskrit reads *sapta*, "seven," a reading followed in the SL translation.

3.3.3. 2.2.2. 11.2.1. 3. Showing the name of the chapter

Regarding the name of this chapter **in the** ***Concise Shrī Herukābhidhāna Tantra***, in Mardo's solo and dual translation it is "the detailed description of the six yoginī ritual actions and the power of speech."[601] While Lochen also translated it as "the detailed description of the power of speech of the six yoginīs,"[602] it was translated by Mal as "the six yoginīs' power of speech and the procedure of summoning,"[603] which accords with Vīravajra's commentary.[604] Since the import [of this] is also better, this is **the forty-fifth chapter** on **the procedure of** accomplishing **the power of speech** with **the six yoginīs'** armor mantra, **and** accomplishing **ritual actions** such as **summoning** and so forth through the achievement of that. This is the explanation of the forty-fifth chapter in the *Illumination of the Hidden Meaning, A Detailed Exegesis of the Concise Saṁvara Tantra Called "The Chakrasaṁvara."*

601. That is, *rnal 'byor ma drug dang tshig gi dngos grub lung bstan pa*, the title found in the PM and SM translations.

602. That is, *rnal 'byor ma drug gi tshig gi dngos grub lung bstan pa.*

603. Tsong Khapa reports that Mal's translation is *rnal 'byor ma drug gi tshig gi dngos grub dang / dgug pa'i cho ga*, which closely accords with the SL translation, *rnal 'byor ma drug gi dngos grub dang / 'gugs pa'i cho ga* (Gray 2012, 473). It also accords most closely to the extant Sanskrit, namely *ṣaḍyoginīkarmavākṣiddhyākarṣaṇavidhi* (2012, 218).

604. As Tsong Khapa notes, Vīravajra's commentary quotes the chapter title in a manner that accords with Mal's translation as well as the extant Sanskrit. It reads: *rnal 'byor ma drug gi tshig grub pa dang dgug pa'i cho ga* (SG 204a.2–3).

Chapter 46

Chapter 46 Outline

3.3.3. 2.2.2. 11.2.2. Ritual success relying on the five *ha* [syllables]

The second part, ritual success relying on the five *ha* [syllables], has three sections: (1) the promise to explain, (2) the promised explanation of the meaning, and (3) showing the name of the chapter.

3.3.3. 2.2.2. 11.2.2. 1. The promise to explain

Next, having explained the forty-fifth chapter, **I will explain**[605] **the accomplishment of all ritual actions**, such as killing **relying upon the five *ha* syllables.** Regarding the need for this, [the text] states that it is because the adept, **through mere knowledge** of them and by putting them into practice, **will rapidly engage with**, i.e., attain, **power (46.1)**.

605. This verb, *bshad*, is found only in the SL translation; it does not occur in the extant Sanskrit or the PM and SM translations.

3.3.3. 2.2.2. 11.2.2. 2. The promised import explained

The second part has three sections: (1) the rite of killing, (2) the rite of shape changing, and (3) the rite of womb transference.

3.3.3. 2.2.2. 11.2.2. 2.1. The rite of killing

The five syllables in the solo Mardo translation are *hai ho hau*[606] *haṁ ha*;[607] the dual translation reads *haṁ ho hi hai ha*.[608] It appears, moreover, in many different [forms] in other translations.[609] It should be taken as previously asserted by Bhava[bhaṭṭa], that *hā hī hū hai hau* results when you apply to *ha* the vowels that remain, *a*, *i*, *u*, *e* and *o* in [the selection of] the previously [discussed] hero's six-armor mantra.[610]

These five syllables should be actually written or visualized on the five spokes of a wheel on one's hand. **Rub with one's hand** which has an arrow **the** written or visualized **five syllables**, the mantra together **with a** word of **command.** Make a fire sacrifice, and visualize that you pierce **his mouth** with a five-pointed needle, such that **blood is drawn** and is collected in a

606. The subscribed letter *'a* was affixed to bottom of the syllable *ho* here; this is evidently an archaic way to transliterate the Sanskrit letter *hau*, found also in some of the older manuscripts and print editions; see Gray 2002, 390, n. 3304; 556, n. 718.

607. This is very close to the mantra as preserved in the SM edition; see Gray 2002, 556.

608. This is close to the mantra as preserved in the PM edition; in my edition of this text I read this mantra as *haṁ hau ho hai haḥ* (Gray 2002, 390). However, there was considerable variance among the manuscripts.

609. It reads for example, as *he ho hu haṁ ha* in the SL translation. The Sanskrit texts reads *haṁ hau ho hai haḥ*, according with the PM translation. Kambala's Sanskrit commentary reads *hā hī hū he ho haḥ*, for a total of six syllables (K 73b.3), while the Tibetan translation attests only five, *ha hi hu he ho* (SN 76a.4).

610. Tsong Khapa here refers to Bhavabhaṭṭa's commentary on these syllables, which occurs as follows: "It is said that *hā hī hai hau haḥ* are the five *ha* syllables. The *ha* syllables are distinguished by the five vowels that remain following the selection of the hero's six-armor mantra" (Pandey 2002, 569: *hakārapañcakam āha hā hī hai hau haḥ iti hakārapañcakam / ṣaṣṭhaṁ svaraṁ vinā ṣaḍvīrakavacamantraoddhāraśeṣapañcasvara-viśeṣito hakāraḥ*; 2002, 835–36: *ha lnga ston te hā hī hai hau haṁ / zhes bya ba ni ha lnga'o / dbyangs drug po gang yin pa'i dpa' bo drug gi go cha'i sngags btu ba'i lhag ma dbyangs lna ni has khyad par du byas pa'o*).

Note that Tsong Khapa's presentation of the five syllables according to Bhavabhaṭṭa and the presentations in the Sanskrit and Tibetan versions of the commentary all differ.

skull bowl. Blood will flow from the victim's mouth, and **one's foe dies instantly** (**46.2**).

Make a wheel with five spokes, and in its center draw the five long vowels ending with *haḥ*, with visarga. Mix together **one's own blood with** that **of one's ring finger** and the blood of a childless woman. **Place**, i.e., put, it in a **skull**, and repeat [the mantra] with the victim's name augment. If you rub it with your hand **until it dries**, by that **the victim will perish** (**46.3**), i.e., die. **Should one**, lacking the two substances,[611] **repeat** the five syllables with a name augment **with eyes** blazing with **anger and reddened**, he who is the victim, illustrated by **the king with his army and mount, will quickly be killed** (**46.4**).

Generate the five fleshes, of **the cat, mongoose, crow, fox**[612] **and crane** from the five syllables over the course of a month and form them into a **ḍākinī** "full of strength," that is, **sacrificial cake**,[613] as a preliminary, and **make a fire offering** [with it]. **There is no doubt that in this tantra one quickly attains the power** (**46.5**) of killing etc. with these meats.

3.3.3. 2.2.2. 11.2.2. 2.2. The rite of shape changing

Make a cord from the hair of rabbit, and so forth, i.e., a jackal etc., **and enchant it a thousand times** with the five *ha* [syllables]. **That** victim **around whose neck it is bound will assume** the form that is **like that** (**46.6**), that of a rabbit etc.

3.3.3. 2.2.2. 11.2.2. 2.3. The rite of womb transference

Having enchanted one's hand one thousand times with the five *ha* [syllables], **if one touches a pregnant woman with an oleander blossom, the embryo is transferred. Enchanting each syllable**[614] means that you

611. The "two substances" (*rdzas gnyis po*) are, apparently, the blood of one's ring finger and blood of a childless woman. Presumably, it would be the latter which might be in short supply.

612. That is, *wa*, in Tibetan translation. The Sanskrit reads *jambūka*, "jackal."

613. The Sanskrit *bali*, "sacrifice," "sacrificial offering," was incorrectly translated into Tibetan as *stobs can*. Tsong Khapa glosses this with the correct translation, *gtor ma*.

614. Tsong Khapa follows the Tibetan in reading "enchant," *mngon bzlas* here. The Sanskrit reads *saṁyojya*, "employing."

enchant one hundred thousand time per the count of each of the five *ha* syllables.[615] This means that they are then employed in the ritual action. When the touch is **released** from the body, **there is liberation** due to the transference of the embryo.

That victim **who is admonished** fiercely and toward whom the mantra is repeated vehemently **is killed**. Furthermore, if the mantra is repeated peacefully and the admonishment is relaxed, she or he **will be restored** (46.7).

3.3.3. 2.2.2. 11.2.2. 3. Showing the name of the chapter

In the *Concise* ***Shrī Herukābhidhāna Tantra***, this is **the forty-sixth chapter** on **the procedure** of accomplishing **ritual actions** relying upon **the five *ha* syllables.** This is the explanation of the forty-sixth chapter in the *Illumination of the Hidden Meaning, A Detailed Exegesis of the Concise Saṁvara Tantra Called "The Chakrasaṁvara."*

615. Presumably this means that you repeat the five-syllable mantra 500,000 times.

Chapter 47

Chapter 47 Outline

3.3.3. 2.2.2. 11.3. Success with the buddhaḍākinī mantra and continual performance of deity visualization

The third part, success with the buddhaḍākinī mantra and continual performance of deity visualization, has two sections: (1) ritual success with the buddhaḍākinī mantra, and (2) continual visualization of the heroes and yoginīs.

3.3.3. 2.2.2. 11.3.1. Ritual success with the buddhaḍākinī mantra

The first part has three sections: (1) the promise to explain, (2) the promised explanation of the meaning, and (3) showing the name of the chapter.

3.3.3. 2.2.2. 11.3.1. 1. The promise to explain

Now, having shown ritual success with the five *ha* [syllables] in the forty-sixth [chapter], one might wonder what **I will explain** thence. It is the quintessence of Vajravārāhī that brings together **all ḍākinīs.** The rites are accomplished via the revelation [of this mantra] in reverse order in the chapter that follows this one.[616]

Although someone states that it is the Vairochanī mantra, other commentaries accord with the name of the chapter, which refers to the buddhaḍākinī mantra.[617] Regarding its necessity, **the mere utterance of** this quintessence mantra **gives rise to all powers** such as subjugation and so forth. **I will explain** (47.1) it due to that.

3.3.3. 2.2.2. 11.3.1. 2. The promised explanation of the meaning

The second part has two sections: (1) success with the rites of controlling and destroying, and (2) success with the rite of transforming into another [state].

3.3.3. 2.2.2. 11.3.1. 2.1. Success with the rites of controlling and destroying

Then, after the preliminary service, if one **repeats the ḍākinīs' great spell**, i.e., the augmented buddhaḍākinī mantra, **one brings all of the social classes,** the military aristocracy (*kṣatriya*), etc. **under one's control.** If that mantra is **repeated constantly, the great glory**, i.e., all good things such as longevity, will be **generated** (47.2.1).

Produce a stake made of human bone, six finger's breadths long, and **enchant it one hundred and eight times** with the [female] partner's mantra. **The lineage of** that victim **in whose door it is infixed will be cut off.** Bhavabhaṭṭa explains that the mantra is repeated eight hundred times, and

616. That is, this mantra is displayed in reverse order in the next chapter.

617. This is Vajravārāhī's essence mantra, revealed in chapter 8. Butön makes the claim that this mantra is the focus of this chapter; see NS 260b.5. Tsong Khapa rejects this idea and advances the thesis that this chapter focuses on Vajravārāhī's buddhaḍākinī quintessence mantra. Bhavabhaṭṭa, on the other hand, following the Indian tradition in general and contra the Tibetan interpretation, identifies the longer sarvabuddhaḍākinī mantra as the essence, and the Vairochanī mantra as the quintessence. See Pandey 2002, 572, 831.

quotes "driven out" [in place of] "cut off."[618] If you dig the earth **in his cattle pen, and in his place for buffalo, elephants, and horses**, and enchant and **implant** the previously explained stake, all of his fields and so forth **will be lost** (47.2.2).[619]

Now, if a wise one wants to control the king or the royal minister, she or he should, in the application of the rite, **make an image** of the victim **eight finger's breadths long out of clay**, that is, the mud that is conglomerated in the hands of a potter. Set the mantra with the victim's name augment written on birch bark etc. on its heart, and **place it**, i.e., dig the earth and bury it, **at the gate of the king** or minister. **Should one, on the first day, immolate three thousand** [times] **citron flowers** and fruit **mixed with** saffron crocus **blossoms**, and afterward offer eight thousand immolations, **he**, the king, etc. **will be subjugated.**

With this buddhaḍākinī **mantra** and with the method of deity visualization and taking the appropriate color of the mantra and so forth, **one can summon**, "subdue" or **paralyze, bewilder, dessicate,**[620] **drain energy,**[621] **steal speech**, i.e., cause muteness, **and also blind** the eye **and make** the tongue **stammer.** If one desires to restore [the victim], if one repeats the mantra with a peaceful intent, one can **release him or her** (47.2.3), i.e., reverse the power of the mantra's ritual application.

3.3.3. 2.2.2. 11.3.1. 2.2. Success with the rite of transforming into another [state]

The second part has six sections: (1) transforming into another gender, (2) transforming into another life form, (3) transforming into another substance, (4) transforming into another mental state, (5) transforming into another form, and (6) turning another man's wealth [into one's own].

618. Tsong Khapa is not quoting Bhavabhaṭṭa here but is referring to the use of the verb *skrod*, "expel, drive out" to translate *ucchāda*, rather than *gcod* as in the canonical translation. This is a translation issue, as the Sanskrit version of the commentary correctly quotes the root text here. See Pandey 2002, 572, 832.

619. That is, his crops and livestock will be destroyed.

620. Tsong Khapa follows the Tibetan, which reads *skems pa*, "parching, drying up." The Sanskrit lists the more common operation, *dveṣaṇa*, "inciting hostility."

621. This operation, *rmugs pa*, occurs in the SL and SM translations, but is omitted in the Sanskrit and PM translation. See Gray 2012, 474, 557.

3.3.3. 2.2.2. 11.3.1. 2.2.1. Transforming into another gender

Next, if a man wishes to become a woman, [he **should assemble**[622]] **and divide into equal portions:**[623]

1. **Flowers from a human corpse**
2. An iron comb[624]
3. **Velvet beans** (*kākaṇḍakīphala*), which are said to be the Mahākāla fruit or the fruit of the "black creeper"[625]
4. **Crows's nail,** i.e., the nail of a crow,[626] regarding which "nail of a ravenous one" also occurs, which is explained to mean the nail of a crow,[627] and is also explained to mean, being ravenous, the nail of a corpse[628]
5. **Skin from the bottom,** i.e., sole, **of the foot.**[629]

Take the seed that has been produced in the previously described skull of a woman, and **pulverize** [the substances listed above] **with rabbit blood. Form** [the mixture] **into eleven pills and dry them in the shade. In this**

622. The verb *saṁgṛhya* is not translated in the Tibetan translations and is thus omitted by Tsong Khapa. I add it here in brackets for the sake of clarity.

623. Tsong Khapa merely lists the items and comments on them. To clarify this, I have organized the items in list form. The numbers were added by me.

624. This item, *lcags kyi so tog*, is not listed in the root text.

625. The name given for this fruit is the *kākaṇḍakīphala*, the fruit of the kākaṇḍa plant or velvet bean, *Mucuna pruriens*. Kambala glosses this as "Mahākāla fruit," *mahākālaphalam* (K 73b.7), which evidently is an alternate name for the fruit of this plant. Tsong Khapa lists "black creeper," *lcug ma nag po*, as another name of the plant.

626. Tsong Khapa glosses *khwa'i sen mo* as *bya khwa ta'i sen mo*.

627. Kambala comments that "ravenous one" indicates a crow. (K 73b.7: *bubhukṣita iti kākaḥ*; SN 76b.1–2: *bkres pa zhes bya ba ni kha ste*).

628. Jayabhadra, on the other hand, quotes a variant reading, *prabhukṣita*, and glosses it as "of a corpse." (Sugiki 2001, 139: *prabhukṣitasyeti mṛtakasya*; CP 67b.5: *rab tu rtogs pa ni mi shi ba'o*).

629. The extant Sanskrit here reads *bubhukṣitasya pādau carmanakhādi*, which I translated as "the skin, nails, and so forth, [from] the feet of one who is ravenous." (Gray 2007, 361–62). The Tibetan translations, however, take them as two separate items, "Nail of a crow and skin from the sole of the foot," (PM, SM: *khwa'i sen mo dang / rkang pa'i 'og gi pags pa*; Gray 2012, 393, 557), while the SL translation translates *bubhukṣitasya* literally and omits any reference to skin, i.e., *bkres pa'i sen mo dang / rkang pa'i 'og gi sen mo*, Gray 2012, 474).

way, take them in **one's hand on a good day,** i.e., at an auspicious time and astrological configuration, and **bind them to** one's fist. Repeat [the mantra] at every juncture of everyday, and **on the twelfth day, he on whose head the** pill **powder is applied will become a woman** (47.2.4). In the case of one who is bald it is as above.

3.3.3. 2.2.2. 11.3.1. 2.2.2. Transforming into another life form

Now, if a man wants to become a dog, he **should place** ***puṣhya*** **iron,**[630] i.e., gold, powdered with saffron **in** the head, i.e., **skull, of** an excellent **mongoose,** i.e., weasel.[631] **Repeat** the mantra **eight thousand times over seven nights,** i.e., days. **On the seventh**[632] **day, balance it with saffron, enchant the powder eight hundred times** with the augmented mantra, **and immolate** it in a hearth for all rites. **He on whose head this ash is applied will transform into a dog. With regard to his restoration,** if one **undertakes at night a great ḍākinī worship** ceremony, **offer a sacrificial cake** and request this, after that **he will return to his original nature** (47.2.5).

3.3.3. 2.2.2. 11.3.1. 2.2.3. Transforming into another substance

If **one wishes to make a** precious **substance**—i.e., gold, silver, etc.—**or a non-**precious **substance, should one immolate golden fruits,** i.e., datura fruits, **one hundred and eight** [times] together with an augment, **there will be** a [precious] **substance** or **non-**[precious] **substance. If one** performs eight hundred **immolations** of eight hundred **yellow myrobalan** [fruits],[633] **it will return to its original nature** (47.2.6).

630. The Sanskrit here is somewhat obscure, with variant readings *puṣyaloha* and *puṣyalohita,* i.e., "Puṣhya iron" or "iron of the Puṣhya asterism." This is translated, literately and obscurely, as *rgyal lcags* (SM; SL: *rgya lcags*), but the PM translation gives an interpretive translation, *skar ma rgyal gyi gnam lcags,* "meteoric iron of the Puṣhya asterism," which I used as the basis of my translation, "meteoric iron." See Gray 2007, 362 and 2012, 221, 394, 474, 557. However, Tsong Khapa follows Kambala, who glossed it as "gold" (K 74a.1: *puṣyalohitam iti suvarṇaṁ*; SN 76b.3: *rgyal gyi lcags zhes bya ba ni gser ro*).

631. Tsong Khapa here glosses "mongoose" (*ne'u le*), an animal not found in Tibet, as "weasel," *sre mo,* a better known related species.

632. The Sanskrit reads "on the seventh day," *saptame divase,* while the Tibetan reads "on the eighth day," *nyin zhag brgyad pa la* (Gray 2012, 222, 394).

633. That is the fruit of the *harītakī* or *a ru ra* tree, i.e., *Terminalia chebula.*

3.3.3. 2.2.2. 11.3.1. 2.2.4. Transforming into another mental state

If **one wishes to be intoxicated,**[634] **should one immolate the abode of the great bird,** that is, the owl[635] with thorn wood, having done preliminary repetition of the mantra eight thousand times over seven days, **on the seventh day, one will be intoxicated. With regard to one** reversal, i.e., **restoration,** if you perform eight thousand **immolations** of rice **chaff** in the fire, **it will be terminated** (47.2.7).

3.3.3. 2.2.2. 11.3.1. 2.2.5. Transforming into another form

Taking hairs of a cat during a lunar eclipse, immolate them eight thousand times **with the mantra and** an augment in which **the name** of the victim is stated. **He upon whose head that ash is placed will turn into a cat. If one repeats** [the mantra] eight thousand times **again** with a peaceful intent, **he will return to his original nature.**

Taking a cord made from **crow sinew,** i.e., tendon, **and enchant** it eight hundred times with the mantra augmented with the victim's name. **He around whose neck it is bound will become a crow.** Illustrated by that, **he to whose neck is bound a cord made of the sinew of whatever** being, **enchanted** eight hundred times with the name augmented mantra, **will become that sort** of being. **Likewise, he may become one who has the form of a crow, pigeon, peacock, heron, owl, or a vulture** (47.2.8).

Make a cord of cow's hair and enchant it eight hundred times with the mantra together with the victim's name augment. **He to whose neck it is bound will become a cow. Make a cord of the hair of any** living being **whatsoever, of a quadruped and so forth,** i.e., of many-legged or legless [beings], **and enchant** it as before with the name augment. He to whose **neck it is bound will have** the **form** of **that** living being. **If** these cords **are removed** from their necks they **are liberated** (47.2.9).

634. See my translation and the note thereto for an alternate interpretation of this passage (Gray 2007, 363, n. 20).

635. Tsong Khapa glosses here the Tibetan translation, *bya chen po'i gnas*. The Sanskrit reads *mahāśakunavāsam*, the *śakuna* being a bird associated with prognostication, and associated with various actual bird species, such as vultures or eagles. Tsong Khapa glosses it with two Tibetan names for the owl, *srin bya* and *'ug pa*.

3.3.3. 2.2.2. 11.3.1. 2.2.6. Turning another man's wealth [into one's own]

Enchanting grain eight thousand times each session over seven days, **cast it into the home of a wealthy man.** After casting it, **consecrate oneself with the remainder,** i.e., water enchanted with the mantra. Should one repeat [the mantra] for seven days, **over seven nights all** of his grain **will be drawn forth** (47.2.10).

3.3.3. 2.2.2. 11.3.1. 3. Showing the name of the chapter

In the *Concise* ***Shrī Herukābhidhāna Tantra,*** this is **the forty-seventh chapter** on **the procedure** of accomplishing **ritual actions** by way of **the sarvabuddhaḍākinī mantra,** i.e., the mantra of all buddhaḍākinīs. This is the explanation of the forty-seventh chapter in the *Illumination of the Hidden Meaning, A Detailed Exegesis of the Concise Saṁvara Tantra Called "The Chakrasaṁvara."*

Chapter 48

Chapter 48 Outline

3.3.3. 2.2.2. 11.3.2. Continual visualization of the heroes and yoginīs

The second part, continual visualization of the heroes and yoginīs, has three sections: (1) the promise to explain, (2) the promised explanation of the meaning, and (3) showing the name of the chapter.

3.3.3. 2.2.2. 11.3.2. 1. The promise to explain

Next, having explained the forty-seventh [chapter], one might wonder what **I will** propound thence. It is that which makes the adept **auspicious,** the mantra that is **the essence of all ḍākinīs,** Vajravārāhī and so forth, **which is the means** by which **the yoginīs achieve all** of the adept's **desired aims (48.1).** [The text] states "I will propound" that, if one thus **shakes the triple world,** the subterranean, terrestrial and celestial **by the mere recollection** in one's mind and repetition **of** the mantra and deity, and if one wanders among the seats, subsidiary seats, and so forth through the process of engaging in service of the yoginīs **just by subsequent recollection** that is not dependent upon fire sacrifice and so forth, then one will **progressively** achieve the state of Saṁvara that is **the authentic power** (48.2).

3.3.3. 2.2.2. 11.3.2. 2. The promised explanation of the meaning

The second part has three sections: (1) the mantra that achieves rites together with its benefit, (2) visualizing the secret mandala, and (3) summarizing the meaning.

3.3.3. 2.2.2. 11.3.2. 2.1. The mantra that achieves rites together with its benefit

Regarding the disclosure of the mantra, it was stated in reverse order, *hā svā* etc., to prevent casual engagement with the tantra. Stated in the correct order it is "***Oṁ sarvabuddhaḍākinīye vajravarṇaṇīye***[636] ***hūṁ hūṁ phaṭ svāhā*** (48.3)." Regarding that, *oṁ* is a salutation. For the sake of whom is it [addressed]? It is for the sake of *sarvabuddhaḍākinīye*, that is the ḍākinī of all buddhas, who has *vajravarṇaṇīye*, the adamantine praise (*rdo rje rab bsngags ma*, **vajrapraśaṁsā*). *Hūṁ hūṁ* is the import in this context on which one is focused, *phaṭ* is illumination, and *svāhā* exhalation.[637]

Regarding **the power of reciting this mantra**, it **is the auspicious accomplishment of all ritual actions** without regard to previous service and so forth due to previous accumulations of merit. With others aside from this, there is only dependence upon previous service and so forth. Whose mantra is this? In short, it is **the ḍākinīs'**, and it is also explained to be **the yoginīs'**. It is also held by all those who abide in the mandala palace, **the khaṇḍarohās, lāmās, and so forth** (48.4).

The mantra of all ḍākinīs that is like this is **this** buddhaḍākinī mantra that is **famous** (48.5ab). Regarding the greatness of this mantra, **whatever ritual actions** (48.6a), pacification and so forth, **occur in the triple world—in the underworld, in heaven** or the celestial realm, **or even moreover in the** terrestrial or **mortal world** (48.5cd)—this buddhaḍākinī **mantra accomplishes all of them**. Since it **accomplishes all powers**, it does so **auspiciously. Aside from this** mantra **that bestows all powers** (48.6bcd),

636. Tsong Khapa represents this as *vajravarniye*.

637. Tsong Khapa here closely follows Butön's commentary; see NS 266b.1–2.

there are no other mantras that are **greater than** it. It is because this mantra is that **through which is shown** well **the approach** to **the unexcelled** (48.7) power.

3.3.3. 2.2.2. 11.3.2. 2.2. Visualizing the secret mandala

The second part has two sections: (1) visualizing the habitat, and (2) visualizing the inhabitant deities.

3.3.3. 2.2.2. 11.3.2. 2.2.1. Visualizing the habitat

Here **I will explain concisely the abode** in which **all ḍākinīs** dwell, **but** I will **not** explain this **extensively**. What is it? **One should draw** with one's mind **the divine mountain**, i.e., eight-peaked Mount Sumeru, which is composed of the seven types of precious substances,[638] and which is adorned **with a variety of flowers and fruit** (48.8). Since the abode is shown concisely, illustrated by that one should visualize from the stacked-up elements up to the mandala palace.

3.3.3. 2.2.2. 11.3.2. 2.2.2. Visualizing the inhabitant deities

Regarding who **one should always visualize on top of that** divine mountain, on petals in the directions and quarters of an eight-petalled lotus within the visualized mandala palace, one should always visualize the deity host of lord Saṁvara, **Ḍākinī** to the east, **and likewise Lāmā** to the north, **Khaṇḍarohā** to the west, Rūpiṇī to the south, **the** thirty-two **yoginīs**, **the hero himself**, Heruka, the principal among **the heroes** (48.9) of the retinue, along with his consort, with **the ḍākinīs' network**, i.e. host, with the laughing one, ***ha ha he he***, and the twenty-four heroes.

Just as the twenty-four yoginīs were shown in reverse order in chapter four, the twenty-four heroes are also shown in reverse order. The eight heroes who abide in the body wheel are: the hero **Vajrasattva**, **Vairochana** (48.10),[639] **Padmanarteshvara**, **Shrī Heruka**, **Ākāshagarbha**, **Hayagrīva**,

638. That is, rubies, sapphire, beryl, emerald, diamond, pearl, and coral.

639. Tsong Khapa glosses the atypical translation found in the SM translation, *rnam snang byed*, with the standard translation *rnam snang mdzad*.

Ratnavajra, and **Mahābala**. The eight heroes who abide in the speech wheel are: **Virūpākṣha**, Mahā**bhairava** (**48.11**),[640] **Vajrabhadra, Subhadra, Vajrahūṁkāra, Mahāvīra, Vajrajaṭila**, and **Aṅkurika**. The eight heroes who abide in the mind wheel are: **Vajradehaka** (**48.12**),[641] **Vajraprabha, Amitābha, Surāvairiṇa, and likewise Vikaṭadaṁṣhṭriṇa, Kaṅkāla, Mahākaṅkāla, and Khaṇḍakapālin**. Here the term **and so forth** (*ādi*, *sogs*; **48.13**) should be taken to mean "foremost" as in Bhavabhaṭṭa's commentary, and it should not be taken to mean "and so forth."[642]

Regarding the body colors and hand implements of these deities many different [accounts] are stated in the explanatory tantras, and it seems that each master has a position regarding this. One should practice as is relevant to whichever [practice tradition one is undertaking].

In this way, the twenty-four internal sites, the head, crown, and so forth of **all beings are pervaded by the twenty-four heroes**, that is, they are visualized as existing [there], along with Prachaṇḍā etc. **The heroes** and **ḍākinīs, the** twenty-four **yoginīs, Prachaṇḍā and so forth** (**48.14**), **should be seen**, i.e., visualized, **as positioned on** the spokes of **the** three body, speech, and mind **wheels** by the adept **who is adept in all rites** or ritual practices, pacification and so forth. This illustrates that, supplemented with the remaining deities, one should visualize the sixty-two-deity [mandala]. One who **desires** to achieve **power should always, well-equipoised**, i.e., without being distracted by other matters, **visualize oneself as the** habitat and inhabitant deity **wheels** (**48.15**). **By means of the method previously taught** in the

640. Tsong Khapa reads *'jigs byed chen po* here, but the Tibetan translations of the root text all read simply *'jigs byed*, matching the Sanskrit, which reads *bhairavaḥ*. See Gray 2012, 225, 399, 476, 560.

641. Tsong Khapa glosses the non-honorific *lus* in the name *rdo rje'i lus* with the honorific *sku*.

642. Bhavabhaṭṭa's commentary here reads as follows: "Regarding **Khaṇḍakapālin and so forth, and so forth** means foremost, which means that you should visualize **Mahākaṅkāla**, etc. with **Khaṇḍakapālin** positioned first" (Pandey 2002, 577: *khaṇḍakapālinādi tv iti ādīty ādau / ādau sthitena khaṇḍakapālinā saha mahākaṅkālādīn bhāvayed ity arthaḥ*; 2002, 844–45: *thod pa'i dumb u dang po zhes pa ni dang po ni thog mar ro / dang por gnas pa'i thod pa'i dum bu dang lhan cig tu keng rus chen po la sogs pa bsgom par bya'o zhes pa'i don to*).

While *ādi* at the end of a compound means "and so forth," its root meaning is "first" or "foremost"; Bhavabhaṭṭa reads its placement after Khaṇḍakapālin as a sign that this deity, coming at the end of the list, should actually be read as the first in the list.

second and third chapters, repeat, that is, **worship,**[643] Chakra**saṁvara** surrounded by the host **of the ḍākinīs' network** (**48.16ab**).[644]

3.3.3. 2.2.2. 11.3.2. 2.3. Summarizing the meaning

This visualization of the yoginīs of **the great wheel** of the mandala and the previously explained worship of it are **the basis of all powers** (**48.16cd**), and are the path **which was well-spoken by tens of millions of buddhas**, Vairochana and so forth, **and by tens of millions of heroes**, Heruka, etc. One should exert oneself upon it.

Regarding showing the greatness of the heroes, each one of the heroes and also **each one of the yoginīs** and each one of the ḍākinīs who are like that **is attended** by a retinue of countless **tens of millions** (**48.17**). Regarding the greatness of the yoginīs, **among the yoginīs,** that actuality of the ḍākinīs, **are Ḍākinī, Rūpiṇī, Khaṇḍarohā, and Lāmā**, and by **and so forth**, there are the eight gate and quarter goddesses and also the count of the ladies' retinues as previously explained. All of them bestow **all powers** and make **the adept auspicious** (**48.18**).

3.3.3. 2.2.2. 11.3.2. 3. Showing the name of the chapter

In the *Concise Shrī Herukābhidhāna Tantra*, this is **the forty-eighth chapter** on **the procedure** of visualizing **the** deity **mandala** that is **hidden**, i.e., in which one visualizes, **the abode**, i.e., Mount Sumeru and so forth, **of all heroes and yoginīs.** This is the explanation of the forty-eighth chapter in the *Illumination of the Hidden Meaning, A Detailed Exegesis of the Concise Saṁvara Tantra Called "The Chakrasaṁvara."*

643. As I noted in my translation of the root text (Gray 2007, 366, n. 13), variant readings here include "worship" *yajet/mchod* and "repeat" *japet/brjod.* Tsong Khapa quotes the latter and glosses it with the former reading.

644. Here Tsong Khapa glosses the compound *ḍākinījālasaṁvaraṁ*, *mkha' 'gro dra ba'i bde mchog.*

Chapter 49

Chapter 49 Outline

3.3.3. 2.2.2. 11.4. Detailed exposition of the examination of the seven-lived one

The fourth part, detailed exposition of the examination of the seven-lived one, has three sections: (1) the promise to explain, (2) the promised explanation of the meaning, and (3) showing the name of the chapter.

3.3.3. 2.2.2. 11.4.1. The promise to explain

Now, having explained the forty-eighth [chapter], **above all I will speak.** Upon what? It is upon **the sacrificial victim,** i.e., the seven-lived one, **achieved** by one who has previously undertaken the donkey yoga **in accordance with the procedure** stated in chapter fourteen. It is said that this is necessary because one **will rapidly achieve the powers** stated below **through mere knowledge of** (**49.1**) the special blessing substance by the adept.

3.3.3. 2.2.2. 11.4.2. The promised import explained

The second part has three sections: (1) making an image of the sacrificial victim from rice powder, (2) the rite of relying on one who has the characteristics of the supreme sacrificial victim, and (3) showing the supremacy of that ritual application.

3.3.3. 2.2.2. 11.4.2. 1. Making an image of the sacrificial victim from rice powder

The mantrin should make an image of **the sacrificial victim**, human and so forth, in winter in **rice flour** pastry with flour of wild rice, the variety [known as] "human corn." Regarding **according to the procedure**, one should make an image of the human, and so forth, according to the procedure.

What can serve as sacrificial victims? They are taken to be **human, tortoise, camel, donkey, jackal, horse, and so forth** (**49.2**). Regarding, **in this way, the variegated hog**, it is said that it is a type of antelope that is multicolored.[645] **These** sacrificial victims that should be made out of rice flour **are known to be the sacrificial victims** (**49.3ab**). This fills the gap regarding the previously [mentioned] image of the donkey placed at the center of the mandala, which is to be made from rice flour or rice pastry.[646]

3.3.3. 2.2.2. 11.4.2. 2. The rite of relying on one who has the characteristics of the supreme sacrificial victim

The second part has three sections: (1) the promise to explain the two

645. This commentary was made by Bhavabhaṭṭa, who wrote "**the variegated hog** is a type of antelope that is multicolored (Pandey 2002, 580: *viśvarāho nānāvarṇo mṛgaviśeṣaḥ*). This may be a reference to the Indian hog deer, *Hyelaphus porcinus*.

646. Tsong Khapa refers to the discussion in section 3.3.3. 2.2.2. 2.2.5. 2.2, in chapter 14, at Gray 2017, 290.

meanings, (2) showing the characteristics of the supreme sacrificial victim, and (3) showing the ritual application relying on him.

3.3.3. 2.2.2. 11.4.2. 2.1. The promise to explain the two meanings

I will explain the ritual action of these seven-lived ones, **in a manner which will accord with their defining characteristics (49.3cd).**

3.3.3. 2.2.2. 11.4.2. 2.2. Showing the characteristics of the supreme sacrificial victim

First, **there are** people **with one birth**, then those in their **second** birth, as well as those in their **third, fourth, fifth, and sixth** birth. **Have no doubt that** those who have been human continually over **seven** [lives] **are the** supreme **sacrificial victim (49.4).** The reason why they are called sacrificial victims was explained previously.[647] Mal's translation lacks "and two, or," which is good.

The person **has a pleasant** lotus-like **scent in his mouth, gazes without blinking, is truthful, is kind** if **seen** by others, **always delights in the true teaching (49.5), knows his own life**, and his or her body's **scent is always pleasant. One who is endowed with these characteristics is one born as a seven-lived one (49.6)** without interruption. There is an extensive [list of] characteristics in the *[Discourse Appendix]* explanatory tantra, as follows:[648]

647. See Section 3.3.3. 2.2.2. 7.2.2. 1 in chapter 32 above.

648. Here I translate the canonical Tibetan translation which Tsong Khapa quotes; it differs significantly from the Sanskrit version of this text (for the Sanskrit and a translation therefrom, see Gray 2007, 206–7, n. 2). The Tibetan text reads as follows: *skal bzang yid 'ong bde bar 'gro / skra yi myu gu de bzhin ring / mig ni dkyus ring mig kyang dmar / padma'i 'dab ma 'dra ba'i gzugs / de yi lus la rdul zhim 'byung / lus las lha yi dri 'byung zhing / kha yi dbugs ni ga bur dri / ldan pas sbrang ma rtag tu 'khor / gci dang phyi sa gla rtsi bro / tshig ni 'jam par gyur pa dang / lag pa dang ni rkang pa 'jam / utpa la yi dri dang ldan / skra dkar gnyer ma las rnam grol / lus kyang snum zhing mnyen pa dang / snying dang thod pa lte ba ste / des na ro tsa na ru 'gyur / grib bdun ngang pa'i 'gros su 'gro / snying rje'i bsam pa can yin te / dkon mchog gsum la rtag tu dad / sbyin dang tshul khrims dag dang ldan / 'di 'dra rnal 'byor pas rtogs na / mi gsod me yis tshig mi 'gyur / srog chags sna tshogs gdug pa dag / gang yang rung bas za mi nus / de ni mtshan mo mi mthong ste / mi snang ba yi dbang phyug mchog* (AU 364a.1–4).

He's an attractive, prosperous Buddhist,[649]
The locks of his hair are likewise quite long,
And his eyes are elongated and red,
Endowed with the shape of lotus petals.
Perspiration[650] is found on his body,
Whence arises a divine aroma.
The breath of his mouth is camphor scented,
And he is ever surrounded by bees.
His urine and excrement are musky,
His speech moreover should be quite gentle,
And his hands and feet are likewise gentle,
Having the scent of *Utpala* lotus.
He is devoid of wrinkles and grey hair.
His body supple and also oiled.
He will have a concretion in his heart,
Or within his head, or in his navel.
He has seven shadows, a goose's gait,
And a compassionate disposition.
He's always devoted to the three jewels,
And he is generous and disciplined.
If a *yogī* finds this sort of [person],
He will neither die or be cremated.[651]
The various malicious living beings
Will never be able to devour him.
If a mantrin finds this sort of [person],
During the night he will remain unseen,
A master of invisibility.

The *Discourse Appendix* [continues], stating that seeing one who has these characteristics, one requests "Give me a gift." Form a pill from his feces,

649. This follows the Tibetan translation, *skal bzang yid 'ong bde bar 'gro* (AU 364a.1). The Sanskrit, here, however, reads "soft-spoken Buddhist," *priyavādī saugato*.

650. Here I follow the Sanskrit *prasvedaṁ*. The Tibetan translation reads *rdul rab*, "particles, dust," which makes less sense. It is likely that *rdul rab* is a corruption for *rngul rab*, a plausible translation for *prasvedaṁ*.

651. Presumably, it is the yogī who gains these powers of immortality and invisibility. As we will see below, the victim dies as result of the ritual being described here.

urine, and spirit of awakening, and wrap it with the three metals. Unite the two organs repeating the quintessence mantra one hundred thousand times, and give that pill into his hand, saying, "Give me a gift." He will die immediately and be reborn in Akṣhobhya's realm. Carry his corpse to an isolated spot and one will succeed.[652]

3.3.3. 2.2.2. 11.4.2. 2.3. Showing the ritual application relying on him

The third part has two sections: (1) success through the rite relying on the supreme sacrificial victim, and (2) success through the rite relying on another sacrificial victim.

3.3.3. 2.2.2. 11.4.2. 2.3.1. Success through the rite relying on the supreme sacrificial victim

Through merely having eaten this flesh of the seven-lived one who is like that **one will assume a divine form. Or** through just **having smelled** the scent of the concretion of his heart, **or having touched it**, the adept **who forms** the concretion **into a drop** (49.7) on his forehead **will accomplish** powers as soon as he forms the drop. **This** yogī **will assume his desired form. The wise one**, in the ritual application, **takes up** the *rocanā*, i.e., concretion, that exists **in the heart of this** (49.8) seven-lived one. The concretion exists in his heart, skull, and head, as was stated in the previously quoted [passage] from the explanatory tantra.[653]

Taking that concretion, **form it into a drop repeating the essence mantras** of the partners. **If one desires to assume the form of whatever sentient being** (49.9), **have no doubt that one will transform into the form of that** sentient being **by** forming **the** previously [described] **drop. If the wise one** in this ritual application **takes up tree sap together with concretion and forms it into a drop on his forehead** (49.10), **there is no doubt that he will assume the form of that** tree.

Should one bring together **the body hair of the sacrificial victim**, and, illustrated by that victim's body hair, **the five limbs**, which also include

652. Tsong Khapa here relates in prose a verse passage in AU that immediately follows the text quoted above. See AU 364a.4–6.

653. See the passage from AU quoted in section 3.3.3. 2.2.2. 11.4. 2.2.2 above.

nails, teeth, skin, and head hair, and **bind it to** [one's] **hand and** another's **head, have no doubt that one will assume the form** (49.11–12) of that animal to which it is bound. With the exception of the text "if one binds the body hair of the victim together with its five limbs to the hand and head," the other two lines do not occur in the commentaries.[654] The oral instruction is that if one releases all of [materials] bound to them they will be freed [from the alteration of their form].[655]

One who has conditioning in deity **yoga and** who has **repeated** the mantra with a name augment will succeed. What is the reason for humans to transform into animals? The reading, "although **humans** have **the capability** to achieve the path, they **incline toward affliction** and sin," is excellent.[656] It is said that since humans are generally oriented toward the practice of sin and the afflictions, they **obstruct the path of the powers** (49.13). On can assume inferior forms in order to turn away from that.

3.3.3. 2.2.2. 11.4.2. 2.3.2. Success through the rite relying on another sacrificial victim

Visualize according to the procedure the flesh of **elephant, horse, donkey, tortoise, camel, hog, fox,**[657] **etc. and crow, owl, vulture, curlew, hawk, or crane** (49.14), i.e., swan,[658] and repeating the mantra, offer the sacrificial cake (*gtor ma, bali*). That adept **can assume good forms** that are **divine forms** as well as **bad forms**, if he so desires. Someone explains that "fox," *wa*, translates the equivalent [Sanskrit] term [meaning] "jackal."[659] Regarding [the text] "good forms and bad forms," in the *Twofold Commentary* there

654. Tsong Khapa seems to be referring to two lines in 49.12, namely *de yi spu dang rnam bsres la* and *de yi gzugs 'gyur the tshom med*. See Gray 2012, 403.

655. Kambala makes this point; see SN 77a.4.

656. Tsong Khapa appears to be referring to, but not directly quoting, Tathāgatarakṣhita's analysis of the second line here as *nyon mongs sdig pa la dga' ba*, which differs from the canonical translation, which is *dka' zhing nyon mongs la dga' ba*. See UN 250a.5–6.

657. Tsong Khapa follows the Tibetan translation in reading *wa*, "fox," which usually translates Sanskrit words designating the jackal.

658. Tsong Khapa gives a transliteration here, *sa ra sa*, from the Sanskrit *sārasa*, "crane," which he glosses as *bzhad*, "swan."

659. Butön makes this point at NS 267b.4.

is the translation "good forms as well as bad forms," which is excellent.[660] **Have no doubt that the** adept **who is a great yogī will give rise to**, i.e., assume, whatever **form** he **desires (49.15)**.

3.3.3. 2.2.2. 11.4.2. 3. Showing the supremacy of that ritual application

There is nothing greater in the triple world than this (**49.16**) ritual application of the seven-lived one.

3.3.3. 2.2.2. 11.4.3. Showing the name of the chapter

In the ***Concise Shrī Herukābhidhāna Tantra***, this is **the forty-ninth chapter** on **the procedure of transforming** the form of oneself and others, and achieving the distinctive powers as stated in chapter eleven depending upon **the seven-lived one**. This is the explanation of the forty-ninth chapter in the *Illumination of the Hidden Meaning, A Detailed Exegesis of the Concise Saṁvara Tantra Called "The Chakrasaṁvara."*

660. Tsong Khapa here compares the canonical translation, *gzugs bzang ba dang gzugs ngan pa*, with the translation found in Tathāgatarakṣhita's commentary, namely *gzugs ngan pa yang gzugs bzang* as he relates it. It occurs as follows in the commentary: "assumes a good form as well as a bad form" (UN 250a.7: *gzugs ngan pa la yang gzugs bzang por 'gyur zhes bya ba'i don to*).

Chapter 50

Chapter 50 Outline

3.3.3. 2.2.2. 11.5. Ritual success with the mother's essence mantra
3.3.3. 2.2.2. 11.5.1. Explaining the fire sacrifice
3.3.3. 2.2.2. 11.5.1. 1. The promise to explain
3.3.3. 2.2.2. 11.5.1. 2. The promised explanation of the meaning
3.3.3. 2.2.2. 11.5.1. 2.1. The fire sacrifice for controlling
3.3.3. 2.2.2. 11.5.1. 2.2. The violent fire sacrifices
3.3.3. 2.2.2. 11.5.1. 2.2.1. The fire sacrifice for dividing
3.3.3. 2.2.2. 11.5.1. 2.2.2. The fire sacrifices for killing and expelling
3.3.3. 2.2.2. 11.5.1. 2.3. The method for continually pacifying obstacles
3.3.3. 2.2.2. 11.5.1. 2.4. The fire sacrifice for enriching
3.3.3. 2.2.2. 11.5.1. 2.4.1. Expanding wealth
3.3.3. 2.2.2. 11.5.1. 2.4.2. Expanding power
3.3.3. 2.2.2. 11.5.1. 2.4.3. Expanding dominion
3.3.3. 2.2.2. 11.5.1. 2.4.4. Extending life
3.3.3. 2.2.2. 11.5.1. 2.5. The fire sacrifice for paralyzing
3.3.3. 2.2.2. 11.5.1. 3. Summarizing the meaning and showing the mantra which achieves the rites
3.3.3. 2.2.2. 11.5.2. Explaining the ten seats etc.
3.3.3. 2.2.2. 11.5.2. 1. The promise to explain
3.3.3. 2.2.2. 11.5.2. 2. The promised explanation of the meaning
3.3.3. 2.2.2. 11.5.2. 2.1. Showing that the seats etc. are the ten stages
3.3.3. 2.2.2. 11.5.2. 2.1.1. The general meaning
3.3.3. 2.2.2. 11.5.2. 2.1.1. 1. The way that the names of the stages such as the joyous are each stated
3.3.3. 2.2.2. 11.5.2. 2.1.1. 2. Avoiding the contradiction of stating [the stages] out of harmony with the seats etc.
3.3.3. 2.2.2. 11.5.2. 2.1.1. 3. The types of disciples for whom they are stated
3.3.3. 2.2.2. 11.5.2. 2.1.2. The auxiliary meanings
3.3.3. 2.2.2. 11.5.2. 2.2. Showing that the ten seats etc. are all pervading
3.3.3. 2.2.2. 11.5.3. Summarizing the meaning
3.3.3. 2.2.2. 11.5.4. Showing the name of the chapter

3.3.3. 2.2.2. 11.5. Ritual success with the mother's essence mantra

The fifth part, ritual success with the mother's essence mantra, has four sections: (1) explaining the fire sacrifice, (2) explaining the ten seats etc., (3) summarizing the meaning, and (4) showing the name of the chapter.

3.3.3. 2.2.2. 11.5.1. Explaining the fire sacrifice

The first part has three sections: (1) the promise to explain, (2) the promised explanation of the meaning, and (3) summarizing the meaning and showing the mantra which achieves the rites application.

3.3.3. 2.2.2. 11.5.1. 1. The promise to explain

Next, after the forty-ninth [chapter], **I will explain the performance of the ritual procedure of the dominion fire sacrifice,** the correct rite of controlling **through which one rapidly obtains the powers** (**50.1**) one desires.

3.3.3. 2.2.2. 11.5.1. 2. The promised explanation of the meaning

The second part has five sections: (1) the fire sacrifice for controlling, (2) the violent fire sacrifices, (3) the method for continually pacifying obstacles, (4) the fire sacrifice for enriching, and (5) the fire sacrifice for paralyzing.

3.3.3. 2.2.2. 11.5.1. 2.1. The fire sacrifice for controlling

Should one mix *gomāṁsa*, i.e., **beef, with liquor,** that is, alcohol, **and immolate it with one's left hand, even the Buddha will be subjugated.** The text mentions the most eminent one, and if this is the case, **what need is there to mention petty humans** (**50.2**), who can be controlled at will? If one performs a fire sacrifice for controlling **with** oblations of mouth water, that is, **saliva, toothpicks, and thus** the bodily filth **that delights one's body**[661] **and liquor, along with** the essence mantra with **a name** augment,

661. The text here calls for the ambiguous ingredient "that which delights one's body," *rang gi lus mnyes pa*. Tsong Khapa's gloss, "bodily filth that delights one's body" seems strange.

one **will bring into** one's **control** the beings of **the three realms** (50.3), that is, the three regions.[662] The victim **will be summoned immediately** if one performs a fire sacrifice **with** a woman's **uterine blood**, **food** that having been eaten is **moistened** and then regurgitated, **along with human hair** (50.4).

3.3.3. 2.2.2. 11.5.1. 2.2. The violent fire sacrifices

The second part has two sections: (1) the fire sacrifice for dividing, and (2) the fire sacrifices for killing and expelling.

3.3.3. 2.2.2. 11.5.1. 2.2.1. The fire sacrifice for dividing

Regarding "one's **own body**" and "**own hair**," Bhavabhaṭṭa quotes "**dog's body**" and "**dog's hair.**"[663] **Should** one perform a divisive fire sacrifice, immolating **that which is regurgitated from the body**, i.e., stomach, **of a dog, dog's hair, and *nimba* wood,** dear friends **will be cleaved in an instant** (50.5).

3.3.3. 2.2.2. 11.5.1. 2.2.2. The fire sacrifices for killing and expelling

Should one who is **well equipoised** in fierce concentration kindle **a fire** with **datura** wood, and **immolate crows' wings treated**, i.e., saturated with, **mustard oil** or black mustard oil and [the victim's] name, for **immediately killing**, [this is done] with a murdering mantra, and for **expelling** (50.6) him or her from a place, [it is done] with a mantra with his or her [name] augment.

However, he derives this gloss from Vīravajra (PD 445b.7), who also lists the five ambrosias (PD 445b.5) among the oblations for the controlling fire sacrifice. These are substances that are conventionally considered "filth" (*dri ma*) but are transformed through creative visualization into "ambrosia" (*bdud rtsi*).

662. Tsong Khapa glosses *khams gsum* as *sa gsum*, namely the celestial, terrestrial, and subterranean realms.

663. Tsong Khapa correctly notes that Bhavabhaṭṭa quotes a textual variant here, reading, *śvakāyaḥ* and *śvakeśāḥ*, rather than **svakāyaḥ* and **svakeśāḥ* (See Pandey 2002, 583–84, 859–61. The Tibetan translations attest the latter reading, *rang gi lus* and *rang skras*, but Tsong Khapa prefers the former.

3.3.3. 2.2.2. 11.5.1. 2.3. The method for continually pacifying obstacles

If the mantrin always repeats the mantra **while** lying on a mat, i.e., **asleep**, not lying down, i.e., **awake**, sitting or **standing,**[664] **eating** food, **engaging in sexual intercourse** and so forth, **there will be no obstacle** (50.7) to this repetition. This shows that if one repeats the mantra, no harm from obstacles will arise in any path of practice.

3.3.3. 2.2.2. 11.5.1. 2.4. The fire sacrifice for enriching

The fourth part has four sections: (1) expanding wealth, (2) expanding power, (3) expanding dominion, and (4) extending life.

3.3.3. 2.2.2. 11.5.1. 2.4.1. Expanding wealth

Regarding **the person who makes offerings of one hundred oblations** for enriching **with** the fire offering substance of **jackal flesh,**[665] **after three months the poverty of** his or her **clan will be destroyed** (50.8). **Should the adept perform fire sacrifice** with the fire offering substance of **great flesh together with** intoxicants, i.e., **liquor, up to one hundred and eight times** every day **in three sessions** (50.9), all **the ground over which he ranges for six months will be subdued** for his enjoyment. **Have no doubt that the ḍākinī satisfied** by the fire sacrifice **will give a kingdom to that** (50.10) adept.

3.3.3. 2.2.2. 11.5.1. 2.4.2. Expanding power

Should one visualize with the concentration of vivid appearance **all the deities** of the mandala individually **and perform fire sacrifice** daily **in two sessions** for three months, **then** the adept **will attain flight**, travelling in space itself, **with one's very own body** (50.11).

664. The PM and SM translations read *'dug pa*, "sitting," while the SL translation and extant Sanskrit read "standing," *uttiṣṭho, langs pa*. Tsong Khapa quotes both readings. See Gray 2012, 229, 405, 478, 562.

665. Tsong Khapa follows the Tibetan translation in reading *wa yi sha*, "fox flesh," which I read as jackal flesh in accordance with his commentary in section 3.3.3. 2.2.2. 11.4.2. 2.3.2 in chapter 49 above.

Although *gomāyu* was translated as "fox," here it seems it should be translated as "jackal." **Should one** [perform] **external fire sacrifice** to the gods in a fire sacrificial hearth and **internal** fire sacrifice **with jackal meat and liquor,** (50.12ab) **enchanting** that meat with **the mantra for a night** (50.13a) and eating it, **all powers will rapidly enter into the hand of that adept** (50.12cd), and he or she can **even overthrow** a great **country. Doing thus,** i.e., the two fire sacrifices and [mantra] repetition, **every day,** that adept **will become a king** (50.13bcd).

As for there being any other enriching rites **more excellent than this** ritual application, **there is nothing in the triple world** or the three realms. With this rite, **the great yogin dies** and is reborn, and with the power of **his desire** he **assumes various forms,** such as gods etc., **enjoying** (50.14) sense pleasures.

3.3.3. 2.2.2. 11.5.1. 2.4.3. Expanding dominion

If one makes a hundred thousand enriching **fire sacrifices with** the fire sacrificial substances of *bilva*, i.e., **wood apple,**[666] and likewise **the flame of the forest,**[667] and **cluster fig,**[668] **one will quickly become a great lord of wealth** (50.15). **Mixing together** *gomāṃsa*, i.e., **beef and liquor,** i.e., alcohol, **it should be immolated by one who desires to be king. Encountering the lady of yogīs,**[669] i.e., the [female] partner, **who has poverty** (50.16)? That is, one will not have it. One will be conducted to the glory of a kingdom.

By performing **fire sacrifice** with *gomāyu*, i.e., **jackal,** flesh, one **will easily obtain** whatever one desires. This expresses praise for making fire sacrificial substances with that flesh. Through *gomāyu*, i.e., **jackal,** flesh **fire sacrifice, one will quickly** attain wealth **equal to a benefactor** (50.17), i.e., the son of Vishrava.[670] The production of fire sacrificial substances

666. That is, *Limonia acidissima*. I presume that it is the wood of these tree species that is called for here, although the text does not specify this.

667. That is, the *palāśa* or *Butea monosperma*.

668. That is, the *uḍumbara* or *Ficus racemose*.

669. The extant Sanskrit reads the feminine "lady of yogīs," *yogīśvarīṃ*, here (Gray 2012, 230), but the Tibetan translations have the ambiguous reading *rnal 'byor dbang phyug*, which Tsong Khapa reproduces. Since he does not indicate the gender, I have followed the gender indicated by the Sanskrit.

670. That is, Vaishravaṇa, one of the four heavenly kings and a god of wealth.

with jackal flesh is stated repeatedly [in this chapter] because it the best in the exposition of this ritual application, as it is said to "easily" [bring about whatever one desires].[671] **Although** one who has **purity** in the external **observances** will not succeed, **one will, however, obtain the powers through this instruction** (50.18ab).

3.3.3. 2.2.2. 11.5.1. 2.4.4. Extending life

Abundant life means an unlimited lifespan. Should one perform an enriching fire sacrifice with *dūrvā* [grass] as a fire sacrificial substance, even one whose lifespan is exhausted should become one with an unlimited lifespan. The commentaries quote "should become one with an unlimited lifespan."[672]

3.3.3. 2.2.2. 11.5.1. 2.5. The fire sacrifice for paralyzing

[The term] ***kuṣhmāṇḍaṁ*** refers to the seed of the tree of that name.[673] *Mudga* is **the mung bean**, *māṣha* is **the *māṣha* bean**,[674] and [*caṇa*] **the chickpea**. "Bee sediment" is **beeswax**.[675] [There is] black **mustard, and the leaves of a household tamāla tree** are said to be the leaves of the *vāsaka*.[676]

671. This is stated in the verse just explicated, 50.17.

672. This section is based upon a single word in the root text, *adhikāyu*, which means "abundant life," and which is translated in the Tibetan translations as *lhag pa'i tshe* (PM, SM) and *lhag pa'i tsher gyur* (SL). See Gray 2012, 407, 479, 563. The commentary Tsong Khapa refers to is Jayabhadra's. It reads: "*Adhikāyuḥ* is an unlimited lifespan" (Sugiki 2001, 141: *adhikāyur aparimitāyur bhavati*).

673. Tsong Khapa repeats the SM transliteration *kuṣmaṇṇaṁ*; the PM translation gives a more accurate transliteration, *kuṣmaṇḍaṁ*, for the Sanskrit *kuṣmāṇḍaṁ*, the winter melon or wax gourd, *Benincasa hispida*. It grows as a vine, not a tree, as Tsong Khapa indicates.

674. The Sanskrit term *māṣa*, like *mudga*, refers to the mung bean. The Sanskrit here reads *mudgamāṣa*, and it probably should be read as a compound referring just to the mung bean.

675. Tsong Khapa glosses the SM translation's *sbrang rtsi'i tshigs ma*, a rendering of the unusual Sanskrit term *madhucchardi*, "honey vomit." Jayabhadra glosses it as *madhusikthaṁ*, "beeswax" (Sugiki 2001, 141).

676. Tsong Khapa refers here to Kambala's commentary, which reads, "**The leaves of a household tamāla tree** are the leaves of the *vāsaka* [plant]; one should make a fire sacrifice with that" (SN 77a.6: *khyim gyi ta ma la'i 'dab ma la zhes bya ba ni bā sa ka'i 'dab ma ste*

Someone explains that it is the smoke that hangs down from above the house.[677] Kambala states that one should draw the form of the victim on a *vāsaka* leaf within the syllable *ga* with the ash of a cremated corpse. Place it inside of the gills of a fish and fill it with *dūrvā* grass and rice chaff. Cover it with fish gill bones, and seal it with beeswax. If you insert it without breathing into excrement, the victim's mouth will be bound.[678]

This is the end of the ritual applications in this tantra. The ritual applications are stated beginning in chapter nine up to this [point]. With the exception of a few in particular they are common to the contexts of both stages. As for accomplishing the powers of pacifying etc., having gone to the limit of the creation stage without cultivation of the perfection stage, this is one who has only practiced the creation stage. However, beings of lesser faculties are controlled relying upon the perfection stage.

3.3.3. 2.2.2. 11.5.1. 3. Summarizing the meaning and showing the mantra which achieves the rites

When one **desires to perform** oneself the previously explained ritual actions such as controlling and so forth, **the yogī** who practices the procedures of those rites **stays wherever he wishes (50.18cd)** accomplishing them. The mantra that accomplishes the rites stated above is *oṁ vajravairocanīye*[679] *hūṁ hūṁ phaṭ svāhā*. As a certain great adept has identified this as the quintessence, and another as the essence, it is acceptable to advocate either position.[680]

---

des sbyin sreg bya'o; K 75b.5: *gṛhatamālapatrer iti vāsapatrer iti homayet*). Tsong Khapa's text represents the name of this plant as *pa śa ka*, but the canonical translation gives a better reading. This is almost certainly a reference to the the *vāsaka* or the Malabar nut shrub, *Adhatoda vasica*, a well-known South Asian medicinal plant.

677. Tsong Khapa appears to be referring to Bhavabhaṭṭa's commentary, which reads, "**leaves of a household** . . . refers to smoke hanging down from above" (CV 240a.2: *khyim gyi 'dab ma ni steng nas 'phyang ba'i dud pa'o*).

678. See SN 77a.6–7.

679. Tsong Khapa's text here reads *badzra bai ro tsa ni ye*.

680. The Indian tradition generally identified this mantra as Vajravārāhī's quintessence, and the longer sarvabuddhaḍākinī mantra as her essence; Bhavabhaṭṭa argues this, as noted above (see Pandey 2002, 572, 831). Durjayachandra, however, identifies the Vajravairochanī mantra as the quintessence (RG 275a.7). The Tibetan tradition appears to have generally followed Durjayachandra's position, which is understandable given his great

3.3.3. 2.2.2. 11.5.2. Explaining the ten seats etc.

The second part has two sections: (1) the promise to explain, and (2) the promised explanation of the meaning.

3.3.3. 2.2.2. 11.5.2. 1. The promise to explain

Next, having explained the ritual applications, **I will explain above all** the meaning of the rites that I previously revealed. What is that? I will explain the symbolic disclosure of **the** ten [bodhisattva] **stages**, the joyous and so forth, with **the seats**, subsidiary seats, **and so forth**, that are symbolically disclosed by **the yoginīs**. Where do the seats and so forth exist? They exist in **the limbs** and minor body parts, such as joints etc., of **Shrī Heruka's body**. Heruka's twenty-four [internal sites], the head and so forth, exist as the nature of the twenty-four sites, and this is the meaning of the ten stages that is symbolically disclosed by that.

All Heruka's limbs **have the nature of being the immobile** habitat **and the mobile (50.19)** inhabitants. Regarding this, the habitat and inhabitants are contained in the three, the celestial, terrestrial, and subterranean [worlds]. It means that the lord of the triple world and the yoginī exist in portions of Heruka's body. Regarding "nature of the mobile and immobile," Bhavabhaṭṭa, quoting the text, "all limbs, the head and power," explains that this means that the head is the form aggregate, and taking "power" as the remaining aggregates, the nature of stages, seats, etc., aggregates, and so forth is Shrī Heruka's limbs and minor body parts.[681]

---

influence on Mal Lotsawa and hence the Tibetan exegetical tradition; Tsong Khapa, of course, is aware of both positions.

681. The canonical version of Bhavabhaṭṭa's commentary does not quote the line that Tsong Khapa attributes to it, *thams cad yan lag spyi bo stobs*. However, he does gloss most of these words in his commentary, which occurs as follows: "Regarding **the limbs and minor body parts**, the limbs are the hands and so forth, and the minor body parts are the joints and so forth. The head is the form aggregate, and the power is feeling and so forth. The nature of the stages, seats, etc., and aggregates, and so forth is Shrī Heruka's limbs and minor body parts" (Pandey 2002, 586: *aṅgāṅgam iti / aṅgaṁ karādi tasyāṅgaṁ parvādi / śiro rūpaskandhaḥ / balā vedanādayaḥ / bhūmipīṭhādiskandhādyātmakaṁ śrīherukasyāṅgāṅ-gam*; 2002, 867: *yan lag nying lag ces pa ni yan lag ni lag pa la sogs pa'o / nying lag ni tshigs la sogs pa'o / spyi bor gzugs kyi phung po'o / stobs ni tshor ba la sogs pa'o / sa dang gnas la sogs pa phung po la sogs pa'i bdag nyid dpal he ru ka'i yan lag dang nying lag go*).

3.3.3. 2.2.2. 11.5.2. 2. The promised explanation of the meaning

The second part has two sections: (1) showing that the seats etc. are the ten stages, and (2) showing that the ten seats etc. are all pervading.

3.3.3. 2.2.2. 11.5.2. 2.1. Showing that the seats etc. are the ten stages

The first part has two sections: (1) the general meaning, and (2) the auxiliary meanings.

3.3.3. 2.2.2. 11.5.2. 2.1.1. The general meaning

The first part has three sections: (1) the way that the names of the stages such as the joyous are each stated, (2) avoiding the contradiction of stating [the stages] out of harmony with the seats etc., and (3) the types of disciples for whom they are stated.

3.3.3. 2.2.2. 11.5.2. 2.1.1. 1. The way that the names of the stages such as the joyous are each stated

It has been explained that in this root tantra the ten [bodhisattva stages], from the joyous up to the cloud of truth [stages] are indicated by the ten [sites], from the seats and subsidiary seats up to the charnel grounds and subsidiary charnel grounds. The explanatory tantra, after adding two [additional sites], the *pīlava* (*'thung gcod*) and *upapīlava* (*nye ba'i thung gcod*), states, "these stages are twelve,"[682] [indicating] that there are twelve [sites], the seats etc., and twelve stages.

Regarding the twelve stages, the two, devoted conduct (*adhimukticaryā*, *mos spyod*)[683] and completely radiant (*samantaprabhā*, *kun tu 'od*),[684] are

682. The line Tsong Khapa quotes occurs at ST 5.1, 102b.7, as follows: *'di rnams sa ni bcu gnyis te*, which in turn is a quote of HT 1.7.11 (Snellgrove 1959, 2.22–23). As Tsong Khapa indicates, this follows a list of the twelve types of sites. ST follows HT in giving a list of twelve types of sites and indicating that they correspond to twelve bodhisattva stages.

683. Regarding this and other stages, see Dayal 1932, 278 ff.

684. These additional stages were part of the traditional bodhisattva stages schema, the *adhimukticaryā* being a preliminary stage that preceded the ten stages proper, while

added to the ten, joyous and so forth, in [commentaries by] Bhavabhaṭṭa,[685] Shāntipa,[686] and Kāṇhapa,[687] the *Hevajra* commentary written by Padmāṅkuravajra,[688] and the *Sheaf of Esoteric Instructions*.[689] It is explained that devoted conduct is the *pīlava* [site], and that the completely radiant [stage] is the *upapīlava* [site].

Regarding the *Gnosis Drop [Tantra]*'s explanation that there are sixteen stages, that very work comments that:[690]

> The joyful sites, the seats and so forth,
> Are articulated by the word "stage."
> Now, devoted conduct is the first stage,
> And the second is joyous,

---

samantaprabhā is the awakened state itself, the final stage, or rather the goal of the bodhisattva path of practice.

685. Bhavabhaṭṭa does not comment thus in this commentary, probably because the root text clearly indicates that there are ten stages. However, he does address this topic in his *Explanatory Exposition on the Shrī Hevajra [Tantra]* (*Śrīhevajravyākhyāvivaraṇa*) commentary on HT 1.7.11; see Tōh. 1182, D 208ab. He also comments on the twelve sites and stages in his commentary on the *Vajraḍāka Tantra*. See VV 65a.5–6.

686. See Ratnākarashānti's *String of Pearls, a Commentary on the Shrī Hevajra* (*Śrīhevajrapañjikā-nāma-muktikāvali*) (Tōh. 1189, 247b.6–48a.3).

687. Tsong Khapa likely refers to either Kṛiṣhṇāchārya's *Jewel Rosary of Yoga, a Commentary on Hevajra* (*Yogaratnamālā*) (see Tōh. 1183, D 19b.5–7; Snellgrove 1959, 122), or his *Source for Recollection, a Commentary on Hevajra* (*Hevajra-nāma-mahātantrarāja-dvikalpamāyāpañjikā-smṛtinipāda* (Tōh. 1187). See D 160b.4–6.

688. See his *kye'i rdo rje zhes bya ba'i rgyud kyi rgyal po'i 'grel pa* (Tōh. 1188, 201a.3–4).

689. For Abhayākaragupta's discussion of this issue, see AM 155a–b.

690. This passage occurs in the *Jñānatilaka-yoginītantrarāja-paramamahādbhuta* as follows: *gnas la sogs pa dga' ba'i gnas / sa yi sgra yis brjod pa yin / sa dang po mos pas spyod pa / gnyis pa rab tu dga' ba / gsum pa dri ma med pa / bzhi pa 'od byed pa / lnga pa 'od 'phro ba / drug pa sbyang dka' ba / bdun pa mngon du gyur pa/ brgyad pa ring du song ba / dgu pa mi g.yo ba/ bcu pa legs pa'i blo gros / de rnams ni byang chub sems dpa'i sa'o / chos kyi sprin ni sangs rgyas kyi sa / kun tu 'od ni yang dag par rdzogs pa'i sangs rgyas kyi sa / kun tu snang ba mched pa'i 'od ni dpal rdo rje sems dpa' bcom ldan 'das kyi sprul pa'i sku'i sa / kun tu snang ba thob pa'i 'od ni longs spyod rdzogs pa'i sku'i sa/ yang dag 'od rab chos kyi sku'i sa / brjod du med pa tshad med pa ni bde ba chen po'i sa ste / de kun dga' ba'i bye brag la/ sar ni kun tu btags pa'o.*

Tsong Khapa omits the line *yang dag 'od rab chos kyi sku'i sa* (Tōh. 422, D *rgyud 'bum* vol. nga, 126a.2–5).

The third is the immaculate,
The fourth is the illuminating,
And the fifth is the effulgent.
The sixth, difficult-to-conquer,
[Is followed by] the seventh, the facing.
The eighth is the far-reaching [stage],
The ninth the immovable,
And the tenth is thus the accomplished.

These are thus the bodhisattva stages. The cloud of truth is the buddha stage, and completely radiant the stage of complete, perfected buddhas. The light that spreads complete radiance is the stage of the emanation body of lord Vajrasattva. The light that attains complete radiance is the stage of the communal enjoyment body. [Supreme true light is the stage of the truth body.][691] Inexpressible and immeasurable is the stage of great bliss. The distinctions of joy of all of these are designated as stages.

Indeed, there are sixteen stages, since that very work also states:[692]

It's taught the eleventh stage is always
By means of the emanation body.
The twelfth is through the enjoyment body.
The thirteenth is through the body of truth,
And the fourteenth is truly of great bliss.
The fifteenth stage is called the gnostic stage,
And the sixteenth is unfathomable.

With respect to that, the devoted conduct stage is the stage of ordinary beings and can be explained in the manner of the adamantine secret as the

691. This line is omitted by Tsong Khapa.

692. This passage occurs in the *Jñānatilaka-yoginītantrarāja-paramamahādbhuta* as follows: *rtag tu sprul pa yi ni skus / sa nib cu gcig pa ru dran / longs spyod rdzogs sku bcu gnyis pa / chos kyi skus nib cu gsum mo / bde ba chen pos bcu bzhi pa / gang zhig bcwa lnga yi ni sa / de ni ye shes sa zhes bya / bcu drug pa ni brtags pa min* (Tōh. 422, 126a.1–2).

four, heat, peak, tolerance, and the supreme,[693] and the remainder of them as the noble stages.[694]

Regarding the distinction between the buddha and complete, perfected buddha [stages] in the *Gnosis Drop [Tantra]*, it is because, as Haribhadra states, "Regarding the tenth stage, one should speak only with respect to the bodhisattvas and buddhas, and not with respect to truly perfected buddhas."[695] The distinction of those two appears to be the intention of the *Ornament of the Universal Vehicle Sutras*, and they are likewise distinguished in *Sheaf of Esoteric Instructions* as well.

If the joyous is taken as the first stage, then the completely radiant is the eleventh. Then the triple body and the body of great bliss characterize four [stages]. Taking each one of these stages, there are fifteen stages. As for there also being a gnostic stage for the gnostic body, while it is fifteenth counting from the first stage, it is sixteenth counting from devoted conduct.[696] Taking it thus, the reality that free of all taints is the reality body, so that which is understood as the gnostic body is the gnostic reality body. Since the *Gnosis Drop [Tantra]* commentary also explains that there are sixteen stages, in this system it is not the case that more than fifteen stages are not accepted.

In addition to the ten stages the joyous and so forth, the explanatory tantra states:[697]

693. The idea here is that this initial stage of practice is correlated with the four "aids to penetration" (*nirvedhabhāgiya*) of the "path of application" (*prayogamārga*), described by Vasubandhu in his commentary on the *Ornament of the Universal Vehicle Sutras* 14.26; see Jamspal et al. 2004, 180–81.

694. This explanation is like Ratnākarashānti's, who identified the first stage as the stage of "ordinary being bodhisattvas," *so so skye bo'i byang chub sems dpa'i sa gcig*. The remainder are ten stages for "master bodhisattvas," and a final buddha stage. See the *String of Pearls, a Commentary on the Shrī Hevajra* (Tōh. 1189, 247b.7).

695. This passage occurs as follows in Haribhadra's *Ārya-Aṣṭasāhasrikā-prajñāpāramitāvyākhyā-abhisamayālaṁkārāloka-nāma*, D *shes phyin* vol. cha, 62b: *sa bcu pa'i byang chub sems dpa' la ni sangs rgyas nyid ces brjod bar bya'i yang dag par rdzogs pa'i sangs rgyas ni ma yin no.* Tsong Khapa's quotation differs slightly, reading: *sa bcu pa la ni byang chub sems dpa' sangs rgyas kho nar brjod bar bya'I / yang dag par rdzogs pa'i sangs rgyas ni ma yin no.*

696. This accounting only works if the gnostic body stage is identified with one of the previously listed sixteen stages, as Tsong Khapa suggests below.

697. Tsong Khapa quotes these lines as *dpe med pa dang ye shes ldan / rdo rje sa ste bcu gsum pa*. Both of these lines, or versions of them, occur in AU ch. 30. The line *rdo rje sa ni bcu gsum pa* occurs first, at AU 316a.1. The line *gzugs med pa dang ye she ldan*, "formless and

Peerless and endowed with gnosis,
The vajra stage is the thirteenth.

As for the meaning of this, the *Sheaf of Esoteric Instructions* explains that the tenth stage is taken as just the tenth, the peerless stage is the path that is distinct from the tenth stage. The endowed with gnosis stage is the path free of the obstacles of the tenth, and the vajradhara stage is completely radiant.[698] The *Vajra Rosary* explanatory tantra explains that with respect to the fourteen stages, the vase consecration [correlates] to the [first] eleven stages, and the three higher consecrations yield fourteen, such that "for each consecration there is a stage."[699] The *Ornament of the Vajra Essence Tantra* states:[700]

The bodhisattva is the light that's clear,
And the completely radiant great stage.

If one takes that as the first, then [the text] states, after the twelfth, "each of the twelve is thus self-cognizant, and the perfection of yogic gnosis."[701] I

endowed with gnosis" occurs at AU 316a.2, following the list of the ten stages to which Tsong Khapa refers, but does not quote.

698. The passage which Tsong Khapa summarizes here occurs at AM 33b.1–2, as follows: *de ltar sa bcu gcig rnams te / mos pa spyod pa'i sa dang lhan cig bcu gnyis dang las dang po pa'i sa dang lhan cig bcu gsum rnams so / yang na khyad par gyi ngo bo dpe med pa'i sa dang lhan cig bcu gnyis te / sangs rgyas kyi sa'i bar chad med pa'i lam gyi bdag nyid ye shes dang ldan pa'i sa dang lhan cig bcu gsum mo zhes pa ji ltar regs par gdul bya'i bsam pa ji lta bar mdo dang rgyud la sogs pa rnams su rnam par gzhag pa'o.*

699. The passage to which Tsong Khapa refers occurs in chapter 2 of the *Vajra Rosary Tantra*, as follows: *dbang bskur ba yi dbye ba ni / dang po'i dbang ni gtzo bo ste / gnyis pa gsang ba'i ming can no / gsum pa kun nas sbyor ba ste / bzhi pa'i don ni dam pa'o / gtso bo dbye ba bcu gcig ste / bcu gnyis pa ni gsang ba 'o / bcu gsum pa ni yang dag sbyor / bcu bzhi pa ni don dam ste / dbang bskur re re sa re'o* (D fol. 212b.2–4)

700. The text that Tsong Khapa cites here as *rdo rje snying po rgyan gyi rgyud* is not the *Vajrahṛdayālaṁkāra-tantra*, *dpal rdo rje snying po rgyan gyi rgyud*, preserved in the Derge canon (Tōh. 451). Rather, it is the *Śrīvajramaṇḍālaṁk[ā]ra-nāma-mahātantrarāja* (*Ornament of the Glorious Vajra Essence, Great King of Tantras*) (D 490), a text also preserved in the Lhasa Kangyur as Hlasa 459 (*rgyud 'bum* vol. nya, 1b–120b). The text, *byang chub sems ni 'od gsal ba / kun tu 'od kyi sa chen po*, occurs at Lhasa fol. 84b.5.

701. The previous quote lies at the beginning of a list of what appears to be twelve stages of consciousness, given names that evoke light. After the list of twelve is the passage Tsong

think it is excellent if you take this in the manner of the exegetical system of the twelve stages of the *mahāpaṇḍita* scholar.[702] It is the intention of the *Gnosis Drop Tantra*, and many Indian scholars have commented upon it.

Regarding [the claim]:[703]

> since it is not stated that there are stages beyond the eleven [ending with] the completely radiant, and since there are many more stages in the Mantric Vehicle than in the Perfections [Vehicle], this has served as the basis for the confusion. Those who abide in the completely radiant [stage] are not ultimate buddhas,

those who uphold the lofty and great should avoid disparaging perfected buddhas.

It is clearly explained that through the system of this vehicle with respect to the stages, there is no realization of anything established above and beyond the realization of the objective reality through subjective, spontaneous, great bliss. Regarding the establishment of the path of preparation beyond the realization of reality through the gnosis that arises through worldly meditation, the establishment of the path of vision beyond the direct realization of what was previously unrealized, truth itself (*chos nyid*, *dharmatā*), the establishment of the path of meditation on which one cultivates what one has seen in that manner, and so forth, these are like [the system of] other vehicles. Furthermore, there is no certainty with respect to the summary of these path's essential points. Regarding this path's establishment of each distinct form of spontaneous bliss as an individual stage, all the distinct forms of joy are designated as stages.[704]

While this is also the identification of one's own stage, it does not thus establish one in all stages, the joyous and so forth. How are the five paths

---

Khapa quotes here, *bcu gnyis so sorb dag rig pa / rnal 'byor ye shes yongs rdzogs nyid*, at fol. 85a.3–4.

702. I am not sure to whom Tsong Khapa refers to as *paṇ chen mkhas pa* here, but I suspect it is Abhayākaragupta and the system of twelve stages that he explains in AM as noted above.

703. Tsong Khapa does not identity his source here; I have not been able to identify it either.

704. Tsong Khapa appears to be paraphrasing another source here. I have not been able to identify it.

arranged if the stages are arranged in this fashion? The paths of ordinary beings and noble ones are distinguished with respect to the attainment or non-attainment of the noble stage with respect to the direct realization or non-realization of reality. If you apply the practice of the [paths of] accumulation and preparation on the path of ordinary beings, the joyous [stage] is the path of accumulation so long as one is unable to actually draw forth the empty state through the dissolution of the wind inserted into the central channel through the force of meditation beginning from that which is common to [these] paths, the path of accumulation to the point at which one has not directly realized reality by means of great bliss through that capacity, and the path of vision in which one has not attained integration through the objective clear light. The [remaining] nine stages are the path of meditation on which one has not progressed to the integration of no more learning from the integration of one who is still learning.

3.3.3. 2.2.2. 11.5.2. 2.1.1. 2. Avoiding the contradiction of stating [the stages] out of harmony with the seats etc.

The *Kiss [Tantra]* states that the seats are four, Pullīramalaya,[705] Jālandhara, Oḍḍiyāna, and Arbuda. The subsidiary seats are four, Godāvarī, Rāmeshvara, Devīkoṭa, and Mālava. Kāmarūpa and Oḍra are the two fields, and Trishakuni and Koshala are the two subsidiary fields. Kaliṅga and Lampāka are the two *chandoha*, and Kāñchi and Himālaya the two *upachandoha*. Pretapurī and Gṛihadevatā are the two meeting places, and Saurāṣhṭra and Suvarṇadvīpa the two subsidiary meeting places. Nagara and Sindhu are the two charnel grounds, and Maru and Kulutā are the two subsidiary charnel grounds.[706] It also occurs thus in [the systems of] Lūipa and Ghaṇṭapā.[707]

In the *Sheaf of Esoteric Instructions*, the lists the names "Bollagiri, Kollagiri, and Pullīramalaya [as] the adamantine seats."[708] The *Kiss [Tantra]*

705. ST lists Kollagiri (*kolla gi ri*) in place of Pullīramalaya. See ST 103a.2.

706. Tsong Khapa summarizes the list found at ST 103a.2–5.

707. This appears to be Tsong Khapa's interpretation; the sites and their classes are not correlated in any of the works attributed to Lūipa or Ghaṇṭapā.

708. Tsong Khapa partially quotes the following line from this source: "The seats are Jālandhara, Oḍḍiyāna, Pullīramalaya, and Arbuda. Bollagiri, Kollagiri, and Pullīramalaya

and other tantras state there are the five that are stated, Kāraṇyapāṭaka, Karmapāṭaka, Harikela, Vindhya, or the forest of the Vindhya range, and Kaumārapaurikā, as well as Charitra as well as that which lies at villages and city boundaries.[709] Regarding the seven sites that are close to the *pīlava*s, they are the *upapīlava*s, the two charnel grounds, namely the ghost complex (*pretasaṁhāta*) and the ocean's shore, and the [two] subsidiary charnel grounds, the garden and lotus pool shore;[710] the yoginīs love to gather in these charnel grounds and subsidiary charnel grounds.

The goddesses of the mandala in the sites such as Pullīramalaya are born from the wombs of brahmins and so forth. This is also explained by the following passage from the *Vajraḍāka*:[711]

> Those who are renowned as the ḍākinīs,
> The adamantine mandala's ladies,
> Are born in their very own birthplaces,
> In various lands, endowed with gnosis.

---

are listed as the 'adamantine seats'" (AM 151a.1: *gnas ni dza landha ra dang / o ḍi ya na dang pullī ra ma la ya dang arbu da'o / bolla gi ri dang kolla gi ri dang pullī ra ma la ya dang rdo rje'i gnas zhes pa rnam grangs so*).

709. Tsong Khapa here seems to be referring to a list of seven sites; I haven't been able to find this list in the *Kiss Tantra* or other tantras. However, this list bears some resemblance to HT 1.7.17, which defines the *pīlava* and *upapīlava* sites. It reads: "The *pīlavas* comprise that which lies on the village boundary, and that belonging to the city, Carita, Kośala, and Vindhyākaumārapaurikā. The *upapīlava* is nearby to that, O Vajragarbha of great compassion" (Snellgrove 1959, 1.70; *pīlavaṁ [ca] grāmantaṣṭhaṁ pīlavaṁ nagarasya ca / caritraṁ kośalaṁ caiva vindhyākaumārapaurikā / upapīlavaṁ tatsanniveśaṁ vajragarbha mahākṛpa*; 1959, 2.24–25: *'thung gcod grong khyer gyi dang yang / 'thung gcod grong ni mthar gnas pa / tsa ri tra ta ko sa la / bin dha gzhon nu'i grong khyer ro / rdo rje snying po snying rje che / nye ba'i thung gcod de nye ba'o.*) The *Saṁpuṭa* commentary on this verse occurs at ST 103a.5.

710. This is a reference to the *Hevajra Tantra*'s identification of the *śmaśāna* and *upaśmaśāna* sites at HT 1.7.18. See Snellgrove 1959, 1.70, 2.24–25.

711. Tsong Khapa here quotes a passage at the opening of VD ch. 8. Tsong Khapa quotes the passage as follows: *mkha' 'gro ma zhes yang dag grags / rdo rje dkyil 'khor gtso mo ste / ye shes ldan rnams yul yul du / rang nyid skye gnas rnams su skye*. Tsong Khapa's quote appears to be a variant reading of this text. It occurs as follows in the canonical translation: *ye shes ldan pa'i rang skye gnas / yul dang yul du mngon par skye / de ni mkha' 'gro ma zhes bya / rdo rje dkyil 'khor gtso mo yin* (VD 48a.5).

Moreover, this is explained in detail in the *Two-sectioned* [*Hevajra Tantra*], which indicates that the seats are Jālandhara, Oḍḍiyāna, Paurṇagiri, and Kāmarūpa. The subsidiary seats are Mālava, Sindhu, and Nagara. The fields are Munmuni, Kāruṇyapāṭaka, Devīkoṭa, and Karmārapāṭaka, and the subsidiary fields are Kulutā, Arbuda, Godāvarī, and Himādri. The *chandoha* are Harikela, Lampāka, Kāñchi, and Saurāṣhṭra, and the *upachandoha* are Kaliṅga, Suvarṇadvīpa, and Koṅkaṇa. The *pīlava*s are five, namely that which lies at villages and city boundaries, Charitra, Koshala, Vindhya, and Kaumārapaurikā, and the *upapīlava*s are five, close to the *pīlava*s. The two charnel grounds are the ghost complex and the ocean's shore, and the subsidiary charnel grounds are the garden and lotus pool shore.[712] This [source] does not indicate at all the meeting places and subsidiary meeting places.

In the *Great Seal Drop* it is clearly written that the seats are Jālandhara, Oḍḍiyāna, Paurṇagiri, and Kāmarūpa.[713] The subsidiary seats are Mālava, Nagara, Sindhu, and Siṁhala. The fields are Munmuni and Devīkoṭa, and the subsidiary fields are Kulutā and Arbuda. The *chandoha* are Godāvarī and Harikela, and the *upachandoha* are Lampāka and Kāñchi. The meeting places are Karmapāṭaka and Suvarṇadvīpa, and subsidiary meeting places are Koṅkaṇa and Vindhya. The charnel grounds are the ghost complex charnel ground[714] and at the ocean's shore. The subsidiary charnel grounds are Charitra and Kaumārapaurikā. The *pīlava*s are Kashmir and the land of Kerala,[715] and the *upapīlava*s are Nepal and Kānyakubja.[716] [717] "The *Rigi*

712. Tsong Khapa appears here to be providing a prose summary of HT 1.7.12–18. See Snellgrove 1959, 1.70, 2.22–25.

713. MT here differs somewhat from Tsong Khapa's summary, indicating that the Oḍḍiyāna is an "adamantine seat," and listing Pullīrama instead of Paurṇagiri, although these may be alternate names for the same place. It reads: *rdo rje gnas ni u rgyan dang / gnas ni dzā lan dha rar ldan / gnas ni pūlli ra ma dang / gnas ni kā ma rū pa'o* (MT 73b.2).

714. This follows the canonical translation, which reads *yi dags 'dus pa'i dur khrod* (MT 73b.4), corresponding to the Sanskrit *śmaśānaṁ pretasaṁhātaṁ* (HT 1.7.18a, Snellgrove 1959, 2.24). Tsong Khapa reads *rab song gi sa gzhi*, which appears to be based on the translation found in the canonical HT translation, *dur khrod rab gson dge 'dun* (Snellgrove 1959, 2.25)

715. "Land of Kerala" is a hypothetical reading of the text preserved in MT, *ke ra da yul* (73b.4). Tsong Khapa here reads *ke ri ta'i dkyil 'khor.*

716. Tsong Khapa here reads *kā nya kub dza*. The canonical text reads *kar no ja* (MT 73b.5).

717. Tsong Khapa here again gives a prose summary of text found in MT ch. 10, 73b.2–5. Divergent readings are noted above.

Ārali Tantra states the sites are [on the continent of] Videha in the East, Jambhudvīpa [in the South], Godanīya [to the West], and Kurava [to the North]."[718]

Don't all of these statements contradict one another? There is no fault. While there seems to be a contradiction between, on the one hand, [the system of this tantra, which] identifies **the seats** with **the joyous stage** [up to] **the subsidiary charnel grounds** with **the cloud of truth** [stage; **50.20a–22b**], with another [system], indications with words such as "seat" (*pīṭha*, *gnas*), "subsidiary seat" (*upapīṭha*, *nye ba'i gnas*) are not contradictory with respect to being right or wrong, existent or nonexistent. This is because a single thing has various names. Therefore, The *Kiss [Tantra]*'s elucidation of Arbuda as a seat does not contradict the *Hevajra* and the *Great Seal Drop*'s explanation that it is a subsidiary seat. Likewise, the *Great Seal Drop*'s explanation that Godāvarī is a *chandoha*, the *Hevajra*'s explanation that it is a subsidiary field, and the *Kiss [Tantra]*'s explanation that it is a subsidiary seat are not contradictory. Through these [examples] one should know that the other [discrepancies] are also non-contradictory.

Moreover, if you apply the outer sites to the internal body, the explanation in the *Great Seal Drop* has many differences from the Saṁvara [system],[719] however this is not contradictory, because they were taught to accord with the mentalities of various disciples. These [arguments for the] avoidance of contradiction are stated in accordance with the intention of the *Sheaf of Esoteric Instructions*.[720]

718. This passage occurs as follows in the *Rigi-ārali-tantrarāja-nāma*: "The ten grounds are distinguished. The seats are Videha in the East, and likewise Godanīya, Kurava in the North, and thus Jambhudvīpa. The four goddesses are in the four continents, and Rigi abides on the tip of Sumeru" (Tōh. 427, D *rgyud* vol. nga, 176a.6–7: *sa bcu rnams ni rab tu phye / gnas ni shar gyi lus 'phags so / de bzhin du ni ba lang spyod / gnas ni byang gi sgra mi snyan / gnas ni de bzhin 'dzam bu gling / gling bzhir lha mo bzhi dang ni / ri rab spyi bor ri gi bzhugs*).

719. MT correlates the sites to the body parts and constituents at fol. 73b.5–7. For a summary of the Chakrasaṁvara system, see Gray 2007, 56–64.

720. Tsong Khapa here paraphrases Abhayākaragupta's argument at AM 152a.1–3. Much of this section is a summary of the opening portion of AM ch. 17, from fol. 150b.2 to 152a.3.

3.3.3. 2.2.2. 11.5.2. 2.1.1. 3. The types of disciples for whom they are stated

In the *Sheaf of Esoteric Instructions*, [Abhayākaragupta] explains that the outer seats and so forth are taught for the sake of those with dull faculties from among the five [types of] disciples. They are taught so that those incapable of yogic meditation avoid attachment to their own lands. The placement of the seats and so forth on the spokes of the triple wheel mandala [are taught] for those of middling faculties. For the lesser of the three great [types of] disciples, the placement of the seats and so forth in the twenty-four sites of the body [are taught]. The middling [among the great], as perfection stage practitioners, visualize the channels in the seats etc. in the head and so forth as goddesses, without reliance on seed syllables and so forth. The greatest [among the great], in terms of abiding in perfection stage practice, place the spirit of awakening of inseparable emptiness and compassion in the seats and so forth that are the joyous [stage etc.] The last is the definitive meaning, and the first four of the five are interpretable meanings. Through faith in the stages such as the joyous correlated to the seats and so forth, would it not be fitting to strive for the sake of the realization of the transcendent stages?[721]

Reality is bestowed on the path of the union of spontaneous bliss and emptiness, as was quoted [in the following passages] in the *Discourse Appendix*:[722]

721. Tsong Khapa summarizes, but does not directly quote, Abhayākaragupta's discussion of the five types of practitioners with respect to this mandala, at AM 152a.4–b.4. See Gray 2007, 69–70 for a translation of this passage.

722. Tsong Khapa's immediate source for this and the following quotation is Abhayākaragupta's AM commentary, which quotes a single long passage from the opening of AU ch. 68. Tsong Khapa quotes most of this passage and divides it into two shorter quotations. This quotation is generally close to the canonical translation of AU; however, it omits a number of lines. It occurs as follows in Abhayākaragupta's commentary: *mkha' 'gro ma kun 'di nyid du / thugs rje ldan rnams rnam par gnas / sangs rgyas byang chub sems dpa' kun / 'gro ba gsum po'ang de nyid du'o / nyi shu bzhi'i dbye ba yis / gnas sogs 'di kho na la gnas / de bas de ru bskor ba yi / skyob bya de nyid can gyis min / gal te de nyid med gyur na / de rnams bskor bas cung zad min / gal te de nyid ldan gyur na / de rnams nskor bas ci zhig dgos / phyi rol rnal 'byor pa de rnams / bskor bas khams rnams zad par 'gyur / de bas phyi rol spangs nas ni / rnal 'byor rol pas gnas par bya / dpal ldan rdo rje rnal 'byor mas / rnam dag ye shes spyan rnams kyis / rdo rje rnal 'byor can rnams gzigs / thugs rjes khyab pa'i thugs kyis ni / de rnams dges pas dngos grub mchog / ji ltar 'dod bzhin stsol par mdzad* (AM 152b.5–53a.1).

Note that *skyob bya* and *dges pas* appear to be corrupt readings; Tsong Khapa quotes the

It is here that the ḍākinīs
Endowed with compassion reside.
Here dwell all perfected buddhas,
Bodhisattvas, and the three worlds.
The seats and so forth, distinguished
As twenty-four, all exist right here.
Those who know reality do not
Exhaust themselves visiting them.
If you don't know reality,
There's no reason to visit them.
And if you know reality,
There's no reason to visit them.
Outer yogīs, visiting them,
Just exhaust their vitality.
Thus, one should shun the external,
And dwell in the play of yoga.
Glorious vajrayoginīs
Will gaze upon vajrayogīs
With their eyes of gnosis that's pure,
And with minds full of compassion.
Being pleased, they will thus bestow
The supreme power one desires.

And also:[723]

Contemplating one's supreme deity,
Reflect upon the sole reality.
Through as little as six months of

---

correct readings, *skyo bya* and *dgyes pas*, respectively. The passage in the ultimate source occurs at AU 368b.6–7, and, following a long passage omitted by Abhayākara, resumes at AU 369a.2–3, and following another omitted passage, continues at AU 369a.5–6.

723. This passage is quoted as follows by Abhayākara: *rang gi lhag pa'i lha dmigs te / de kho nan yid gcig pu bsam / lkugs pa'i dngos por rab gyur pa'i / zla drug tsam gyis nges par ni / rnal 'byor ma yis nyer bstan pa'i / rnal 'byor chen po 'digs la 'gyur / ye shes 'od zer mchog mthong nas / rnal 'byor ma rnams legs 'du ste / padma'i 'byung gnas nyams dga' bar / ngang pa'i tshogs 'du ji bzhin no / dpal ldan rdo rje 'dzin dngos su / 'gyur bar 'di la the tshom med / mig 'phrul mkhan bzhin 'jig rten du / sems can kun gyi don byed rnams / sems ni dag par gyis shig ces / sems can rnams la bdag gsol 'debs* (AM 153a.3–5; cf. AU 369b.1–3).

Maintaining a state of silence,
The great yogī is radiant
And attended[724] by yoginīs.
Seeing this supreme gnostic light,
Yoginīs gather around him,
Just as a gaggle of geese flock
To a lovely lotus-filled lake.
Have no doubt that he will become
A glorious vajradhara.
Like a magician, he will then secure
The welfare of all the world's beings.
My request to sentient beings
Truly is, "Purify your minds!"[725]

3.3.3. 2.2.2. 11.5.2. 2.1.2. The auxiliary meanings

The seats that satisfy immeasurable sentient beings with generosity are **the joyous** stage (50.20a), the first stage. One should know that in this tantra the third stage, the **illuminating** stage, are **the fields** (50.20c) that give rise to perfections such as clairvoyance through the power of patience. The [syllables] *chanda* of ***chandoha*** means "desire," while the [syllables] *uha*, from which the letter *u* derives [prior to sandhi] means "comprehending," hence [*chandoha*] means "comprehending desire" (*'dun rtog*).[726] Desire here is seeking perfection for the sake of oneself and others, and comprehension is acting accordingly for the sake of this. This is the fifth stage, **the very-difficult-to-conquer** (50.21a) stage.[727] **The meeting place,** through

724. This translates the reading preserved by Tsong Khapa and AU, *nyer bsten na* (AU 369b.1). AM here reads *nyer bstan na* (AM 153a.3).

725. This translates the Tibetan preserved in the AM and AU texts, *sems ni dag par gyis shig ces* (AM 153a.5, AU 369b.3) and the Sanskrit, *kriya[n]tāṁ śuddhacetasaḥ* (J 317.7). Tsong Khapa's text here has the corrupt reading *sems ni dga' bar gyis shig ces.*

726. This analysis of *chandoha* as a compound of the words *chandas* and *ūha* is a folk etymology.

727. In the root text, the *chandoha* are linked to the facing (*abhimukhī*) stage, and the *upachandoha* to the *sudurvijayā* stage, reserving the usual order of these stages. Tsong Khapa appears to be correcting this discrepancy.

indeterminable exertion in concentration, clairvoyance, and so forth with the power of the perfection of skillful means, is the seventh stage, **the far-reaching** (**50.21c**). Selflessly realizing the sphere of reality that is like a charnel ground, one endeavors to teach the Dharma, and so forth, in order that sentient beings will realize that. Those **charnel grounds** are the ninth stage, **the accomplished** (**50.22a**).

The subsidiary seats, are **the immaculate** second stage (**50.20b**), and **the subsidiary fields** are **the effulgent** fourth stage (**50.20d**). **The *upachandoha*** are **the facing** sixth stage (**50.21b**), **the subsidiary meeting places** are **the immovable** eighth stage (**50.21d**). **The subsidiary charnel grounds** are **the cloud of truth** tenth stage. The meanings of the names of the five subsidiary sites are similar to those of the five former names [that they share]. The subsidiary status implies connection to those in need of assistance and those who assist. One should know that the significance of subsidiarity also implies coming to eminence from the previous five, and the five [sites] signified as subsidiary are positioned close to the outer sites. It means that, depending upon the previous [sites], they correspond to them.

In this way, **this practice,** regarding the seats, subsidiary seats and so forth, **in the teaching of Shrī Heruka**[728] **concerns the inner** ten **stages** (**50.22cd**) as characterized by the definitive meaning. **With respect to the stages**, the joyous and so forth, having the nature of **the ten perfections**, generosity and so forth, **the** symbolic **language of the yoginīs** reveals that they are the seats etc. Since "symbolic" and **barbaric language** (**50.23ab**) are common equivalents, although you can translate [*mlecchabhāṣaṁ*] as "barbaric language," someone states that this is not a good translation.[729]

728. Tsong Khapa follows the Tibetan translation, *śrī he ru ka gzhung spyod pa'i / 'di ni*. The Sanskrit, *śrīherukamatiś cāyaṁ*, lacks a word corresponding to "practice," *spyod pa*.

729. Tsong Khapa here comments on the translation of the Sanskrit *mlecchabhāṣaṁ*, which is translated as "symbolic language," *brda yi skad*. This would be a good translation of *cchomakabhāṣaṁ*, but not *mlecchabhāṣaṁ*, which would be more accurately translated as *kla klo'i skad*. I have not been able to identify the unnamed author to whom Tsong Khapa refers here. It may have been Abhayākara, who glosses *kla klo'i skad* with *brda'i skad* (AM 155b.3).

3.3.3. 2.2.2. 11.5.2. 2.2. Showing that the ten seats etc. are all pervading

How are all the parts of Heruka's body the seats and so forth? It is said that Heruka is the very identity of all things **mobile and** immobile, due to the inseparability of **the hero** Heruka**'s body** and reality, namely the inhabitants who range **in heaven**, i.e., the mind wheel, those who range **in the mortal world**, i.e., the speech wheel, and those who range **in the underworld** (**50.23cd**), i.e., the body wheel, as well as all twenty-four spokes of each of those habitat wheels. Regarding the what is intended by that, **the teaching regarding Pullīramalaya, and so forth**, which implies the remaining twenty-three sites as well, **is that they exist** as the very identity of what is **outside** and **inside**. It is explained that the outer exists in the inner body, and the definitive meaning of them is the inseparability of bliss and emptiness.

Since the great king Shrī Heruka has mastered the enjoyment of **all desires**, he is **the powerful lord** that one can achieve with this path (**50.24**). What is Heruka like? He has **hands and feet, and eyes, faces, and heads** and **hearing.**[730] In what way does he have these six, hands and so forth? The meaning of **everywhere**, applied to the six [parts and faculties], is that he is able to activate the function of the hand with all body parts, hence he has hands everywhere. One should also know this with respect to the other five. In the *Sheaf of Esoteric Instructions*, [Abhayākaragupta] explains that he exists covering, that is, pervading, all worlds.[731] In this manner, he undertakes the function of grasping with a hand **in all worlds.** One should also know this with respect to the remaining [body parts and functions]. The term "**covering**" (*g.yogs*) occurs as "pervading" (*khyab*) in other translations (**50.25**).[732]

As quoted in the *Sheaf of Esoteric Instructions*, the *Origin of the Power of Faith Scripture* states that:[733]

730. Tsong Khapa here glosses the term *gsan pa* as *thos pa*. The former term is used in the SM, and the latter in the PM and SL translations.

731. Tsong Khapa paraphrases Abhayākara's comments at AM 308a.4–5.

732. The PM, SL, and SM translations all read *g.yogs* here. However, Abhayākara's commentary quotes this passage, and here the translation *khyab par byas* is used instead (AM 308a.5). The former is a more literal translation of the Sanskrit *āvṛtya*.

733. As Tsong Khapa indicates his source again is Abhayākara's commentary, where it occurs as follows: *de bzhin du de bzhin gshegs pas gtsug tor gyis kyang gzigs so / de bzhin du*

The Tathāgata also sees with his or her cranial protuberance, and likewise sees with the hair tuft as well, and in this way with every mark. S/he thus sees in an instant of time all of the billions of worldly realms in the ten directions.

3.3.3. 2.2.2. 11.5.3. Summarizing the meaning

Through him who has become firm in the yoga of Heruka who is like that, there is **the attainment of all powers with a mind endowed with the meditative states** of the two stages. **This secret reality was stated** by the Lord **for the sake of the welfare of the adepts** (50.26).

3.3.3. 2.2.2. 11.5.4. Showing the name of the chapter

In the *Concise* ***Shrī Herukābhidhāna Tantra***, this is **the fiftieth chapter** on **the procedure of** fire sacrifice, such as **the domination fire sacrifice, and of the teaching of the** ten **stages in relation to the** ten **seats and so forth**. This is the explanation of the fiftieth chapter in the *Illumination of the Hidden Meaning, A Detailed Exegesis of the Concise Saṁvara Tantra Called "The Chakrasaṁvara."*

---

mdzod spus kyang gzigs so / de ltar mtshan re res so / de ltar dus cig car du phyogs bcu rnams su 'jig rten gyi khams rab 'byam thams cad du gzigs so (AM 308a.6–7).

Chapter 51

Chapter 51 Outline

3.3.3. 2.3. The fifty-first chapter's summarization of the previous [chapters]

The third part, showing the fifty-first chapter's summarization of the previous [chapters], has three sections: (1) the promise to explain, (2) the promised explanation of the meaning, (3) and showing the chapter count.

3.3.3. 2.3.1. The promise to explain

Now, after the fiftieth chapter, aside from the significance of each of the previously explained chapters, **I will expound** a general summary of the significance of the previous explanations.

3.3.3. 2.3.2. The promised explanation of the meaning

The second part has five sections: (1) showing the esoteric instruction for this tantra that is very hard to obtain, (2) showing the fourteen realities that are the method for easily obtaining it, (3) the benefits of practice in the fourteen, and the fault of lacking faith, (4) the method of comprehensive meditation on the fourteen realities, and (5) showing the method for not forsaking any of the Buddha's scriptures.

3.3.3. 2.3.2. 1. Showing the esoteric instruction for this tantra that is very hard to obtain

It was stated, that is, taught, to Vajrapāṇi that, excepting those who are realized through revering and serving the great guru, **the esoteric instructions** of all buddhas **are very hard to obtain** (**51.1ab**), since otherwise one will not be able to obtain them due to suffering.[734] The oral instructions that are hard to obtain concern the great seal that wanders the field that integrates the two bodies of the purified conventional and the ultimate clear light that engages exactly the reality of one's own mind and things, which is the complete buddha's awakening made manifest by the great seal that moves through the integration that is steadfast in the two truths.[735]

Regarding this, "complete buddha" refers to the magic body, and "awakening" to the clear light. It is explained that this integration is the very clear procedure of practice and spiritual discipline for the adept to engage the ultimate goal of the practice and completely understand unerringly in accordance with the stages of the esoteric instructions. Having embarked upon the creation stage and depending upon the perfection stage, one will equal Shrī Heruka's state.[736] Thus it is taught that it is hard to obtain the esoteric instruction for understanding unerringly the esoteric instructions

734. Tsong Khapa here refers to the opening of Kambala's commentary on this chapter. It occurs as follows: *de nas gzhan yang bshad bya ba / gzhung lugs shin tu rnyed dka' ba / zhes bya ba ni 'dir yang phyag na rdo rje la bos te gsungs pa'o* (SN 77b.1–2).

735. Tsong Khapa here paraphrases Kambala's commentary, which occurs as follows: *shin tu rnyed dka' ste / chos kyi de kho nan yid ji ltar 'gyur bas na / bden pa gnyis la legs par gnas pa'i zung du 'jug pa rgyu ba ste / phyag rgya chen pos mngon par rdzogs pa'i sangs rgyas byang chub pa'o* (SN 77b.2–3).

736. Tsong Khapa here paraphrases Kambala's commentary at SN 77b.3–4.

of the great saints that create the conditions for achieving the state of integration, and which contain the practice of the two stages for progressing to this [state]. Thorough understanding of integration depends upon thorough understanding of these esoteric instructions. The commentary states:[737]

> One cultivates the gnosis of wisdom
> Through hearing, reflecting, and meditating on
> The oral instructions passed one to another,
> Being supreme coming from the supreme,
> The Buddha's eye, possessing the answer,
> That have the means to induce[738] and apply
> The yoginīs' command, the position
> Of the buddhas' awakening, great seal
> That perfects the meditation drawn from
> The unification of all buddhas,
> The network of the ḍākinīs.
> Through regular contact with yoginīs,
> There's the fortune of unending meaning,
> Ripening and purifying.
> It is the secret in all the tantras
> Derived from this scriptural tradition.
> The great secret of all buddhas exists
> As the three-hundred-thousand[-stanza text],
> That's derived from the extensive tantra.

Regarding the meaning of the first three lines of that [passage], attainment through the illusory concentration of the ḍākinīs' network, the unification

737. Tsong Khapa here quotes a verse section of Kambala's commentary, which reads as follows: *sangs rgyas kun dang mnyam sbyor ba / mkha' 'gro dra ba'i sdom pa las / byung ba'i ting 'dzin rdzogs pa yi / sangs rgyas byang chub phyag rgya che'i / las gnas rnal 'byor ma yi bka' / 'dren zhing nye bar spyod pa bcas / lan dang bcas shing sangs rgyas sbyan / mchog las mchog tu gyur pa dang / gcig nas gcig brgyud man ngag ste / thos dang bsam pa sgom pa yis / shes rab ye shes goms pa ni / rnal 'byor rgyun chags rab 'brel pas / rgyun mi chad don skal ba can / yongs su smin cing yongs su byung / snod ldan de yi phyir bstan pas / 'ong ba gang yin 'dir gzhung lugs / rgyud rnams kun du gsungs pa gang / gsang chen sangs rgyas kun gnas pa / 'bum phrag sum 'gyur gang yin nyid / rab rgyas rgyud la 'ongs pa'o* (SN 77b.4–6).

738. This translates the reading in Kambala's commentary, *'dren* (SN 77b.4). Tsong Khapa's text reads *bden* here.

of all buddhas, is the enlightened activity that achieves the the great seal of the inseparable two truths, the "complete buddha" which is the conventional magic body and clear light of "ultimate awakening." With respect to the two lines, "position" and so forth, it seems that they occur as "closely affixed, arising from the command of the yoginīs of the seats," in another translation of Kambala's commentary. [The text] "possessing the answer" (*lan dang bcas*) does not occur in other translations.[739] "The Buddha's eye" means cherished like an eye. Here "scriptural tradition" is the previously explained esoteric instructions that are hard to obtain. The remainder is easy [to understand].

[The passage] occurs in verse in Gö's translation,[740] and in prose in the translation by Shākya Tsöndru.[741] "Three hundred thousand" occurs in Gö's translation. The translation "three thousand" in the other translation and Devagupta's commentary was made from a corrupt text.[742] Regarding the meaning of [the secret] being thus derived from the three-hundred-thousand[-stanza] tantra, it is **hidden by me**, Vajradhara, as **symbolically spoken by the hero (51.1cd)** through being free of the afflictions having meditated upon the fourteen realities depending upon the creation stage and having reached the limit of the perfection stage.

Where is it hidden? It is said that "[it is hidden] in other tantras, in the action, practice, yoga and unexcelled [tantras]."[743] "In other tantras" refers to the three classes of lower tantras. As for being hidden in two [places], it is hidden without being revealed at all with regard to both the three lower classes of tantra and the genre of sutras. Although "in the supreme yoginīs"

739. Unfortunately, it does not appear that any alternate translations of Kambala's commentary survived. The extant Sanskrit manuscript is also missing its last few folio, corresponding to chapter 51, so it is not possible to compare the canonical translation with the Sanskrit text either.

740. Tsong Khapa refers here to the translator of the canonical translation of Kambala's commentary, Gö Lotsawa Shönu Pal.

741. Shākya Tsöndru was an eleventh century translator who translated works associated with the yoginī tantra traditions. He likely was the earliest translator of this work, but his translation has not, to my knowledge, survived.

742. Devagupta's commentary contains a prose version of this text, at SS 155b.1–4. As Tsong Khapa notes, it contains the variant reading *stong phrag gsum*.

743. Tsong Khapa quotes Kamabala's commentary, which here reads: *gang du zhe na rgyud gzhan dag tu ste bya ba dang spyod pa dang rnal 'byor dang rnal 'byor bla ma rnams su'o* (SN 77b.7).

occurs in the fourth line in another translation, this refers to the unexcelled [tantras].[744]

The text is not clear regarding what is hidden, even though it is for the sake of those tantras. They are hard to obtain for this reason. The oral instructions that are thus hard to obtain in general pertain to the practice of Heruka's two stages. In particular, they are the difficult to obtain method for achieving integration by means of the concentration of the magic body. The main essential points are explained by Kambala the Blanketed and Devagupta.

3.3.3. 2.3.2. 2. Showing the fourteen realities that are the method for easily obtaining it

As for to the second [section], having shown what is thus difficult to obtain and the reason that it is difficult to obtain, with respect to the method for easily obtaining it, it is necessary to summarize and then explain the fourteen realities. It has two [parts]: (1) explaining the literal meaning of the fourteen realities, and (2) the explanation applicable to the two stages.

3.3.3. 2.3.2. 2.1. Explaining the literal meaning of the fourteen realities

Although the reliable commentaries on the root tantra do not explain the manner in which the enumeration of the fourteen realities is made, there are actual statements of the number of the realities. Regarding the first reality, the reality of **the garb, five insignia, and so forth** (**52.2a**), the equivalent term for "garb" (*gos*) is *vasanaṁ*, and it is asserted by the learned translators that it can designate both an "abode" and "garb," which is excellent.[745] Therefore, following the two explanations in the commentaries of *gos/nivasanaṁ* as "tiger hide" and "mandala palace,"[746] although there is a

744. The alternate reading, *rnal 'byor ma mchog rnams su'o*, occurs in Devagupta's commentary at SS 155b.6.

745. The Sanskrit term here is actually *nivasanaṁ*, which, like *vasanaṁ*, also has the double meaning as Tsong Khapa explains here.

746. Kambala glosses *gos/nivasanaṁ* as "tiger hide," *stag gi pags pa'o* (SN 77b.7). Bhavabhaṭṭa also includes the elephant hide that Heruka wears (Pandey 2002, 588 *nivasanaṁ vyāghracarma gajacarma ca*; cf. 873). Devagupta follows Kambala in glossing *gos/*

single, simple [equivalent] in the Tibetan language, based upon the equivalent terms, with respect to "abode" (*gnas*) there is both the abode of the practitioner and the abode of the mandala deities. Regarding the "five insignia," they consist of the following five: (1) a diadem or wheel on the crown, (2) earrings, (3) necklace, (4) bracelet and (5) sacred thread. It is explained that "and so forth" includes ash.[747] Kāṇha's *Mandala Rites* also includes [other] ornaments such as a garland of heads, a dreadlock crest, and artificial hair.[748] This is the method of engaging in the clothing of an adept in the adept's abode.

The second, the reality of **the wisdom** [consort]'s **body**, is explained as being embraced by the skull staff or the body of the consort.[749] Kāṇha's *Mandala Rites* also states "the wisdom [consort]'s body atop the cushion,[750] which means that the consort should be taken as being on the cushion, as previously [explained].

The third is the reality of **the stake and the cage (51.2b)**, that is, the adamantine stake and adamantine cage. Illustrated by that is are the adamantine fence and canopy, the adamantine ground, the net of arrows, the garland of fire and so forth. This is the visualization of the wheel of protection.

Uttering the garland of **vowels and consonants (51.2c)**, through their circulation at the horizon, it is explained that they are visualized in the form of the moon and sun.[751] The method of visualizing the moon from the vowels and the sun from the consonants is also explained by Durjayachandra.[752] Illustrated by that one should also apprehend the generation of

---

nivasanaṁ as "tiger hide," but adds that it can also designate the mandala palace (SS 155b.7: *gos zhes pa ni stag gi pags pa'o / yang na gos zhes pa ni gzhal yas khang brtsegs pa'o*).

747. Tathāgatarakṣhita indicates this; see UN 251b.1.

748. After listing the standard five insignia, Kāṇha does indeed list these other ornaments. See his *Mandala Rites* (*Bhagavacchrīcakrasaṁvaramaṇḍalavidhi*) (Tōh. 1446), D fol. 284b.1–2.

749. Both of these interpretations are advanced by Kambala; see SN 78a.1.

750. This text, the *shes rab yan lag stan gyi steng*, occurs at the *Mandala Rites* (Tōh. 1446), D fol. 284b.1. The text in the sDe-dge reprint reads *sting* rather than *steng*.

751. That is, they are visualized circling one at the horizon like these celestial bodies. Kambala makes this comment at SN 78a.2.

752. Durjayachandra briefly comments on this, evidently following Kambala. He wrote, "Regarding **uttering the vowels and consonants**, they should be in the form of the moon

the two white and red moons and the single moon. Here the reality of the vowels and the reality of the consonants should be taken as two, thus being the fourth and the fifth realities.

The sixth reality is **the preliminary** that is **devoid of cause**. Since [the term] "first" is applied to it, the equivalent term to **and so forth (51.2d)** in Mardo's tradition,[753] it can be explained as having first undertaken, the store of merit that is the cause, one accumulates both [that and] the store of gnosis by meditating on emptiness. However, in the commentaries it is explained in terms of "and so forth." If one explains as stated in Vīravajra's and [Tathāgatarakṣhita's] *Twofold Commentary* [commentaries], "*he* is the emptiness of cause and so forth,"[754] it can be applied as well to meditation on emptiness prior to the generation of the habitat. If taken in this manner, it is a preliminary practice for the generation of the habitat and inhabitant [deities].

"Cause" is that which brings about generation, while "and so forth" includes all things that are generated. Regarding these things being "empty," it is explained in terms of the gnosis that achieves the four [modes of emptiness,].[755] The intention here is that since the moon, sun and seeds exist distinctly, they are mixed into one empty [state].

Regarding the seventh reality of **the sound of manifestation, and so forth (51.3a)**, another translation of Kambala's commentary explains that:[756]

---

and sun" (RG 314a.7: *ā li kā li zhes brjod pa / zhes bya ba ni zla ba dang nyi ma'i gzugs su gyur pa'o*).

753. Tsong Khapa is referring to the word *ādi* in the compound *hetvādiśūnyapūrvakaṁ*, which literally means "first," but in compound means "and so forth."

754. I have not been able to find the line Tsong Khapa quotes here, *he ni rgyu sogs stong pa nyid*, in either of Vīravajra's commentaries or Tathāgatarakṣhita's UN commentary. The former, in his PD commentary, quotes CT 51.2d, *rgyu sogs stong pa sngon 'gro yin*, and then quotes the traditional etymology of Heruka, which begins with the line *he ni rgyu tshogs spangs pa ste*. See PD 448a.2.

755. Tsong Khapa paraphrases Kambala's commentary here, which states: "As for **the preliminary devoid of cause and so forth**, 'cause' is that which produces [something], and 'and so forth' with respect to that is 'cause and so forth,' namely the product generated. This is the gnosis that achieves the four modes of emptiness with respect to those [things]" (SN 78a.2: *rgyu sogs stong pa sngon 'gro ba'i / zhes bya ba la rgyu ni byed pa'o / de la sogs pa ni rgyu sogs te / bskyed pa'i bya ba la sogs pa'o / de rnams kyi stong pa ni bzhi pa bya ba grub pa'i ye shes sp*).

756. Tsong Khapa quotes this passage as follows: *sgra la sogs pas bsdus pa zla nyi dang phyag mtshan rnams rgyu rdo rje 'dzin pa ji srid pa de srid du 'jug pa dang / 'jug pa'i mtshan ma*

> by **sound . . . and so forth**, the causal Vajradhara manifests insofar as the moon, sun, and hand emblems are drawn back. The sign of manifestation, its cause or "mere sound," is the [syllable] *hūṁ* which exists in the context of the fourth [stage of] manifest awakening.

Another translation quotes "abiding in the sound of apprehension and so forth," and this is explained as "one embraces the reality of the three syllables and sound as the cause that apprehends or manifests, thus generating, Heruka."[757] "And so forth" implies the radiation of the deities of the three wheels from the three syllables.

The eighth reality that **has the employment of condensation** is said to be applying the condensation of the seed, moon and sun into a single mass in the context of achieving the ritual actions.[758] Someone explains that through the preliminary of benefitting sentient beings with the radiated deities, they are condensed into the three syllables, and quotes "condensation in such a way."[759] The meaning of "from" and **insofar (51.3b)** is from the meditation on the manifest awakenings up until their perfection.

The ninth reality of **being satisfied with ambrosia**, is delighting oneself as Vajradhara with the gnosis of total purity. It is furthermore outer and inner worship with the ambrosias. The tenth reality of **cessation (51.3c)** is condensing the deities into oneself at the conclusion of meditation on the

---

ste rgyu ni sgra tsam zhes pa mngon byang bzhi pa skabs su gnas pa'i hūṁ mo. An alternate version of this passage is preserved in the canonical translation: *'jug pa sgra la sogs pa nas / zhes bya ba la rgyu rdo rje 'dzin pa ni 'jug pa'o / 'jug pa'i rgyu ni sgra ste gnas skabs bzhi pa'i yi ge huṁ ngo / sogs pa zhes bya ba zla ba dang nyi ma dang mtshan ma'i bar du'o / ji srid bsdus pa'i sbyor ldan pa* (SN 78a.3).

757. Tsong Khapa here refers to Tathāgatarakṣhita's commentary, although the line quoted does not occur in the canonical translation of that work exactly as Tsong Khapa indicates; he quotes this line as *bzung ba nā da sogs par gnas.* The quote and commentary occur as follows in the canonical commentary: *'jug pa nā da sogs par gnas / zhes pa ni he ru ka 'jug cing bskyed pa'i rgyur yi ge gsum gyi nā da'i ngo bos yongs su gzung ba'o* (UN 251b.2–3).

758. Tsong Khapa paraphrases Kambala's comment at SN 78a.3–4.

759. This someone is Tathāgatarakṣhita, who does indeed quote an alternate reading for 51.3b. He wrote: *ji ltar bsdus pa'i sbyor ldan pa / zhes pa ni lha de rnams kyis 'gro ba'i don byed pa sngon du 'gro bas yi ge gsum la bsdu'o* (UN 251b.3–4).

mandala. The eleventh reality of **hand worship** includes both worship on the hand and worship with the hand. It is explained extensively elsewhere.[760]

The twelfth reality of **consecration (51.3d)** is said to include the following fourteen [consecrations]: the water, crown, vajra, royal, name, master, vow, prophesy, encouragement, honoring, preaching the Dharma, the secret, gnosis of the consort, and the fourth.[761] This also illustrates deity empowerment.

The thirteenth reality of **being guarded by the great armor (51.4a)** involves placement of drops containing the twenty-four syllables—*pu*, *ja*, *la*, and so forth—on solar seats in the twenty-four bodily sites such as the crown. This is the "great armor," and illustrated by that, one is protected having placed the two armors of the partners.

The fourteenth reality of **worshipping with all mantras (51.4b)** is worship reciting the mantras of all deities as explained by Lūipa;[762] one should repeat the mantra of each deity while visualizing each deity's form. Someone claims that you worship the mantra in order to praise with the eight-line mantra.[763] Others claim it is recollecting the meaning of mantras such as the vowels and consonants etc.[764] Regarding **these fourteen realities being concisely stated (51.4cd)** as was previously explained in this manner, it is a statement summarizing the meaning of the previous fifty chapters.

3.3.3. 2.3.2. 2.2. The explanation applicable to the two stages

There are four realities that are common to both [the creation and perfection] stages. Among them is the reality of consecration, which makes one a suitable vessel for the tantras. It occurs first. [Next] is the reality of hand worship. With respect to protecting the commitments and vows obtained at the time of consecration, it is the latter among those two [i.e., the vows] that are not common [to the two stages], as they are generally taught in the context of the heteropraxy, however, among these two, it is the

760. See section 3.3.3. 2.2.2. 7.1.2 in chapter 31 above.

761. Vīravajra makes this claim; see SS 206b.4–5.

762. See Lūipa's *Glorious Lord's Realization* (*Śrībhagavad-abhisamaya*), Tōh. 1427, D 191a.4–b.5.

763. Tathāgatarakṣhita makes this claim; see UN 251b.5.

764. Vīravajra makes this claim; see SS 206b.6.

commitments that are primary. The reality of the garb, five insignia, and so forth, along with the previous two make three. The reality of the wisdom [consort]'s body is necessary in three contexts, at the time of consecration and at the time or context of the two stages. That makes four that are common to both stages.

For an explanation connecting them to the creation stage, you can apply them to the entire creation stage, such as the explanation that there is an infinite creation stage etc. as occurs in the *Discourse Appendix*. However, if you explain relying on the exegetical traditions of Lūipa, Ghaṇṭapā, and Kāṇhapa, whose prescriptions are essential here, the reality of the stake and the cage, brings together the three, the extensive, middling and abridged protection wheels. Regarding the need to know the main parts of the spiritual discipline (*sgrub thabs dngos gzhi*) such as the [deity] union and host assembly etc. illustrated by that, they should be known from the explanatory tantras such as the *Discourse Appendix*.

Regarding Kambala's linking of the five manifest awakenings with the four lines beginning with "vowels and consonants" (**51.2c–3b**), it is suitable to apply it as well to the meditation manuals of the trio, i.e., Lūipa, Ghaṇṭapā, and Kāṇhapa, excepting just a few distinctions that precede [this passage]. Regarding its application to the created bodies of the mandala deities as well as explained in other commentaries, one should be able to understand this through my previous commentary.

"Sound . . . and so forth" also includes other syllables that illustrate the intermediate states. "Manifestation" is the descent onto the lunar disk in the simultaneous creation of the habitat and inhabitants, or the face of the [male] partner in the causal Vajradhara deity couple union. Existing in the heart and so forth, [the syllables] go into the [female] partner's lotus. "From" means that they are "taken thence."

The reality of having the employment of condensation means for as long as the two deities, the commitment hero and gnosis hero, are united into one. This is sufficient as applied in [the meditation manuals of] both Lūipa and Ghaṇṭapā. Regarding accepting this in the manner of Kāṇha as I previously explained, it is done up to the point employing the condensation into one of the thirty-seven deities and thirty-seven aids to awakening. Here is it also connected to the sealing by the clan lord in the consecration of the deity of one portion of the consecration. The reality of being satisfied with ambrosia includes internal worship and worship with sacrificial cakes and so forth. [The realities of] cessation, armor, and mantra worship are as previously [stated].

Regarding the method of indicating the perfection stage, the meaning of the fourteen realities are explained in the context of showing below the creation of Heruka along with his retinue. The above presentation of fourteen realities was shown as easily found in the oral instructions; however, it is not easily found when the root and explanatory [tantras] are not well applied, due to the fact that the explanatory tantras are the norm on the basis of which the root tantra's oral instructions are derived. However, their application is not lacking in the explanations by the gurus who know the oral instructions of the great saints, such as the trio Lūipa, Kāṇhapa, and Ghaṇṭapā.

3.3.3. 2.3.2. 3. The benefits of practice in the fourteen, and the fault of lacking faith

The third part has two sections: (1) the benefits of practice in the fourteen realities, and (2) the fault of lacking faith in this path.

3.3.3. 2.3.2. 3.1. The benefits of practice in the fourteen realities

The first part has two sections: (1) showing in general the outer benefits of this, and (2) showing in particular the benefit that arises at the time of death.

3.3.3. 2.3.2. 3.1.1. Showing in general the outer benefits of this

The excellent man who practices in the two stages with the previously explained fourteen realities, becomes one **whose nature is purified of all** previously accumulated **sins**, and **attains** in this life **the stage** of the gnosis of the **tathāgata** that is purified of all taints of the two obscurations. If one does not obtain that [state] in this manner due to not embarking upon this [path of] marvelous meditation, what will one become at that time? **In life after life (51.5) one is born into the sugata clan**, that is, in a happy destiny realm in a class of tantric practitioners in particular, and **one becomes a Dharma-practicing king** of that sort of clan.

What will become at that time if one who is very sinful meditates on the fourteen realities? Regarding "previous and so forth," it is translated as "previously accumulated" by Mal, which is good.[765] Hence, **one who is deficient with regard to**, i.e, has exhausted, **all of the** [good] **qualities** due to **however many sins previously accumulated** with one's body, speech and mind will **become the lord of all desires on earth** (51.6). How are they exhausted? An adept exhausts sin by the concentration of **meditating constantly on these** fourteen realities.

How is previously accumulated sin extinguished by meditating on Heruka with the distinctive features of his faces and arms? The text gives an example of this. **Just as if a pot filled with butter** and smeared with impurities **is placed in the midst of a fire** (51.7), **the ghee in** it **melts**, and the sticky impurity of the pot's **taint is destroyed. Likewise**, just as in case of what remains after the ghee, **sin is destroyed**, i.e., exhausted, **by means of** one meditation **on the name "Shrī Heruka"** (51.8), **through meditation** on the distinctive features of his faces and arms and emptiness. Having purified sin through **mere reflection**, i.e., contemplation of the meditative image of Heruka in one's mind, or through **reading, recitation, or writing** of the text of the root tantra, **one attains the** happy destiny realm and **pleasures of heaven or of a universal monarch** (51.9).

3.3.3. 2.3.2. 3.1.2. Showing in particular the benefit that arises at the time of death

If one has not attained power in this life due to distraction, there is benefit **at the time of death**. When **yogīs** and yoginīs of this path pass from this world to the world beyond, **the heroes and yoginīs and so forth**—including the **glorious** blood drinker, i.e., **Heruka**, and the lady Vārāhī—**conduct one to the aerial state with various offerings** of **flowers**, different sorts of incense, **various banners and flags**, and **varied sounds of instruments and** delightful **songs** (51.10–11).

Three commentaries, taking "the aerial state" to be clear light, explain that one is established in that state.[766] This is an explanation of the definitive

765. Tsong Khapa quotes here *sngon sogs*, which is apparently an alternate reading of the SM translation; the versions I consulted have the archaic reading *sngon stsogs*. The PM and SL translations read *sngon bsags*, which Tsong Khapa attributes to Mal.

766. Durjayachandra makes this claim; see RG 314b.6.

meaning [of this term]; death exists manifestly as clear light. In the *Twofold Commentary*, [Tathāgatarakṣhita] explains on the basis of a literal reading that "ultimately, the adept goes [there] having forsaken the previous sites and relied upon the sites of the noble ones in particular."[767] This refers to the aerial state of interpretable meaning. Durjayachandra quotes [the line 51.11d as] "carried to the place of the ḍākinīs";[768] this is the aerial state qua the ḍākinīs' place of residence.

Here the one who attains flight that is mainly described as being attained by those with human forms is not the adept who practices in accordance with the method of this path. However, a few people, for the mere power of flight and so forth via the magical force of mantra or [magical] substances and so forth, having abided in particular in the state of the realm of space of the ḍākas and ḍākinīs who are distinguished by forms of luminous mantric practice, [attain] the state of practicing the supreme mantras that is the aerial state. These practitioners are able to progress with human forms without abandoning their bodies, and to achieve flight.

If one does not succeed in this life, regarding succeeding in a later life, one may achieve flight in another life; there are many stages in flying in this manner. The system for achieving flight in this life can be achieved through the power of the path of the two stages, and there is also [the possibility of] being actually conducted there by several distinctive ḍākinīs and heroes. Likewise, one can practice in particular regions of the human world, and there are also many extraordinary sites for tantric practice for the many beings who uphold esoteric lore. Therefore, regarding what **the worldly thought of "death" (51.11c)** designates, the death of extraordinary yogīs is letting go of an auspicious state and entering into [another] auspicious [state]. This is greater [than the worldly thought], just as one does not say "death" when [someone] moves from one good house to another.

Regarding the statement that **the great heroes**—Shrī Saṁvara, Khaṇḍakapālin, etc.—**and the yoginīs**—Prachaṇḍā etc.—to whom are attributed good qualities **of this sort are difficult to attain on earth (51.12ab)**, this

767. The passage occurs as follows at UN 252a.3: *don dam pa na sngon gyi gnas yongs su btang ste shin tu khyad par du 'phags pa'i gnas rnams la brten nas rnal 'byor pa 'gro'o.*

768. Durjayachandra quotes this line as follows: *mkha' 'gro'i gnas su 'khyer bar 'gyur* (RG 314b.6). In the canonical translation, this line occurs as follows: *mkha' spyod gnas su 'khrid par byed* (Gray 2012, 410). The former is almost certainly a variant translation of the Sanskrit *nīyate khecarīpade.*

means that it is very difficult to attain [the state of] heroes and yoginīs who are like this who persevere in meditation. Thus, the deity, the great heroes, and the yoginīs are difficult to attain on earth. Since it is indicated that they are difficult to attain, it is understood that they are very difficult to obtain when one has the opportunity to practice on this sort of path. Hence, it shows that one should make an effort in learning, contemplating, and meditating on this path!

3.3.3. 2.3.2. 3.2. The fault of lacking faith in this path

Whoever knows Shrī Heruka's great tantra yet is not devoted to it (**51.12cd**) **will always have poverty**, i.e., be destitute with respect to all powers, **and the agony of dissatisfaction** (**51.13ab**) of the lower realms and so forth. What need is there to speak of those who act without knowledge or faith? On account of this, if one makes an effort to know this great tantra, knowing it one will be extremely devoted to it.

3.3.3. 2.3.2. 4. The method of comprehensive meditation on the fourteen realities

If the benefit of contemplating the meaning of the fourteen realities and the fault of not having faith are [both] very great, how does one undertake the method of contemplating their meaning? Relevant here is the [statement] below that "one should contemplate the meaning of the fourteen realities that are the means for achieving the supreme position of the great king Shrī Heruka." How should one meditate? One should visualize Shrī Heruka. and so forth endowed with **bracelets** and **anklets**, ornaments on both shoulders, **earrings, a sacred thread** (**51.13cd**), **a necklace** which is **a rosary** of wet heads, a diadem of dry **skulls**, and a girdle with **tinkling bells**.

Moreover, in visualizing the deities, through what method should they be generated? There is Lūipa's method of generating the habitat and the inhabitants from the intermixture of the moon and seed, i.e., perfecting at one time both the habitat and the inhabitants, through the transformation of both the clockwise and counterclockwise rotation of the two sets of sixteen **vowels, and** the clockwise and counterclockwise rotation of the two sets of forty **consonants.** This is at the center of the small variegated lotus, which is atop the double vajra in the center of **the great variegated lotus** on the top of **Mount** Sumeru (**51.14**) and the stacked-up elements which were explained in the context of chapter thirty-two [above].

If you take the habitat and inhabitants as earlier and later, respectively, the habitat is the previously generated divine palace atop Mount Sumeru, in the midst of which Heruka is generated from the five manifest awakenings, the vowels and consonants etc. It is necessary to apply [this method] to the many meditation manuals taught in the *Discourse Appendix*; it not applicable to Lūipa's and Kāṇha's [meditation manuals] only. However, it can be applied to [them] in a partial manner in some contexts.

The Heruka generated from the manifest awakenings **treads** with his feet **upon** both **Gaurī**, the goddess Umā, and **her lord**, Rudra. His first set of hands, which hold **a vajra** and **bell**, **embraces** Vārāhī's body. While there are explanations that **half of twenty-four**, or twelve, refers to either his twelve arms or the twelve mothers,[769] the explanation with respect to his arms is better, since it accords with the *Conduct Tantra*.[770]

Being endowed with arms in this manner, the other hand implements should be known from the clear realization [practice] stated in the explanatory tantra[771] and as established in accordance with the meditation manuals composed by Lūipa and Ghaṇṭapā. Since "embracing the body" also indicates the [female] partner, one should visualize the mandala consisting of the principal deity couple surrounded **with a host of heroes and yoginīs** (**51.15**). Lochen here translated "surrounded by a host of heroes and yoginīs.[772]

769. Tathāgatarakṣhita explains this as his twelve arms; see UN 252a.7. Bhavabhaṭṭa explains this in terms of the twelve mothers; see Pandey 2002, 592, 883.

770. The *Yoginīsaṁcāra Tantra* contains a parallel passage to this text at 17.23 in the Pandey edition, although its interpretation, too, is an open question. Interestingly, Tathāgatarakṣhita's commentary explains this text in terms of a set of twelve goddesses, the four essence yoginīs and the eight guardian goddesses. He comments "Next, **endowed with half of twenty-four** means that one visualizes the tetrad, Ḍākinī, etc., and the octet Kākāsyā, surrounded by the syllables *lāṁ*, *māṁ*, *pāṁ*, and *tāṁ* and the eight *ha* syllables. One should visualize them revolving around him, positioned with their arms and colors as previously described" (Pandey 1998, 154: *tadanu caturviṁśatisaṁyuktam iti lāṁ māṁ pāṁ tāṁ hākārāṣṭakaparāvṛtyā ḍākinyādicatuṣṭayaṁ kākāsyādyaṣṭakaṁ ca vibhāvya tena parivṛtaṁ pūrvapratipāditavarṇabhujasaṁsthānaṁ vibhāvayet*).

771. I presume that the *Discourse Appendix Tantra* is the reference here, as noted above.

772. Tsong Khapa reports that Lochen's translation of line 51.15d reads *dpa' bo rnal 'byor ma tshogs bskor*, a reading preserved in the SL translation. The PM and SM translation read

In the middle of the retinue of all twenty-four of the heroes, Khaṇḍakapālin, and so forth, and of the thirty-six yoginīs, Ḍākinī, and so forth, **is the one who has the yoga** (**51.16cd**) of the equipoise of the primary deity couple, **who has the nondual nature** of bliss and emptiness that creates **delight** in **all** of the deities, and **brings about emanation**, i.e., the generation of the wheel deities, **and recollection** (**51.17ab**) of them into oneself.

The adept who has thus obtained all of the consecrations at the beginning undertakes the protection wheel, yoga, and accumulations. [Such a one] generating and visualizing all of the deities, both the habitat and inhabitants, protecting the commitments, worshipping, and so forth is the import of the fourteen realities. Since the essential among them are shown here, this is meditation on the essentials of the meanings of the fourteen realities. The definitive meaning of the habitat, the stacked-up elements, and so forth and the definitive meaning of clear realization process, and thence the perfection of Heruka and so forth, were explained in detail in chapter one.

In particular, the attainment of integration by means of the concentration of the magic body is achieved via the entry of the magic body into clear light. If one wishes to know this fully, it should be known from the *Glorious Esoteric Communion [Tantra]*.

3.3.3. 2.3.2. 5. Showing the method for not forsaking any of the Buddha's scriptures

The various beings, i.e., disciples, who **have faith** in the various diverse arrangements and topics of the body of doctrinal teaching **are taught the various** and diverse **practices** (**51.17cd**) by the Buddha. **They are instructed through diverse means** that accord with their own capacities in **the discipline with various methods. Were one to thus have faith due to instruction in the** very **profound teaching** (**51.18**) of the Dharma, that Dharma [teaching] **should not be repudiated**; the profound **Dharma** that is expressed in scripture **should be contemplated**, regarded as **inconceivable** (**51.19ab**). Since it is difficult to generate even-minded devotion toward all, even if one cannot give rise to that sort of faith, it is said that if one can

---

dpa' bo rnal 'byor ma tshogs dang, which is closer to the Sanskrit, *vīrayoginīvṛndakaiḥ*. See Gray 2012, 235, 411, 481, 566.

remain composed and not disparage [anything], then there is no fault. The the *Ornament of the [Universal Vehicle] Sutras* [states]:[773]

> An evil mind's naturally deficient,
> Unfit even for unsuitable things,
> There's no need to mention doubtful teachings.
> Thus, equanimity's good; there's no fault.

And the *Jewel Rosary* also states:[774]

> The Tathāgata's intentional speech
> Is not easy to understand; therefore,
> He taught one vehicle, three vehicles.
> Protect oneself with equanimity.
> There is no sin with equanimity.
> With hate there's sin; there will be no virtue.

How one should contemplate the inconceivable? **With regard to this** great secret, one who **does not have the scope** of an alienated individual should think, **"I do not know the reality (51.19cd)** of things nor the means whereby [this is known]; this **is known by the completely awakened** buddhas **and their offspring** who have attained the **great spirit** stage." The *Bodhisattva Stages* also states:[775]

773. This quote is the final verse in chapter 2 of Asaṅga/Maitreyanātha's *Ornament of the Universal Vehicle Sutras*; it occurs as follows: *yid kyi nyes pa rang bzhin gdug pa ste / mi rigs pa yi gzugs la'ang mi rigs na / the tshom za ba'i chos la smos ci dgos / de phyir btang snyoms gzhag legs nyes pa med* (Tōh. 4020, D *sems tsam* vol. phi, 3a.2; cf. Jamspal et al. 2004, 15).

774. This passage occurs as follows in Nāgārjuna's *Jewel Rosary, a Letter to the King* (*Rājaparikathāratnamālā*): *de bzhin gshegs dgongs gsungs pa rnams / shes par bla min de yi phyir / theg gcig theg pa gsum gsungs pas / btang snyoms kyis ni bdag bsrung bya / btang snyoms kyis ni sdig mi 'gyur / sdang bas sdig 'gyur dger mi 'gyur* (Tōh. 4158, *spring yig* vol. ge, 121b.2–3).

775. This passage is from chapter 10 of Asaṅga's *Bodhisattva Stages* and occurs as follows in Dutt's edition: *bhavati khalu bodhisattvasya gambhīrāṇi paramagambhīrāṇi sthānāni śrutvā cetaso 'nadhimokṣaḥ / tatra śraddhenāśaṭhena bodhisattvenedaṁ pratisaṁśikṣitavyam / na me pratirūpaṁ syād andhasyācakṣuṣmatas tathāgatacakṣuṣaivānuvyavaharatas tathāgatasandhāya bhāṣitaṁ pratikṣeptum* (1966, 119). The Tibetan translation occurs as follows: *byang chub sems dpa' zab cing mchog tu zab pa'i gnas dag thos nas / sems mos par gyur na / de la byang chub sems dpas dad pa dang g.yo med pas 'di ltar*

> Having heard these profound and supremely profound subjects, a bodhisattva may not have a devotional attitude. Regarding this, a faithful and honest bodhisattva should train her or himself as follows: "It is not right that I, being blind and eyeless, operating only in accordance with the Tathāgata's eye, should reject the Tathāgata's esoteric statements."

Regarding whether or not [a scripture] was "intentional speech" [of the tathāgata], there is a supreme strategy for not accepting the karmic obscuration of abandoning the Dharma. However, it is said that it is difficult to realize as the karmic obscuration of abandoning the Dharma is extremely subtle. Since [this problem] is also commonplace at the present time, one should endeavor to recognize well [the fault of] abandoning the Dharma and to not be sullied by it.

Regarding the reason, they are inconceivable, are **buddhas produced or not** (51.20)? Since they exist as does **the all-pervasive reality, lacking loss, and gain,** they are **inconceivable**. If you take "reality" (*chos nyid, dharmatā*) here in terms of the actual state of existence, it does not apply to the reason of it being unacceptable to abandon the profound teachings on the nature of things. Moreover, the reality that exists devoid of production and cessation is not relevant to the reason for not abandoning the teaching of the Dharma itself (*chos nyid*). Therefore, it should be taken as a reason for abandoning neither the teaching [itself] nor things as they are [to which the former pertains].

Moreover, regarding statements in scripture that "this arises from that," "this does not arise from that," "this is or is not thus,"[776] I have explained that they simply exist in the manner of the reality of things, lacking "gain" or increase and "loss" or annihilation. Since all of them are not in one's experiential scope, they are "inconceivable." **Contemplating thus**, that this "is known by the Buddha, but not known by me," that which was taught for the sake of **worldly** disciples **should not be faulted** (51.21). **The way**

---

bdag ni long bar gyur te / mig med la de bzhin gshegs pa'i spyan gyis rjes su spyod par zad pas / de bzhin gshegs pas dgongs te gsungs pa spangs pa ni bdag gi cha ma yin no zhes yang dag par bslab par bya'o (Tōh. 4037, *sems tsam* vol. wi, 94a.2–3).

776. Tsong Khapa here refers to various scriptural accounts of dependent arising, *pratītyasamutpāda*.

or disposition **of that** world of the disciples is **inconceivable**, because the performance **of the buddhas' play** or emanations that accord with it is also **inconceivable**.

What are the teachings that are stated in accordance with the disciples' dispositions? From the perspective of the **sutra** canon and tantra canon, the sutra canon includes the *Extensive Play* (*Lalitavistara*) and so forth. The outer collection is the triple basket (*tripiṭaka*). The tantra collection includes **action** tantras such as the *Accomplished Solitary Hero*,[777] and it is stated that **practice** tantras include the *Taming of the Ghosts*,[778] in other words, the *Complete Awakening of Vairochana*,[779] and so forth. **Yoga** tantras include the *Compendium of Reality*[780] and so forth. The **final secret** tantras are the unexcelled yoga tantras. Regarding the differentiation via these **divisions**, they were taught so as to **delight** on their own path **each and every sentient being**, i.e., disciple, who are [differently] **disposed through faith** (**51.22**) in their path. Hence, they are not to be disparaged.

A certain Tibetan has [claimed] that, in addition to the three classes of tantra as previously stated,[781] that "secret" indicates unexcelled yoga tantras, "final" indicates unexcelled yoginī tantras, and "division" indicates the even further unexcelled Chakrasaṁvara, thus positing six classes of tantras, which is the "system of Kambala."[782] However, this is utterly unreasonable, since the meaning of "division" refers to divisions into the above [stated classes]. That explanation does not actually engage with the syntactic meaning. This is because the import here is the differentiation into four [classes of tantra], since it is shown that the "final secret" refers to the unexcelled ultimate [class] of secret mantra, because there is no explanation of this sort in any of the commentaries, and because there is also no explanation of this sort in Kambala's text.[783]

777. That is, the *Siddhaikavīra-mahātantrarājā*, Tōh. 544.

778. Tsong Khapa here is following Tathāgatarakṣhita, who gives one example of each scriptural class, but stops for some reason after the *caryātantra* class. See UN 252b.3. The tantra to which Tathāgatarakṣhita refers is the *Bhūtaḍāmara-mahātantrarājā*, Tōh. 747.

779. That is, the *Mahāvairocanābhisaṁbodhi Tantra*, Tōh. 494.

780. That is, the *Sarvatathāgatatattvasaṁgraha-nāma-mahāyāna-sūtra*, Tōh. 479.

781. That is, the action, practice, and yoga classes.

782. Sachen does indeed analyze the text in this fashion. See PG 380.2 and my discussion of this at Gray 2007, 382, n. 28.

783. Tsong Khapa is correct that Sachen seems to be alone in advancing this interpretation

Bhavabhaṭṭa, quoting "delight in each and every," explains that all tantras were taught in their entirety, and this is for the purpose of "praise by the compiler and so forth."[784] Regarding this, since there many different [versions of] the text, it is not suitable if it is similar to the Tibetan text unless there is an alternate text for the above verse.[785] We have heard, reflected, and meditated on the meaning summarized by the first chapter, stated at length in [next] forty-nine [chapters], and the stages of the path of creation and perfection brought together by the fifty-first [chapter]. The teachings of the *Shrī Saṁvara* are expanded upon in the tantras of this and other [traditions].

3.3.3. 2.3.3. Showing the chapter count

This concludes the fifty-first chapter of the great king of yoginī tantras, which, if you condense the name, is **called the *Shrī-Chakrasaṁvara*, the appendix** of the extensive root tantra that is **primordially established**, meaning it establishes or is the basis for the rapid bestowal of the awakened state since beginning-less time. Regarding what is achieved **through the recitation of the great hero Shrī Heruka**, while one quickly attains awakening through reciting the tantra, one is also **unsurpassed by all others**, meaning it is not surpassed by other vehicles and the lower classes of tantra. It outshines all of them. It is **the highest** or best of all the yoginī tantras, **included within** or derived from **the one-hundred-thousand**-stanza **king of tantras** extensive root tantra, **the *Discourse of Shrī Heruka*.** This is the explanation of the fifty-first chapter in the *Illumination of the Hidden Meaning, A Detailed Exegesis of the Concise Saṁvara Tantra Called "The Chakrasaṁvara."*

---

of 51.23. Kambala's commentary contains no explanation of this verse whatsoever. However, Sachen does not attribute this idea to Kambala; perhaps this claim was made by a later Sakya scholar.

784. Tsong Khapa seems to be referring to Bhavabhaṭṭa's comments at Pandey 2002, 893, CV 245a.2–3. However, I do not know the source of the quote *sdud pa po la sogs pa thams cad kyis mngon par bstod do*, which does not seem to occur in Bhavabhaṭṭa's commentary or any of the other canonical commentaries.

785. I presume that Tsong Khapa is referring to 51.22; the line he attributes to Bhavabhaṭṭa, *de dang de la dga' ba yin*, is the last line of this verse; it occurs in the canonical PM translation as *de dang de la dga' ba bzhin* (Gray 2007, 412).

Colophon

Chapter Outline

3.3.4. The meaning of the conclusion
3.3.4. 1. How the text concluded
3.3.4. 2. How [the text] was translated in Tibet

3.3.4. The meaning of the conclusion

The fourth part, the meaning of the conclusion, has two sections: (1) how the text concluded, and (2) how [the text] was translated in Tibet.

3.3.4. 1. How the text concluded

This completes the fifty-first chapter of the highest and primordially established root tantra that is abbreviated, that is unsurpassed and is achieved by reciting the great hero Shrī Heruka, which is the king or principal of all treatises, that astounds the minds of all scholars, and is marvelous for the achievement of power in this very life. It is the ritual text (*rtog pa*, *kalpa*) for achieving the supreme great seal included within the one hundred thousand *Shrī Heruka*.[786]

3.3.4. 2. How [the text] was translated in Tibet

[The text] **was translated**,[787] i.e., originally translated, from Sanskrit to

786. Tsong Khapa here summarizes the text's colophon which he analyzed in more detail in section 3.3.3. 2.3.3 above.

787. Tsong Khapa in this section comments upon the colophon to the SM translation,

Tibetan **by the Indian scholar Padmākaravarma**, i.e., he whose armor produces lotuses,[788] **and the monk Rinchen Zangpo, the chief editor and translator** (*lo tsā ba*), the verbal meaning of which is *loka*, "world" and *chandoha*, "zest," hence "zest for the world" (*'jig rten 'dun pa*). Literally speaking, they **proofread** it and **finalized** it through explanation and listening.

Later, **the Indian scholar Sūryagupta**[789] **and the Tibetan translator Gö Lotsawa Shönu Pal** (*'gos lo tswa ba gzhon nu dpal*) **revised** Lochen's translation **according to Kambala's commentary. Subsequently the Indian scholar Sumatikīrti and the Tibetan** translator and **great scholar Marpa Chökyi Wangchuk** (*mar pa chos kyi dbang phyug*), famed as Marpa Dopa, **proofread** Gö's translation, and finalized it through explanation and listening.

The king of tantras, the *Chakrasaṁvara*, this harbor for millions of lords of yoga,
Blazing brightly with the glory of millions of virtues in the glorious tantric canon,
Producing joy and wonder with its vast display of the two powers' joy,
Transforming the world with the two stages, at the peak of pure empowerment and the commitments.
The subtle and difficult points in this
Are bound by the code of the yoginīs,
But are clear with the hero's own comments,
And many explanatory tantras.
They're then revealed in the saints' instructions
By the saints who have reached the highest state,
And the many Indian scholars too
Realized according to this method.

---

which occurs at 567 in my 2012 edition. The words in bold are words actually found in this colophon.

788. Tsong Khapa transliterates Padmākaravarma's name, as *padma ka ra war ma*, following the SM edition, and he translates it accordingly (and accurately) as *padma byed pa'i go cha*. However, the SM edition omits the long *a* vowel; a better translation of *padmākaravarma* would be "he whose armor is a multitude of lotuses."

789. Tsong Khapa corrects the translation of his name in the SM edition, *sbas pa'i nyi ma*, to *nyi ma sbas pa*.

The fulfiller known as Nārotapā,
Famed as the constellations' master light,
Before whom are scholars strewn like jasmine blooms,
Whose stainless system derives from the best,
Is the eye of Snowy Land's disciples.
In the lineage of the omniscient ones
In this era of conflict and of strife,
This commentary brings together all
Indian and Tibetan good teachings,
Relying on his way of explaining
With dual aptitude in both languages.
May it be a treasure of the two feats,
The wondrous storehouse of the serpent kings.
Relying upon the oral instructions
Of Lūipa, Ghaṇṭapā, and Kāṇha,
When one elucidates the root tantra
Via the explanatory tantras,
Abiding in stainless empowerment
And in the commitments, the root tantra
Manifests as the foremost instruction.
Knowing how to reveal in the tantra
The ways to reach the vajradhara stage
By progressing well with the two stages
And the achievement of infinite feats,
May scholars who see the mantric method
Know what a "tantric practitioner" is.
Long familiar with Saṁvara literature,
And with scriptural commentaries in general,
Even if they're well applied, I confess
Earnestly that it is replete with faults
Due to my ordinary intellect.
May myself and all others, through wholesome
Virtues attained with tremendous effort,
Enter this fine Chakrasaṁvara path
And quickly attain Heruka's station.

The glory that is the learned monk Tsong Khapa Lozang Drak-ba, once he was well familiar with the *Shrī Saṁvara Root Tantra*, all of the explanatory and corresponding portion tantras, and the Saṁvara literature in general, the texts of Lūipa, Ghaṇṭapā, and Kāṇha in particular, and the many Saṁvara commentaries, conceived this *Illumination of the Hidden Meaning, A Detailed Exegesis of the Concise Saṁvara Tantra Called "The Chakrasaṁvara"* as a mnemonic note in order to heal the deterioration of the theory and practice of the Saṁvara tradition. Rinchen Pal, an adept in the four teachings,[790] was the copyist at work in Ganden Namgyal-ling at the highland mountain.

Oṁ svasti (Om, may it be good!)
Augment this slowly moving stream
That endlessly bestows Dharma,

The grove that gathers the Victor's
Teachings, these being welfare's source,
In the great school of the Dharma
That's naturally blessed for practice,

For the good end of liberation
Of the vast array of all beings.

Sarvamaṅgalaṁ (Blessings for all)

790. That is, *bka' bzhi pa*, one who has mastered Madhyamaka, Prajñāpāramitī, Vinaya, and Abhidharma.

Appendixes, Glossaries, Bibliographies, and Indexes

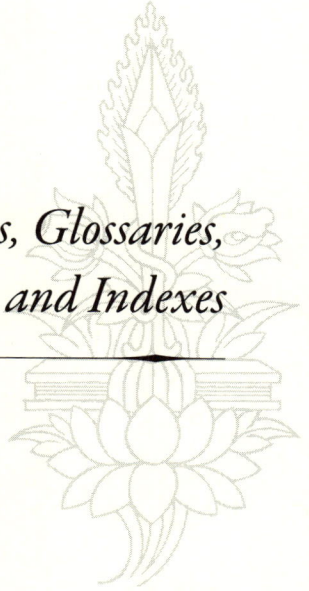

Appendix I
Tsong Khapa's General Outline (sa bcad) of the Entire Illumination of the Hidden Meaning (Chs. 1–51)

[VOLUME ONE]	
[INTRODUCTION]	
1.	The general arrangement of all the teachings
2.	The particular arrangement of the great bliss tantras
2.1.	Identifying the root tantra, explanatory tantras, and intertextual tantras
2.1.1.	Identifying the noncontroversial tantras
2.1.2.	Discussing the controversial explanatory tantras
2.2.	Showing the time and place of the original proclamation of the *Chakrasaṁvara Tantra*
2.3.	The way in which the explanatory tantras explain the root tantra
2.3.1.	Identifying the main points by which the explanatory tantras explain the root tantra
2.3.2.	How the uncommon explanatory tantras explain
2.3.2. 1.	How the *Discourse Appendix* and *Vajraḍāka* explain
2.3.2. 1.1.	How the *Discourse Appendix* explains
2.3.2. 1.1.1.	How the creation stage is explained
2.3.2. 1.1.1. 1.	How the creation stage is not clear in the root tantra
2.3.2. 1.1.1. 2.	How this explanatory tantra explains clearly
2.3.2. 1.1.2.	How the perfection stage is explained
2.3.2. 1.2.	How the *Vajraḍāka* explains
2.3.2. 2.	How the *Origin of Saṁvara* and the *[Yoginī]saṁcāra* explain

2.3.2. 2.1.	How the *Origin of Saṁvara* explains
2.3.2. 2.2.	How the *[Yoginī]saṁcāra* explains
2.3.3.	How the common explanatory tantras explain
3.	Introduction to the way in which the concise root tantra is explained
3.1.	The explanation based on the instructions of the mahāsiddhas
3.2.	Showing the method of explanation based upon them [the instructions of the mahāsiddhas]
3.2.1.	Significance of the count of fifty-one chapters
3.2.2.	Applying the threefold explanation to the fifty-one chapters
3.2.3.	Showing the relevance of the summary of each chapter
3.2.3. 1.	Showing the summary of each [chapter]
3.2.3. 1.1.	Summary of bestowing consecration and showing reality therein
3.2.3. 1.2.	The summary of the selection of mantras and achieving the powers
3.2.3. 1.3.	The summary of attaining both powers through the kindness of the messengers
3.2.3. 1.4.	The summary of impact-heightening conduct and the vow as a friend on the path
3.2.3. 1.5.	The summary of the four seals such as the great seal
3.2.3. 1.6.	The summary on understanding the signs of the rapid attainment of the powers
3.2.3. 2.	The arrangement in one of the stages of the path
3.2.3. 3.	The method of the lineage from Nāropā

[Chapter 1]	
3.3.	The actual method of explaining the root tantra
3.3.1.	The meaning of the name
3.3.1. 1.	The translation of the name
3.3.1. 2.	The explanation of the name
3.3.2.	The salutation of the translators
3.3.3.	The meaning of the text
3.3.3. 1.	The reason "Thus have I heard" is not stated in the beginning
3.3.3. 2.	The actual explanation of the text's meaning
3.3.3. 2.1.	The first chapter's introduction to the significance of the entire tantra
3.3.3. 2.1.1.	The actual text
3.3.3. 2.1.1. 1.	The promise to explain the secret
3.3.3. 2.1.1. 2.	The exhortation to listen to the secret
3.3.3. 2.1.1. 2.1.	The secret that should be heard
3.3.3. 2.1.1. 2.1.1.	Showing in brief the presentation of the secret
3.3.3. 2.1.1. 2.1.1. 1.	Explaining the interpretable meaning
3.3.3. 2.1.1. 2.1.1. 2.	Explaining the definitive meaning
3.3.3. 2.1.1. 2.1.2.	Explaining the presentation somewhat more extensively
3.3.3. 2.1.1. 2.1.2. 1.	The actual meaning

3.3.3. 2.1.1. 2.1.2. 1.1.	Explaining the two lines [that begin with] "the secret . . . supreme" [1.2cd]
3.3.3. 2.1.1. 2.1.2. 1.1.1.	Explaining in terms of the interpretable meaning
3.3.3. 2.1.1. 2.1.2. 1.1.1. 1.	Explaining as applicable to the narrative preface "Thus have I heard . . ."
3.3.3. 2.1.1. 2.1.2. 1.1.1. 1.1.	Stating the exact words of the narrative preface
3.3.3. 2.1.1. 2.1.2. 1.1.1. 1.2.	Explaining their meaning
3.3.3. 2.1.1. 2.1.2. 1.1.1. 2.	The explanation applicable to the creation stage
3.3.3. 2.1.1. 2.1.2. 1.1.2.	Explaining in terms of the definitive meaning
3.3.3. 2.1.1. 2.1.2. 1.1.2. 1.	The definitive meaning as applied to the narrative preface
3.3.3. 2.1.1. 2.1.2. 1.1.2. 2.	The definitive meaning as applied to the creation stage
3.3.3. 2.1.1. 2.1.2. 1.1.2. 3.	Explaining the sixteen syllables in reference to alchemy
3.3.3. 2.1.1. 2.1.2. 1.2.	Explaining the four lines [that begin with] "made of all ḍākinīs" [1.3]
3.3.3. 2.1.1. 2.1.2. 1.2.1.	The explanation applied to the goal
3.3.3. 2.1.1. 2.1.2. 1.2.2.	The explanation applied to the perfection stage of the path
3.3.3. 2.1.1. 2.1.2. 1.3.	Explaining the two lines that begin with *arising* [1.4ab]
3.3.3. 2.1.1. 2.1.2. 1.3.1.	Explaining the interpretable meaning
3.3.3. 2.1.1. 2.1.2. 1.3.2.	Explaining the definitive meaning
3.3.3. 2.1.1. 2.1.2. 2.	The difficult to obtain
3.3.3. 2.1.1. 2.1.2. 3.	Showing an example of the union of bliss and emptiness
3.3.3. 2.1.1. 2.2.	The actual exhortation to listen
3.3.3. 2.1.1. 3.	The method for making progress in the secret of the path

3.3.3. 2.1.1. 3.1.	Worship of the clanswoman
3.3.3. 2.1.1. 3.1.1.	General worship of the clanswoman
3.3.3. 2.1.1. 3.1.2.	The attainment of power depending upon the clanswoman together with worship
3.3.3. 2.1.1. 3.1.3.	The benefits of worshipping the clanswoman
3.3.3. 2.1.1. 3.2.	Protecting the commitments
3.3.3. 2.1.1. 3.2.1.	Maintaining the commitments to be protected
3.3.3. 2.1.1. 3.2.2.	Protecting the food commitments
3.3.3. 2.1.1. 3.3.	Meditation on the four seals
3.3.3. 2.1.1. 4.	Showing the place for practicing the secret
3.3.3. 2.1.2.	Showing the name of the chapter
[CHAPTER 2]	
3.3.3. 2.2.	The detailed exegesis of the meaning by the remaining forty-nine [chapters]
3.3.3. 2.2.1.	Becoming a suitable vessel for meditating on the two stages, and so forth
3.3.3. 2.2.1. 1.	Drawing the mandala, and its worship upon completion
3.3.3. 2.2.1. 1.1.	The characteristics of the master
3.3.3. 2.2.1. 1.2.	How he performs the rite
3.3.3. 2.2.1. 1.2.1.	The rites of the ground
3.3.3. 2.2.1. 1.2.1. 1.	Purifying the ground
3.3.3. 2.2.1. 1.2.1. 2.	Occupying the ground

3.3.3. 2.2.1. 1.2.2.	The rite of drawing and completing the mandala
3.3.3. 2.2.1. 1.2.2. 1.	Drawing the mandala
3.3.3. 2.2.1. 1.2.2. 1.1.	Drawing with marking string
3.3.3. 2.2.1. 1.2.2. 1.2.	Drawing with color
3.3.3. 2.2.1. 1.2.2. 2.	Completing the mandala
3.3.3. 2.2.1. 1.2.3.	Making and placing the vases
3.3.3. 2.2.1. 1.2.4.	The rite of mandala worship
3.3.3. 2.2.1. 1.2.4. 1.	Ornamenting the mandala
3.3.3. 2.2.1. 1.2.4. 2.	Worshipping the mandala
3.3.3. 2.2.1. 1.3.	Showing the name of the chapter
[CHAPTER 3]	
3.3.3. 2.2.1. 2.	Bestowing consecration in the completed mandala
3.3.3. 2.2.1. 2.1.	Pleasing the guru and the deities in the beginning
3.3.3. 2.2.1. 2.2.	Entering the mandala and bestowing consecration
3.3.3. 2.2.1. 2.2.1.	Entering the mandala
3.3.3. 2.2.1. 2.2.2.	Bestowing consecration upon the entrant
3.3.3. 2.2.1. 2.2.2. 1.	The actual consecration bestowal
3.3.3. 2.2.1. 2.2.2. 1.1.	Bestowing the vase consecration
3.3.3. 2.2.1. 2.2.2. 1.2.	Bestowing the higher consecrations

3.3.3. 2.2.1. 2.2.2. 2.	The salutation at the end of that
3.3.3. 2.2.1. 2.3.	Offering the fee and its benefit
3.3.3. 2.2.1. 2.3.1.	Offering the fee
3.3.3. 2.2.1. 2.3.2.	The benefit of offering
3.3.3. 2.2.1. 2.4.	Showing the definite need for consecration
3.3.3. 2.2.1. 2.5.	Showing the significance of consecration
3.3.3. 2.2.1. 2.5.1	Showing the supremacy of this consecration
3.3.3. 2.2.1. 2.5.2.	Addendum on the difficulty of getting this consecration
3.3.3. 2.2.1. 2.6.	Showing the name of the chapter
[CHAPTER 4]	
3.3.3. 2.2.2.	The detailed exegesis of the secret for suitable vessels
3.3.3. 2.2.2. 1.	The detailed exegesis of the secret of the path
3.3.3. 2.2.2. 1.1.	The four realities of the creation stage
3.3.3. 2.2.2. 1.2.	The four realities of the perfection stage
3.3.3. 2.2.2. 1.3.	Showing the name of the chapter
[CHAPTER 5]	
3.3.3. 2.2.2. 2.	The detailed exegesis of attainment by means of mantra and meditation
3.3.3. 2.2.2. 2.1.	Selecting the mantra to be repeated
3.3.3. 2.2.2. 2.1.1.	Selecting the root mantra's consonants

3.3.3. 2.2.2. 2.1.1. 1.	The actual text
3.3.3. 2.2.2. 2.1.1. 1.1.	Preparing the basis for mantra selection
3.3.3. 2.2.2. 2.1.1. 1.1.1.	The interpretable explanation
3.3.3. 2.2.2. 2.1.1. 1.1.2.	The definitive explanation
3.3.3. 2.2.2. 2.1.1. 1.2.	Selecting the mantra from that [basis]
3.3.3. 2.2.2. 2.1.1. 1.2.1.	Selecting the eight-line root mantra
3.3.3. 2.2.2. 2.1.1. 1.2.1. 1.	Selecting the first four lines
3.3.3. 2.2.2. 2.1.1. 1.2.1. 2.	Selecting the latter four [lines]
3.3.3. 2.2.2. 2.1.1. 1.2.2.	Selecting the *kara kara* root mantra
3.3.3. 2.2.2. 2.1.1. 1.2.2. 1.	Selecting the mantra's first set of eight [lines]
3.3.3. 2.2.2. 2.1.1.1.2.2. 2.	Selecting the mantra's middle set of eight
3.3.3. 2.2.2. 2.1.1. 1.2.2. 3.	Selecting the mantra's final set of eight [lines]
3.3.3. 2.2.2. 2.1.1. 1.3.	Showing the greatness of the selected mantra
3.3.3. 2.2.2. 2.1.1. 2.	Showing the name of the chapter
[Chapter 6]	
3.3.3. 2.2.2. 2.1.2. 1.	The actual text
3.3.3. 2.2.2. 2.1.2. 1.1.	The enumeration of the two mantras' syllables together with the selection of the armor mantra
3.3.3. 2.2.2. 2.1.2. 1.2.	Showing the places on which the armor [mantras] are set down
3.3.3. 2.2.2. 2.1.2.	Selecting the hero's armor mantra

3.3.3. 2.2.2. 2.1.2. 2.	The name of the chapter
[Chapter 7]	
3.3.3. 2.2.2. 2.1.3.	Selecting the root mantra's vowels
3.3.3. 2.2.2. 2.1.3. 1.	The actual selection of the auxiliary vowels
3.3.3. 2.2.2. 2.1.3. 1.1.	Selecting the vowels of the eight-line [mantra]
3.3.3. 2.2.2. 2.1.3. 1.1.1.	Selecting the vowels of the first four lines
3.3.3. 2.2.2. 2.1.3. 1.1.2.	Selecting the vowels of the last four [lines]
3.3.3. 2.2.2. 2.1.3. 1.2.	Selecting the vowels of the *kara* etc. [mantra]
3.3.3. 2.2.2. 2.1.3. 1.2.1.	Selecting the vowels of the first set of eight [lines]
3.3.3. 2.2.2. 2.1.3. 1.2.2.	Selecting the vowels of the middle set of eight [lines]
3.3.3. 2.2.2. 2.1.3. 1.2.3.	Selecting the vowels of the final set of eight [lines]
3.3.3. 2.2.2. 2.1.3. 2.	The greatness of the selected mantra
3.3.3. 2.2.2. 2.1.3. 3.	Selecting the root mantra's first and last syllables
3.3.3. 2.2.2. 2.1.3. 4.	Showing the name of the chapter
[Chapter 8]	
3.3.3. 2.2.2. 2.1.4.	Selecting the reversed order essence mantra and the heroine's armor mantra
3.3.3. 2.2.2. 2.1.4. 1.	The essence mantra
3.3.3. 2.2.2. 2.1.4. 2.	The armor mantras together with the four treasures

3.3.3. 2.2.2. 2.1.4. 3.	The method of performing the mantra authorization
3.3.3. 2.2.2. 2.1.4. 4.	The name of the chapter
[CHAPTER 9]	
3.3.3. 2.2.2. 2.2.	The way of achieving the powers through mantra repetition
3.3.3. 2.2.2. 2.2.1.	Ritual success with the root mantra
3.3.3. 2.2.2. 2.2.1. 1	The promise to explain, and its greatness
3.3.3. 2.2.2. 2.2.1. 2	Detailed exegesis of the actual host of ritual actions
3.3.3. 2.2.2. 2.2.1. 2.1.	The general principles of the methods for performing the ritual actions
3.3.3. 2.2.2. 2.2.1. 2.2.	Showing each of the methods for performing ritual actions
3.3.3. 2.2.2. 2.2.1. 2.2.1.	The rites that largely destroy and incidentally benefit
3.3.3. 2.2.2. 2.2.1. 2.2.2.	The host of destructive rites
3.3.3. 2.2.2. 2.2.1. 2.2.3.	Showing the way to perform rites that incidentally benefit
3.3.3. 2.2.2. 2.2.1. 2.2.4.	The destructive rites of killing and restoring life
3.3.3. 2.2.2. 2.2.1. 2.2.5.	Showing other beneficial rites
3.3.3. 2.2.2. 2.2.1. 3.	Showing the necessity of understanding the reality of mantra for those [rites]
3.3.3. 2.2.2. 2.2.1. 4.	Showing the name of the chapter
[CHAPTER 10]	
3.3.3. 2.2.2. 2.2.2.	Ritual success with the essence [mantra]
3.3.3. 2.2.2. 2.2.2. 1.	Chapter ten
3.3.3. 2.2.2. 2.2.2. 1.1.	Accomplishing the triple body

3.3.3. 2.2.2. 2.2.2. 1.1.1.	The promise to explain
3.3.3. 2.2.2. 2.2.2. 1.1.2.	Showing the adept's accomplishment of the triple body
3.3.3. 2.2.2. 2.2.2. 1.1.2. 1.	The general meaning
3.3.3. 2.2.2. 2.2.2. 1.1.2. 2.	The auxiliary meaning
3.3.3. 2.2.2. 2.2.2. 1.2.	The collection of rites of the essence [mantra]
3.3.3. 2.2.2. 2.2.2. 1.2.1.	The promise to explain
3.3.3. 2.2.2. 2.2.2. 1.2.2.	The actual collection of rites
3.3.3. 2.2.2. 2.2.2. 1.3.	Showing the name of the chapter
[Chapter 11]	
3.3.3. 2.2.2. 2.2.2. 2.	Chapter eleven
3.3.3. 2.2.2. 2.2.2. 2.1.	The promise to explain
3.3.3. 2.2.2. 2.2.2. 2.2.	The method of examining the one born seven times
3.3.3. 2.2.2. 2.2.2. 2.3.	Ritual success relying upon the concretion of the one born seven times
3.3.3. 2.2.2. 2.2.2. 2.4.	Showing the name of the chapter
[Chapter 12]	
3.3.3. 2.2.2. 2.2.3.	Ritual success with the quintessence [mantra]
3.3.3. 2.2.2. 2.2.3. 1.	The promise to explain
3.3.3. 2.2.2. 2.2.3. 2.	The actual ritual applications
3.3.3. 2.2.2. 2.2.3. 2.1.	Showing the four ritual applications of earthquakes etc.
3.3.3. 2.2.2. 2.2.3. 2.2.	The ritual applications depending on the eye

3.3.3. 2.2.2. 2.2.3. 2.3.	The ritual application of the pill that achieves flight
3.3.3. 2.2.2. 2.2.3. 2.4.	The six rites of drawing blood etc., together with their remedies
3.3.3. 2.2.2. 2.2.3. 2.5.	The seven rites of invisibility etc., together with their remedies
3.3.3. 2.2.2. 2.2.3. 2.6.	The five rites of reversing the flow of a river etc., together with their remedies
3.3.3. 2.2.2. 2.2.3. 3.	Showing the name of the chapter
[Chapter 13]	
3.3.3. 2.2.2. 2.2.4.	Ritual success with the armor mantras
3.3.3. 2.2.2. 2.2.4. 1.	The promise to explain
3.3.3. 2.2.2. 2.2.4. 2.	The actual collection of rites
3.3.3. 2.2.2. 2.2.4. 2.1.	The eight rites of dispelling fear etc., together with subsequent release
3.3.3. 2.2.2. 2.2.4. 2.2.	The collection of rites of subjugating and relying on cotton clothing
3.3.3. 2.2.2. 2.2.4. 2.3.	The ordinary methods of accomplishing ritual actions
3.3.3. 2.2.2. 2.2.4. 2.4.	The two rites of turning into a tree etc., together with the subsequent release
3.3.3. 2.2.2. 2.2.4. 3.	The name of the chapter
[Chapter 14]	
3.3.3. 2.2.2. 2.2.5.	Showing other rites accomplished with the essence
3.3.3. 2.2.2. 2.2.5. 1.	The promise to explain
3.3.3. 2.2.2. 2.2.5. 2.	The actual ritual applications
3.3.3. 2.2.2. 2.2.5. 2.1.	The literal explanation
3.3.3. 2.2.2. 2.2.5. 2.2.	The symbolic explanation

3.3.3. 2.2.2. 2.2.5. 3.	The benefits of attainment
3.3.3. 2.2.2. 2.2.5. 4.	The method of attainment
3.3.3. 2.2.2. 2.2.5. 5.	Praise for that
3.3.3. 2.2.2. 2.2.5. 6.	The name of the chapter
[CHAPTER 15]	
3.3.3. 2.2.2. 3.	The detailed exegesis of worship of the clanswoman
3.3.3. 2.2.2. 3.1.	The syllabic speech signs for generally recognizing the ḍākinīs
3.3.3. 2.2.2. 3.1.1.	The promise to explain
3.3.3. 2.2.2. 3.1.2.	The actual display of the signs
3.3.3. 2.2.2. 3.1.3.	The synopsis and showing the method of imparting [the signs]
3.3.3. 2.2.2. 3.1.4.	Showing the name of the chapter
[CHAPTER 16]	
3.3.3. 2.2.2. 3.2.	The way to recognize the particular ḍākinī clans
3.3.3. 2.2.2. 3.2.1.	Showing each of the clans of the six ḍākinīs
3.3.3. 2.2.2. 3.2.1. 1.	The promise to explain
3.3.3. 2.2.2. 3.2.1. 2.	The actual disclosure of that to be explained
3.3.3. 2.2.2. 3.2.1. 2.1.	The division into seven clans
3.3.3. 2.2.2. 3.2.1. 2.2.	The abridgement into six clans
3.3.3. 2.2.2. 3.2.1. 3.	Showing the name of the chapter

[Chapter 17]	
3.3.3. 2.2.2. 3.2.2.	Enumeration of the names of the seven ḍākinīs
3.3.3. 2.2.2. 3.2.2. 1.	The promise to explain
3.3.3. 2.2.2. 3.2.2. 2.	Showing the characteristics of the seven ḍākinīs
3.3.3. 2.2.2. 3.2.2. 3.	Showing their symbolic insignia
3.3.3. 2.2.2. 3.2.2. 4.	Showing the name of the chapter
[Chapter 18]	
3.3.3. 2.2.2. 3.2.3.	The classification of the ḍākinī clans
3.3.3. 2.2.2. 3.2.3. 1.	The promise to explain
3.3.3. 2.2.2. 3.2.3. 2.	The characteristics of each of the yoginī [clans]
3.3.3. 2.2.2. 3.2.3. 2.1.	Padmanarteshvara's clan
3.3.3. 2.2.2. 3.2.3. 2.2.	Heruka's clan
3.3.3. 2.2.2. 3.2.3. 2.3.	Vajravārāhī's clan
3.3.3. 2.2.2. 3.2.3. 2.4.	Khaṇḍarohā's clan
3.3.3. 2.2.2. 3.2.3. 2.5.	Heruka's clan
3.3.3. 2.2.2. 3.2.3. 2.6.	Vināyaka's clan
3.3.3. 2.2.2. 3.2.3. 3.	Summarizing the meaning of these
3.3.3. 2.2.2. 3.2.3. 4.	Showing the name of the chapter
[Chapter 19]	
3.3.3. 2.2.2. 3.2.4.	The classification of the lāmā clans

3.3.3. 2.2.2. 3.2.4. 1.	The promise to explain
3.3.3. 2.2.2. 3.2.4. 2.	Stating the characteristics of each of the lāma clans
3.3.3. 2.2.2. 3.2.4. 2.1.	Amitābha's clan
3.3.3. 2.2.2. 3.2.4. 2.2.	Ratnasambhava's clan
3.3.3. 2.2.2. 3.2.4. 2.3.	Akṣhobhya's clan
3.3.3. 2.2.2. 3.2.4. 2.4.	Vairochana's clan
3.3.3. 2.2.2. 3.2.4. 2.5.	Amoghasiddhi's clan
3.3.3. 2.2.2. 3.2.4. 3.	Showing the name of the chapter
[CHAPTER 20]	
3.3.3. 2.2.2. 3.3.	The physical signs for generally recognizing the ḍākinī clans
3.3.3. 2.2.2. 3.3.1.	The hand seal signs
3.3.3. 2.2.2. 3.3.1. 1.	The promise to explain
3.3.3. 2.2.2. 3.3.1. 2.	The actual display of the signs
3.3.3. 2.2.2. 3.3.1. 3.	What should be done once the signs are displayed
3.3.3. 2.2.2. 3.3.1. 4.	The name of the chapter
[CHAPTER 21]	
3.3.3. 2.2.2. 3.3.2.	The signs characterized by the limbs
3.3.3. 2.2.2. 3.3.2. 1.	The promise to explain

3.3.3. 2.2.2. 3.3.2. 2.	The actual display of the signs
3.3.3. 2.2.2. 3.3.2. 3.	Showing the name of the chapter
[Chapter 22]	
3.3.3. 2.2.2. 3.3.3.	The characteristics of the distinctive gestures
3.3.3. 2.2.2. 3.3.3. 1.	The promise to explain
3.3.3. 2.2.2. 3.3.3. 2.	The actual display of the signs
3.3.3. 2.2.2. 3.3.3. 3.	Their summary
3.3.3. 2.2.2. 3.3.3. 4.	Showing the name of the chapter
[Chapter 23]	
3.3.3. 2.2.2. 3.4.	Things to know for ascertaining [the messenger's] devotion to oneself
3.3.3. 2.2.2. 3.4.1.	The promise to explain
3.3.3. 2.2.2. 3.4.2.	Worshipping for the sake of devotion
3.3.3. 2.2.2. 3.4.3.	Displaying the signs of devotion
3.3.3. 2.2.2. 3.4.4.	The drawn signs that should be known
3.3.3. 2.2.2. 3.4.5.	Showing the name of the chapter
[Chapter 24]	
3.3.3. 2.2.2. 3.5.	Verbal signs that are combinations of multiple syllables for generally recognizing the ḍākinīs
3.3.3. 2.2.2. 3.5.1.	The promise to explain
3.3.3. 2.2.2. 3.5.2.	The actual verbal signs that are combinations of multiple syllables

3.3.3. 2.2.2. 3.5.3.	Summarizing their meaning
3.3.3. 2.2.2. 3.5.4.	Showing the extraordinary distinguishing features of this tantra
3.3.3. 2.2.2. 3.5.5.	Showing the name of the chapter
	[VOLUME TWO]
[CHAPTER 25]	
3.3.3. 2.2.2. 4.	Showing the root mantra, and the detailed explanation of the commitments to be protected
3.3.3. 2.2.2. 4.1.	The clear exposition of the root mantra
3.3.3. 2.2.2. 4.1.1.	The way in which the root mantra is made unclear
3.3.3. 2.2.2. 4.1.2.	The way in which the root mantra is clarified in this chapter
3.3.3. 2.2.2. 4.1.2. 1.	Explaining in terms of the interpretable meaning
3.3.3. 2.2.2. 4.1.2. 2.	Explaining in terms of the definitive meaning
3.3.3. 2.2.2. 4.1.2. 2.1.	The definitive meaning of the first set of eight
3.3.3. 2.2.2. 4.1.2. 2.2.	The definitive meaning of the latter set of eight
3.3.3. 2.2.2. 4.1.3.	Showing the name of the chapter
[CHAPTER 26]	
3.3.3. 2.2.2. 4.2.	Showing the eight commitments
3.3.3. 2.2.2. 4.2.1.	Demonstrating the greatness of the root mantra
3.3.3. 2.2.2. 4.2.2.	The bestowal of all powers through the worship of the messenger
3.3.3. 2.2.2. 4.2.3.	The procedures of the commitments and vows

3.3.3. 2.2.2. 4.2.3. 1.	The promise to explain
3.3.3. 2.2.2. 4.2.3. 2.	Heteropraxy together with worship
3.3.3. 2.2.2. 4.2.3. 3.	Showing each of the commitments
3.3.3. 2.2.2. 4.2.3. 4.	Their concise meaning
3.3.3. 2.2.2. 4.2.4.	The cause of delighting the messenger
3.3.3. 2.2.2. 4.2.5.	The procedure of examining the disciple
3.3.3. 2.2.2. 4.2.6.	Showing the name of the chapter
[CHAPTER 27]	
3.3.3. 2.2.2. 5.	The detailed exegesis of the conceptually elaborate practices
3.3.3. 2.2.2. 5.1.	The general arrangement of practices
3.3.3. 2.2.2. 5.2.	The conceptually elaborate practices shown by three chapters
3.3.3. 2.2.2. 5.2.1.	The practice of the observances together with the offerings and sacrificial cakes
3.3.3. 2.2.2. 5.2.1. 1.	The promise to explain
3.3.3. 2.2.2. 5.2.1. 2.	The actual explanation
3.3.3. 2.2.2. 5.2.1. 2.1.	The way of practicing the conduct and observances
3.3.3. 2.2.2. 5.2.1. 2.1.1.	Having sought the messenger the way in which one conducts oneself toward her
3.3.3. 2.2.2. 5.2.1. 2.1.2.	How the rites and observances should be practiced
3.3.3. 2.2.2. 5.2.1. 2.1.2. 1.	How the rites should be practiced
3.3.3. 2.2.2. 5.2.1. 2.1.2. 2.	How the observances should be practiced

3.3.3. 2.2.2. 5.2.1. 2.1.3.	The worship of the purities, and its benefit
3.3.3. 2.2.2. 5.2.1. 2.1.3. 1	The worship of the purities
3.3.3. 2.2.2. 5.2.1. 2.1.3. 2	The benefit of doing thus
3.3.3. 2.2.2. 5.2.1. 2.2.	The sacrificial procedure
3.3.3. 2.2.2. 5.2.1. 3.	Showing the name of the chapter
[CHAPTER 28]	
3.3.3. 2.2.2. 5.2.2.	The procedure of the inner fire sacrifice together with one clan
3.3.3. 2.2.2. 5.2.2. 1.	The inner fire sacrifice, along with a section on what should and should not be done
3.3.3. 2.2.2. 5.2.2. 1.1.	The procedure of inner fire sacrifice
3.3.3. 2.2.2. 5.2.2. 1.2.	Showing the difference between appropriate and inappropriate actions
3.3.3. 2.2.2. 5.2.2. 2.	Heteropraxy and the one clan procedure
3.3.3. 2.2.2. 5.2.2. 2.1.	Heteropraxy
3.3.3. 2.2.2. 5.2.2. 2.2.	The one clan procedure
3.3.3. 2.2.2. 5.2.2. 3.	Showing other procedures of fire sacrifice
3.3.3. 2.2.2. 5.2.2. 4.	The one clan procedure together with its benefit
3.3.3. 2.2.2. 5.2.2. 5.	Showing the name of the chapter
[CHAPTER 29]	
3.3.3. 2.2.2. 5.2.3.	The characteristics of the messenger and procedures for the state of heat or power
3.3.3. 2.2.2. 5.2.3. 1.	The promise to explain
3.3.3. 2.2.2. 5.2.3. 2.	The actual explanation

3.3.3. 2.2.2. 5.2.3. 2.1.	The characteristics of the messenger
3.3.3. 2.2.2. 5.2.3. 2.2.	The procedure of power
3.3.3. 2.2.2. 5.2.3. 2.3.	Praise for Mahāyoga
3.3.3. 2.2.2. 5.2.3. 2.3.1.	The consequences of hating and rejecting Mahāyoga
3.3.3. 2.2.2. 5.2.3. 2.3.2.	The benefits of establishing oneself in Mahāyoga
3.3.3. 2.2.2. 5.2.3. 3.	Showing the name of the chapter
[CHAPTER 30]	
3.3.3. 2.2.2. 6.	Selecting the protective mantra that removes obstacles
3.3.3. 2.2.2. 6.1.	The promise to explain
3.3.3. 2.2.2. 6.2.	Explaining the promised import
3.3.3. 2.2.2. 6.2.1.	Performing ground cleansing etc. and selecting the mantra
3.3.3. 2.2.2. 6.2.1. 1.	Assembling the basis on which the mantra is selected
3.3.3. 2.2.2. 6.2.1. 2.	Showing the yoga by which one selects
3.3.3. 2.2.2. 6.2.1. 3.	Placing the basis from which one selects
3.3.3. 2.2.2. 6.2.1. 4.	The actual method of mantra selection
3.3.3. 2.2.2. 6.2.1. 4.1.	Summary of mantra selection
3.3.3. 2.2.2. 6.2.1. 4.2.	The definitive meaning of the basis of selection and the summary
3.3.3. 2.2.2. 6.2.1. 4.3.	Detailed exegesis of mantra selection
3.3.3. 2.2.2. 6.2.1. 4.3.1.	Selecting the mantra's first line
3.3.3. 2.2.2. 6.2.1. 4.3.2.	Selecting the mantra's second line

3.3.3. 2.2.2. 6.2.1. 4.3.3.	Selecting the mantra's third line
3.3.3. 2.2.2. 6.2.1. 4.3.4.	Selecting the mantra's fourth line along with the first and final syllables
3.3.3. 2.2.2. 6.2.2.	The greatness of the selected [mantra] and its procedure
3.3.3. 2.2.2. 6.2.2. 1.	The mantra's greatness
3.3.3. 2.2.2. 6.2.2. 2.	The mantra's procedure
3.3.3. 2.2.2. 6.2.3.	Arranging the four mantras in a series and showing them
3.3.3. 2.2.2. 6.3.	Showing the name of the chapter
[Chapter 31]	
3.3.3. 2.2.2. 7.	The detailed exegesis of the food commitments
3.3.3. 2.2.2. 7.1.	The chapter on the procedure of the hand signs
3.3.3. 2.2.2. 7.1.1.	Explanation of the scope of engagement of heteropraxy
3.3.3. 2.2.2. 7.1.2.	Detailed exegesis of heteropraxy
3.3.3. 2.2.2. 7.1.2. 1.	Heteropraxy in general
3.3.3. 2.2.2. 7.1.2. 2.	Worship with the left hand in particular
3.3.3. 2.2.2. 7.1.3.	Acting to hide and disclose this method
3.3.3. 2.2.2. 7.1.4.	Showing the name of the chapter
[Chapter 32]	
3.3.3. 2.2.2. 7.2.	The chapter on the procedures of the achievement of the sacrificial victim and zombie and the creation stage
3.3.3. 2.2.2. 7.2.1.	The promise to explain

3.3.3. 2.2.2. 7.2.2.	Explaining the promised import
3.3.3. 2.2.2. 7.2.2. 1.	The achievement of the sacrificial victim for the sake of fire sacrifice
3.3.3. 2.2.2. 7.2.2. 2.	The achievement of the zombie for the sake of great power
3.3.3. 2.2.2. 7.2.2. 3.	Showing the yoga of the creation stage that is essential for all of them
3.3.3. 2.2.2. 7.2.2. 3.1.	Creation of the habitat
3.3.3. 2.2.2. 7.2.2. 3.2.	Creation of the inhabitant deities
3.3.3. 2.2.2. 7.2.3.	Showing the name of the chapter
[Chapter 33]	
3.3.3. 2.2.2. 7.3.	The chapter on the secret and reverential worship
3.3.3. 2.2.2. 7.3.1.	The promise to explain
3.3.3. 2.2.2. 7.3.2.	Explaining the promised import
3.3.3. 2.2.2. 7.3.2. 1.	The reverential worship
3.3.3. 2.2.2. 7.3.2. 2.	The secret worship
3.3.3. 2.2.2. 7.3.2. 3.	The benefit of worship
3.3.3. 2.2.2. 7.3.3.	Showing the name of the chapter
[Chapter 34]	
3.3.3. 2.2.2. 8.	The detailed exegesis of the secret of the four [types of] worship
3.3.3. 2.2.2. 8.1.	The chapter that shows the great seal
3.3.3. 2.2.2. 8.1.1.	The promise to explain
3.3.3. 2.2.2. 8.1.2.	Explaining the promised import

3.3.3. 2.2.2. 8.1.2. 1.	Detailed exegesis of the import to be explained
3.3.3. 2.2.2. 8.1.2. 1.1.	Explaining in terms of the interpretable meaning
3.3.3. 2.2.2. 8.1.2. 1.2.	Explaining in terms of the definitive meaning
3.3.3. 2.2.2. 8.1.2. 1.2.1.	The explanation that occurs in the oral instructions of previous gurus
3.3.3. 2.2.2. 8.1.2. 1.2.2.	Kambala the Blanketed's explanation
3.3.3. 2.2.2. 8.1.2. 1.2.2. 1.	The explanation in terms of the yoga of the drop
3.3.3. 2.2.2. 8.1.2. 1.2.2. 2.	The explanation in terms of subtle yoga
3.3.3. 2.2.2. 8.1.2. 2.	Summary of the explained import
3.3.3. 2.2.2. 8.1.3.	Showing the name of the chapter
[CHAPTER 35]	
3.3.3. 2.2.2. 8.2.	The chapter that shows the reality seal
3.3.3. 2.2.2. 8.2.1.	The promise to explain
3.3.3. 2.2.2. 8.2.2.	Explaining the promised import
3.3.3. 2.2.2. 8.2.2. 1.	Explaining in terms of the interpretable meaning
3.3.3. 2.2.2. 8.2.2. 1.1.	The method of repeating [the mantra]
3.3.3. 2.2.2. 8.2.2. 1.2.	The method of achieving ritual actions with Khaṇḍarohā
3.3.3. 2.2.2. 8.2.2. 2.	Explaining in terms of the definitive meaning
3.3.3. 2.2.2. 8.2.3.	Showing the name of the chapter
[CHAPTER 36]	
3.3.3. 2.2.2. 8.3.	The chapter that shows both the symbolic and actual seals through a single approach

3.3.3. 2.2.2. 8.3.1.	The promise to explain
3.3.3. 2.2.2. 8.3.2.	Explaining the promised import
3.3.3. 2.2.2. 8.3.2. 1.	The worship of reality
3.3.3. 2.2.2. 8.3.2. 1.1.	Worship depending on the two [types of] seals
3.3.3. 2.2.2. 8.3.2. 1.2.	Explaining somewhat the classification of the four seals
3.3.3. 2.2.2. 8.3.2. 2.	The procedure for ritual success depending on that
3.3.3. 2.2.2. 8.3.3.	Showing the name of the chapter
[Chapter 37]	
3.3.3. 2.2.2. 8.4.	The chapter on subjugating the actual seal (consort)
3.3.3. 2.2.2. 8.4.1.	The promise to explain
3.3.3. 2.2.2. 8.4.2.	Explaining the promised import
3.3.3. 2.2.2. 8.4.2. 1.	Subjugating the victim relying upon food
3.3.3. 2.2.2. 8.4.2. 2.	Subjugating the victim relying upon fire sacrifice
3.3.3. 2.2.2. 8.4.2. 3.	Showing praise for the subjugation procedure
3.3.3. 2.2.2. 8.4.3.	Showing the name of the chapter
[Chapter 38]	
3.3.3. 2.2.2. 9.	The detailed exegesis the two remaining [modes of] conduct
3.3.3. 2.2.2. 9.1.	The promise to explain
3.3.3. 2.2.2. 9.2.	The promised import explained

3.3.3. 2.2.2. 9.2.1.	Showing the commitment to protect the performance of conduct etc.
3.3.3. 2.2.2. 9.2.1. 1.	Showing the commitments that pertain to what the yogī should not do
3.3.3. 2.2.2. 9.2.1. 2.	Showing the commitments that pertain to what should be done
3.3.3. 2.2.2. 9.2.2.	Showing conduct performance together with the locations
3.3.3. 2.2.2. 9.3.	Showing the name of the chapter
[Chapter 39]	
3.3.3. 2.2.2. 10.	Examining the signs of the attainment of power
3.3.3. 2.2.2. 10.1.	The chapter on vision and "*ha ha*" laughter
3.3.3. 2.2.2. 10.1.1.	The promise to explain
3.3.3. 2.2.2. 10.1.2.	Explaining the promised import
3.3.3. 2.2.2. 10.1.2. 1.	The method of giving rise to vision through laughter
3.3.3. 2.2.2. 10.1.2. 2.	Showing the consequence of fear when [they] are seen
3.3.3. 2.2.2. 10.1.2. 3.	Showing the benefit of not being afraid when [they] are seen
3.3.3. 2.2.2. 10.1.3.	Showing the name of the chapter
[Chapter 40]	
3.3.3. 2.2.2. 10.2.	The chapter on subjugating the five classes, and serving the great seal
3.3.3. 2.2.2. 10.2.1.	The promise to explain
3.3.3. 2.2.2. 10.2.2.	Explaining the promised import
3.3.3. 2.2.2. 10.2.2. 1.	Outer and inner fire sacrifice
3.3.3. 2.2.2. 10.2.2. 2.	The number relative to each [type of] victim

3.3.3. 2.2.2. 10.2.2. 3.	The benefit of doing so
3.3.3. 2.2.2. 10.2.3.	Showing the name of the chapter
[Chapter 41]	
3.3.3. 2.2.2. 10.3.	The chapter on the placement of the mandala of twenty-four syllables
3.3.3. 2.2.2. 10.3.1.	The promise to explain
3.3.3. 2.2.2. 10.3.2.	Explaining the promised import
3.3.3. 2.2.2. 10.3.2. 1.	Classifying the ritual actions to be achieved
3.3.3. 2.2.2. 10.3.2. 2.	Showing the cause of their achievement
3.3.3. 2.2.2. 10.3.2. 2.1.	The concise exposition
3.3.3. 2.2.2. 10.3.2. 2.2.	The detailed exposition
3.3.3. 2.2.2. 10.3.2. 2.2.1.	Showing in detail the sites with the ḍākinīs
3.3.3. 2.2.2. 10.3.2. 2.2.2.	Recognizing the chief among the sites
3.3.3. 2.2.2. 10.3.2. 2.2.2. 1.	Showing the twenty-four sites
3.3.3. 2.2.2. 10.3.2. 2.2.2. 2.	The way to engage with the blessings of the yoginīs there
3.3.3. 2.2.2. 10.3.2. 2.2.2. 3.	Those who are included with the yoginīs
3.3.3. 2.2.2. 10.3.2. 2.2.3.	Showing protection by means of meditation and worship
3.3.3. 2.2.2. 10.3.3.	Showing the name of the chapter
[Chapter 42]	
3.3.3. 2.2.2. 10.4.	The chapter on the laughter mantra and the cause of the ḍākinīs' forms
3.3.3. 2.2.2. 10.4.1.	The promise to explain

3.3.3. 2.2.2. 10.4.2.	The actual explanation
3.3.3. 2.2.2. 10.4.2. 1.	The first exegetical method
3.3.3. 2.2.2. 10.4.2. 1.1.	The method of laughter
3.3.3. 2.2.2. 10.4.2. 1.2.	The signs of laughter together with the remainder
3.3.3. 2.2.2. 10.4.2. 2.	The second exegetical method
3.3.3. 2.2.2. 10.4.3.	Showing the name of the chapter
[CHAPTER 43]	
3.3.3. 2.2.2. 11.	Showing other methods for the attainment of mundane powers
3.3.3. 2.2.2. 11.1.	Ritual success with the father's quintessence and armor [mantras]
3.3.3. 2.2.2. 11.1.1.	Success relying upon the father's quintessence
3.3.3. 2.2.2. 11.1.1. 1.	The promise to explain
3.3.3. 2.2.2. 11.1.1. 2.	The promised explanation of the meaning
3.3.3. 2.2.2. 11.1.1. 2.1.	Places in which they glance
3.3.3. 2.2.2. 11.1.1. 2.2.	Naked worship
3.3.3. 2.2.2. 11.1.1. 2.3.	The mantra that protects against obstacles
3.3.3. 2.2.2. 11.1.1. 2.4.	Ritual success relying on the attainment of mantric power
3.3.3. 2.2.2. 11.1.1. 2.4.1.	Methods for gaining particular mantric powers
3.3.3. 2.2.2. 11.1.1. 2.4.2.	Methods for success in rites relying upon them
3.3.3. 2.2.2. 11.1.1. 2.4.2. 1.	Ritual success in invisibility and tree summoning

3.3.3. 2.2.2. 11.1.1. 2.4.2. 2.	Ritual success in dream interpretation and the descent of the divinatory image
3.3.3. 2.2.2. 11.1.1. 2.4.2. 3.	Ritual success in the pacification of illness etc.
3.3.3. 2.2.2. 11.1.1. 2.4.2. 3.1.	Pacifying illness relying upon mantra and a wheel
3.3.3. 2.2.2. 11.1.1. 2.4.2. 3.2.	Fire sacrifice for subjugation, along with the options
3.3.3. 2.2.2. 11.1.1. 2.4.2. 3.3.	Showing the different colors for the different ritual actions
3.3.3. 2.2.2. 11.1.1. 2.4.2. 3.4.	Methods for destroying poison, plague, etc.
3.3.3. 2.2.2. 11.1.1. 2.4.2. 3.5.	Victory in gambling and fighting, and additional matters
3.3.3. 2.2.2. 11.1.1. 2.5.	Techniques for achieving ritual power
3.3.3. 2.2.2. 11.1.1. 3.	Showing the name of the chapter
[Chapter 44]	
3.3.3. 2.2.2. 11.1.2.	Success relying upon his and the mother's armor
3.3.3. 2.2.2. 11.1.2. 1.	The promise to explain
3.3.3. 2.2.2. 11.1.2. 2.	The promised explanation of the meaning
3.3.3. 2.2.2. 11.1.2. 2.1.	The rite of summoning from the perspective of dominion
3.3.3. 2.2.2. 11.1.2. 2.1.1.	Summoning relying on a wheel
3.3.3. 2.2.2. 11.1.2. 2.1.2.	Summoning relying on fire sacrifice
3.3.3. 2.2.2. 11.1.2. 2.2.	The rite of suppression and subsequent release
3.3.3. 2.2.2. 11.1.2. 2.3.	The rite of maddening and subsequent release
3.3.3. 2.2.2. 11.1.2. 3.	Showing the name of the chapter

[Chapter 45]	
3.3.3. 2.2.2. 11.2.	Ritual success relying on the heroine's armor and five *ha* [syllables]
3.3.3. 2.2.2. 11.2.1.	Procedures for achieving the heroine's armor and the power of speech
3.3.3. 2.2.2. 11.2.1. 1.	The promise to explain
3.3.3. 2.2.2. 11.2.1. 2.	Explaining the promised import
3.3.3. 2.2.2. 11.2.1. 2.1.	The method for achieving the power of speech
3.3.3. 2.2.2. 11.2.1. 2.2.	Success in multiple rites of summoning relying on that
3.3.3. 2.2.2. 11.2.1. 2.2.1.	Summoning in reliance on binding the vulva seal
3.3.3. 2.2.2. 11.2.1. 2.2.2.	Summoning in reliance on fire sacrifice
3.3.3. 2.2.2. 11.2.1. 2.2.3.	Ritual success relying on the oleander flower
3.3.3. 2.2.2. 11.2.1. 2.3.	Achieving the power of speech relying on other methods
3.3.3. 2.2.2. 11.2.1. 2.4.	Having obtained that, achieving many different rites with speech
3.3.3. 2.2.2. 11.2.1. 2.4.1.	Rites of summoning and destroying
3.3.3. 2.2.2. 11.2.1. 2.4.2.	Explaining the rite of summoning in particular
3.3.3. 2.2.2. 11.2.1. 3.	Showing the name of the chapter
[Chapter 46]	
3.3.3. 2.2.2. 11.2.2.	Ritual success relying on the five *ha* [syllables]
3.3.3. 2.2.2. 11.2.2. 1.	The promise to explain
3.3.3. 2.2.2. 11.2.2. 2.	Explaining the promised import
3.3.3. 2.2.2. 11.2.2. 2.1.	The rite of killing

3.3.3. 2.2.2. 11.2.2. 2.2.	The rite of shape changing
3.3.3. 2.2.2. 11.2.2. 2.3.	The rite of womb transference
3.3.3. 2.2.2. 11.2.2. 3.	Showing the name of the chapter
[CHAPTER 47]	
3.3.3. 2.2.2. 11.3.	Success with the buddhaḍākinī mantra and continual performance of deity visualization
3.3.3. 2.2.2. 11.3.1.	Ritual success with the buddhaḍākinī mantra
3.3.3. 2.2.2. 11.3.1. 1.	The promise to explain
3.3.3. 2.2.2. 11.3.1. 2.	Explaining the promised import
3.3.3. 2.2.2. 11.3.1. 2.1.	Success with rites of controlling and destroying
3.3.3. 2.2.2. 11.3.1. 2.2.	Success with the rite of transforming into another [state]
3.3.3. 2.2.2. 11.3.1. 2.2.1.	Transforming into another gender
3.3.3. 2.2.2. 11.3.1. 2.2.2.	Transforming into another life form
3.3.3. 2.2.2. 11.3.1. 2.2.3.	Transforming into another substance
3.3.3. 2.2.2. 11.3.1. 2.2.4.	Transforming into another mental state
3.3.3. 2.2.2. 11.3.1. 2.2.5.	Transforming into another form
3.3.3. 2.2.2. 11.3.1. 2.2.6.	Turning another man's wealth [into one's own]
3.3.3. 2.2.2. 11.3.1. 3.	Showing the name of the chapter
[CHAPTER 48]	
3.3.3. 2.2.2. 11.3.2.	Continual visualization of the heroes and yoginīs
3.3.3. 2.2.2. 11.3.2. 1.	The promise to explain

3.3.3. 2.2.2. 11.3.2. 2.	Explaining the promised import
3.3.3. 2.2.2. 11.3.2. 2.1.	The mantra that achieves rites, with its benefit
3.3.3. 2.2.2. 11.3.2. 2.2.	Visualizing the secret mandala
3.3.3. 2.2.2. 11.3.2. 2.2.1.	Visualizing the habitat
3.3.3. 2.2.2. 11.3.2. 2.2.2.	Visualizing the inhabitant deities
3.3.3. 2.2.2. 11.3.2. 2.3.	Summarizing the meaning
3.3.3. 2.2.2. 11.3.2. 3.	Showing the name of the chapter
[CHAPTER 49]	
3.3.3. 2.2.2. 11.4.	Detailed exposition of the examination of the one born seven times
3.3.3. 2.2.2. 11.4.1.	The promise to explain
3.3.3. 2.2.2. 11.4.2.	Explaining the promised import
3.3.3. 2.2.2. 11.4.2. 1.	Making an image of the sacrificial victim from rice powder
3.3.3. 2.2.2. 11.4.2. 2.	The rite of relying on one who has the characteristics of the supreme sacrificial victim
3.3.3. 2.2.2. 11.4.2. 2.1.	The promise to explain the two meanings
3.3.3. 2.2.2. 11.4.2. 2.2.	Showing the characteristics of the supreme sacrificial victim
3.3.3. 2.2.2. 11.4.2. 2.3.	Showing the ritual application relying on him
3.3.3. 2.2.2. 11.4.2. 2.3.1.	Success through the rite relying on the supreme sacrificial victim
3.3.3. 2.2.2. 11.4.2. 2.3.2.	Success through the rite relying on another sacrificial victim

3.3.3. 2.2.2. 11.4.2. 3.	Showing the supremacy of that ritual application
3.3.3. 2.2.2. 11.4.3.	Showing the name of the chapter
[CHAPTER 50]	
3.3.3. 2.2.2. 11.5.	Ritual success with the mother's essence mantra
3.3.3. 2.2.2. 11.5.1.	Explaining the fire sacrifice
3.3.3. 2.2.2. 11.5.1. 1.	The promise to explain
3.3.3. 2.2.2. 11.5.1. 2.	Explaining the promised import
3.3.3. 2.2.2. 11.5.1. 2.1.	The fire sacrifice for controlling
3.3.3. 2.2.2. 11.5.1. 2.2.	The violent fire sacrifices
3.3.3. 2.2.2. 11.5.1. 2.2.1.	The fire sacrifice for dividing
3.3.3. 2.2.2. 11.5.1. 2.2.2.	The fire sacrifices for killing and expelling
3.3.3. 2.2.2. 11.5.1. 2.3.	The method for continually pacifying obstacles
3.3.3. 2.2.2. 11.5.1. 2.4.	The fire sacrifice for enriching
3.3.3. 2.2.2. 11.5.1. 2.4.1.	Expanding wealth
3.3.3. 2.2.2. 11.5.1. 2.4.2.	Expanding power
3.3.3. 2.2.2. 11.5.1. 2.4.3.	Expanding dominion
3.3.3. 2.2.2. 11.5.1. 2.4.4.	Extending life
3.3.3. 2.2.2. 11.5.1. 2.5.	The fire sacrifice for paralyzing
3.3.3. 2.2.2. 11.5.1. 3.	Summarizing the meaning and showing the mantra that achieves the rites
3.3.3. 2.2.2. 11.5.2.	Explaining the ten seats etc.

3.3.3. 2.2.2. 11.5.2. 1.	The promise to explain
3.3.3. 2.2.2. 11.5.2. 2.	Explaining the promised import
3.3.3. 2.2.2. 11.5.2. 2.1.	Showing the ten seats etc.
3.3.3. 2.2.2. 11.5.2. 2.1.1.	The general meaning
3.3.3. 2.2.2. 11.5.2. 2.1.1. 1.	The way that the names of the stages such as the joyous are each stated
3.3.3. 2.2.2. 11.5.2. 2.1.1. 2.	Avoiding contradiction of stating [the stages] out of harmony with the seats etc.
3.3.3. 2.2.2. 11.5.2. 2.1.1. 3.	The types of disciples for whom they are stated
3.3.3. 2.2.2. 11.5.2. 2.1.2.	The auxiliary meanings
3.3.3. 2.2.2. 11.5.2. 2.2.	Showing that the ten seats etc. are all pervading
3.3.3. 2.2.2. 11.5.3.	Summarizing the meaning
3.3.3. 2.2.2. 11.5.4.	Showing the name of the chapter
[CHAPTER 51]	
3.3.3. 2.3.	The chapter's summary of the previous [chapters]
3.3.3. 2.3.1.	The promise to explain
3.3.3. 2.3.2.	Explaining the promised import
3.3.3. 2.3.2. 1.	Showing the esoteric instruction for this tantra that is very difficult to obtain
3.3.3. 2.3.2. 2.	Showing the fourteen realities that are the method for easily obtaining it

3.3.3. 2.3.2. 2.1.	Explaining the literal meaning of the fourteen realities
3.3.3. 2.3.2. 2.2.	The explanation applicable to the two stages
3.3.3. 2.3.2. 3.1.	The benefits of practice in the fourteen realities
3.3.3. 2.3.2. 3.	The benefits of practice in the fourteen, and the fault of lacking faith
3.3.3. 2.3.2. 3.1.1.	Showing in general the outer benefits of this
3.3.3. 2.3.2. 3.1.2.	Showing in particular the benefit that arises at the time of death
3.3.3. 2.3.2. 3.2.	The fault of lacking faith in this path
3.3.3. 2.3.2. 4.	The method of comprehensive meditation in the fourteen realities
3.3.3. 2.3.2. 5.	Showing the method for not forsaking any of the Buddha's scriptures
3.3.3. 2.3.3.	Showing the chapter count
[COLOPHON]	
3.3.4.	The meaning of the conclusion
3.3.4. 1.	How the text concluded
3.3.4. 2.	How [the text] was translated in Tibet

Appendix II
Tibetan Names (Phonetic-Transliterated Equivalents)

Phonetic Rendition	Wylie Transliteration
Büton	Bu-ston
Gö Hlaytsay	’Gos Lhas-btsas
Kunga Nyingpo (*See* Sachen [Kunga Nyingpo])	Kun-dga’ sNying-po
Lochen (Rinchen Zangpo)	Lo-chen (Rin-chen bZang-po)
Mal, Malgyo (Lotsawa)	Mal-gyo (Lo-tsā-ba)
Mar Chökyi Gyalpo	Mar Chos-kyi rGyal-po
Mardo (Lotsawa)	Mar-do (Lo-tsā-ba)
Marpa Chökyi Wangchuk (*See* Mardo [Lotsawa])	Mar-pa Chos-kyi-dBang-phyug
Marpa Dopa (*See* Mardo [Lotsawa])	Mar-pa Do-pa
Rinchen Pal	Rin-chen dPal
Rinchen Zangpo (*See* Lochen [Rinchen Zangpo])	Rin-chen bZang-po. *See* Lo-chen (Rin-chen bZang-po)
Sachen (Kunga Nyingpo)	Sa-chen (Kun-dga’ sNying-po)
Shākya Tsöndru	Sha’-kya brTson-’grus

Glossaries

English–Sanskrit–Tibetan Glossary

English	Sanskrit	Tibetan
accomplished, achieved	siddha	grub pa
accomplishment, power	siddhi	dngos grub
action	kriyā	bya ba
adept	sādhaka	sgrub pa po
aerial state	khecarīpada	mkha' spyod gnas mkha' la 'gro ba'i gnas
affliction	kleśa	nyon mongs
ambrosia	amṛta	bdud rtsi
appendix	uttaratantra	rgyud phyi ma
armor	kavaca	go cha
art	upāya	thabs
asceticism	tapas	dka' thub
astral spirit	graha	gdon
auspicious	śubha	dge ba
awakening spirit	bodhicitta	byang chub sems
narrative preface	nidāna	gleng gzhi
barbarian	mleccha	kla klo
beast	paśu	phyugs

English	Sanskrit	Tibetan
being	sattva	sems dpa'
beneficiary	sādhya	bsgrub bya
benefit, benefiting	anugraha	phen 'dogs
binding	saṁvara	sdom pa
birth place	yoni	skye gnas
Blessed Lady	bhagavatī	bcom ldan 'das ma
Blessed Lord	bhagavān	bcom ldan 'das
bliss	sukha	bde ba
blood	rakta, rudhira	khrag
body	aṅga	lus
	kāya	sku, lus
	gātra, deha, mūrti, vigraha, śarīra	lus
body wheel	kāyacakra	sku kyi 'khor lo
cake	saṁkulikā	snum 'khur
celestial musician	gandharva	dri za
centaur	kinnara	mi'am ci
central channel	avadhūti	rtsa dbu ma
characteristic	lakṣaṇa	mtshan nyid
charnel ground	śmaśāna	dur khrod
chastity	brahmacārya	tshangs spyod
clan	kula	rigs
clanswoman	kulikā	rigs ldan
commitment	samaya	dam tshig
communal enjoyment body	sambhogakāya	longs spyod rdzogs pa'i sku

ENGLISH	SANSKRIT	TIBETAN
concentration	samādhi	ting nge 'dzin
conception, conceptualization	vikalpa	rnam par rtog pa
concretion	rocanā	gi wang
conduct	caryā	spyod pa
consecration	abhiṣeka	dbang bskur ba
countergesture	pratimudrā	phyag rgya'i lan
creation stage	utpattikrama	bskyed rim
cyclic existence	saṁsāra	'khor ba
dead person	preta	yi dags
death	mṛtyu, māra	'chi ba, bdud
demon	rākṣasa	srin po
demoness	rākṣasī	srin mo
destroying	nigraha	tshar gcod
devil	māra	bdud
divinatory image	prasena	pra se na
disciple	śrāvaka	nyan thos
disposition	śīla	mos pa
dissatisfaction	duḥkha	sdug bsngal
distinguishing mark	lakṣaṇa	mtshan nyid
dryad	yakṣiṇī	gnod sbyin mo
emanation	nirmāṇa	sprul pa
enveloping, intercourse, kiss	saṁpuṭa	kha sbyar ba
esoteric instruction	āmnāya	man ngag

English	Sanskrit	Tibetan
essence	hṛdaya	snying po
experiential scope	gocara	spyod yul
experiential unity	ekarasa	ro gcig
explanatory tantra	vyākhyātantra	bshad rgyud
father tantra		pha rgyud
fee	dakṣiṇā	yon
field	kṣetra	zhing
fierce one	khrodha	khro bo
fire sacrifice	homa	sbyin sreg
flight	khecaratvaṁ	nam mkhar rgyu
floating	khecara	mkha' spyod, mkha' la rgyu ba
flying	khecara	mkha' spyod, mkha' la rgyu ba
	khecarī	mkha' la spyod
fury fire	caṇḍālī	gtum mo
gesture	mudrā	phyag rgya
ghost	preta	yi dags
goblin	pīśāca	sha za
gnosis	jñāna	ye shes
gnosis hero	jñānasattva	ye shes sems dpa'
great seal	mahāmudrā	phyag rgya chen po
great serpent	mahoraga	lto 'phye chen po
habitual propensity	vāsanā	bag chags
happiness	sukha	bde ba
heretic	tīrthika	mu stegs

English	Sanskrit	Tibetan
hero	vīra	dpa' bo
	sattva	sems dpa'
Heruka	heruka	he ru ka, khrag 'thung ba
heteropraxy	vāmācāra	g.yon pa'i kun spyod
inauspicious	aśubha	mi dge ba
insight	vipaśyanā	lhag mthong
insignia	mudrā	phyag rgya
intercourse, enveloping, kiss	saṁpuṭa	kha sbyar ba
joy	ānanda	dga' ba
joy of cessation	viramānanda	dga' bral
khatvanga staff	khaṭvāṅga	kha ṭvāṁ ga
knowledge	jñāna	she pa
lady	yoṣit	btsun mo
left channel	lalanā	rtsa rkyang ma
life force	prāṇa	srog
limb	aṅga	yan lag
magical diagram	yantra	'khrul 'khor
emanation body	nirmāṇakāya	sprul pa'i sku
means of achievement	sādhana	sgrub byed
means of achieving	sādhaka	sgrub byed
meditation, meditative state	dhyāna	bsam gtan
meeting place	melāpaka	'dus pa
menstruating	puṣpavatī	me tog dang ldan pa
messenger	dūtī	pho nya mo

English	Sanskrit	Tibetan
mind wheel	cittacakra	thugs kyi 'khor lo
mother tantra		ma rgyud
natural	sahaja	lhan cig skyes pa
natural joy	sahajānanda	lhan cig skyes pa'i dga' ba
nature	ātman prakṛti	bdag nyid rang bzhin
net, network	jāla	dra ba
nonconceptual	nirvikalpa	rnam par mi rtog pa
nonconceptuality	nirvikalpatvam	mi rtog pa nyid
nondual	advaya	gnyis med
observance	vrata	brtul zhugs
obstacle demon	vināyaka	log 'dren rnam par log 'dren
omen	utpāta	ltas ngan
oral instruction	upadeśa	man ngag
partner		yab, yum
partners		yab yum
penis	liṅga	ling ga
perfected one	siddha	grub pa
perfection stage	niṣpannakrama	rdzogs rim
power	śaktika	nus pa
power, accomplishment	siddhi	dngos grub
practice	caryā	spyod pa
procedure	vidhi	cho ga
quiescence	śamathā	zhi gnas

English	Sanskrit	Tibetan
quintessence	upahṛdaya	nye snying
reality	tattva	de nyid
	dharmatā	chos nyid
reality body	dharmakāya	chos kyi sku
reality source	dharmodaya	chos 'byung ba
red	rakta	dmar po
right channel	rasanā	rtsa ro ma
rite	vidhi	cho ga
ritual action	karma	las
	kriyā	bya ba
root tantra	mūlatantra	rtsa rgyud
sacred knowledge	vidyā	rig pa
sacrificial cake	bali	gtor ma
sacrificial victim	paśu	phyugs
sea monster	makara	chu srin
seal	mudrā	phyag rgya
seal consort	mudrā	phyag rgya ma, phyag rgya mo
seat	pīṭha	gnas
secret	guhya, rahasya	gsang ba
seed syllable	bīja	sa bon
semen	śukra	khu ba
seminal fluid	retas	rdzas
sentient being	sattva	sems dpa'
serpent deity	nāga	klu

English	Sanskrit	Tibetan
serpent	uraga	lto 'phye
	sarpa	sbrul
sign	cihna, cchomaka, liṅga	brda, mtshan ma, ling ga
solitary buddhas	pratyekabuddha	rang rgyal ba
speech wheel	vākcakra	gsung gi 'khor lo
spell	vidyā	rig pa
spell consort	vidyā	rig ma
sphere of reality	dharmadhātu	chos kyi dbyings
spiritual discipline	sādhana	sgrub byed
strategy	upāya	thabs
subsidiary charnel ground	upaśmaśāna	nye ba'i dur khrod
subsidiary field	upakṣetra	nye ba'i zhing
subsidiary meeting place	upamelāpaka	nye bar 'dus pa
subsidiary seat	upapīṭha	nye gnas
suffering	duḥkha	sdug bsngal
supreme bliss	saṁvara	bde mchog
supreme joy	paramānanda	mchog dga'
tantric feast	gaṇacakra	tshogs kyi 'khor lo
titan	asura, dānava	lha min
tree spirit	yakṣa	gnod sbyin
triple wheel	tricakra	'khor lo gsum
triple world	triloka, trailokya	'jig rten gsum
unexcelled yoga	niruttarayoga	rnal 'byor bla med
unification	samāyoga	mnyam 'byor

English	Sanskrit	Tibetan
union	yoga	rnal 'byor
	saṁyoga	yang dag 'byor
	saṁvara	sdom pa
universal monarch	cakravartin	'khor los sgyur ba
untimely death	apamṛtyu	dus min 'chi
uterine blood	rakta, rajas	khrag
vase	kalaśa	bum pa
vassal lord	sāmanta	rgyal phran
vermilion	rakta	dmar
victim	sādhya	bsgrub bya
victor	jina	rgyal ba
vow	saṁvara	sdom pa
vulva	yoni	skye gnas
	dharmodaya	chos 'byung ba
	bhaga	bha ga
war machine	yantra	'khrul 'khor
wisdom	prajñā	shes rab
wisdom consort	prajñā	shes rab ma
yogic posture	yantra	'khrul 'khor
zombie	vetāla	ro langs

Sanskrit–Tibetan–English Glossary

Sanskrit	Tibetan	English
aṅga	lus	body
	yan lag	limb
advaya	gnyis med	nondual
anugraha	phen 'dogs	benefit, benefiting
apamṛtyu	dus min 'chi	untimely death
abhiṣeka	dbang bskur ba	consecration
amṛta	bdud rtsi	ambrosia
avadhūti	rtsa dbu ma	central channel
aśubha	mi dge ba	inauspicious
asura	lha min	titan
ātman	bdag nyid	self, nature, oneself
ānanda	dga' ba	joy
āmnāya	man ngag	esoteric instruction
uttaratantra	rgyud phyi ma	appendix
utpattikrama	bskyed rim	creation stage
utpāta	ltas ngan	omen
upakṣetra	nye ba'i zhing	subsidiary field
upadeśa	man ngag	oral instruction

Sanskrit	Tibetan	English
upapīṭha	nye gnas	subsidiary seat
upamelāpaka	nye bar 'dus pa	subsidiary meeting place
upaśmaśāna	nye ba'i dur khrod	subsidiary charnel ground
upahṛdaya	nye snying	quintessence
upāya	thabs	art, strategy
uraga	lto 'phye	serpent
ekarasa	ro gcig	experiential unity
karma	las	ritual action
kalaśa	bum pa	Vase
kavaca	go cha	armor
kāya	sku, lus	body
kāyacakra	sku kyi 'khor lo	body wheel
kinnara	mi'am ci	centaur
kula	rigs	clan
kulikā	rigs ldan	clanswoman
kriyā	bya ba	action, ritual action
kleśa	nyon mongs	affliction
kṣetra	zhing	field
khaṭvāṅga	kha ṭvāṁ ga	khatvanga staff
khecara	mkha' spyod, mkha' la rgyu ba	flying, floating
khecaratvaṁ	nam mkhar rgyu	flight
khecarī	mkha' la spyod	flying
khecarīpada	mkha' spyod gnas, mkha' la 'gro ba'i gnas	aerial state

Sanskrit	Tibetan	English
khrodha	khro bo	fierce one
gaṇacakra	tshogs kyi 'khor lo	tantric feast
gandharva	dri za	celestial musician
gātra	lus	body
guhya	gsang ba	secret
gocara	spyod yul	experiential scope
graha	gdon	astral spirit
cakravartin	'khor los sgyur ba	universal monarch
cakrasaṁvara	'khor lo sdom pa	
caṇḍālī	gtum mo	fury fire
caryā	spyod pa	conduct, practice
cittacakra	thugs kyi 'khor lo	mind wheel
cihna	mtshan ma	sign
cchomaka	brda	sign
jāla	dra ba	net, network
jina	rgyal ba	victor
jñāna	ye shes shes pa	gnosis knowledge
jñānasattva	ye shes sems dpa'	gnosis hero
tattva	de nyid	reality
tapas	dka' thub	asceticism
tricakra	'khor lo gsum	triple wheel
triloka, trailokya	'jig rten gsum	triple world
ḍākinī	mkha' 'gro ma, phra men ma	

Sanskrit	Tibetan	English
dakṣiṇā	yon	fee
dānava	lha min	titan
duḥkha	sdug bsngal	dissatisfaction, suffering
dūtī	pho nya mo	messenger
deha	lus	body
dharmakāya	chos kyi sku	reality body
dharmatā	chos nyid	reality
dharmadhātu	chos kyi dbyings	sphere of reality
dharmodaya	chos 'byung ba	reality source, vulva
dhyāna	bsam gtan	meditation, meditative state
nāga	klu	serpent deity
nigraha	tshar gcod	destroying
nidāna	gleng gzhi	narrative preface
nirmāṇa	sprul pa	emanation
nirmāṇakāya	sprul pa'i sku	emanation body
nirvikalpa	rnam par mi rtog pa	nonconceptual
nirvikalpatvam	mi rtog pa nyid	nonconceptuality
niṣpannakrama	rdzogs rim	perfection stage
paramānanda	mchog dga'	supreme joy
paśu	phyugs	beast, sacrificial victim
pīṭha	gnas	seat
pīśāca	sha za	goblin
puṣpavatī	me tog dang ldan pa	menstruating
prakṛti	rang bzhin	nature

Sanskrit	Tibetan	English
prajñā	shes rab, shes rab ma	wisdom, wisdom consort
pratimudrā	phyag rgya'i lan	countergesture
prasena	pra se na	divinatory image
prāṇa	srog	life force
preta	yi dags	ghost, dead person
bali	gtor ma	sacrificial cake
bīja	sa bon	seed syllable
bodhicitta	byang chub sems	awakening spirit
brahmacārya	tshangs spyod	chastity
bhaga	bha ga	vulva
bhagavatī	bcom ldan 'das ma	Blessed Lady
bhagavān	bcom ldan 'das	Blessed Lord
makara	chu srin	sea monster
mahāmudrā	phyag rgya chen po	great seal
mahoraga	lto 'phye chen po	great serpent
māra	bdud	devil, Death
mudrā	phyag rgya, phyag rgya ma, phyag rgya mo	seal, seal consort, gesture, insignia
mūrti	lus	body
mūlatantra	rtsa rgyud	root tantra
mṛtyu	'chi ba	death
melāpaka	'dus pa	meeting place
mleccha	kla klo	barbarian
yakṣa	gnod sbyin	tree spirit
yakṣiṇī	gnod sbyin mo	dryad

SANSKRIT	TIBETAN	ENGLISH
yantra	'khrul 'khor	magical diagram, yogic posture, war machine
yoga	rnal 'byor	union
yogin	rnal 'byor pa	
yoginī	rnal 'byor ma	
yoni	skye gnas	vulva, birth place
yoṣit	btsun mo	lady
rakta	dmar, dmar po, khrag	red, vermilion, blood, uterine blood
rajas	khrag	uterine blood
rasanā	rtsa ro ma	right channel
rahasya	gsang ba	secret
rākṣasa	srin po	demon
rākṣasī	srin mo	demoness
rudhira	khrag	blood
retas	seminal fluid	rdzas
rocanā	gi wang	concretion
lakṣaṇa	mtshan nyid	characteristic, distinguishing mark
lalanā	rtsa rkyang ma	left channel
liṅga	ling ga	penis, sign
vākcakra	gsung gi 'khor lo	speech wheel
vāmācāra	g.yon pa'i kun spyod	heteropraxy
vāsanā	bag chags	habitual propensity
vikalpa	rnam par rtog pa	conception, conceptualization

Sanskrit	Tibetan	English
vigraha	lus	body
vidyā	rig pa, rig ma	spell, sacred knowledge, consort
vidhi	cho ga	procedure, rite
vināyaka	log 'dren, rnam par log 'dren	obstacle demon
vipaśyanā	lhag mthong	insight
viramānanda	dga' bral	joy of cessation
vīra	dpa' bo	hero
vetāla	ro langs	zombie
vyākhyātantra	bshad rgyud	explanatory tantra
vrata	brtul zhugs	observance
śaktika	nus pa	power
śamathā	zhi gnas	quiescence
śarīra	lus	body
śīla	mos pa	disposition
śukra	khu ba	semen
śubha	dge ba	auspicious
śmaśāna	dur khrod	charnel ground
śrāvaka	nyan thos	disciple
sattva	sems dpa'	(sentient) being, hero
samaya	dam tshig	commitment
samādhi	ting nge 'dzin	concentration
samāyoga	mnyam 'byor	unification
saṁkalpa	rnam par rtog pa	conception, conceptualization

Sanskrit	Tibetan	English
saṁkulikā	snum 'khur	cake
saṁpuṭa	kha sbyar ba	enveloping, intercourse, kiss
saṁyoga	yang dag 'byor	union
saṁvara	sdom pa	binding, sanctuary, vow, union
	bde mchog	supreme bliss
saṁsāra	'khor ba	cyclic existence
sarpa	sbrul	serpent
sahaja	lhan cig skyes pa	natural
sahajānanda	lhan cig skyes pa'i dga' ba	natural joy
sādhaka	sgrub pa po	adept
	sgrub byed	means of achieving
sādhana	sgrub byed	means of achievement, spiritual discipline
sādhya	bsgrub bya	victim, beneficiary
sāmanta	rgyal phran	vassal lord
siddha	grub pa	accomplished, achieved, perfected one
siddhi	dngos grub	accomplishment, power
sukha	bde ba	bliss, happiness
hṛdaya	snying po	essence
heruka	he ru ka, khrag 'thung ba	Heruka
homa	sbyin sreg	fire sacrifice

Tibetan–Sanskrit–English Glossary

Tibetan	Sanskrit	English
kla klo	mleccha	barbarian
klu	nāga	serpent deity
dka' thub	tapas	asceticism
sku	kāya	body
skye gnas	yoni	vulva, birth place
bskyed rim	utpattikrama	creation stage
kha ṭvāṁ ga	khaṭvāṅga	khatvanga staff
kha sbyar ba	saṁpuṭa	enveloping, intercourse, kiss
khu ba	śukra	semen
khrag	rakta	blood, uterine blood
	rajas	uterine blood
	rudhira	blood
khro bo	khrodha	fierce one
mkha' 'gro ma	ḍākinī	
mkha' spyod	khecara	flying, floating
mkha' spyod gnas, mkha' la 'gro ba'i gnas	khecarīpada	aerial state

Tibetan	Sanskrit	English
mkha' la rgyu ba	khecara	flying, floating
'khor ba	saṁsāra	cyclic existence
'khor lo sdom pa	cakrasaṁvara	"binding of the wheels"
'khor lo gsum	tricakra	triple wheel
'khor los sgyur ba	cakravartin	universal monarch
'khrul 'khor	yantra	magical diagram, yogic posture, war machine
gi wang	rocanā	concretion
go cha	kavaca	armor
grub pa	siddha	accomplished, achieved, perfected one
gleng gzhi	nidāna	narrative preface
dga' ba	ānanda	joy
dga' bral	viramānanda	joy of cessation
dge ba	śubha	auspicious
rgyal phran	sāmanta	vassal lord
rgyal ba	jina	victor
rgyud phyi ma	uttaratantra	appendix
sgrub pa po	sādhaka	adept
sgrub byed	sādhaka	means of achieving
	sādhana	means of achievement
bsgrub bya	sādhya	victim, beneficiary
dngos grub	siddhi	accomplishment, power
bcom ldan 'das	bhagavān	Blessed Lord
bcom ldan 'das ma	bhagavatī	Blessed Lady
chu srin	makara	sea monster

Tibetan	Sanskrit	English
cho ga	vidhi	procedure, rite
chos kyi dbyings	dharmadhātu	sphere of reality
chos kyi sku	dharmakāya	reality body
chos nyid	dharmatā	reality
chos 'byung ba	dharmodaya	reality source, vulva
mchog dga'	paramānanda	supreme joy
'chi ba	mṛtyu	death
'jig rten gsum	triloka, trailokya	triple world
nyan thos	śrāvaka	disciple
nye snying	upahṛdaya	quintessence
nye gnas	upapīṭha	subsidiary seat
nye ba'i dur khrod	upaśmaśāna	subsidiary charnel ground
nye ba'i zhing	upakṣetra	subsidiary field
nye bar 'dus pa	upamelāpaka	subsidiary meeting place
nyon mongs	kleśa	affliction
gnyis med	advaya	nondual
mnyam 'byor	samāyoga	unification
snying po	hṛdaya	essence
ting nge 'dzin	samādhi	concentration
gtum mo	caṇḍālī	fury fire
gtor ma	bali	sacrificial cake
ltas ngan	utpāta	omen
lto 'phye	uraga	serpent
lto 'phye chen po	mahoraga	great serpent
brda	cchomaka	sign

Tibetan	Sanskrit	English
brtul zhugs	vrata	observance
thabs	upāya	art, strategy
thugs kyi 'khor lo	cittacakra	mind wheel
dam tshig	samaya	commitment
dur khrod	śmaśāna	charnel ground
dus min 'chi	apamṛtyu	untimely death
de nyid	tattva	reality
dra ba	jāla	net, network
dri za	gandharva	celestial musician
gdon	graha	astral spirit
bdag nyid	ātman	self, nature, oneself
bdud	māra	devil, Death
bdud rtsi	amṛta	ambrosia
bde mchog	saṁvara	supreme bliss
bde ba	sukha	bliss, happiness
'dus pa	melāpaka	meeting place
sdug bsngal	duḥkha	dissatisfaction, suffering
sdom pa	saṁvara	binding, sanctuary, vow, union
nam mkhar rgyu	khecaratvaṁ	flight
nus pa	śaktika	power
gnas	pīṭha	seat
gnod sbyin	yakṣa	tree spirit
gnod sbyin mo	yakṣiṇī	dryad
rnam par rtog pa	vikalpa, saṁkalpa	conception, conceptualization

Tibetan	Sanskrit	English
rnam par mi rtog pa	nirvikalpa	nonconceptual
rnam par log 'dren	vināyaka	obstacle demon
rnal 'byor	yoga	union
rnal 'byor pa	yogin	
rnal 'byor bla med	niruttarayoga	unexcelled yoga
rnal 'byor ma	yoginī	
snum 'khur	saṁkulikā	cake
pra se na	prasena	divinatory image
dpa' bo	vīra	hero
spyod pa	caryā	conduct
spyod yul	gocara	experiential scope
sprul pa	nirmāṇa	emanation
sprul pa'i sku	nirmāṇakāya	emanation body
pha rgyud		father tantra
phen 'dogs	anugraha	benefit, benefiting
pho nya mo	dūtī	messenger
phyag rgya	mudrā	seal, insignia, gesture
phyag rgya ma	mudrā	seal consort
phyag rgya mo	mudrā	seal consort
phyag rgya chen po	mahāmudrā	great seal
phyag rgya'i lan	pratimudrā	countergesture
phyugs	paśu	beast, sacrificial victim
phra men ma	ḍākinī	
bag chags	vāsanā	habitual propensity
bum pa	kalaśa	vase

Tibetan	Sanskrit	English
byang chub sems	bodhicitta	awakening spirit
dbang bskur ba	abhiṣeka	consecration
sbyin sreg	homa	fire sacrifice
sbrul	sarpa	serpent
bha ga	bhaga	vulva
ma rgyud		mother tantra
man ngag	upadeśa	oral instruction
	āmnāya	esoteric instruction
mi dge ba	aśubha	inauspicious
mi rtog pa nyid	nirvikalpatvam	nonconceptuality
mi'am ci	kinnara	centaur
mu stegs	tīrthika	heretic
me tog dang ldan pa	puṣpavatī	menstruating
mos pa	śīla	disposition
dmar	rakta	vermilion
dmar po	rakta	red
btsun mo	yoṣit	lady
mtshan ma	cihna	sign
rtsa rkyang ma	lalanā	left channel
rtsa rgyud	mūlatantra	root tantra
rtsa dbu ma	avadhūti	central channel
rtsa ro ma	rasanā	right channel
tshangs spyod	brahmacārya	chastity
tshar gcod	nigraha	destroying
tshogs kyi 'khor lo	gaṇacakra	tantric feast

TIBETAN	SANSKRIT	ENGLISH
mtshan nyid	lakṣaṇa	characteristic, distinguishing mark
rdzas	retas	seminal fluid
rdzogs rim	niṣpannakrama	perfection stage
zhi gnas	śamathā	quiescence
zhing	kṣetra	field
yan lag	aṅga	limb
yang dag 'byor	saṁyoga	union
yab		[male] partner
yab yum		partners
yi dags	preta	ghost, dead person
yum		[female] partner
ye shes	jñāna	gnosis
ye shes sems dpa'	jñānasattva	gnosis hero
yon	dakṣiṇā	fee
rang bzhin	prakṛti	nature
rig pa	vidyā	spell, sacred knowledge
rig ma	vidyā	spell consort
rigs	kula	clan
rigs ldan	kulikā	clanswoman
ro gcig	ekarasa	experiential unity
ro langs	vetāla	zombie
las	karma	ritual action
ling ga	liṅga	penis, sign
lus	aṅga, kāya, gātra, deha, mūrti, vigraha, śarīra	body

Tibetan	Sanskrit	English
log 'dren	vināyaka	obstacle demon
sha za	pīśāca	goblin
shes pa	jñāna	knowledge
shes rab	prajñā	wisdom
shes rab ma	prajñā	wisdom consort
bshad rgyud	vyākhyātantra	explanatory tantra
sa bon	bīja	seed syllable
sems dpa'	sattva	(sentient) being, hero
srin po	rākṣasa	demon
srin mo	rākṣasī	demoness
srog	prāṇa	life force
gsang ba	guhya, rahasya	secret
gsung gi 'khor lo	vākcakra	speech wheel
bsam gtan	dhyāna	meditation, meditative state
lha min	asura, dānava	titan
lhag mthong	vipaśyanā	insight
lhan cig skyes pa	sahaja	natural
lhan cig skyes pa'i dga' ba	sahajānanda	natural joy

Selected Bibliographies
Indian and Tibetan Texts

Abhayākaragupta. *Sheaf of Esoteric Instructions* (*Āmnāyamañjarī, man ngag gi snye ma*) (AM). *Śrīsaṁpuṭatantrarājaṭīkāmnāyamañjarī-nāma, dpal yang dag par sbyor ba'i rgyud kyi rgyal po'i rgya cher 'grel pa man ngag gi snye ma zhes bya ba*. Tōh. 1198, D rgyud 'grel vol. cha, 1b–316a.

Accomplished Solitary Hero (*Siddhaikavīra-mahātantrarājā-nāma, dpa' bo gcig bu grub pa zhes bya ba'i rgyud kyi rgyal po chen po*). Tōh. 544, D rgyud 'bum vol. pa, 1b–13a.

Adamantine Terror Tantra (*Śrī-vajrabhairava-kalpa-tantrarājā, dpal rdo rje 'jigs byed kyi rtog pa'i rgyud kyi rgyal po*). Tōh. 470, D rgyud 'bum vol. ja, 167b–73b.

Asaṅga. *Bodhisattva Stages* (*Yogacāryābhūmau-bodhisattvabhūmi, rnal 'byor spyod pa'i sa las byang chub sems dpa'i sa*). Tōh. 4037, D sems tsam vol. wi, 1b–213a.

Asaṅga/Maitreyanātha. *Ornament of the Universal Vehicle Sutras* (*Mahāyānasūtrālaṁkāra-nāma-kārikā, theg pa chen po mdo sde'i rgyan zhes bya ba'i tshig le'ur byas pa*). Tōh. 4020, D sems tsam vol. phi, 1b–39a.

*Avalokitavrata (spyan ras gzigs brtul zhugs). *Commentary on the Lamp of Wisdom* (*Prajñāpradīpaṭīkā, shes rab sgrol ma rgya cher 'grel pa*). Tōh. 3859. D *shes phyin* vol. wa, 1b–287a.

Bhavabhaṭṭa. *Commentary on the Shrī Vajraḍāka, Great King of Tantras* (*Śrīvajraḍāki-nāma-mahātantrarājasya-vivṛtti, rgyud kyi rgyal po chen po dpal rdo rje mkha' 'gro zhes bya ba'i rnam par bshad pa*) (VV). Tōh. 1415, D rgyud 'grel vol. tsha, 1–208b.

———. *Detailed Commentary on the Chakrasaṁvara* (*Cakrasaṁvara-vivṛtti, dpal 'khor lo sdom pa'i dka' 'grel*) (CV). Tōh. 1403, D rgyud 'grel vol. ba, 141a–246b. Sanskrit and Tibetan edited in Pandey 2002.

———. *Explanatory Exposition on the Shrī Hevajra [Tantra]* (*Śrīhevajra-vyākhyāvivaraṇa-nāma, dpal dgyes pa'i rdo rje'i rnam bshad rnam par 'grel pa zhes bya ba*). Tōh. 1182, D rgyud 'grel vol. ka, 173b–275a.

Bhavyakīrti. *Heroes' Delight, a Commentary on the Shrī Chakrasaṁvara* (*Śrīcakrasaṁvarapañjikā-śūramanojñā-nāma, dpal 'khor lo sdoṃ pa'i dka' 'grel dpa' bo'i yid du 'ong ba zhes bya ba*) (BC). Tōh. 1405, D rgyud 'grel vol. ma, 1–41a.

Buddhashrījñānapāda. *Direct Speech [of Mañjushrī]* (*Dvikramatattva-bhāvana-nāma-mukhāgama, rim pa gnyis pa'i de kho na nyid bsgom pa zhes bya ba'i zhal lung*). Tōh. 1853, D rgyud 'bum vol. di, 1b–17b.

Butön Rinchendrup. *Illumination of the Hidden Reality* (*bde mchog rtsa rgyud kyi rnam bshad gsang ba'i de kho na nyid gsal bar byed pa*) (NS). In *The Collected Works of Bu-ston*, ed. Lokesh Chandra. New Delhi: International Academy of Indian Culture, 1966. vol. cha, pp. 141–718.

Chakrasaṁvara Tantra (*Cakrasaṁvara Tantra, 'khor lo sdom pa'i rgyud*) (CT). Tōh. 368. Sanskrit and Tibetan edited in Gray 2012.

Compendium of Reality (*Sarvatathāgatatattvasaṁgraha-nāma-mahāyāna-sūtra, de bzhin gshegs pa thams cad kyi de kho na nyid bsdus pa zhes bya ba theg pa chen po'i mdo*). Tōh. 479, D rgyud 'bum vol. nya, 1b–142a (vol. 84).

Complete Awakening of Vairochana (*Mahāvairocanābhisambodhi-vikurvatī-adhiṣṭhāna-vaipulya-sūtra-indrarājā-nāma-dharmaparyāya, rnam par snang mdzad chen po mngon par rdzogs par byang chub pa rnam par sprul pa byin gyis rlob pa shin tu rgyas pa mdo sde'i dbang po'i rgyal po zhes bya ba'i chos kyi rnam grangs*). Tōh. 494, D rgyud 'bum vol. tha, 151b–260a.

Conduct of the Yoginīs [Tantra] (*Yoginīsaṁcāra, rnal 'byor ma'i kun tu spyod pa*) (YS). Tōh. 375, D rgyud 'bum vol. ga, 34a–44b. Sanskrit and Tibetan edited in Pandey 1998.

Ḍākārṇava-mahāyoginītantrarāja, mkha' 'gro rgya mtsho rnal 'byor ma'i rgyud kyi rgyal po chen po (DA). Tōh. 372, D rgyud 'bum, vol. kha, 137a–264b.

Ḍākinīs' Vajra Pavillion (*Ḍākinīvajrapañjara, mkha' 'gro ma rdo rje gur*) (DV) (*Āryaḍākinīvajrapañjara-mahātantrarājakalpa, 'phags pa mkha' 'gro ma rdo rje gur zhes bya ba'i rgyud kyi rgyal po chen po*). Tōh. 419, D rgyud 'bum vol. nga, 30a–65b.

Devagupta. *Storehouse for Shrī Chakrasaṁvara Practice Manuals, a Commentary* (*Śrīcakrasaṃvarasādhanasarvaśālā-nāma-ṭīkā, dpal 'khor lo sdom pa'i sgrub thabs gnas thams cad rgya cher 'grel pa*) (SS). Tōh. 1407, D vol. ma, 69a–156b.

Discourse Appendix Tantra (*Abhidhānottara-Tantra, mngon par brjod pa'i rgyud bla ma*)

(AU) Tōh. 369, D rgyud 'bum vol. ka, 247a–370a.

(H) Institute for Advanced Studies of World Religions (Carmel, NY) microfiche no. MBB-I-100. Incomplete; consisted of a total 194 folia, 6 of which are missing. Written on palm leaves in Bhujimol script by the scribe Paramānanda. Dated N. S. 258, 1138 ce.

(I) Institute for Advanced Studies of World Religions (Carmel, NY) microfiche no. MBB-I-26. Consists of 92 folia on Nepali paper in Nevārī script. Dated N. S. 863, 1743 ce.

(J) A late ms. of 160 folia in Devanāgarī on Nepali paper, reproduced in Lokesh Chandra, ed. Abhidhānottara-Tantra: A Sanskrit Manuscript from Nepal. Śata-piṭaka series vol. 263. New Delhi: Sharada Rani, 1981.

Durjayachandra. *Jewel Assembly, a Commentary [on the Chakrasaṁvara]* (*Ratnagaṇa-nāma-pañjikā, rin po che'i tshogs kyi dka' 'grel zhes bya ba*) (RG). Tōh. 1404, D rgyud 'grel vol. ba, 246b–315a.

Esoteric Communion Tantra (*Guhyasamāja Tantra, gsang ba 'dus pa'i rgyud*) (GT) (*Sarvatathāgatakāyavākcittarahasya-guhyasamāja-nāma-mahākalparāja, de bzhin gshegs pa thams cad kyi sku gsung thugs kyi gsang chen gsang ba 'dus pa zhes bya ba brtag pa'i rgyal po chen po*). Tōh. 442, 443. D rgyud 'bum vol. ca, 90a–157b. Sanskrit edited in Matsunaga 1978.

Extensive Play Sutra (*Ārya-lalitavistara-nāma-mahāyāna-sūtra, 'phags pa rgya cher rol pa zhes bya ba theg pa chen po'i mdo*). Tōh. 95, mdo sde vol. kha, 1b–216b.

Ghaṇṭapā. See Vajraghaṇṭa.

Glorious Primal Supreme (*Śrī-paramādya-nāma-mahāyāna-kalparājā, dpal mchog dang po zhes bya ba theg pa chen po'i rtog pa'i rgyal po*). Tōh. 487, D rgyud 'bum vol. ta, 150b–73a.

Gnosis Drop Tantra (*Jñānatilaka-yoginītantrarāja-paramamahādbhuta, dpal ye shes thig le rnal 'byor ma'i rgyud kyi rgyal po chen po mchog tu rmad du byung ba*). Tōh. 422, D rgyud 'bum vol. nga, 96b–136b.

Great Seal Drop (*Mahāmudrātilaka, dpal phyag rgya chen po'i thig le*) (MT) (*Śrīmahāmudrātilakaṁ-nāma-mahāyoginī-tantrarāja-adhipati, dpal phyag rgya chen po'i thig le zhes bya ba rnal 'byor ma chen mo'i rgyud kyi rgyal po mnga' bdag*). Tōh. 420, D rgyud-'bum, vol. nga, 66a–90b.

Haribhadra. *Splendid Ornament of Realization, a Commentary on the Noble Eight-thousand-stanza Perfection of Wisdom* (*Ārya-Aṣṭasāhasrikā-prajñāpāramitāvyākhyā-abhisamayālaṁkārāloka-nāma, 'phags pa shes rab kyi pha rol tu phyin pa brgyad stong pa'i bshad pa mngon par rtogs pa'i rgyan gyi snang ba*). Tōh. 3791, D shes phyin vol. cha, 1bz–341a.

Hevajra-tantrarājā, kye'i rdo rje zhes bya ba rgyud kyi rgyal po (HT). Tōh. 417, D rgyud 'bum vol. nga, 1b–30a. Sanskrit and Tibetan edited in Snellgrove 1959.

Indrabhūti. *Saṁvara Compendium on the Shrī Chakrasaṁvara King of Tantras, a Commentary* (*Śrīcakrasaṁvaratantrarāja-saṁvarasamuccaya-nāma-vṛtti, dpal 'khor lo sdom pa'i rgyud kyi rgyal po bde mchog bsdus pa zhes bya ba'i rnam par bshad pa*) (IC). Tōh. 1413, D rgyud 'grel vol. tsa, 1a–119b.

Jayabhadra. *Commentary on the Chakrasaṁvara* (*Cakrasaṁvarapañjikā, dpal 'khor lo sdom pa'i rtsa ba'i rgyud kyi dka' 'grel*) (CP). Tōh. 1406, D rgyud 'grel vol. ma, 41a–69a. Sanskrit edited in Sugiki 2001.

Jñānabodhi. *Summary on Commitments for Beginners* (*Prathamakarma-samayasūtrasaṁgraha, las dang po pa'i dam tshig mdor bsdus pa*). Tōh. 3726, D rgyud 'grel vol. tshu, 49b–54b.

Kambala. *Treasury of Practice Manuals, a Commentary on the Shrī Chakra-saṁvara* (*Sādhananidhi-śrīcakrasaṁvara-nāma-pañjikā, dpal 'khor lo sdom pa'i dka' 'grel sgrub pa'i thabs kyi gleng gzhi zhes bya ba*)

(K) National Archives of Nepal, ms. no. 4–122, *bauddhatantra* 87. Mf. B31/20, Moriguchi #610. This work consists of 73 palm leaf folia, in Newārī script. No date. Note that it is catalogued under the title *Herukāvidhāna*.

(SN) Tōh. 1401, D rgyud 'grel vol. ba, 1b–78a; PTT. 2118, vol. 48, pp. 173.5–207.5.

Kambalāmbara. *Commentary on the Realization of Shrī Chakrasaṁvara* (*Śrīcakrasaṁvarābhisamayaṭīkā*, *dpal 'khor lo bde mchog gi mngon par rtogs pa'i 'grel pa*). PTT. 4661, vol. 82, pp. 90.1–98.1.

Kāṇha. *Jewel Rosary of Yoga, a Commentary on Hevajra* (*Yogaratnamālā-nāma-hevajrapañjikā*, *dgyes pa'i rdo rje'i dka' 'grel rin po che'i phreng ba zhes bya ba*). Tōh. 1183, D rgyud 'grel vol. kha, 1b–61a. Sanskrit edited in Snellgrove 2010, 103–59.

———. *Mandala Rites of the Glorious Lord Chakrasaṁvara* (*Bhagavacchrī-cakrasaṁvaramaṇḍalavidhi*, *bcom ldan 'das dpal bde mchog 'khor lo'i dkyil 'khor gyi cho ga*). Tōh. 1446, D rgyud 'grel vol. wa, 276b–92b.

———. *Meditation Manual on the Shrī Chakrasaṁvara* (*Śrīcakrasaṁvara-sādhana*, *dpal 'khor lo sdom pa zhes bya ba'i sgrub thabs*). Tōh. 1445, D rgyud 'grel vol. wa, 272b–76b.

———. *Source for Recollection, a Commentary on Hevajra* (*Hevajra-nāma-mahātantrarāja-dvikalpamāyāpañjikā-smṛtinipāda*, *rgyud kyi rgyal po chen po dgyes pa'i rdo rje zhes bya ba sgyu ma brtag pa gnyis pa'i dka' 'grel dran pa'i 'byung gnas*). Tōh. 1187. D rgyud 'grel vol. ga, 146b–94a.

Kiss of the Four Yoginīs Tantra (*Caturyoginīsaṁpuṭatantra*, *rnal 'byor ma bzhi'i kha sbyor gyi rgyud*). Tōh. 376, D rgyud 'bum vol. ga, 44b–52b.

Kiss Tantra (*Saṁpuṭa Tantra*, *yang dag par sbyor ba zhes bya ba'i rgyud*)

(ST) Tōh. 381, D rgyud 'bum vol. ga, 73b–158b; PTT. 26, vol. 2, pp. 245.5–80.1.

(L) Microfiche scan of Sanskrit manuscript; Institute for Advanced Studies of World Religions (Carmel, NY) microfiche no. MBB-I-17.

Sanskrit partially edited in Skorupski 1996 and Sugiki 2003.

Lūipa. *The Glorious Lord's Realization* (*Śrībhagavad-abhisamaya*, *dpal bcom ldan 'das mngon par rtogs pa*). Tōh. 1427, D rgyud 'grel vol. wa, 186b–93a.

Nāgārjuna. *Crushing the Categories* (*Vaidalya-nāma-prakaraṇa*, *zhib mo rnam par 'thag pa zhes bya ba'i rab tu byed pa*). Tōh. 3830, D dbu ma vol. tsa, 99b–110a.

———. *Jewel Rosary, a Letter to the King* (*Rājaparikathāratnamālā*, *rgyal po la gtam bya ba rin po che'i phreng ba*). Tōh. 4158, D spring yig vol. ge, 107a–26a.

Network of Ḍākinīs, Unification of all Buddhas Tantra (*Sarvabuddha-samāyoga-ḍākinījālasaṁvara-nāma-uttaratantra, dpal sangs rgyas thams cad dang mnyam par sbyor ba mkha' 'gro ma sgyu ma bde ba'i mchog ces bya ba'i rgyud phyi ma*) (JS). Tōh. 366, D rgyud 'bum vol. ka, 151a–93a.

Origin of Heruka (*Herukābhyudaya, khrag 'thung mngon par 'byung ba*) (HA). Tōh. 374, D rgyud 'bum vol. ga, 1b–33b.

Origin of Saṁvara Tantra (*Saṁvarodaya Tantra, bde mchog 'byung ba'i rgyud*)

(SU) Tōh. 373, D rgyud 'bum vol. kha, 265a–311a.

(M) Microfiche scan of Sanskrit manuscript; Institute for Advanced Studies of World Religions (Carmel, NY) microfiche no. MBB-II-89. This manuscript is entitled *Herukābhidhāna-mahātantrarāja*.

Sanskrit and Tibetan partially edited in Tsuda 1974.

Ornament of the Glorious Vajra Essence, Great King of Tantras (*Śrīvajra-maṇḍālaṁkara-nāma-mahātantrarāja, dpal rdo rje snying po rgyan ces bya ba'i rgyud kyi rgyal po chen po*). Lhasa Kangyur 459, rgyud 'bum vol. nya, 1b–120b. Tōh. 490, D rgyud 'bum vol. tha, 1b–82a.

Padmāṅkuravajra. *Commentary on the Hevajra Tantra* (**Hevajra-nāma-tantrarājaṭīkā, kye'i rdo rje zhes bya ba'i rgyud kyi rgyal po'i 'grel pa*). Tōh. 1188. D rgyud 'grel vol. ga, 194b–220b.

Padmavajra. *Esoteric Accomplishment* (*Guhyasiddhi, dpal gsang ba grub pa*). Tōh. 2217, D rgyud 'grel vol. wi, 1b–28b. Sanskrit and Tibetan edited in Samdhong and Dwivedi 1988, 5–62, 1–107.

Prajñārakṣhita. *Glorious Realization, a Commentary [on Luipa's Chakrasaṁvara Sādhana]* (*Śrī-abhisamaya-nāma-pañjikā, dpal mngon par rtogs pa zhes bya ba'i dka' 'grel*). Tōh. 1465, D rgyud 'grel vol. zha, 34a–45b.

Ratnākarashānti. String of Pearls, a Commentary on the Shrī Hevajra (*Śrīhevajrapañjikā-nāma-muktikāvali*, dpal dgyes pa'i rdo rje'i dka' 'grel mu tig phreng ba zhes bya ba). Tōh. 1189. D rgyud 'grel vol. ga, 221a–97a.

Ratnarakṣhita. *The Lotus, a Commentary on the Glorious Origin of Saṁvara, King of Tantras* (*Śrīsaṁvarodayamahātantrarāja-padminī-nāma-pañjikā, dpal sdom pa 'byung ba'i rgyud kyi rgyal po chen po'i dka' 'grel padma can zhes bya ba*). Tōh. 1420, D rgyud 'grel vol. wa, 1b–101b.

Rigi Ārali Tantra (*Rigi-ārali-tantrarāja-nāma, ri gi A ra li'i rgyud kyi rgyal po zhes bya ba*). Tōh. 427, D rgyud 'bum vol. nga, 176a–80b.

Sachen Kunga Nyingpo. *Pearl Garland* (*dpal 'khor lo bde mchog gi rtsa ba'i rgyud kyi ṭīka mu tig phreng ba*) (PG). In *The Complete Works of the Great Masters of the Sa Skya Sect of the Tibetan Buddhism. Vol. 1. The Complete Works of Kun dga' snying po*. bSod nams rgya mtsho, compiler. Tokyo: The Toyo Bunko, 1968, 288.3–380.3.

Saraha. *Treasury of Songs* (*Dohakoṣagīti, do ha mdzod kyi glu*). Tōh. 2224, D rgyud 'grel vol. wi, 70b–77a.

*Shāśvatavajra (rtag pa'i rdo rje). *Śrītattvaviśada-nāma-śrīsaṁvaravṛtti, dpal sdom pa'i 'grel pa dpal de kho na nyid mkhas pa zhes bya ba*. Tōh. 1410, D rgyud 'grel vol. ma, 253a–352a.

Secret Moon Drop (*Candraguhyatilaka, zla gsang thig le*) (*Śrīcandraguhyatilaka-nāma-mahātantrarāja, dpal zla gsang thig le zhes bya ba rgyud kyi rgyal po chen po*). Tōh. 477, rgyud 'bum vol. ja, 247b–303.

Sumatikīrti. *Intended Import of the Chapters of the Concise Saṁvara Tantra* (*Laghusaṁvaratantrapaṭalābhisandhi, sdom pa'i rgyud chung ngu'i mtshams sbyor*) (LA). Tōh. 1411, D vol. ma, 352a–53a; PTT. 2127, Q vol. 49, pp. 161.4–62.2.

Taming of the Ghosts Tantra (*Bhūtaḍāmara-mahātantrarājā-nāma, 'byung po 'dul ba zhes bya ba'i rgyud kyi rgyal po chen po*). Tōh. 747, D rgyud 'bum vol. dza, 238a–63a.

Tathāgatarakṣhita. *Commentary on the Conduct of the Yoginīs* (*Yoginīsaṁcāranibandha, rnal 'byor ma kun tu spyod pa'i bshad sbyar*). Tōh. 1422, D rgyud 'grel vol. wa, 120a–39a. Sanskrit edited in Pandey 1998.

———. *Twofold Commentary* (*Ubhayanibandha, gnyis ka'i bshad sbyar*) (UN). Tōh. 1409. D rgyud 'grel vol. ma, 207a–53a.

Treasury of Secrets Tantra (*Guhyakośa, gsang ba'i mdzod*). This may be an alternate name, or perhaps even the correct name, of the *Guhyagarbha* (*gsang ba'i snying po*), Tōh. 832. See note 171 above.

Tsong Khapa. *rje tsong kha pa'i gsung 'bum*. sku 'bum par ma. 19 vols. TBRC work number 22272.

———. *bcom ldan 'das dpal 'khor lo bde mchog gi mngon par rtogs pa'i rgya cher bshad pa 'dod pa 'jo ba*, vol. ta. (*Wish-granting Cow, an Extensive Commentary on the Glorious Lord Chakrasaṁvara's Realization*.)

———. *bde mchog bsdus pa'i rgyud kyi rgya cher bshad pa sbas pa'i don kun gsal ba* (KS).

(B) TBRC scan of the *bla brang bkra shis 'khyil* print of KS; vol. nya, *sbas don* 1a–248a; pp. 485–979. TBRC work number W22273.

(D) TBRC scan of the *de dge dgon chen* print of KS; vol. nya, *sbas don* 1a–254a; pp. 407–909. TBRC work number W22274.

(Q) The Otani reprint of KS in the Tibetan Tripitaka, Beijing edition. *Btsoṅ-kha-pa Bkaḥ-ḥbum* vol. da, 1a–229b. Photo-reproduced in *The Tibetan Tripitaka: Peking Edition*, ed. Daisetz T. Suzuki, 168 vols. Tokyo-Kyoto: Tibetan Tripitaka Research Institute, 1955–1961. PTT 6157, vol. 157, pp. 2.1–94.1.

(T) *bkra shis lhun po par rnying* edition of KS. Photographic reprint. Delhi: Ngawang Gelek Demo, 1980, vol. nya, *sbas don* 1a–251b.

———. *bde mchog rim lnga'i bshad pa sbas don lta ba'i mig rnam par 'byed pa*, vol. tha. (*Exegesis that is the Eye that Sees the Hidden Meaning Stated in the Saṁvara Five Stages*.)

———. *dpal 'khor lo bde mchog lūipa'i mngon rtogs ngag 'don gyi cho ga'i rim pa*. vol. ta. (*Stages of the Rites for Reciting Lūipa's Glorious Chakrasaṁvara Realization*.)

———. *gsang 'dus rim lnga'i rab tu gsal ba'i sgron me*, vol. ja.

Vajra Rosary Tantra (*Vajramālā, rdo rje phreng ba*). (*Śrīvajramālābhidhā namahāyogatantra-sarvatantrahṛdaya-rahasyavibhaṅga, rnal 'byor ma chen mo'i rgyud dpal rdo rje phreng ba mngon par brjod pa rgyud thams cad kyi snying po gsang ba rnam par phye ba*). Tōh. 445, D rgyud 'bum vol. ca, 208a–77b.

Vajraḍāka Tantra, rdo rje mkha' 'gro'i rgyud. Śrīvajraḍāka-nāma-mahātantrarāja, rgyud kyi rgyal po chen po dpal rdo rje mkha' 'gro zhes bya ba (VD). Tōh. 370, D rgyud-'bum vol. kha, 1b–125a. Sanskrit partially edited in Sugiki 2002 and 2003.

Vajraghaṇṭa. *Five Stages of Shrī Chakrasaṁvara* (*Śrīcakrasaṁvarapañcakrama, dpal 'khor lo sdom pa'i rim pa lnga pa*). Tōh. 1433, D rgyud 'grel vol. wa, 224b–27a.

Vasubandhu. *Ornament of the [Universal Vehicle] Sutras Commentary* (*Sūtrālaṁkārabhāṣya, mdo sde'i rgyan gyi bshad pa*). Tōh. 4026, D sems tsam vol. phi, 129b1-206a7; PTT. 5527, Q vol. 108, pp. 56-117. Edited in Jamspal, et al. 2004.

Vīravajra. *Abode of Universal Virtue, a Commentary [on the Chakrasaṁvara Tantra]* (*Samantaguṇaśālinī-nāma-ṭīkā, yon tan ma lus pa'i gnas zhes bya ba'i 'grel pa*) (SG). Tōh. 1408, D rgyud 'grel vol. ma, 156b–207a.

———. *Illumination of the Meaning of the Words, a Commentary on the Shrī Saṁvara Root Tantra* (*Padārthaprakāśikā-nāma-śrīsaṁvaramūlatantraṭīkā, dpal bde mchog gi rgya cher bshad pa tshig don rab tu gsal ba zhes bya ba*) (PD). Tōh. 1412, D rgyud 'grel vol. ma, 353b–450a.

Vṛddhakāyastha. *Very Clear Commentary on the Kiss [Tantra]* (*Suviśadasampuṭaṭīkā, rab tu gsal ba'i kha sbyor gyi rgya cher 'grel pa*). Tōh. 1190. D rgyud 'grel vol. nga, 1b–236a.

Editions and Secondary Sources

Bagchi, S., ed. 1970. *Mahāyāna-Sūtrālakāra of Asaṅga*. Buddhist Sanskrit Texts no. 13. Darbhanga: The Mithila Institute.

Beyer, Stephan. 1973. *The Cult of Tārā: Magic and Ritual in Tibet*. Los Angeles: University of California Press.

Davidson, Ronald M. 2006. "The Problem of Secrecy in Indian Tantric Buddhism." In *The Culture of Secrecy in Japanese Religion*, edited by Bernhard Scheid and Mark Teeuwen, 60–77. London: Routledge.

Dayal, Har. 1932. *The Bodhisattva Doctrine in Buddhist Sanskrit Literature*. London: Routledge & Kegan Paul. Reprint, Delhi: Motilal Banarsidass, 1970.

Dutt, Nalinnaksa, ed. *Bodhisattvabhūmi, Being the XVth Section of Asangapada's Yogacarabhumi*. Tibetan Sanskrit Works Series VII. Patna: K. P. Jayaswal Research Institute, 1966.

Gray, David B. 2001. "On Supreme Bliss: A Study of the History and Interpretation of the Cakrasamvara Tantra." PhD diss., Columbia University.

———. 2007. *The Cakrasamvara Tantra: A Study and Annotated Translation*. New York: American Institute of Buddhist Studies.

———. 2010. "On the Very Idea of a Tantric Canon: Myth, Politics, and the Formation of the Bka' 'gyur." Journal of the International Association of Tibetan Studies, no. 5 (December 2009; published in October 2010): 1–37.

———. 2012. *The Cakrasamvara Tantra: Editions of the Sanskrit and Tibetan Texts*. New York: American Institute of Buddhist Studies.

———. 2017. *Illumination of the Hidden Meaning: Maṇḍala, Mantra, and the Cult of the Yoginīs, Chapters 1–24*. New York: American Institute of Buddhist Studies.

Jackson, Roger R. 2004. *Tantric Treasures: Three Collections of Mystical Verse from Buddhist India*. Oxford: Oxford University Press.

Jamspal, L., J. Wilson, L. Zwilling, M. Sweet, and R. Thurman, trans. *The Universal Vehicle Discourse Literature, Mahāyānasūtrālaṁkāra. By Maitreyanātha/Āryāsaṅga*. New York: American Institure of Budhhist Studies, 2004.

Matsunaga, Yukei. 1978. *The Guhyasamāja Tantra*. Osaka: Toho Shuppan.

Pandey, Janardan Shastri. 1998. *Yoginīsaṁcāratantram with Nibandha of Tathāgatarakṣita and Upadeśānusāriṇīvyākhyā of Alakakaśala*. Rare Buddhist Texts Series no. 21. Sarnath: Central Institute of Higher Tibetan Studies.

———. 2002. *Śrīherukābhidhānam Cakrasaṁvaratantram with the Vivṛti Commentary of Bhavabhaṭṭa*. Rare Buddhist Texts Series no. 26. Sarnath: Central Institute of Higher Tibetan Studies, 2 vols.

Rigzin, Tsepak. 1986. *Tibetan-English Dictionary of Buddhist Terminology*. Dharamsala: Library of Tibetan Works and Archives.

Samdhong Rinpoche and Vrajvallabh Dwivedi. 1988. *Guhyādi-Aṣṭasiddhi-Saṅgraha*. Rare Buddhist Text Series 1. Sarnath, Varanasi: Central Institute of Higher Tibetan Studies.

Sanderson, Alexis. 2009. "The Śaiva Age: The Rise and Dominance of Śaivism During the Early Medieval Period." In *Genesis and Development of Tantrism*, edited by Shingo EINOO, 41–349. Tokyo: Institute of Oriental Culture, University of Tokyo.

Schaeffer, Kurtis R. 2005. *Dreaming the Great Brahmin: Tibetan Traditions of the Buddhist Poet Saint Saraha*. Oxford: Oxford University Press.

Snellgrove, David L. 1959. *The Hevajra Tantra: A Critical Study*. London: Oxford University Press, 2 vols.

Sugiki, Tsunehiko. 2001. "On the Making of the *Śrīcakrasaṁvaratantra*, with a Critical Sanskrit Text of Jayabhadra's *Śrīcakrasaṁvarapañjikā*." *Chisan Gakuho* (智山学報) 50: 91–141.

———. 2002. "A Critical Study of the Vajraḍākamahātantrarāja (I): Chapter 1 and 42." *Chisan Gakuho* (智山学報) 51: 81–115.

———. 2003. "A Critical Study of the Vajraḍākamahātantrarāja (II): Sacred Districts and Practices Concerned." *Chisan Gakuho* (智山学報) 52: 53–106.

Suzuki, Daisetz T., ed. *The Tibetan Tripitaka: Peking Edition*. 168 vols. Tokyo-Kyoto: Tibetan Tripitaka Research Institute, 1955–1961.

Thurman, Robert A.F. 1976. *The Holy Teaching of Vimalakīrti, A Mahāyāna Scripture*. University Park: Pennsylvania State University Press.

Tsuda, Shiníchi. 1974. *The Saṁvarodaya-Tantra: Selected Chapters*. Tokyo: The Hokuseido Press.

Ui, Hakuju, et al. 1934. *A Complete Catalogue of Tibetan Buddhist Canons (Bkaḥ-ḥgyur and Bstan-ḥgyur)*. Sendai: Tōhoku Imperial University.

Wedemeyer, Christian K. 2007. *Āryadeva's Lamp That Integrates the Practices (Caryāmelāpakapradīpa): The Gradual Path of Vajrayāna Buddhism according to the Esoteric Community Noble Tradition*. New York: American Institute of Buddhist Studies.

Indexes

Index of Canonical Texts Cited

Index of Canonical Authors Cited

Indian Authors

Abhayākaragupta, 160, 272, 276, 280, 281, 282, 284, 285

Asaṅga, 8, 42, 85, 303

Avalokitavrata, 198

Bhavabhaṭṭa, 7, 15, 17, 18, 19, 20, 21, 22, 23, 24, 26, 27, 28, 30, 32, 33, 34, 35, 37, 53, 54, 56, 57, 66, 69, 70, 85, 114, 115, 117, 120, 121, 124, 143, 144, 146, 147, 149, 150, 171, 178, 183, 196, 197, 210, 211, 214, 218, 227, 230, 238, 242, 243, 252, 256, 265, 269, 270, 272, 291, 301, 306

Bhavyakīrti, 28, 34, 35, 49, 53, 72, 100, 102, 105, 107, 108, 109, 112, 117, 118, 121, 125, 126, 127, 158, 160, 161, 163, 164, 171, 174, 186, 191, 200, 201, 202, 212, 228, 229

Buddhashrījñānapāda, 126

Devagupta, 26, 31, 32, 36, 52, 57, 68, 71, 72, 91, 93, 94, 117, 118, 120, 124, 126, 161, 199, 200, 208, 233, 290, 291

Durjayachandra, 12, 29, 37, 54, 55, 100, 101, 105, 121, 125, 127, 139, 140, 144, 150, 222, 227, 269, 292, 298, 299

Haribhadra, 8, 274

Indrabhūti, 60

Jayabhadra, 27, 33, 34, 35, 36, 37, 38, 39, 42, 48, 49, 51, 53, 54, 55, 70, 71, 72, 85, 89, 97, 100, 102, 106, 108, 109, 113, 117, 118, 127, 133, 143, 147, 164, 171, 174, 178, 191, 200, 201, 202, 212, 214, 226, 228, 229, 244, 268. *See also* Koṅkanapa

Jñānabodhi, 172

Kambalāmbara, 60, 61, 101, 176

Kāṇha (Kṛiṣhṇāchārya), xii, 7, 118, 119, 120, 121, 122, 149, 153, 272, 292, 296, 297, 301, 309, 310

Koṅkanapa, 34, 36, 37, 38, 117, 118, 127, 133, 174, 191. *See also* Jayabhadra

Kṛiṣhṇāchārya. *See* Kāṇha (Kṛiṣhṇāchārya)

Laṅka. *See* Jayabhadra; Koṅkanapa

Lūipa, xii, 7, 61, 101, 109, 121, 122, 156, 277, 295, 296, 297, 300, 301, 309, 310

Nāgārjuna, 107, 118, 303

Nāropa, xii, 5, 53, 138, 158, 189, 308

Padmākaravarma, 307, 308

Padmāṅkuravajra, 272

Padmavajra, 44

Prajñākīrti, 54

Prajñārakṣhita, 156

Ratnākarashānti, 272, 274

Ratnarakṣhita, 62

Saraha, 206, 207

Sumatikīrti, 6, 8, 27, 98, 119, 147, 175, 308

Sūryagupta, 8, 308

Tathāgatarakṣhita, 117, 146, 157, 158, 211, 218, 229, 231, 260, 261, 292, 293, 294, 295, 299, 301, 305

Vajraghaṇṭa (Ghaṇṭapāda), xii, 7, 118, 119, 141, 157, 160, 277, 296, 297, 301, 309, 310

Vasubandhu, 42, 274

Vīravajra, 33, 35, 38, 39, 48, 49, 53, 55, 106, 108, 109, 113, 114, 117, 118, 125, 133, 171, 186, 191, 211, 212, 214, 218, 226, 228, 229, 235, 265, 293, 295

Vṛddhakāyastha, 182

Tibetan Authors

General Index

A

accomplishment(s) (siddhi). *See also* power(s) (siddhi)
action tantra(s), 36, 69, 290, 305
adamantine songs (vajragīta), 67, 68
Akṣhobhya Buddha, 47, 259
alchemy, 38, 77, 116
alcohol, 57, 59, 67, 83, 104, 196, 264, 267. *See also* intoxicant(s)/intoxication; liquor
ambrosia(s), 47, 57, 89, 149, 199, 218, 265, 294, 296. *See also* charu oblation(s)
  five, 51, 52, 57, 108, 109, 124, 134, 141, 149, 210, 211, 212, 265
Amitābha Buddha, 252
appendix tantra (uttaratantra) (genre), 186, 306
art (upāya), 17, 19, 22, 23, 51, 74, 140, 145, 152, 174, 200

B

bliss, 18, 22, 23, 27, 34, 52, 53, 55, 57, 58, 75, 80, 116, 119, 136, 137, 174, 175, 206, 207, 276
  emptiness and. *See* emptiness: union of bliss and
  great, 22, 27, 28, 38, 52, 66, 67, 75, 94, 102, 118, 119, 134, 136, 137, 142, 151, 159, 160, 161, 172, 179, 196, 197, 201, 273, 274, 276, 277
  natural, 19, 22, 34, 55, 156, 202
  sexual, 152
  supreme, 11, 75, 108, 151
bodhisattva(s), xii, 59, 66, 173, 175, 204, 270, 271, 272, 273, 274, 275, 282, 304
body mandala, 51, 164, 189, 197, 204
Brahmā, 99, 114
buddha bodies, 142. *See also* Vajradhara: body of
  communal enjoyment body (sambhogakāya), 91, 160, 273
  emanation body (nirmāṇakāya), 91, 159, 273, 305
  gnostic body (jñānakāya), 49, 179, 274
  reality body (dharmakāya), 91, 105, 160, 273, 274

C

caru oblation(s), 57, 68
chaṇḍāla(s), 85, 183, 190, 223
channel(s), 36, 37, 45, 72, 74, 119, 132, 133, 136, 138, 140, 142, 146, 150, 151, 152, 153, 158, 159, 160, 161, 200, 228, 229, 277, 281
charnel ground(s), 44, 60, 116, 120, 136, 175, 178, 187, 223, 224, 231, 271, 277, 278, 279, 280, 284
charu oblation(s), 47, 68. *See also* ambrosias
Chumbikā, 109, 189, 191, 192
clan(s), 142, 158, 191, 266, 297
  of consorts, 45, 47
  five, 160
  four, of consorts, 80
  immovable (akṣobhya), 75
  jewel (ratna), 75
  lāmā, 191
  lord, 296
  of messengers, 78
  mistress/goddess, 189, 191

actual (karmamudrā), 34, 43, 70, 131, 137, 152, 153, 155, 156, 158, 159, 160, 161, 166, 176, 197, 201, 221, 234
consort (phyag rgya mo), 47, 205, 207
four, 43, 137, 156, 159
gnostic (jñānamudrā), 34, 44, 155, 156, 159, 176
great (mahāmudrā), 26, 44, 49, 52, 67, 127, 131, 137, 138, 159, 160, 177, 184, 288, 289, 290, 307. *See also* power(s) (siddhi): supreme
achievement of, 50, 57, 179, 183, 197, 199
reality (dharmamudrā), 131, 137, 153, 159, 160
reality-source (dharmodayamudrā), 227, 228
symbolic (samayamudrā), 131, 137, 156, 158, 159, 160, 161, 176
vulva (yonimudrā), 225, 227, 228, 234
sex, sexuality, 77
sexological treatises (kāmaśāstra), 28, 207
sexual fluids, 34, 35, 37, 38, 51, 72, 76, 77, 83, 196
sexual intercourse, 28, 29, 33, 37, 47, 71, 266
sexual positions (karaṇa), 28
sexual practices, 48
sexual union, 33, 196, 207
sexual yoga(s), 35
Shākyamuni Buddha, 3, 4
Shiva, 114
siddhi. *See* accomplishment(s) (siddhi); power(s) (siddhi)
site(s), xii, 187, 188, 189, 190, 191, 218, 271, 272, 277, 278, 280, 284, 299
inner, 169, 252, 270, 280, 281, 285, 295
outer, 280, 284, 285
twenty-four, 62, 169, 188, 189, 190, 193, 252, 270, 281, 282, 295
soma, 54, 57, 67, 71, 72
spell consort (rig ma), 47, 127, 202, 228

T

thatness, 33, 34
triple body. *See* buddha bodies
triple realm, 93, 94, 141, 142, 206, 265, 267
triple world, 26, 73, 84, 99, 107, 117, 166, 174, 175, 191, 199, 207, 210, 211, 249, 250, 261, 267, 270, 282, 285

U

unexcelled yoga tantra(s), xi, xii, 290, 291, 305
universal monarch, 99, 104, 231, 298

V

Vairochana Buddha, 107, 251, 253
Vajradhara, 3, 30, 49, 58, 69, 75, 78, 172, 283, 290, 294
body of, 104, 120, 126, 127. *See also* buddha bodies
causal, 121, 149, 294, 296
clan of. *See* clan(s): Vajradhara
reality of, 84
stage, 275, 309
two, 122
unmanifest, 126
womb-born, 121
worship of, 126, 127
Vajrapāṇi (bodhisattva), 197, 288
Vajrasattva Buddha, 28, 101, 107, 116, 120, 251, 273
Vajravārāhī, 53, 106, 109, 120, 126, 157, 158, 175, 191, 200, 242, 249, 251, 267, 298, 301
victim(s) (sādhya), 76, 148, 149, 165, 166, 182, 183, 222, 223, 224, 228, 229, 230, 231, 234, 239, 240, 242, 243, 246, 258, 260, 265, 269
subjugation of, 163, 164, 165, 166
Viṣhṇu, 99, 114, 119
vow(s), 25, 29, 35, 42, 44, 73, 295. *See also* commitment(s)

W

wisdom consort (shes rab ma), 139, 159, 182, 193
women, 27, 29, 30, 31, 34, 37, 47, 52, 70, 71, 74, 82, 107, 128, 163, 164, 165, 190, 192, 228, 229, 232, 234, 239, 244, 245. *See also* clanswoman